POPULAR WRITING
a college reader

POPULAR WRITING

a college reader

Harold Stolerman
and
Helene O'Connor
Queensborough Community College

Holt, Rinehart and Winston

New York Chicago San Francisco Philadelphia
Montreal Toronto London Sydney
Tokyo Mexico City Rio de Janeiro Madrid

Library of Congress Cataloging in Publication Data
Stolerman, Harold.
    Popular writing.

    Includes index.
    1. College readers.   2. English language—Rhetoric.
3. Readers—Mass media.   4. Mass media—United States—
Addresses, essays, lectures.   I. O'Connor, Helene.
II. Title.
PE1417.S757   1986   808'.0427   85-7600
ISBN 0-03-071117-7

Copyright © 1986 by CBS College Publishing

Address correspondence to:
383 Madison Avenue
New York, N.Y. 10017

All rights reserved

Printed in the United States of America
Published simultaneously in Canada

6 7 8 9 090   9 8 7 6 5 4 3 2 1

CBS COLLEGE PUBLISHING
Holt, Rinehart and Winston
The Dryden Press
Saunders College Publishing

PREFACE

The most powerful influence on contemporary American society is the mass media. Some people might quibble about the use of the superlative, but few would dispute the widespread influence of the print media—newspapers, magazines, and books—and the electronic media—radio, television, and film. These methods of mass communication are ubiquitous and immediate in today's world. Television screens are in hospital nurseries, so we are introduced at birth to the media. We know how often television serves as babysitter, companion, entertainer, and educator. Sounds of radio emanate from elevators, offices, and even from electronic necklaces and rings. As if this electronic barrage were not enough, we are deluged with newspapers, magazines, and paperbacks in such numbers that they defy any individual attempt to keep pace.

It is imperative that we who live in this highly charged media milieu become discerning critics of it. The yellow brick road to passivity is all too tempting. Television is on in many American homes for an average of six to seven hours a day and radio anywhere from 18 to the full 24 hours. Like muscles, brains can atrophy from disuse. As much as we look and listen, we must also reflect, observe carefully, and evaluate. To succeed in our complex society, we must understand the mass media and their impact on our lives.

To aid in this endeavor is the purpose of this book. It presents essays, articles, questions, and writing suggestions designed to stimulate analytical thinking and writing about popular culture and the mass media. It is ultimately through writing—that crucial step from passive viewing, listening, and reading to active expression—that we learn more about ourselves and our ideas and values. The pen has always been the medium of the mind. If we can express our ideas we may attain insight. *Popular Writing: A College Reader* can be, we hope, an instrument toward that end.

ACKNOWLEDGMENTS

We are grateful to all those who have contributed in various ways to this text: for their invaluable insights and expertise, Sheena Gillespie, Linda Stanley, Tony Pipolo, John Morales, Gerry O'Connor; for their artwork Barret and Marianne O'Connor and Maureen Conlon-Peirce; and for their helpful suggestions: John Bayer, St. Louis Community College at Meramec; Richard Elias, Ohio Wesleyan University; Ruth Gardner, University of Arizona; Dorothy Guinn, Arizona State University; Hugh Ingrasci, De Paul University; Walter Minot, Gannon University.

We also wish to acknowledge all the talented and cooperative people at Holt, Rinehart and Winston who have made working on this book so enjoyable: in particular our fearless and tireless editors, Charlyce Jones-Owen, Charlotte Smith, and Maruta Mitchell.

Finally, for their encouragement, patience, and support through a long and difficult passage: Gladys Stolerman, and Mark and Elliot Stolerman. And, J.M., and Maeve, Rhu, and Colin.

CONTENTS

1 Writing About Popular Culture   1

2 Popular Culture   13

    Ray B. Browne   Popular Culture: Notes toward a Definition   15

    Barbara Goldsmith   The Meaning of Celebrity   22

    Robert Sargent   The Mystique of the Empire State Building   32

    Leslie A. Fiedler   Up, Up and Away—the Rise and Fall of Comic Books   35

    John Skow   Games that Play People   42

    Barbara W. Tuchman   The Decline of Quality   49

3 Communications   60

    Peter M. Sandman, David M. Rubin, and *David B. Sachsman*   American Mass Communication   62

Anthony Smith The New Form of Power: Information	72
Stanley N. Wellborn A World of Communications Wonders	77
Roger Rosenblatt The Mind in the Machine	84

4 News: Print and Broadcast 93

Donald H. Johnston What Is News?	95
American Society of Newspaper Editors A Statement of Principles	102
The Institute for Propaganda Analysis How to Detect Propaganda	104
Thomas Collins TV, Newspaper Journalists Abide by Different Rules	110
Ronald Steel How Politicians Seduce Journalists	113
Lewis H. Lapham Sculptures in Snow: Notes on the Uses of the Press	118
John Leo Journalese as a Second Tongue	123
David Saltman No Verbs Tonight . . . the Reasons . . . the Consequences	126
Jonathan Friendly Drawing a Privacy Line inside Publicity's Glare	129
Howard Polskin Save a Life or Get the Story?	133

5 Popular Print: Magazines and Books 139

MAGAZINES

John R. Bittner Magazines	142
Beverly Beyette He Moves in Close to Bring the Big Stories Vividly to Life	149
Associated Press Magazine Runs Hydrogen Bomb Diagram	153

BOOKS

Alfred Kazin	American Writing Now	155
Herbert Mitgang	Average U.S. Author's Writings Bring in Less than $5,000 a Year	161
Carol Thurston and *Barbara Doscher*	Supermarket Erotica: 'Bodice-busters' Put Romantic Myths to Bed	167
Rod Townley	Wait Till You Read/See the Book/Show	174
Elizabeth Peer with *Lea Donosky* and *George Hackett*	Why Writers Plagiarize	180
Rita Ciolli	The Textbook Wars	183
Bill McGowan, Jr.	25 Million Americans Can't Read This	189

6 Advertising 195

Marjorie Burns	The Advertiser's Bag of Tricks	198
Rod Townley	So Long, Ring Around the Collar! Welcome Paper Blob!	206
Bob Wiemer	Those Packages Aren't Just Selling Deodorant	212
Bernice Kanner	The Fizz Biz	215
John Cheever	Don't Leave the Room During the Commercials	220
Henryk Skolimowski	The Semantic Environment in the Age of Advertising	224
John Crichton	Morals and Ethics in Advertising	233
Selected Ads for Study		243

7 Television 257

Harry F. Waters	Life According to TV	259
Peggy Charren and *Cynthia Alperowicz*	TV Violence Breeds Violent Children	268

Mike Oppenheim, M.D. TV Isn't Violent *Enough*	270
Combined News Services TV Fan, 15, Leaps to His Death	274
Peter Goodman Orwellian Implications of Two-Way Television	275
Susan Jacoby Washing Our Minds Out with Soaps	280
David Hinckley It's Nothing to Smile About: The Decline of TV Sit-Coms	283
David Friedman Ball Games or Brawl Games?	287
Fred A. Keller Television and the Slow Death of the Mind	290

8 Radio — 296

Karl E. Meyer Radio's Born-Again Serenity	298
Kevin L. Goldman Radio's Latest Boom: Late-Night Talk Shows	303
Robert Palmer Will Video Clips Kill Radio as Maker of Rock's Top 10?	306
Jeff Bailey Stereo "Box": Big Bucks in Big Sounds	309
The New York Times Tuning Out Controls on Radio	312

9 Popular Music — 315

Lance Morrow They're Playing *Ur*-Song	317
Lionel Tiger Why, It Was Fun!	320
John Rockwell Country Music Is No Small-Town Affair	324
Benjamin DeMott Ordinary Critics: Immanuel Kant and the Talking Heads	329
John Rockwell A Pink Floyd Album Marks 10 Years as a Best Seller	336
Wayne Robins Heavy Metal	339

Louis Menand Transforming Elvis into a Suffering Culture Hero	341
Daniel Goleman Psychologists Examine Appeal of Michael Jackson	345
Richard Corliss The Medium Is the Maximum	348

10 Film 353

Tony Pipolo P.O.V., *Psycho,* and *E.T.*	354
Roger Ebert Why Movie Audiences Aren't Safe Any More	365
Janet Maslin Unreal Heroes for the 80's	371
Gerald Clarke In the Footsteps of Ulysses	374
Marilyn Milloy A Cinematic Schism in Black and White	376
Vincent Canby Longevity—the Real James Bond Mystery	382
Pauline Kael Movies on TV	386
Charles Champlin The Critic as Image Maker	389

The Pulitzer Hoax: A Casebook 394

Thomas Collins Wash. Post Story a Hoax, Paper Returns Pulitzer	395
Newsday Aftermath of a Pulitzer Hoax	398
Les Payne The Faked Story: When Ambition Replaces the Truth	399
Ellen Goodman Faked News Reports and the Destruction of the Public's Trust	402
Al Cohn Ex-reporter Recalls Costly Fear of Failure	403
James A. Michener On Integrity in Journalism	405

RHETORICAL TABLE OF CONTENTS

Following is a selected index of articles that illustrate rhetorical techniques.

CAUSE AND EFFECT

Barbara W. Tuchman The Decline of Quality	49
Ronald Steel How Politicians Seduce Journalists	113
Alfred Kazin American Writing Now	155
Carol Thurston and *Barbara Doscher* Supermarket Erotica: 'Bodice-busters' Put Romantic Myths to Bed	167
Bill McGowan, Jr. 25 Million Americans Can't Read This	189
Bob Wiemer Those Packages Aren't Just Selling Deodorant	212
Bernice Kanner The Fizz Biz	215
Peggy Charren and *Cynthia Alperowicz* TV Violence Breeds Violent Children	268
Peter Goodman Orwellian Implications of Two-Way Television	275
Fred A. Keller Television and the Slow Death of the Mind	290
Robert Palmer Will Video Clips Kill Radio as Maker of Rock's Top 10?	306
Louis Menand Transforming Elvis into a Suffering Culture Hero	341
Charles Champlin The Critic as Image Maker	389

CLASSIFICATION

Ray B. Browne Popular Culture: Notes toward a Definition	15
Peter M. Sandman, David M. Rubin, and *David B. Sachsman* American Mass Communication	62
Stanley N. Wellborn A World of Communications Wonders	77
Donald H. Johnston What Is News?	95

The Institute for Propaganda Analysis   104
    How to Detect Propaganda

Ronald Steel   How Politicians Seduce Journalists   113

John R. Bittner   Magazines   142

Herbert Mitgang   Average U.S. Author's Writings   161
    Bring in Less than $5,000 a Year

Marjorie Burns   The Advertiser's Bag of Tricks   198

Henryk Skolimowski   The Semantic Environment in   224
    the Age of Advertising

John Crichton   Morals and Ethics in Advertising   233

Daniel Goleman   Psychologists Examine Appeal of   345
    Michael Jackson

COMPARISON AND CONTRAST

Barbara W. Tuchman   The Decline of Quality   49

Anthony Smith   The New Form of Power: Information   72

Thomas Collins   TV, Newspaper Journalists   110
    Abide by Different Rules

Beverly Beyette   He Moves in Close to Bring the Big   149
    Stories to Life

Alfred Kazin   American Writing Now   155

Rod Townley   So Long, Ring Around the Collar!   206
    Welcome Paper Blob!

Janet Maslin   Unreal Heroes for the 80's   371

Gerald Clarke   In the Footsteps of Ulysses   374

Marilyn Milloy   A Cinematic Schism in Black   376
    and White

Pauline Kael   Movies on TV   386

DEFINITION

Ray B. Browne   Popular Culture: Notes   15
    toward a Definition

Barbara Goldsmith   The Meaning of Celebrity   22

Barbara W. Tuchman   The Decline of Quality   49

Donald H. Johnson What is News? — 95
The Institute for Propaganda Analysis How to Detect Propaganda — 104
John Leo Journalese as a Second Tongue — 123
Marjorie Burns The Advertiser's Bag of Tricks — 198
Lance Morrow They're Playing *Ur*-Song — 317
Richard Corliss The Medium is the Maximum — 348

DESCRIPTION
Howard Polskin Save a Life or Get the Story? — 133
Wayne Robins Heavy Metal — 339

EXAMPLE AND ILLUSTRATION
John Skow Games that Play People — 42
Barbara W. Tuchman The Decline of Quality — 49
John Leo Journalese as a Second Tongue — 123
David Saltman No Verbs Tonight . . . the Reasons . . . the Consequences — 126
Jonathan Friendly Drawing a Privacy Line inside Publicity's Glare — 129
Howard Polskin Save a Life or Get the Story? — 133
John R. Bittner Magazines — 142
Alfred Kazin American Writing Now — 155
Carol Thurston and *Barbara Doscher* Supermarket Erotica: 'Bodice-busters' Put Romantic Myths to Bed — 167
Rod Townley Wait Till You Read/See the Book/Show — 174
Elizabeth Peer with *Lea Donosky* and *George Hackett* Why Writers Plagiarize — 180
Rita Ciolli The Textbook Wars — 183
Marjorie Burns The Advertiser's Bag of Tricks — 198
Bob Wiemer Those Packages Aren't Just Selling Deodorant — 212
Bernice Kanner The Fizz Biz — 215

Henryk Skolimowski The Semantic Environment in the Age of Advertising — 224

David Friedman Ball Games or Brawl Games? — 287

EXPOSITION

John Skow Games that Play People — 42

Peter M. Sandman, David M. Rubin, and *David B. Sachsman* American Mass Communication — 62

Stanley N. Wellborn A World of Communications Wonders — 77

Donald H. Johnston What Is News? — 95

Jonathan Friendly Drawing a Privacy Line inside Publicity's Glare — 129

John R. Bittner Magazines — 142

Beverly Beyette He Moves in Close to Bring the Big Stories Vividly to Life — 149

Herbert Mitgang Average U.S. Author's Writings Bring in Less than $5,000 a Year — 161

Rita Ciolli The Textbook Wars — 183

Marjorie Burns The Advertiser's Bag of Tricks — 198

Kevin L. Goldman Radio's Latest Boom: Late-Night Talk Shows — 303

Tony Pipolo P.O.V., *Psycho,* and *E.T.* — 354

Thomas Collins Wash. Post Story a Hoax, Paper Returns Pulitzer — 395

PERSUASION

Ray B. Browne Popular Culture: Notes toward a Definition — 15

Barbara Goldsmith The Meaning of Celebrity — 22

Robert Sargent The Mystique of the Empire State Building — 32

Barbara W. Tuchman The Decline of Quality — 49

Roger Rosenblatt The Mind in the Machine — 84

Lewis H. Lapham Sculptures in Snow: Notes on the Uses of the Press	118
Alfred Kazin American Writing Now	155
Carol Thurston and *Barbara Doscher* Supermarket Erotica: 'Bodice-busters' Put Romantic Myths to Bed	167
John Cheever Don't Leave the Room During the Commercials	220
Henryk Skolimowski The Semantic Environment in the Age of Advertising	224
John Crichton Morals and Ethics in Advertising	233
Mike Oppenheim, M.D. TV Isn't Violent *Enough*	270
Susan Jacoby Washing Our Minds Out with Soaps	280
Fred A. Keller Television and the Slow Death of the Mind	290
The New York Times Tuning Out Controls on Radio	312
Benjamin DeMott Ordinary Critics: Immanual Kant and the Talking Heads	329
Tony Pipolo P.O.V., *Psycho*, and *E.T.*	354
Janet Maslin Unreal Heroes for the 80's	371
Les Payne The Faked Story: When Ambition Replaces the Truth	399

NARRATION

Leslie A. Fiedler Up, Up and Away—the Rise and Fall of Comic Books	35
Howard Polskin Save a Life or Get the Story?	133
John Cheever Don't Leave the Room During the Commercials	220

PROCESS ANALYSIS

Ronald Steel How Politicians Seduce Journalists	113

POPULAR WRITING
a college reader

1

WRITING ABOUT POPULAR CULTURE

Good writing is like many other accomplishments we find admirable. When we ask ourselves why we admire a particular work, whether it is a film, a piece of art, a record album, or a television program, we often find what we are responding to is a harmonious fusion of concept and execution. Although the specific work may convey a kind of appealing effortlessness, we are aware that that grace has not been arrived at accidentally; it is the felicitous combination of method and idea.

We respond to the same appeal in good writing. We admire not only what has been said but also the unerringly 'right' way in which it has been expressed. How do we go about achieving the same results in our own writing? Clearly, effective approaches have been developed over the many centuries since man first picked up a stylus.

Effective writing first requires effective thinking and preparation. As with anything we care about, we must devote to it the time and concentration that it merits. Writing is an acquired ability, functioning on three levels. It is a physical process with a tangible product that embodies intellectual content. As with other physical endeavors from swimming to guitar lessons, practice—and more practice—helps. Simply writing—just to write—can sometimes aid in overcoming that occasional and universal ailment known as writer's block. Writing without the pressure of any assignment or deadline—free writing—can also bring about the realization that writing is not only a thoughtful but also a genuinely pleasurable activity, one that can heighten our sense of self-worth and accomplishment, as do other forms of self-expression that we enjoy.

Assignments should not diminish our pleasure in writing. Our feeling of delight in doing something well will increase commensurate with the difficulty of the writing goals we set for ourselves. Writing is a process of self-discovery, but it is also a voyage of exploration into the world: past, present, and future.

Writing about popular culture provides an excellent embarkation point for that exploration, as it makes us look at that vast audience of which we are a part that is our contemporary society. Just what is popular culture? Ray Browne notes in his definitive essay in Chapter Two that a workable definition can be arrived at by examining some of the culture's "salient and quintessential aspects"—its artistic creations. Today, the majority of our artistic creations are created for or by the mass media and transmitted to us through them—specifically, newspapers, magazines, books, television, radio, records, and film. The media select the information and entertainment our society receives and determine in what manner it will be presented. Their influence on our popular culture is undeniable. Whether, as some critics have charged, the media have partially created that culture is speculative, but most observers agree that the most accurate reflection of it can be found in the different media. To write about popular culture then, we must examine the media, reflect upon them and their impact on us. What does each medium reveal about us as a people? Why do we read (or not read) what we do in newspapers, books, and magazines? Why do we watch those favorite films or television programs and listen to that special kind of music on radio or records? What about us as individuals; what do our choices and tastes say about us as human beings, about our perceptions and values? We cannot write about any of the mass media that consume so many hours of our lives unless we examine both them and their audience—ourselves.

AUDIENCE

The media invite our immediate attention to a key factor in all writing: audience. Media and audience are inseparable; today, the mass media survive and thrive on the size and strength of the audience they attract. In the print media, many newspapers have folded and others are facing financial crises because of declining audience. That vast audience of potential readers (of which we are part) must somehow be moved to choose a particular newspaper to purchase and read. Correspondingly, the newspaper must recognize and attract its audience with devices such as headlines and photographs, "grabbers" as they are called, precisely because they do grab our attention. The editors and advertisers of the *New York Times*, for example, have researched their audience thoroughly, and the newspaper reflects this awareness. The differences between it and a rural daily or even a paper in the nationwide Murdoch chain are too obvious to need explanation.

Just as familiar to us as the headlines in the tabloids is television's Nielsen Rating Service. Television, the medium that contributed the term and concept "sudden death" to the sportsworld, is the medium where actors, programs, and careers flourish and fade by an immediate audience vote, the rating system. Three weeks, six weeks, and we, the audience, speak electronically and it's all over—or—it's fame! Television more than any of the other mass media is audience directed and, thus, audience controlled. Everything on television is aimed at grabbing us in some way. Television is a medium; if it is also a means, then audience is the end.

Writing about the media thrusts us immediately from our comfortable seat in that audience to the director's chair. Instead of a camera or recording equipment, the pen is our instrument of creativity. Through the positive, energetic mental and physical activity of writing, we move from being passive members of the audience, waiting to be intrigued, entertained, manipulated, wooed, perhaps even sold, to become those who decide what is actually said and to whom it is said. As writers we determine initially for whom we are writing, our audience, and how we may best approach them. We speak to our distinct audiences through our writing, and it is we who can choose to intrigue, entertain, manipulate, if we wish, through our words. A piece on video games, for example, would probably be very different in vocabulary and tone if written for a gathering of potential franchisers or for a collection of teenage devotees than if written for a group of concerned parents.

Determination of audience influences approach and also topic; there are some topics that are simply inappropriate for some audiences. We must know for whom we are writing, and then most importantly have something to say and have some plan or pattern of organization and development by which to say it.

In film and television, because they are *mass* media the techniques of organization used are often so familiar to us that we do not pause to consider them as such. We are all experienced enough viewers to identify the close-up, the zoom shot, the pan, the fade-out, the flashback, to name a few of the most popular. Yet, most of us are not directors. However, we are writers, and we can use writing principles of organization and development to enhance the clarity and impact of our work, just as the director uses a variety of shots with the camera to achieve goals. Rhetoric is the ancient name for the study of language, the body of principles for composition. As we learn these writing principles and apply them to our reading and writing, we will find that although the vocabulary differs, we have seen many of these techniques and their functions in some adaptation in the other media.

TOPIC

We have a sense of our audience. Now, we must determine our topic and then our aim in writing. We may decide to write about television. Shazam! We have a topic. Television, however, is much too broad a topic to tackle in a brief essay. We must then limit our topic. Television news, sitcoms, sports, soaps, children's shows, talk shows, and so on, are but some of the many different classifications within the category of television. Keep in mind that it is usually better to discuss an aspect of a given subject concretely and with some development than to generalize loosely on some much broader topic. Suppose we decide to write an essay on soap operas (see "Washing Our Minds Out with Soaps," Chapter Seven). We will naturally produce better writing if we are familiar with our subject. If soap means Ivory to you, try an alternative subject.

AIMS

Just what is it that we wish to say about soap operas? Perhaps we wish to give information about them, explain what they are. If so, we will be writing an *expository* essay.

What is our opinion of soaps? Are they satisfying psychological entertainment, enjoyable escapism, or tedious trash? If we wish to persuade our readers of our opinion, we will do it by appealing to their reason and to their emotions. We will then be writing a *persuasive* essay.

If we wish to communicate to our readers the vivid impressions we receive from soap operas, we may want to write a *descriptive* essay. Descriptive writing features details included and ordered for emotional value. It is not simply giving information as in expository writing.

Use of detail can also contribute greatly to a fourth option in our preparation for writing. Do we want to tell our readers a story, a soap opera plot, perhaps? Then we will have a *narrative* aim.

THESIS

Whichever of the four aims we select—expository, persuasive, descriptive, or narrative—we have chosen our topic, limited it, and decided on an approach. We are now ready to formulate a thesis statement. This is a specific sentence or two that contains the overall idea of the essay—what we are really attempting to say. The thesis statement should always answer that question English instructors like to ask, "What is the point of your paper?" A good thesis statement will be clearly focused, specific, concisely phrased, and will usually contain within it an implied mode of organization and development.

SAMPLES OF THE FOUR WRITING AIMS

Expository

Thesis: The soaps are truly operas without song; their histrionic scenes and layers of subplots are worthy of any Verdi libretto.

The paper will explain, with specific examples whenever possible, the elements of the soap opera form.

Persuasive

Thesis: Instead of bursting bubbles, critics of soap operas should admire the shimmering flights of fantasy they provide.

The paper will defend soap operas as escapism.

Descriptive

Thesis: The often traumatic realism of its medical scenes contributes greatly to the popularity of "General Hospital."

The paper will describe the hospital atmosphere and its impact on viewers.

Narrative

Thesis: An experience in my doctor's office last Thursday convinced me that I was living out a soap.

The paper will recount an experience within a particular time sequence.

BRAINSTORMING

Suppose we decide to write a persuasive paper on the soaps as fabulous fantasies. Take a piece of paper and jot down everything that comes to mind.

1. Beautiful people
2. Expensive clothes
3. Women perfect—hair and makeup
4. Men—distinguished elegance
5. Young men—casual charm
6. Rich interiors—custom decor
7. Costly leisure pastimes
8. Golf, tennis, skiing, sailing
9. Work rarely shown
10. No real depiction of poverty
11. Only emotional needs
12. No insoluble problems
13. Travel, money, new relationships—redemption, renewal

From random jottings like these we will be able to order our ideas into a more structured outline for the paper. However rough it may be, brainstorming is a good habit to acquire. Ideas are committed to paper before they are forgotten.

ORGANIZATION

A film or television director decides on the material and approach and with these in mind assembles cast and production crew and then structures the work. We too have determined our audience, our aim, selected and limited our topic, jotted down relevant facts and ideas, and formulated a thesis statement. Our next step in the process of writing an essay is organization.

Organization in writing is essential. Disorganized writing is like anything disorganized—confusing and vaguely irritating. One traditional rhetorical method of organization is called the heuristic wherein the writer gathers and arranges information in an honest attempt to find an answer or solution to a situation. Here the aim can be expository, descriptive, and/or persuasive and the thesis can come at the conclusion of the essay. This method generates a sense of discovery for both writer and reader. In the eristic or argumentative method, where the aim is usually persuasive, the thesis is already formulated and precedes a series of examples or arguments of increasing power. Either method, heuristic/discovery or eristic/argumentative, can proceed from the general to the particular or vice versa. Logic determines the order as it does for all but one of the following modes or patterns of development. The only exception is process analysis where chronology, the time sequence of events or steps, sets the order. In short, however it proceeds to its conclusion a paper should present a coherent line of thought. It should make sense.

MODES

Modes or patterns of development are organizing devices to aid the writer in achieving clarity and coherence in developing his thesis. The six commonly used modes of development are:

1. Example and illustration
2. Definition
3. Classification
4. Process analysis
5. Comparison and contrast
6. Cause and effect

It is important to note that these modes work equally well within an individual paragraph or as a structural pattern for an entire essay.

Example

With virtually any kind of statement we make, oral or written, we illustrate our comment whenever possible with an example to clarify what we have written or said. Advertising (Chapter Six) has created an empire and perhaps even an art form with this mode. What, after all, is an advertisement, either print ad or commercial, but a persuasive example? Both paragraph and essay structures utilize examples in one or more of three ways: listing of facts, detailed description, and anecdote or incident. Readings in this text notable for their extensive use of examples are the Goldsmith and Tuchman essays in Chapter Two. The mode, however, is so versatile that it appears in almost every type of writing.

Definition

Definition, like example, is a mode of development useful in many forms of writing. We cannot explain, persuade, describe, or recount unless we define our terms. Definition is closely allied to audience, since potential disaster looms when we define terms differently from our readers. Ray Browne's article in Chapter Two is a fine example of an essay of definition. Browne's aim is expository: to define and explain popular culture, using numerous examples in each aspect of his definition. In contrast, Wayne Robins' evocative piece "Heavy Metal" in Chapter Nine relies on description for its definition.

Classification

Definition is also a prelude for another mode of development. We must define before we can classify. If our aim is expository or persuasive, it is often effective to define our topic and then divide it into composite groups. What is popular music? "Between rock and a soft place" is Stephen King's definition. We can, however, more precisely classify popular music into several different categories: country-western, mor(middle-of-the-road), jazz, and rock and roll. Here we can see just how thorough a mode classification can be, for our last category, rock and roll, can then be broken down into subclassifications such as heavy metal, new wave, fusion rock, rockabilly, and so on. The propaganda essay in Chapter Four of this text presents seven different classifications of its subject.

Process Analysis

The three previous modes, example, definition, and classification, can be incorporated into a fourth mode—process analysis. This mode quite simply offers directions on how to do something or explains how something works, step by step. The mode has a specific function, exposition, and our success with it can be easily measured since the clarity of our expression will influence the outcome of the process considerably. If we write a process analysis on how to assemble and connect up a stereo system, follow our own directions, and get white noise or worse, no sound at all, we may have to revise our process analysis somewhat.

Comparison/Contrast

One of the most popular modes in all types of writing is comparison/contrast. Comparisons direct attention to similarities, while contrasts point out differences. This mode and the following one, cause and effect, are vital for clear thinking and writing. If we can figure out similarities and differences and what causes certain effects and why, then we are capable of solid intellectual analysis. Some of the profound questions raised by articles in this book are framed in the comparison/contrast mode: celebrity/character, entertainment/art, quality/nonquality.

Outlines for this mode usually follow one of two patterns. We will select our subjects from advertising where comparison/contrast is an extremely popular sales technique. Let's compare a Datsun 280Z with a Ford station wagon in relation to function, economy, and consumer appeal (status, and so on).

Method One

Introduction of topic—Datsun, Ford comparison/contrast
Discussion of Datsun in terms of

    a. function
    b. economy
    c. consumer appeal

Transition to Ford
Discussion of Ford in comparison/contrast to Datsun in terms of

    a. function
    b. economy
    c. consumer appeal

Conclusion

Method Two

This method requires more clarity in expression from the writer.

    Introduction of topic—Datsun, Ford comparison/contrast
    Discussion Datsun/Ford in terms of a. function

Discussion Datsun/Ford in terms of b. economy
Discussion Datsun/Ford in terms of c. consumer appeal
Conclusion

Naturally, the nature of the topics being compared and contrasted will affect the choice of outline method.

Cause and Effect

Cause and effect is the final mode of development we will discuss. Again, it is an analytic mode where clear, logical thinking is a prerequisite. In general, if the paper focuses on causes, it will explain why something has occurred or exists; and if it focuses on effects, it will detail just what those effects are. A longer paper, of course, will consider both aspects of a situation. The articles on violence in television in Chapter Seven are examples of cause and effect essays.

OUTLINING

Now that we are familiar with the modes of development, only one step remains in our prewriting activities: outlining. This ensures that our paper will have unity and coherence.

    An essay illustrating good if complex organization is Ray Browne's "Popular Culture: Notes Toward a Definition." Here is a rough outline for his essay:

Aim: Exposition—to explain what popular culture is
Audience: General—no special knowledge of popular culture required
Thesis: Popular culture consists of the broadly intellectual and creative elements of life that are generally disseminated by the mass media
Approach: Heuristic—an unbiased search for a workable definition

1. Difficulty of defining popular culture
2. Types of culture
3. Critics and defenders of popular culture
4. Major differences between high or elite and popular culture
5. Interrelationship among the types of culture
6. Workable definition

Before Browne wrote his essay, he took the following steps:

1. Chose a subject—culture
2. Limited it—popular culture

3. Collected facts, ideas, and examples—types of culture, opponents and supporters of popular culture, elite and popular artists
4. Decided on his central aim—which determined the type of writing—exposition—and the audience
5. Formulated a thesis statement—an inclusive workable definition of popular culture shaped for a general audience
6. Chose a heuristic approach using four modes of development—definition expanded by analysis and classification (the four categories of culture); comparison/contrast (similarities and differences between high and popular culture, specifically, popular, mass, and folk culture); and example (Melville, Shakespeare, Johnny St. Cyr, and Liberace)

Some instructors prefer a more succinct outline, usually in topic or sentence form. The topic outline indicates the order and relationships of topics by using a noun and its modifiers for each heading. The sentence outline is similar in structure to the topic outline but uses a complete sentence for each heading and subheading. The advantage of the sentence outline is that it provides a fuller and clearer development of the topic and the relationship of its parts. Here is an example of a sentence outline of Ray Browne's essay.

Sentence Outline

Thesis: Popular culture is all those broadly intellectual and creative elements of life that are generally disseminated by the mass media.

I. "Popular Culture" is a difficult term to define.
   A. Most critics either do not completely agree on what popular culture is or do not attempt to define it.
   B. Previous attempts to divide or classify culture have been superficial or incomplete.
II. There are basically four main areas of culture.
   A. Elite or high culture is those elements of life that appeal to the minority because they are too sophisticated to be distributed to a mass audience.
   B. Popular culture is those elements that are distributed to the general public through limited mass media.
   C. Mass culture is those elements that are distributed to a wider or mass audience through wider mass media.
   D. Folk culture or folklore is those elements that are or were at one time disseminated by oral and nonoral methods.
III. The serious study of popular culture has its critics and defenders.

A. Dwight Macdonald, Edmund Wilson, and William Gass are elitist critics who have insisted that real culture is that which is not widespread but rather limited to the elite, aristocratic, and the minority—those who are capable of understanding and appreciating esthetic intention and accomplishment.
B. On the other hand, writers and critics like Tom Wolfe, Susan Sontag, Marshall McLuhan, and Abraham Kaplan all recognize the validity, accomplishment, and significance of popular culture as an artistic and social force.

IV. The four areas of culture are sufficiently distinct.
A. Elite culture differs from popular and mass culture because it is too sophisticated for the mass media.
B. Both popular and mass artists are less interested than elite artists in individual expression and in experimenting with or thoroughly investigating reality.
C. The popular artist, like Johnny St. Cyr, is superior to the mass artist, like Liberace, because he is truly creative in both intent and accomplishment.

V. Despite their differences, the four areas of culture are closely related.
A. Elite art draws heavily from both folk and popular arts.
   1. The elite and folk artists are close in motivation since both value personal expression, explore new art forms, and seek individuality and originality in expression and feeling.
   2. Like elite art, but to a lesser degree, popular art is concerned with probing reality.
   3. Shakespeare is an excellent example of both an elite and a popular artist.
B. Popular culture includes and is similar to mass culture.
   1. Both are disseminated through the mass media.
   2. The popular and mass artists are chiefly interested in restating the old and accepted ideas and conventions.
C. Popular culture draws from and also includes folk culture.
   1. "Sir Patrick Spens," one of the greatest songs (poems) ever written, was originally a folk ballad.
   2. Woody Guthrie and Larry Gorman are popular artists who draw upon folklore in their songs.
D. Folk culture borrows from and imitates both popular and elite cultures.
   1. Both folk and elite art have much that is mediocre and inferior.
   2. Both elite and folk artists are similar in motivation.

VI. Despite the difficulty, it is advantageous to formulate a viable though tentative definition of popular culture.
A. Two scholars believe popular culture is what people do when they play.
B. Based on the definition of one serious scholar, one can formulate a comprehensive definition of popular culture that embraces all levels of our society and culture other than the elite.

This definition by Browne is the thesis statement of his essay.

> **TOPICS FOR INVESTIGATION**
>
> We declared initially that writing was a voyage of exploration into the world: past, present, and future. For that reason we have included at the end of each chapter a list of topics for investigation. These suggestions are meant to stimulate speculation and research on some of the origins and dynamics of the mass media explosion of the twentieth century. We cannot help but know about the mass media in our world, but it may be that what we learn from the past can influence our thinking and actions—and writing is taking action—in the future.

2

POPULAR CULTURE

Popular culture is the name of an international association and a journal. It is a degree program at some universities, but—what is it?

In the initial essay in this section Ray B. Browne provides some perceptive "notes toward a definition" of that inclusive and increasingly important term. Our examination of the mass media must begin with popular culture since that is the material that the mass media transmit to us. All our preferences, tastes, even idiosyncracies so accurately reflected back to us by the media reveal our social customs and our basic values as a society. The media mirror us for ourselves in our popular culture.

The essays in this section focus on various significant examples of our American popular culture. Literary critic Leslie Fiedler probes the influences of comic books on his childhood and his scholarship. Robert Sargent chooses the fiftieth birthday of the Empire State Building as an opportunity to examine both the skyscraper in the United States and various other architectural constructs throughout history as mythic representatives of their respective societies. John Skow and his staff at *Time* have researched a more recent phenomenon, the video game craze that has swept the United States.

Two essays in this chapter, those by Goldsmith and Tuchman, are seminal. The questions they raise about the values of our culture resound through the pages of the book, as specific media and their related issues are considered. Goldsmith and Tuchman present strong negative arguments that our highly popular culture has resulted in a decline in character and quality in our society. Where Browne's opening essay defines and classifies popular culture affirmatively, they explore its weaknesses, and Tuchman, especially, argues for total rejection of it. Whatever opinions we form, this section is a good reminder to us that even pebbles can make waves.

Readings

> **Ray B. Brown,** who received his Ph.D. from the University of California, is a major figure in popular culture studies. His extensive and seminal writing has done much to ensure scholarly recognition and stimulate programs and research in the area. A professor in the Department of Popular Culture at Bowling Green University, Browne is an editor of the *Journal of Popular Culture* and the *Journal of American Culture.*

Popular Culture: Notes toward a Definition

Ray B. Browne

"Popular Culture" is an indistinct term whose edges blur into imprecision. Scarcely any two commentators who try to define it agree in all aspects of what popular culture really is. Most critics, in fact, do not attempt to define it; instead, after distinguishing between it and the mass media, and between it and "high" culture, most assume that everybody knows that whatever is widely disseminated and experienced is "popular culture."

Some observers divide the total culture of a people into "minority" and "majority" categories. Other observers classify culture into High-Cult, Mid-Cult and Low-Cult, or High-Brow, Mid-Brow and Low-Brow, leaving out, apparently, the level that would perhaps be called Folk-Cult or Folk-Brow, though Folk culture is now taking on, even among the severest critics of popular culture a high class and achievement unique unto itself. Most of the discriminating observers agree, in fact, that there are perhaps actually four areas of culture: Elite, Popular, Mass and Folk, with the understanding that none is a discrete unity standing apart and unaffected by the others.

One reason for the lack of precise definition is that the serious study of "popular culture" has been neglected in American colleges and universities. Elitist critics of our culture—notably such persons as Dwight MacDonald and Edmund Wilson—have always insisted that whatever was widespread was artistically and esthetically deficient, therefore unworthy of study. They have taught that "culture" to be worthwhile must necessarily be limited to the elite, aristocratic, and the minority. They felt that mass or popular culture—especially as it appeared in the mass media—would vitiate

Reprinted by permission of Ray Browne.

real culture. This attitude persists today among some of the younger critics. William Gass, for example, the esthetician and critic, takes the extreme position that "the products of popular culture, by and large, have no more esthetic quality than a brick in the street. . . . Any esthetic intentions are entirely absent, and because it is desired to manipulate consciousness directly, achieve one's effect there, no mind is paid to the intrinsic nature of its objects; they lack finish, complexity, stasis, individuality, coherence, depth, and endurance."

Such an attitude as Gass' is perhaps an extreme statement of the elitist critic's point of view. Luckily the force of numerous critics' arguments is weakening such attitudes. Popular Culture has a dimension, a thrust and—most important—a reality that has nothing to do with its esthetic accomplishment, though that has more merit than is often given to it.

This point of view is demonstrated by the talented young stylist Tom Wolfe, who, perhaps writing more viscerally than intellectually, thumbs his nose at the prejudice and snobbery that has always held at arms length all claims of validity if not esthetic accomplishment of the "culture" of the masses.

Susan Sontag, a brilliant young critic and esthetician, is more effective in bludgeoning the old point of view. Far from alarmed at the apparent new esthetic, she sees that it is merely a change in attitude, not a death's blow to culture and art:

> What we are getting is not the demise of art, but a transformation of the function of art. Art, which arose in human society as magical-religious operation, and passed over into a technique for depicting and commenting on secular reality, has in our own time arrogated to itself a new function—neither religious, nor serving a secularized religious function, nor merely secular or profane . . . Art today is a new kind of instrument, an instrument for modifying consciousness and organizing new modes of sensibility.

To Sontag the unprecedented complexity of the world has made inevitable and very necessary this change in the function of art. This is virtually the same attitude held by Marshall McLuhan:

> A technological extension of our bodies designed to alleviate physical stress can bring on psychic stress that may be much worse . . . Art is exact information of how to rearrange one's psyche to anticipate the next blow from our own extended psyches . . . in experimental art, men are given the exact specifications of coming violence to their own psyche from their own counter-irritants or technology. For those parts of ourselves that we thrust out in the form of new inventions are attempts to counter or neutralize collective pressures and irritations. But the counterirritant usually proves a greater plague than the initial irritant like a drug habit. And it is here that the artist can show us how to "ride with the punch," instead of "taking it on the chin."

An equally important aspect of popular culture as index and corrector is its role as a comic voice. Popular humor provides a healthy element in a nation's life. It pricks the pompous, devaluates the inflated, and snipes at the overly solemn. For example, such organs of popular culture as the magazines spoofed Henry James' pomposity during his lifetime, spoofed his "high" seriousness and in general tended to humanize him.

A more reasonable attitude than Gass' and one that is becoming increasingly acceptable is that held by the philosopher Abraham Kaplan: That popular culture has considerable accomplishment and even more real possibilities and it is developing but has not realized its full potential. All areas draw from one another. The Mass area, being largely imitative, draws from the others without altering much. Elite art draws heavily from both folk and, perhaps to a slightly lesser degree, popular arts. Popular art draws from Elite and Mass, and Folk, but does not take any without subjecting it to a greater or lesser amount of creative change. That popular culture has "no more esthetic quality than a brick in the street" or at least no more esthetic potential is a contention refuted by America's greatest writers—Hawthorne, Melville, Whitman, Twain, to name only four—as well as the greatest writers of all times and countries—Homer, Shakespeare, Dickens, Dostoevski, Tolstoi, for example.

Melville provides an excellent case in point. *Moby Dick* is the greatest creative book written in America and one of the half dozen greatest ever written anywhere. Its greatness derives from the sum total of its many parts. It is a blend of nearly all elements of all cultures of mid-nineteenth century America. Melville took all the culture around him—trivial and profound—Transcendentalism and the plumbing of the depths of the human experience, but also demonism, popular theater, the shanghai gesture, jokes about pills and gas on the stomach, etc., and boiled them in the tryworks of his fiery genius into the highest art.

Many definitions of popular culture turn on methods of dissemination. Those elements which are too sophisticated for the mass media are generally called Elite culture, those distributed through these media that are something less than "mass," that is such things as the smaller magazines and newspapers, the less widely distributed books, museums and less sophisticated galleries, so-called clothes line art exhibits, and the like—are called in the narrow sense of the term "popular," those elements that are distributed through the mass media are "mass" culture, and those which are or were at one time disseminated by oral and non-oral methods—on levels "lower" than the mass media—are called "folk."

All definitions of such a complex matter, though containing a certain amount of validity and usefulness, are bound to be to a certain extent inadequate or incorrect. Perhaps a workable definition can best be arrived at by looking at one of the culture's most salient and quintessential aspects—its artistic creations—because the artist perhaps more than any one else draws from the totality of experience and best reflects it.

Shakespeare and his works are an excellent example. When he was producing his plays at the Globe Theater, Shakespeare was surely a "popular" author and his works were elements of "popular" culture, though they were at the same time also High or Elite culture, for they were very much part of the lives of both the groundlings and the nobles. Later, in America, especially during the nineteenth century, all of his works were well known, his name was commonplace, and he was at the same time still High art, Popular (even mass) art and Folk art. In the twentieth century, however, his works are more distinguishble as parts of various levels. *Hamlet* is still a play of both High and Popular art. The most sophisticated and scholarly people still praise it. But *Hamlet* is also widely distributed on TV, radio and through the movies. It is a commonplace on all levels of society and is therefore a part of "popular culture" in the broadest sense of the term. Other plays by Shakespeare, however, have not become a part of "popular" culture. *Titus Andronicus*, for example, for any of several reasons, is not widely known by the general public. It remains, thus, Elite culture.

Wideness of distribution and popularity in this sense are one major aspect of popular culture. But there are others. Many writers would be automatically a part of popular culture if their works sold only a few copies—Frank G. Slaughter and Frank Yerby, for example. Louis Auchincloss also, though his works are of a different kind than Slaughter's and Yerby's, because his subject is Wall Street and high finance, and these are subjects of popular culture.

Aside from distribution another major difference between high and popular culture, and among popular culture, mass culture and folk culture, is the motivation of the persons contributing, the makers and shapers of culture. On the elite or sophisticated level, the creators value individualism, individual expression, the exploration and discovery of new art forms, of new ways of stating, the exploration and discovery of new depths in life's experiences.

On the other levels of culture there is usually less emphasis placed upon, and less accomplishment reached in, this plumbing of reality. Generally speaking, both popular and mass artists are less interested in the experimental and searching than in the restatement of the old and accepted. But there are actually vast differences in the esthetic achievements attained in the works from these two levels, and different aspirations and goals, even within these somewhat limited objectives. As Hall and Whannel have pointed out:

> In mass art the formula is everything—an escape from, rather than a means to, originality. The popular artist may use the conventions to select, emphasize and stress (or alter the emphasis and stress) so as to delight the audience with a kind of creative surprise. Mass art uses the stereotypes and formulae to simplify the experience, to mobilize stock feelings and to 'get them going.'

The popular artist is superior to the mass artist because for him "stylization is necessary, and the conventions provide an agreed base from which true creative invention springs." It is a serious error therefore to agree with Dwight MacDonald (in *Against the American Grain*) that all popular art "includes the spectator's reactions in the work itself instead of forcing him to make his own responses." Consider, for example, the reactions of two carriers of non-Elite culture, the first of popular culture, the banjo player Johnny St. Cyr. He always felt that the creative impulses of the average person and his responses in a creative situation were immense:

> You see, the average man is very musical. Playing music for him is just relaxing. He gets as much kick out of playing as other folks get out of dancing. The more enthusiastic his audience is, why the more spirit the working man's got to play. And with your natural feelings that way you never make the same thing twice. Every time you play a tune new ideas come to mind and you slip that one in.

Compare that true artist's philosophy with that of Liberace, to whom the "whole trick is to keep the tune well out in front," to play "the melodies" and skip the "spiritual struggles." He always knows "just how many notes (his) audience will stand for," and if he has time left over he fills in "with a lot of runs up and down the keyboard."

Here in condensed form is the difference between popular and mass art and popular and mass artists. Both aim for different goals. St. Cyr is a truly creative artist in both intent and accomplishment. His credentials are not invalidated merely by the fact that he works in essentially a popular idiom. Given the limitations of his medium—if indeed these limitations are real—he can still be just as great a creator as—perhaps greater than—Rubenstein. It is incorrect to pit jazz against classical music, the popular against the elite. They are not in competition. Each has its own purposes, techniques and accomplishments. They complement each other rather than compete.

Another fine example can be found among the youth of today and their rebellion against what they consider the establishment. They are obviously not a part of the static mass, to whom escape is everything. Instead they are vigorously active, and in their action create dynamic and fine works of art, as examination of their songs, their art, their movies, etc., dramatically demonstrates.

It is also unfair to give blanket condemnation to mass art, though obviously the accomplishments of mass art are less than those of "higher" forms. Liberace does not aspire to much, and perhaps reaches even less. His purposes and techniques are inferior, but not all his, or the many other workers in the level, are completely without value.

All levels of culture, it must never be forgotten, are distorted by the lenses of snobbery and prejudice which the observers wear. There are no hard and fast lines separating one level from another.

Popular culture also includes folk culture. The relationship between folk culture and popular and elite cultures is still debatable. In many ways folk culture borrows from and imitates both.

Historically folk art has come more from the hall than from the novel, has depended more upon the truly creative—though unsophisticated—spirit than the mediocre imitator. "Sir Patrick Spens," one of the greatest songs (poems) ever written, was originally the product of a single creative genius. Today's best folklore-to-be, that is the most esthetically satisfying folklore which is working into tradition today, is that of such people as Woody Guthrie, Larry Gorman and such individual artists.

To a large number of observers, however, folklore is felt to be the same as popular culture. To another large number folklore derives directly from popular culture, with only a slight time lag. To them, today's popular culture is tomorrow's folklore. Both notions are gross and out of line.

Esthetically folk culture has two levels. There is superb folk art and deficient, mediocre folk art. Esthetically folk art is more nearly akin to Elite art, despite the lack of sophistication that much folk art has, than to popular. Elite art has much that is inferior, as even the most prejudiced critic must admit. In motivation of artist, also, folk art is close to Elite, for like the elite artist the truly accomplished folk artist values individualism and personal expression, he explores new forms and seeks new depths in expression and feeling. But there are at the same time workers in folklore who are mere imitators, just trying to get along—exactly like their counterparts in mass culture.

Thus all elements in our culture (or cultures) are closely related and are not mutually exclusive one from another. They constitute one long continuum. Perhaps the best metaphorical figure for all is that of a flattened ellipsis, or a lens. In the center, largest in bulk and easiest seen through is Popular Culture, which includes Mass Culture.

On either end of the lens are High and Folk Cultures, both looking fundamentally alike in many respects and both having a great deal in common, for both have keen direct vision and extensive peripheral insight and acumen. All four derive in many ways and to many degrees from one another, and the lines of demarcations between any two are indistinct and mobile.

Despite the obvious difficulty of arriving at a hard and fast definition of popular culture, it will probably be to our advantage—and a comfort to many who need one—to arrive at some viable though tentative understanding of how popular culture can be defined.

Two scholars who do attempt a definition, following George Santayana's broad distinctions between work and play, believe that "Popular Culture is really what people do when they are not working." This definition is both excessively general and overly exclusive, for it includes much that is "high" culture and leaves out many aspects which obviously belong to popular culture.

One serious scholar defines a total culture as "The body of intellectual and imaginative work which each generation receives" as its tradition. Basing our conclusion on this one, a viable definition for Popular Culture is all those elements of life which are not narrowly intellectual or creatively elitist and which are generally though not necessarily disseminated through the mass media. Popular Culture consists of the spoken and printed words, sounds, pictures, objects and artifacts. "Popular Culture" thus embraces all levels of our society and culture other than the Elite—the "popular," "mass" and "folk." It includes most of the bewildering aspects of life which hammer us daily.

Such a definition, though perhaps umbrella-like in its comprehensiveness, provides the latitude needed at this point, it seems, for the serious scholar to study the world around him. Later, definitions may need to pare edges and change lighting and emphasis. But for the moment, inclusiveness is perhaps better than exclusiveness.

I. VOCABULARY

disseminate   coherence   pomposity
elite   esthetic   salient
stasis   continuum   quintessential

II. QUESTIONS ON CONTENT

1. What is Browne's definition of popular culture?
2. Browne calls William Gass an "elitist critic." Explain what that means.
3. What does Susan Sontag say the function of art today is?
4. What is happening to "folk art," as Browne defines it, in our society today?
5. List the five attributes Browne cites as characteristics of popular culture.
6. Select some examples of popular culture in the United States from the following areas: food, fashion, sports, music, business, and art.
7. What does our popular culture say about American civilization?

III. QUESTIONS ON FORM

1. How many actual definitions can you find within Browne's essay?
2. For what audience is the essay written?
3. What is Browne's attitude toward popular culture?
4. Which approach does Browne use in this essay: expository, persuasive, descriptive, or narrative? Why?

IV. SUGGESTIONS FOR WRITING

1. Describe the area of popular culture that interests you most.
2. Using specific examples, defend "elite culture."
3. Recount your experiences at a popular culture locale or event (concert, disco, video arcade, and so on) that you have attended recently.
4. Analyze a recent popular culture phenomenon (fast food, designer jeans, punk rock music, and so on) and its impact on U. S. culture.

Barbara Goldsmith is an author and social historian. She has also been an editor on numerous magazines and has written extensively for television. Her most recent book is *Little Gloria, Happy at Last* (1980).

The Meaning of Celebrity

Barbara Goldsmith

At a recent Manhattan dinner party, the celebrity guests included a United States Senator, an embezzler, a woman rumored to spend $60,000 a year on flowers, a talk-show host, the chief executive officer of one of America's largest corporations, a writer who had settled a plagiarism suit and a Nobel laureate.

The line between fame and notoriety has been erased. Today we are faced with a vast confusing jumble of celebrities: the talented and untalented, heroes and villains, people of accomplishment and those who have accomplished nothing at all, the criteria for their celebrity being that their images encapsulate some form of the American Dream, that they give enough of an appearance of leadership, heroism, wealth, success, danger, glamour and excitement to feed our fantasies. We no longer demand reality, only that which is real seeming.

Our age is not one in which the emperor's golden nightingale is exposed as valueless when the true pure voice of the real bird pours forth, but one in which the synthetic product has become so seductive and malleable that we no longer care to distinguish one from the other.

Synthetic celebrities are our own creation, the modern equivalent of biblical graven images. In bowing down to them, we absent ourselves from the everyday ethical and moral judgments that insure the health of a society.

Copyright © 1983 by The New York Times Company. Reprinted by permission.

We cling to outmoded standards in according these fabricated celebrities all the substantial rewards we once reserved for those who deserved our adulation: social acceptance, head-of-the-line access, public acclaim, monetary gains and the ability to influence the power structures and institutions of our nation.

In rewarding these individuals, our society often exempts them from hard moral rules and equal justice.

When the film executive Robert Evans was convicted of cocaine use, his sentence was to create a program to deter young people from using drugs. When the Hollywood studio head David Begelman pleaded no contest to the charges of embezzling funds from Columbia Pictures, he was ordered to continue his psychiatric care. When the international celebrity art dealer Frank Lloyd was convicted of falsifying his books on the purchase and sale prices of the late Mark Rothko's paintings, thereby defrauding Rothko's two children of millions of dollars, his sentence was to donate $100,000 to the Fund for Public Schools to be used in educating children in art.

Contrast these sentences to the one given William James Rummel for three nonviolent crimes that netted him a total of $230.11—life imprisonment (a judgment upheld by the Supreme Court). Or that of Jerry Helm, also sentenced to life imprisonment (a sentence recently overturned by the Supreme Court) for writing a check for $100 on a nonexistent account.

The rewards of villainy and heroism often prove equal. A decade down the road from Watergate, there have been 169 books written about this affair; they have generated an estimated total of $100 million in profits, much of the money garnered by President Nixon and his men, several of whom were imprisoned for their deeds.

Our inability or lack of concern in questioning the qualifications of people to be celebrated represents an increasingly pernicious phenomenon, for it is axiomatic of a society that we are who we celebrate.

The evolution from reality to image has been relatively rapid. In 1962, the social historian Daniel J. Boorstin alerted Americans to what then seemed a distant threat: "We risk being the first people in history to have been able to make their illusions so vivid, so persuasive, so realistic, that they can live in them." What Boorstin could not have predicted was how the swiftness of our technological achievements, combined with the personal disillusionments of the last two decades, would encourage us to manufacture our fantasies while simultaneously destroying our former role models and ripping away the guideposts of the past. The result is that we have created synthetic celebrities whom we worship, however briefly, because they vicariously act out our noblest or basest desires.

Earlier this century, the proliferation of magazines, newspapers, network radio and Hollywood movies propelled celebrities into prominent positions in the national psyche. Now images can be instantly transmitted across the nation, indeed, the world, sometimes with disastrous results. Marshall

McLuhan, the late masscommunications expert, credited television with turning terrorism from an isolated phenomenon into an international spectacle by allowing its practitioners to make free use of electronic facilities to publicize their causes. Political protesters inform the news media of their intentions, then stage demonstrations in front of the cameras. Even intimate tragedies become public events, turning those involved into momentary celebrity performers.

In today's highly technological world, reality has become a pallid substitute for the image reality we fabricate for ourselves, which in turn intensifies our addiction to the artificial. Anyone who has attended a political convention or a major sporting event knows that watching the proceedings on television, where cameras highlight the most riveting moments, then replay and relate them to similar situations, provides us with more stimulating and complex perceptions than being there does.

Next year's visitors to the Grand Canyon need not see it. One mile from the boundary will be a $5 million complex where they will be able to view a film of the way the canyon looks during all four seasons and take a simulated raft ride through artificial rapids.

Thomas Hoving, former director of New York's Metropolitan Museum of Art, predicts that within the next decade there will be a "quantum leap in the appreciation of art." By pushing a button in our living room, we will be able to exactly replicate any work of art in any museum in the world.

"Andy Warhol's Overexposed: A No-Man Show," will star a $400,000 computerized robot of the artist that has such sophisticated pre-programmed speech that it can hold press conferences and answer questions. In creating his robot, Warhol, who frequently serves as a bellwether of our celebrity society, has simply severed his image from himself, thus defining the ultimate in synthetic celebrity.

"Technology," wrote the author Max Frisch, "is the knack of so arranging the world that we don't have to experience it."

Paralleling the technological advances of the last two decades have been a series of moral and ethical blows to the American psyche that have produced a crisis in confidence in the validity of our perceptions. No longer are there immutable standards by which to judge ourselves, or positive role models to provide a pattern for conduct. These have all but vanished in the wake of the assassinations of John Fitzgerald Kennedy, Martin Luther King Jr. and Robert F. Kennedy, in the moral ambiguity of Vietnam, in the senseless violence of Kent State and in the traumatic aftermath of the "third-rate burglary" of Watergate.

But the need to celebrate other human beings—some symbolic, some real—is a continuing psychic and societal fact. Throughout history, the accomplishments of these individuals have provided a pattern for our aspirations, their frailties have bolstered our self-images. Celebrity worship, the psychoanalyst Ernest van den Haag says, is directly traceable to the basic and continuing need for authority figures, the first of whom are our parents.

In the past, Americans celebrated such positive examples as Johnny Appleseed, Horatio Alger and a father who "Knows Best." As societal needs changed, so did the nature of celebrity. In the second half of the 19th century, those who in the words of social scientist Thorstein Veblen received "the deference of the common people" were men who epitomized the Industrial Revolution—Carnegie, Morgan, Rockefeller, Vanderbilt. These captains of industry, crude and rapacious though they were, felt a sense of moral obligation rooted in the puritan ethic. They endowed hospitals, museums, churches, universities; contributed to the poor, and, observed Veblen, served as a "guide to literature and art, church and state, science and education, law and morals—the standard container of civic virtue." The trade-off seemed an equable one: preferential treatment in exchange for providing role models and economic support.

Though our deep-seated need to have individuals to celebrate has remained stable, our society has not. Many people wish to be admired, not respected, to be perceived as successful and glamorous, not as hard working and righteous. Among the worthy now are synthetic celebrities, famed for their images not their deeds. They need not have a sense of moral or ethical obligation, and often use our approbation for their own cynical purposes. The trade-off is no longer fair.

In a society where the details of private lives are subjected to public scrutiny, role models have all but vanished. In the past, we often provided those we celebrated with a protective cloak to cover their fallibilities and frailties. It was an unwritten law, for example, that the press never photographed President Franklin Delano Roosevelt except from the waist up, so that the dispirited society of the 1930's would not be reminded its leader was physically crippled. Today such amenities are not practiced, nor are figures from the past spared. Long after their deaths, we are informed that Presidents Franklin D. Roosevelt, Eisenhower, Kennedy and Johnson all were unfaithful to their wives.

The public appetite for celebrity and pseudo-event has grown to Pantagruelian proportions, and for the first time in history, the machinery of communications is able to keep up with these demands, even to outrun them, creating new needs we never knew existed.

To one extent or another, all the branches of the media have become complicitous to this pursuit. People magazine is prototypical. In one issue, novelist E. L. Doctorow is mentioned, but so are Joanie and Gary McGuffin, an Ontario couple on a 6,200-mile canoeing honeymoon across Canada. Elizabeth Taylor appears, but so does Frank Spisak, a neo-Nazi murderer. The ersatz and the real appear side by side, and the willingness to distinguish between them has been abdicated.

Charlotte Curtis of The New York Times was one of hundreds of members of the news media who interviewed a current celebrity, and wrote: "While she was here, she said, she put the couple's spacious Fifth Avenue duplex on the market. . . . the asking price is expected to exceed $6 million. . . . 'We'll move to the New Jersey place.'. . . a $3.5 million, 430-acre estate in Bedminster. Besides the 25-room Georgian mansion . . . there are guest cottages, a cattle barn and stables."

In the not-so-distant past, this description could only have been of a member of high society. It was written, however, about Cristina DeLorean. When her auto-executive husband was arrested on charges of cocaine dealing, both DeLoreans became instant synthetic celebrities. John Z. DeLorean achieved what he admitted was one of his goals in life, though presumably not in the manner he expected: to appear on the cover of Time magazine. (He also appeared on the covers of New York and People magazines.) The couple also announced that they had been offered millions for their story.

The image of a titan standing at the pinnacle of society was maintained in the coverage of the trial and the subsequent appeals of the guilty verdict handed down to Claus von Bülow, accused of injecting his heiress wife with insulin in an attempt to murder her.

At the latest Whitney Museum of American Art Biennial Exhibition, the painter Eric Fischl depicts a couple in the act of sexual intercourse. A video camera records their actions and projects them on a television screen in front of the couple. The man's eyes are riveted to his own image on the television set, which is clearly more exciting than the act itself. The most primal and basic of human acts has become secondary to its own image.

The rise of synthetic celebrity coincides with what the writer Jules Henry calls "the erosion of the capacity for emulation, the loss of the ability to model oneself consciously after another person." When Lisa Birnbach, a young writer who is currently preparing a comprehensive guide to American universities, asks students to name their heroes, many say they have none. A typical explanation is that they are no longer willing to admire any person. (Indeed, Marilyn Monroe, James Dean, Elvis Presley, Humphrey Bogart and the like may have become enduring deities precisely because they are dead and can no longer manipulate or disappoint us.) Those students who do name their heroes often include the name of Blake Carrington, the unprincipled tycoon character in the television series "Dynasty."

Daily, the concept of the melding of heroes and villains plays itself out on prime-time television where notorious, immoral, self-centered individuals, often the perpetrators of heinous crimes, are pseudoheroes. J. R. Ewing of "Dallas" is a scoundrel, but he is vigorous, rich, powerful and successful.

George Gerbner, dean of the University of Pennsylvania's Annenberg School of Communications, estimates that by the time a typical American child reaches adulthood, he or she will have absorbed more than 30,000 electronic "stories." These have, he suggests, replaced the socializing role of the pre-industrial church in creating "a cultural mythology" that establishes the norm of approved behavior and belief. Gerbner concludes that watchers of prime-time television are receiving a highly synthetic picture of the real world, but that they accept it *more readily* than reality itself.

Credibility and plausibility have replaced truth. During the Watergate investigation, the American public was given explanations that seemed believable. As facts were discovered that rendered them implausible, President Nixon's press secretary, Ron Ziegler, admitted that his previous statements had become "inoperative." Writer Christopher Lasch noted in "The Culture of Narcissism" that "many commentators assumed Ziegler was groping for a euphemistic way of saying that he had lied. What he meant, however, was that his earlier statements were no longer believable. Not their falsity but their inability to command assent rendered them 'inoperative.' The question of whether they were true or not was beside the point."

A university student recently ventured the opinion that if the present Republican Administration wished to remain in power it must give the appearance of helping the poor. When the student was asked should they not simply help the poor, the reply was that, of course, that would be preferable, but if it were done invisibly it would not accomplish the desired end. The subject was, after all, remaining in power and only the visible appearance of helping would win the necessary sympathy and dissipate potential anger. This cynical understanding of the importance of image reality is formidable, and frightening. What counts is that our President project an image of decisiveness and self-confidence, not that he actually be able to solve the country's problems.

We deal openly in terms of image. Universities, religious groups, business organizations, charities, law firms, all speak of their desire to create a favorable image. The woman in a Pine Power television commercial laments, "This mop will ruin my image." Designer Bill Blass says that while he will license such products as chocolate and perfume, he will never lend his name to tires, which would damage his image.

With success as the primary goal, the temptation to take shortcuts is pervasive. The present art market is glutted with Jungian nightmares, full of energy but devoid of intellect. In recent years, there has been a rash of plagiarism suits against prominent writers. Businessman-author Michael Thomas says that today much of business is about "accounting not accountability."

Narcissists, Lasch believes, have the best chance of becoming celebrities because they present pseudoheroic images, are often possessed of magnetic personalities and have "no compunctions about manipulating people or their environment, and no feelings of obligation toward truth." Sociopaths, too, by virtue of the fact that they are totally amoral, incapable of guilt or shame, qualify as excellent material.

The rewards of celebrity are so substantial and seductive that genuinely talented and otherwise level-headed individuals in the arts, business and the humanities are willing to sacrifice their privacy and sense of self to commingle with the synthetic members of this privileged group.

The longer one remains a celebrity, the longer one continues to be rewarded. In explaining why he had signed up yet another book on Henry Kissinger, Summit Books' president James H. Silberman said that he had great confidence in Kissinger's "ability to keep himself in the public eye." Norman Mailer, who recently signed a deal with Random House to write four books over a nine-year period for $4 million, has written of himself, "of necessity, part of Mailer's remaining funds of sensitivity went right into the war of supporting his image and working for it." Early on, Mailer created a renegade literary image for himself, tied to drinking and violence. Now he strenuously objects when the news media clings to his old image and does not print more about his refurbished one as a paterfamilias and partygoer.

Because it is fabricated, image can be altered at will. Andy Warhol owes the longevity of his celebrity to the fact that his image keeps changing to suit the temper of the times. His 1960's go-go image of black-leather motorcycle jacket, patched dungarees and drugged companions has given way to the conservative tailored suits and socialite parties of the 1980's.

Image is essential to the celebrity because the public judges him by what it sees—his public posture as distinguished from his private person. Entertainers are particularly adept at perfecting their images, learning to refine the nuances of personality. Indeed, the words "celebrity" and "personality" have become interchangeable in our language. Public-relations people, who are paid to manufacture celebrities for public consumption, are often referred to as image makers.

Celebrities are invariably accepted as instant authorities. Advertising takes advantage of this, fusing the celebrity with the product to be sold. Robert Young's long association with a physician role on television helped solidify his image as a medical authority, adding credence to his endorsement of Sanka. A similar case is the endorsement of Scoundrel perfume by the actress Joan Collins, the bad girl of television's "Dynasty" series.

Former Senator Sam Ervin, who came close to genuine heroism in the Watergate affair, reduced his stature to synthetic celebrity by using his familiar countryboy locutions in television commercials while never leaving home without his American Express card.

So accustomed are we to seeing celebrities identified with products that those who are not initially celebrities become them as a result of their appearances in advertisements. Leona Helmsley, president of Helmsley Hotels, utilizes the image of a queen, bountifully dispensing her largess to potentional guests in advertisements that rely heavily on the public's identification with her life style, which includes a phone in the bath, magnifying mirror, king-size bed, etc.

It has become common practice to use charity to bolster one's celebrity.

Benefits proliferate, often with no more involvement on the part of celebrities than a lending of their names. Television talk-show host Phil Donahue, who on many occasions has served as host at fund-raisers, said in an article he wrote for Television Quarterly that Americans have been lulled into thinking that "celebrity appearances can solve the problems of human misery. As long as we continue to congratulate ourselves for working on the 'gala' charity dinner, or the telethon, or the celebrity auction . . . we delay the time when we finally face up to the painful fact that this country's priorities are wrong. . . . Sick children ought to receive . . . a piece of our public money pie . . . Show business should be out of *this* business."

The combination of crime and the minutiae of private lives is also a sure-fire guarantee of celebrity. Truman Capote established the pattern in modern times when he reached into the criminal element to write "In Cold Blood" and escalated two men who had wiped out an entire family to celebrity. Recently, there have been two books on Jean Harris, who became an instant celebrity when she killed the Scarsdale Diet doctor, Herman Tarnower. Even in prison, she is a media draw. She was recently interviewed at the Bedford Hills Correctional Facility for radio and television news programs.

The brigand, the flamboyant person who "beats the system," has always been an appealing figure in our culture. Those who operate outside the system gain particular popularity in times of economic stress, when people feel they have little control over their own destinies. Today's social climate has much in common with that of the early 1930's. Then, too, the notorious were invited to dine at the finest tables. Fanny Brice and mobster Nicky Arnstein became media idols. Bank robber Willie Sutton gave speeches at Rotary Club meetings across the nation. But then our admiration for the outlaw was tempered by moral and ethical strictures. Crimes of true villainy or violence were never condoned. As our sense of reality was undermined, so were our standards. In the 1930's, kidnapping was considered one of the most heinous crimes. In the recent film, "King of Comedy," it is through kidnapping that the protaganist achieves his dream of becoming a celebrity.

Because our diets are so glutted with reprocessed images and events, any vestige of spontaneous reality can create a sensation. In 1970, the writer Tom Wolfe noted the phenomenon of "radical chic," whereby members of celebrity society associated with renegades in order to feel the shock of adrenalin that comes from experiencing the sensation of danger without any real threat. Wolfe equated this with the 19th-century French phenomenon of *nostalgie de la boue,* in which the aristocracy could be revitalized by taking on certain styles of the lower orders. But there has always been a clear understanding of who was the patron and who the patronized, and a certain moral code applied.

A recent poll conducted by Yankelovich, Skelly and White Inc. revealed that 63 percent of the American public is ambivalent about embracing a totally self-centered, self-fulfilled style of life, asserting that the old standards are still important. However, 80 percent admitted that they have been deeply affected by the new mentality and feel that their own need for sensation, novelty and ego fulfillment takes precedence over the needs of *all* other people.

Synthetic celebrities are, after all, but reflections of ourselves and in deifying them we are holding a mirror to our own foibles. This reflected image cannot illuminate, it can only destroy our capacity to take an interest in anything outside of ourselves. A society that exalts flights from reality sets a dangerous course. Only a culture that acknowledges power without moral obligation could spawn such celebrity monsters as Charles Manson and the Rev. Jim Jones. John Lennon's assassin, Mark David Chapman, wanted nothing more than forever to be identified with the singer he idolized. Now he is.

The meretricious aspects of synthetic celebrity have been consistently explored by the film director Martin Scorsese. The plot of his "Taxi Driver" revolves around Travis Bickle, a psychotic loser who sets out to assassinate a Presidential candidate but fails. He succeeds, however, in murdering three men. The movie's penultimate scene shows Bickle's bedroom wall covered with numerous newspaper articles about his heroism, as well as a fulsome note of gratitude from the parents of the young prostitute, played by Jodie Foster, whose pimp was one of those he murdered. In the closing frames of the film, a young woman who has been the object of Bickle's sexual desires, a woman who has previously ignored him, now notices him. As a celebrity, he has become worthy of her attention.

When asked why he attempted to assassinate President Reagan, John W. Hinckley Jr., a young drifter, said he did it "to impress Jodie Foster." Hinckley says he saw "Taxi Driver" 15 times and had absorbed its implicit message with stunning acuity: It isn't what you do, it's doing something that will impress enough to project you into the realm of celebrity.

Hinckley was judged not guilty by reason of insanity.

As our lives become more and more difficult to comprehend, we become so accustomed to retreating into our illusions that we forget we have created them ourselves. We treat them as if they were real and in so doing we make them real. Image supersedes reality. Synthetic celebrities become the personification of our hollow dreams.

I. VOCABULARY

synthetic	encapsulate	proliferation	immutable
plagiarism	adulation	psyche	frailties
notoriety	pernicious	fabricate	complicitous

ambivalent	Pantagrulian	pervasive	protagonist
rapacious	emulation	posture	meretricious
scrutiny	meld	credence	fulsome
amenities	heinous	flamboyant	acuity

II. QUESTIONS ON CONTENT

1. Why, according to the essay, do we need to celebrate other human beings? Who is your hero or heroine? Why?
2. What kinds of celebrities did Americans admire in the past? Why? Can you name some others who should have been included?
3. What is a celebrity? What are the rewards of celebrity?
4. What is a synthetic celebrity? How does he or she differ from a genuine celebrity? Do you agree with the author's distinction?
5. What recent changes in our society have given rise to the synthetic celebrity?
6. What role do the media, especially television, play in creating and perpetuating synthetic celebrities and pseudoheroes? How can these people become enslaved by the media?
7. List at least five synthetic celebrities cited by the author. Can you add any others to the list?
8. Why do we create synthetic personalities? What does this tell us about ourselves? About our society? Why does the author regard this overtaking of reality by image as dangerous?
9. How does Barbara Tuchman's criticism of mass culture in "The Decline Of Quality" help to explain the prevalence of the synthetic personality?

II. QUESTIONS ON FORM

1. How does the author attract the reader's attention in the first paragraph of the essay?
2. For what audience is this essay intended? Is this the same audience as the one Tuchman addresses in "The Decline of Quality"? Explain.
3. Goldsmith is an author and social historian. Is she therefore qualified to write on the meaning of celebrity? Why or why not?
4. How does the author define the synthetic celebrity? Compare this method with those used by Browne and Tuchman in their definitions of popular culture and of quality.
5. What is the author's attitude toward synthetic celebrities? Where is this attitude best expressed?
6. What examples are given to support the idea that celebrities are usually accepted as instant authorities? Are these examples sufficient and appropriate?
7. What is the function of the last section of the essay?

III. SUGGESTIONS FOR WRITING

1. Formulate your own definition of the synthetic celebrity and develop it by specific examples and comparison and contrast.
2. Describe your image of yourself. Then explain why you have this image and whether or not you are satisfied with it.
3. Using the paragraph on Andy Warhol as a model, choose a celebrity and trace the changes in his or her image over a decade or more.
4. Should "villains" be rewarded for their illegal or immoral actions?
5. Reality, says Goldsmith, is preferable to image or illusion. Argue pro or con.

Robert Sargent is an associate professor and chairperson of the English Department at Hofstra University.

The Mystique of the Empire State Building

Robert Sargent

Today is the 50th birthday of the Empire State Building, whose outline against the sky has represented for me, since childhood, the power and grandeur of New York City and of America. Yet this building which seemed to me as a child so permanent, so strongly rooted, is actually only nine years older than I am.

I think to myself, "We're both middle-aged." No—I'm middle-aged but this 50-year-old is still an infant so far as the lives of great buildings in the world go. Is the celebration of its birthday, then mere nostalgia? Are we Americans only able to feel for a past we ourselves have known?

We may have a rush of memories as we watch Mayor Edward Koch celebrate the building's anniversary tonight on the 11 o'clock news. I believe, however, that it is worth more thought than that. For good and bad, the Empire State Building symbolizes better than any other structure (including the White House) what we have been and are becoming as Americans.

Joseph Campbell, the mythologist, has said that we may see what a civilization values by what it chooses to make its tallest buildings.

The tallest structures of the ancient world are the pyramids of Egypt, the tombs of the god-kings; of the medieval world, the great cathedrals of Europe; of the Renaissance-modern world, structures that are associated

Reprinted by permission of Robert Sargent.

with political power or national leaders (our own Washington Monument, 555 feet high, is a relatively late example.) In our time, skyscrapers like the Empire State Building symbolize the dominance of economic power and of commercial values.

Most American define their life's goals in terms of work and evaluate their success in terms of money. The metaphors we use to measure our progress come from movement in space—"getting ahead" or "climbing the ladder." We associate spectacular achievement and power with being "on top" or gaining the room at the top, the executive suite of offices or the penthouse.

However, we have also inherited myths from the ancient Greeks and Hebrews that suggest it is dangerous to get too far off the ground, that in forgetting human limitations we risk defeat and destruction.

There is Icarus of Greek myth, who flew too close to the sun on wings of feathers and wax and who, when the wax melted, fell into the sea and drowned.

The Bible has the story of the Tower of Babel, in which Noah's descendants tried to construct a tower with its top in the heavens. God punished its builders for their presumption, scattering them throughout the world and confusing their language so that they could not understand one another's speech, making it impossible for them to complete the tower.

Not all Americans have been or are comfortable with the tremendous impact of economic forces on the cultural life of our society.

Long before the end of the 1920s, the time at which the Chrysler and Empire State Buildings were being constructed, some American intellectuals and artists left for Europe in search of the past, for a civilization that still valued the spiritual and esthetic dimensions of life.

Others remained in the United States, embracing the new order—recognizing its faults, but admiring its ease and energy.

Although those who stayed were aware that the giant buildings and the forces they represented had the power to dwarf the individual and make him or her a faceless member of the crowd, they felt that these buildings, in reaching for the sky, embodied the aspiration and sense of opportunity of Americans, just as the movement into the vast unsettled terrain of the continental United States had represented these things for earlier generations of Americans.

Henry James, the novelist, and his brother, William James, the philosopher, took opposing views regarding the skyscraper and the economic forces it represented. Henry felt more comfortable and creative living and working in London than in New York. He complained that the skyline of New York was a "pincushion in profile" and that the city in the future would be "a huge, continuous 50-floored conspiracy against the very idea of the ancient graces." History and beauty would be replaced by "mere economic convenience." William felt differently; he viewed the skyscrapers and the noise and movement of the city with excitement and pleasure.

34 Popular Writing

The construction of the Empire State Building required ingenuity and risk, inventing a means that allowed one to go up in space, to go further into the unknown than had been gone before. The space shuttle is a recent example of the energy, ingenuity and risk-taking of Americans. Even if the space shuttle is used in the future more for commercial and military purposes than for the exploration of space, its flight involves a heroic gesture.

In the same way, to see the Empire State Building only as a commercial building is to undervalue it. It is a piece of sculpture, capable of surprising and overwhelming us, when all of a sudden we encounter it, whether crossing Herald Square or from high points on Long Island or in New Jersey. And yet, as a commercial building it is in keeping with its time and place, unlike St. Patrick's Cathedral, which though Gothic in style, seems strangely new in contrast to the ancient cathedrals of Europe, like those at York and Chartres.

There has been a major change that has altered what the Empire State Building signifies. It was the addition to the building's top, on May 1, 1951, of the television tower.

This signaled the beginning of a complex revolution through which we are still passing. Some people blame all contemporary ills on television. Others proclaim that it has made the whole world one "electronic village," that we are in a postindustrial society in which the transfer of information is more important than the manufacturing and selling of goods. It is a fact that, since 1951, the tallest structures that have been built, according to the "Guinness Book of World Records," are all radio or television masts. And circling high above these are the communication satellites.

So if Joseph Campbell is right when he says that the purpose for which the tallest buildings are used signify what is valued most in a society, then we are moving from an age of commerce into an age of communication, from an age of personal and national economic assertion into an age in which ideas and information are valued and shared.

I. VOCABULARY

mystique ingenuity metaphor
Renaissance Icarus symbol

II. QUESTIONS ON CONTENT

1. Sargent's article states that the Empire State Building symbolizes certain values to Americans. What are they?
2. What addition has the Empire State Building acquired? What values are imparted to this addition?
3. Paragraph five presents some examples associating height with power.

Does the world still align height with ascendency? Select some examples to support your view.
4. The essay cites Joseph Campbell's view that the values of a civilization are revealed by its tallest buildings. What other structures could indicate social values? Give some supporting examples.
5. How does Anthony Smith's essay in the second part of this chapter comment on Sargent's views on telecommunication?

III. QUESTIONS ON FORM

1. Identify Sargent's thesis sentence.
2. What is Sargent's pattern of organization here? Cite the transitional paragraphs.
3. What is the author's purpose in discussing the brothers Henry and William James?
4. This is a persuasive essay. What methods has Sargent used to persuade you of his point of view? Has he succeeded?

IV. SUGGESTIONS FOR WRITING

1. Have you ever been to the Empire State Building or to another one of America's famous skyscrapers? Describe your experience and emotions.
2. Write an essay describing the most impressive monument, ruin, or other structure created by man that you have seen. Explain why.
3. Write an essay espousing the power and impact of small objects and/or people on our civilization.

An astute commentator on popular culture, **Leslie A. Fiedler** is the author of numerous critical works, including *Love and Death in the American Novel* (1960, rev. 1966) and *The Inadvertent Epic* (1979). He is Samuel L. Clemens Professor of English at the State University of New York at Buffalo.

Up, Up and Away—
The Rise and Fall of Comic Books

Leslie A. Fiedler

I read my first comic book on a school playground in Newark, N.J., sometime in the late 1920's, with a sense of entering a world not only forbidden but magical, like the world of my unconfessable dreams. It was an "eight-page

Copyright © 1976 by The New York Times Company. Reprinted by permission.

Bible" slipped to me by the class Bad Boy: a pornographic burlesque of the comic strip "Tillie the Toiler" in which she and her usually impotent admirer, Mac, performed sexual acts beyond the scope of my unaided 12-year-old fantasy. That they had bodies at all under the conventional garb they never shucked in their daily adventures seemed to me wondrous enough, and that they had usable genitals as well at once blasphemous and miraculous.

I have, however, recently looked at a scholarly collection of such erotic travesties once bootlegged across the border from sunlit Tijuana, where all was permitted, to darkest Newark, where all was forbidden; and I have been appalled to discover how illdrawn, perfunctorily plotted and anaphrodisiac they now seem. Yet neither the magic nor the threat of subversion has wholly departed from me, either from those Bibles themselves or indeed from the whole genre to which they introduced me.

True, comic books had to make a somewhat more respectable second start in the late 1930's before they were accepted as fit for children in whose innocence parents were still pretending to believe. Moreover, the children themselves demanded more than parody of the daily scripts in which sex was absent and violence trivialized; they yearned for a new mythology neither explicitly erotic, overtly terrifying nor frankly supernatural, yet essentially phallic, horrific and magical. Such a mythology was waiting to be released in pulp science fiction, a genre re-created in the United States in 1926 by Hugo Gernsback, who published the first magazine devoted entirely to the genre. He did not invent the name, however, until 1929, just one year before a pair of 16-year-olds, Jerry Siegel and Joe Shuster, reviewed Philip Wylie's "Gladiator" in one of the earliest s.f. fanzines—journals dedicated to amateur criticism of fiction ignored by the critical establishment.

Out of that novel, at any rate, emerged the first and most long-lived of all comic book characters, Superman, whose adventures Siegel and Shuster were already trying to peddle in 1933, though not until 1938 did they persuade a publisher to buy the rights to Superman's name and legend for $130, thus launching the series with which the classic comic book began. Other mythological figures have moved through such publications in the four decades since, ranging from Donald Duck to Dracula. But at its most authentic and popular, the form has belonged always to the avatars of Superman, beginning most notably with Captain Marvel, Batman and Wonder Woman and toward the end including the Fantastic Four of Stan Lee's Marvel Comics.

Yet it required the imminence of World War II before the super-goy dreamed up by a pair of Jewish teenagers from Cleveland in the Great Depression could reach an audience of hundreds of millions starved for wonder but too ill at ease with Gutenberg forms to respond even to science fiction. Only then did the paranoia that is their stock in trade become endemic—the special paranoia of men in cities anticipating in their shared nightmares the saturation bombing that lay just ahead and the consequent end of law and order, perhaps of man himself. The suffering city, Metropolis, which under various names remains the setting for all subsequent Superheroes, is helpless before its external enemies because it is sapped by corruption and fear at its very heart.

But the old American promise of an end to paranoia is there, too, the equivocal dream that had already created the Ku Klux Klan and the vigilantes and the lynch mob, as well as the cowboy hero and the private eye—the dream of a savior in some sense human still, but able to know, as the rest of us cannot, who the enemy really is and to destroy him as we no longer can—not with technology, which is in itself equivocal, but with his bare hands. Small wonder that those who went off to war and in most cases found only boredom, machine-tending, paper shuffling, meaningless drill and endless waiting made the comic books their favorite reading. To them, the dream of meaningful violence was a fantasy as dear and unreal as any they had left at home.

My second exposure to the form came in 1942 as I too moved toward that war and discovered that the Indian boy who accompanied me on the first leg of my journey carried in his paper valise nothing but a spare suit of underwear and half a hundred comic books. Moreover, each time our train stopped, some concerned old lady would thrust into my hands a pack of cigarettes, a candy bar and the latest issue of "Superman" or "Captain Marvel"—tokens of condescension and good will, the last of which I must confess disconcerted me a little, since I was by then, despite my sailor suit, already a professor of literature. But I could not resist reading material pressed on me in much the same spirit as I had been pressing T. S. Eliot and Henry James on my equally reluctant students. I had actually not looked at any comic books since my days in the schoolyard, and this time around the appeal of the tabooed was gone. But I was determined to find out why such kid stuff satisfied large numbers of men moving perhaps toward death, as the high literature whose apostle I then was, did not.

And in fairly short order I was hooked, though I scarcely confessed the fact even to myself. What I discovered behind the seemingly artless style— more grunts and exclamations than words, more image than idea—was old-fashioned *plot*, right down to the O. Henry "hook" that I had taught my students was destroyed forever by Chekhov and Joyce, Gertrude Stein and Hemingway. But by virtue of that very fact, perhaps, there was also a sense of wonder able to compel even in me an ecstatic lifting up of the heart and a kind of shameful excitement in the gut, prompted this time not by sex, which I had grown enlightened enough to think desirable, but by unbridled violence, which I had learned to fear as my parents and teachers had once feared erotic porn.

But I found pathos as well in the double identity of the hero, that Siegel and Shuster invention, product of God knows what very Jewish irony undercutting what it seemed to celebrate. He was a man of steel in one guise, but in the other a short-sighted reporter, a crippled newsboy, an epicene playboy flirting with a teen-age male companion. Phallic but impotent, supermale but a eunuch, incapable of consummating love or begetting a successor; and, therefore, he was a *last hero*, doomed to lonely immortality and banned by an ultimately inexplicable taboo from revealing the secret that would make it possible at least to join the two halves of his sundered self and thus end his comic plight of being forever his own rival for the affection of his best beloved. Ultimately, therefore, the Siegel and Shuster Superman turns out to be not a hero who seems a shlemiel, but a hero who *is* a shlemiel. If this is not essentially funny (and none of the men who read comic books beside me throughout a long war could be persuaded it was so), it is because the joke was on all of us and there was no one left to laugh—not even when the war was over and it had become clear that what it had achieved was the end of heroism rather than of paranoia.

After all, that conflict was resolved not by hand-to-hand struggle but by the dropping (from an invisible machine) of a device contrived in laboratories by white-coated men indistinguishable from the hooked-nose eggheads against whom the Superheroes typically fight for the salvation of the city; and World War II was followed almost immediately by a contest between those forces, East and West, who for the duration were both labeled "good," not just for territory and power but for the exclusive right to that title.

Although the American comic book heroes continued to fight on behalf of the West as if nothing had really changed—substituting Commies for Nazis and, once the Korean War had begun, Chinks for Japs—somehow all conviction had departed. The images of bombed villages, raped and massacred civilians and especially the smashed-in, slant-eyed faces under the steel helmets satisfied for a while the hunger for apocalypse in those growing up at the moment when wartime ennui gave way to the boredom of back-to-school and work. But the world was no longer at war; only a handful of soldiers was engaged in a combat more dubious than mythological and heading toward inevitable stalemate. Besides, the notions of patriotism and heroism destroyed for intellectuals by World War I had begun to wear out for even the most naïve by the end of World War II—especially for the young to whom the only uncompromised law seemed violence for its own sake and the real enemy, therefore, the forces of law and order who sought to make violence a monopoly of the state.

The old Supercomics had been too compromised by their espousal of offical patriotism to satisfy the new hunger for unmediated violence and the new attempt to allay paranoia by identifying with the criminal rather than his victim or even the heroic crime fighter. What was needed was a new adversary literature, and once more the comic books proved resilient enough to respond. In the 1950's, E. C. Comics under the direction of William M. Gaines set the pattern by moving from priggish Superheroes at war to tales of war for violence's sake, to crime and finally to sadomasochistic fantasy. They found an audience particularly among the overprotected children of the white middle classes, for whom the crime in the street available to the poor and the black could be enjoyed only vicariously in a kind of unwitting dream rehearsal of the war against established society which their younger brothers and sisters would act out in the great demonstrations of the late 1960's, becoming the Commies and criminals threatening Metropolis as a new kind of paranoia overtook the adult world.

Embattled bourgeois parents, of the 1950's, convinced by their shrinks that even the unexpurgated Grimms' fairy tales, on which they themselves had been reared, bred anti-social violence in the young, were appalled to find their children reading in such comic books accounts of ball games played with the severed heads of a victim whose entrails had been used to make the baselines. Finding it impossible to believe that such atrocities were produced in response to something within their children themselves— whether an impatience with the very notion of childhood innocence or a lust for naked aggression in a world that had outgrown its old social uses— parents were ready to believe almost any conspiracy theory that exculpated their kids at the expense of someone else: a conspiracy of the masters of media to profit by deliberately corrupting the young (as argued by Frederic Wertham in "Seduction of the Innocent") or a cabal of homosexuals (a favorite theory in Gershon Legman's "Love & Death") against the straight world they resented and envied.

These parents embraced a new kind of paranoia, not resolvable like the earlier ones by the comic books, since comic books themselves were the source of their illusive fears. Comics, therefore, had to learn to censor themselves or be suppressed by a new Puritanism disguised as an enlightened liberalism. What followed was the scandalous 1954 Comics Code, a "voluntary" set of restrictions that the publishers of comic books imposed on themselves as embattled parents, teachers and even Congressional committees closed in for the kill. No one was finally sent to jail, as Gershon Legman had continued to urge, but E. C. Comics, the most creative as well as the best drawn and plotted of the time, was driven out of business by the pious resolve of its less successful competitors to prove that the "medium . . . having come of age on the American cultural scene" could "measure up to its responsibilities by banning all scenes of horror, excessive bloodshed . . . depravity, lust, sadism, masochism" as well as discouraging the "excessive use" of slang and colloquialisms and promising to employ "good grammar" wherever possible.

It was at this point that I came out of the closet and defended the comics in public print. For this I was accused of being not only an enemy of high culture but also a crypto queer and a C.I.A. agent. The cultural cold war and the great repression that followed seemed to me at the time unmitigated disasters; but in retrospect it is clear that the comic books finally benefited by being thus reminded of their disreputable origins and their obligation to remain at all costs part of an adversary culture, colloquial, irreverent, and unredeemably subversive.

The kind of children who preserved behind the backs of their parents old copies of E. C. Horror Comics, identifying them with other forbidden pleasures like rock music, fairy tales, pornography and marijuana, later constituted an audience—unprepared ever to admit that they had grown too old for comic books, just as they had begun by refusing to grant that they were too young—for the new comics that emerged in the 1960's. These were, first the psychedelic fantasies of Stan Lee and Jack Kirby, which subverted the code from within, replacing the beautiful Superhero with a Superfreak, repulsive monsters with soap-opera hangups like the Hulk: then the autobiographical Head Comix of R. Crumb and Gilbert Shelton, in which freaked-out characters, scarcely distinguishable from their dropout middle-class white authors, dedicate their life to pursuits, chiefly sex, sadism and dope, portrayable only by deliberately breaking every taboo of the Comics Code—which is to say bringing back porn "for adults only" more shamelessly than the "eight-page Bibles" ever dared and proffering models of violence more favorably than the ambivalent makers of E. C. Comics were willing to do.

But the 1960's are over and with them, it would seem, the heyday of the comic books that had served once as the scriptures of the cultural revolution at its height and have now become its most trustworthy record. Not that all such publications ceased—Marvel Comics continue to roll off the presses in New York and Head Comix off those in San Francisco and Berkeley where the cultural revolution has gone to die. Even Superman still appears, having survived a score of artists and writers as well as translation into a daily comic strip, radio, movies and TV.

But one does not have to consult the circulation figures, falling for Superman as for all comics characters, to know he will not survive the makers of anthologies, dictionaries, self-congratulatory retrospectives, encyclopedias and histories, which at the moment are piled so high on my desk I can scarcely see the shelves across the room that hold the handful of original comic books I have somehow managed to preserve. Why I agreed in the first place to review these great fat mortuary books I can no longer remember.

It is an absurd way to end a relationship that began in shame and passion, matured in the anguish of a great war and climaxed in an unfashionable defense of what the righteous had agreed to condemn in a time of repression. Yet I have been unable to resist becoming an accomplice in a process that threatens to turn what was once living myth into dead mythology. Perhaps I am writing in the hope of somehow mythicizing my own relationship to the form or even for one instant of magically transforming myself from a fat man with a gray beard who has just spilled a forgotten cup of coffee over his manuscript to the Superhero I have never ceased to be from the moment I realized he was also a Supershlemiel like me—as is only fitting for a fantasy bred by teenage paranoia and doomed to end in middle-aged scholarship.

I. VOCABULARY

blasphemous   pathos   endemic
travesties   psychedelic   schlemiel
genre   ennui   equivocal
paranoia   myth

II. QUESTIONS ON CONTENT

1. Fiedler says that comics bring out the paranoic element in society. What does he mean by that? He also mentions rock music as an inciter of social paranoia. Do you agree?
2. Superman, according to Fiedler, is a "schlemiel." Define this word as you understand it. Do you agree with Fiedler? Does the term apply to other comic book heroes and heroines?
3. What is a myth? Are comic book characters genuine mythic superheroes and heroines?
4. Fiedler writes, "the suffering city, Metropolis . . . helpless before its external enemies because it is sapped by corruption and fear at its very heart." From your own experiences and reading can you apply this description and its implications to other cities?
5. What is the attitude toward comics in society today? Have comics changed? For better or worse?

III. QUESTIONS ON FORM

1. Why does Fiedler present his remarks on comic books in an autobiographical format?
2. Examine carefully Fiedler's final paragraph. Why does he mention the spilled coffee?
3. Does the author approve of comics? What tone does he use throughout the essay?
4. Make a chart of Fiedler's chronological span. With what era does he begin? Where does he conclude?

III. SUGGESTIONS FOR WRITING

1. Recount an anecdote concerning comic books from your own childhood.
2. Describe a comic book hero or heroine and analyze the source of his or her appeal.
3. Children should not be permitted to read a great number of comic books. Argue pro or con.
4. Describe the comics in *Mad Magazine*. How do they differ from "true" comics? Do they represent a development or deterioration of the original?
5. Collecting and selling old comic books is fashionable today. Explain the reasons for this fad.

At home in two different worlds, **John Skow** is a New England based free-lance writer, avid skier, and mountain climber who has written for *Backpacker* and *Outdoor*. He has also written feature articles on celebrities for *Playboy* and *Time* magazines, including the *Time* cover stories on Linda Ronstadt and Cheryl Tiegs.

Games That Play People

John Skow

Skeptical citizens might do well to pay attention to a peculiar clinking sound audible across the land. The noise is made by the estimated 20 billion quarters that poured last year into the arcade monsters. This is a figure that may be the public relations roar of a healthy young industry beating its chest, but one that investment analysts who specialize in the entertainment industry agree is not far wrong. While they spent this $5 billion, video-game addicts also were spending 75,000 man-years playing the machines.

These figures do not include an estimated $1 billion that consumers paid for video-game consoles that hook up to home television sets, and for the expensive cassettes that make them work. For comparison, $5 billion is exactly twice the reported take in the last fiscal year of all of the casinos in Nevada. It is almost twice the $2.8 billion gross of the U. S. movie industry. And it is three times more than the combined television revenues and gate receipts last year of major league baseball, basketball and football.

From what vast aquifer of cash does this astonishing gush of money flow? From the lunch money of schoolchildren, say angry parents who are determined, so to speak, to give video games no quarter. The town fathers

Copyright © 1982 by Time Inc. All rights reserved. Reprinted by permission from TIME.

of Irvington, N.Y. (pop. 6,000), rose up in wrath last July and passed an ordinance designed "to protect the adolescents of the village against the evils associated with gambling" (though video games offer no cash payoff and indeed almost never click out a single free game); they limited each establishment to three machines. Ralph Provenzano, owner of a deli opposite the Irvington Middle School, resents the suggestion that he is corrupting the youth, but agreed to turn off his three machines (Defender, Pac Man and Centipede) before the start of classes each morning. With some justice, he says, "I baby-sat a bunch of kids here all summer. It may have cost them money, but they were here, they were safe, and they didn't get into trouble."

The fears that occasionally are voiced of drug-buzzed, beery teen-agers hanging around video parlors in menacing packs seem absurdly exaggerated, and the likelihood is that communities with troublemaking youngsters had them before the arcades opened. But the video games are enormously addictive, and they do eat a lot of quarters. Atari, one of the leading videogame manufacturers, advertises a cheerful, fast-moving and very popular arcade game called Centipede with the words "Chomp. Chomp. Chomp. Chomp. Chomp" above a drawing of a voracious-looking centipede gnawing a coin.

An adult observer in New London, N.H. (pop. 3,000), wanders into Egan's, a pizza parlor with twelve video games, which has become the town's teen hangout since it opened a few months ago. The place is clean and friendly, with no smell of funny cigarettes (many arcades sternly forbid smoking of any kind) and nothing in sight more menacing than an anchovy pizza. But a conversation with a twelve-year-old boy who is holding his own against Scramble, a Stern Electronics game in which the player tries to fly a jet through what looks like Mammoth Cave, produces unsettling information. "I usually bring $20," says the boy, when asked how much money he spends. As the observer is digesting this, the boy adds, "But today I brought $40." Proprietor Bob Egan, an insurance broker in New Jersey before he moved to New Hampshire last year, says that he too was surprised, but yes, the boy did change $40.

In Orlando, Fla., the consensus of fifth-graders at Blankner Elementary School is that $3 is a "minimum satisfactory amount" to take to an arcade, but several children talked of spending $10 or $20. "I used to spend money on my bike," one boy said ruefully. Not all game players throw huge sums into the coin chutes, but they agree that it takes an investment of between $20 and $50 to become proficient at any game challenging enough to be fun. There is no question that the money drain is one reason why such communities as Babylon, Long Island, Oakland, Calif., Pembroke Pines, Fla., and Durham, N.H., have passed ordinances restricting play by teen-agers of various ages. The New Hampshire Civil Liberties Union asked that enforcement be postponed till the U.S. Supreme Court rules on an ordinance passed in Mesquite, Texas, forbidding play by people under 17. Lower courts have twice struck down the ordinance.

The fact is, however, that teen-agers hoping to bankrupt themselves blissfully with a session of Asteroids or Missile Command may be frustrated not by a prejudicial ordinance but by a lunchtime crowd of adults monopolizing the machines. The Station Break Family Amusement Center in Washington's L'Enfant Plaza opens at 7 a.m.; by 7:15 a dozen men in business suits are blasting away at the games while coffee in plastic cups grows cold. L'Enfant Plaza is within walking distance of at least five major Government agencies. "Office workers seem to need to blow it out" in their fantasies more than other people, says Tom McAuliffe, 33, vice president for operations of the 51-store chain that owns the arcade.

Eric Mondres, 26, a Department of Agriculture staffer, is less cheerful about his addiction. "It's like a drug," he says. "You see the same people here week after week. I've tried to wean myself. I'd like to have back all the money I've spent." Near by, wearing a wet raincoat and steamy glasses, a middle-aged man jabs furiously at the thruster of a Star Castle game. He admits to being an attorney in private practice, but says, "I'd really rather you didn't use my name. This is my secret place. It would drive my wife crazy. I really don't come here very often." Two hours later, he is still there battling the machine's alien psychology—and his own.

An onlooker watching such a scene and disposed to gloom would have no trouble detecting the smell of society's burning insulation. Contrariwise, an optimist sees these lunchless loners as sensible adults wisely granting themselves a period of therapeutic play, avoiding the intake of cholesterol and booze, and emptying their minds of clutter by a method quite as effective as meditation. In Japan, where many of the games originate, a 29-year-old magazine executive named Shozo Kimura, who admits the games have hooked him, views the mass addiction moodily: "Tokyo is a big town. You think you are not lonely, but it is the opposite. People have nothing to do. They don't care about anything. They can't buy houses. They can do nothing with their money except play the games."

The video-game craze, more frenzied even than the universal lust for designer jeans and Kalashnikov assault rifles, has spread across the globe. In West Germany, merchandisers are toting up astonishing Christmas season sales figures that may reach $88 million for home-video consoles and cartridges. In Australia, the quarter-eaters, actually 20¢-piece eaters, bring in $182 million a year. Fascination with the games, often accompanied by cosmic brooding about their presumed bad effect on faith, morals and school attendance, seems to be universal. The games have appeared in Arab settlements in Israel, and in Soweto, Johannesburg's huge black township. Brazil's laws forbid the importing of video games, so they are manufactured locally, and are given the necessary touch of international chic with such English names as Aster Action and Munch Man. In Mexico City, the hot arcade is Chispas ("Sparks"). Video arcades are replacing pool halls as the traditional lounging places for young men in Madrid.

Homosexual cruising is a problem in Amsterdam's arcades. In Stockholm, the games are associated in the public mind with teen-age hoodlumism involving drugs, prostitution and illegal hard liquor. Video addicts under 18 are banned from arcades in West Germany, although younger teen-agers manage to play on home sets in department stores.

In Hollywood, on the other hand, Producer Frank Marshall thinks the video games are "great if you want to take 15 minutes and block everything out. When you're shooting a movie, you're constantly on this high level of adrenaline, and these games use that level to completely absorb you." He kept an Asteroids machine in his office during preproduction work on *Raiders of the Lost Ark*. "It got out of hand," he confesses. "People actually got fired for spending too much time on it."

Nevertheless, there are a Defender, Missile Command and a Donkey Kong game in the offices he shares with Director Steven Spielberg and Producer Kathleen Kennedy. Not many citizens can afford video-arcade games that cost up to $3,500, but two Manhattan dentists, Phil Pierce and Jeanette Tejada, have a Space Invaders on order for their waiting room. There are also machines at other odd way-stops: a Y.M.C.A. in Grand Haven, Mich.; a Baptist church in Merritt Island, Fla.; the basement of Yale's freshman dorm. At Fort Eustis, Va., the Army employs a modified Battlezone as a weapons-training device. The Epilepsy-Center at Johns Hopkins University Medical School uses three specially wired Atari sets to determine the effects of anticonvulsant drugs on learning and ability. The advantage of the games, according to Dr. Eileen Vining, associate director of the center, is that children are eager to make their best efforts in eye-hand coordination tests. The Capital Children's Museum in Washington uses video-game techniques, including wildly changing colors and fast interaction between machine and operator, to teach preschoolers about computers. Children learn measurement by playing with a hungry cartoon worm that eats centimeter segments of lines.

Last year Dun & Bradstreet held a conference for 120 of its managers at Bagatelle Place, a "VIP amusement complex," in the Rye Town, N.Y., Hilton Hotel, which offers a library, a *cappuccino* bar and 33 video games. This classy arcade enforces a dress code after 6 p.m., and serves banquets at which the changemaking attendants, upon request, dress in dinner jackets.

Although Bagatelle staffers deny it, experience suggests tht unless these black-tie dinners are stag affairs, they are almost certain to be social disasters. The reasons are that male arcade players tend to outnumber females by about 20 to 1, and that women, especially if they are wives, generally resent the games, and quite often regard them with outright loathing. Ask men and women at random to explain this undeniable phenomenon, and you get chauvinistic patronizing or matronizing of the worst pop-psychological kind. The most temperate analyst is likely to mention that most women are not conditioned as children to be comfortable with complicated gadgets, or to play shooting games. Ear-weary males, their backs welted with wifely sarcasm, may grumble that women are afraid to look foolish in public, or that they simply do not know how to play (a glib reduction comparable to the feminist slur of a few years ago that men do not know how to cry). They say that women view the games as black holes, soaking up male attention, and that even liberated wives are made nervous when their male protectors act like little boys. Women say they are too sensitive to enjoy the bloodthirsty games, and men counter that, no, women are simply too literal-minded to see that the blood is not real and that the games are harmless fantasy. (Though it is hard to deny that some of the fantasies are fairly creepy. As Producer Frank Marshall admits, when you lose your last city—there goes Cleveland—in Missile Command, "it's depressing.")

The sunny and cheerful exception to the prevalent theme of electronic *Gotterdämmerung,* and one of the few games so far that women play in large numbers, is Bally's Pac Man. Pop psychologizers note that it is not a game of shooting, but—aha!—engulfing. It may also be the ultimate eating disorder; the player directs a happy-looking yellow disc around a maze, as it gobbles cookie-shaped dots, and tries to avoid some not-very-menacing monsters. It is by no means easy to play, though some men feel it is unworthy of serious attention because it has only one hand control. Linda Starkweather, 29, who runs a beauty salon in Union Park, Fla., got hooked on a Pac Man she discovered near by at Jake's Ice Cream Shop. So did her two women employees. They they found another Pac Man at a neighborhood sandwich shop and began straggling back late from lunch hour.

When Starkweather found herself struggling to limit herself at each session to $3 or $4, the obvious next step was to install a Pac Man in her shop. "We've spent all our tips already this morning," she said not long ago, laughing. Ann Williams, one of her former operators and now a Tupperware saleswoman, calls herself a "closet Pacperson." She admits to spending $15 on one session, and although for a while she didn't tell her husband, she feels no guilt: "It's my money; I earned it. There's not a lot of fun things in life. It's taken away my boredom. I've never been as serious about anything as Pac Man."

Serious? Listen to Los Angeles Screenwriter Jeffrey Alan Fiskin, who discovered Pac Man earlier this year during the Hollywood writers' strike: "Oh, pipe down, all you fans of Asteroids and Defenders," he wrote in *California* magazine. "Take your arrested adolescence elsewhere! . . . We want philosophical rigor, a metaphor for life . . ." The task of Pac Man, Fiskin notes solemnly, is to clear a labyrinth, and as he succeeds, he collects point-scoring rewards, all very symbolic: first food in the form of fruit, then keys—"the key to wisdom, the key to the next level; ah, the pure Jungian simplicity of it." Fiskin warns that "you will pay and pay to learn the intricacies of this labyrinth, these demons. The parallel to psychoanalysis has, perhaps, not escaped you . . ."

Mere earthlings, meanwhile, cope as best they can. As might be expected, with-it doctors have detected such video-related maladies as Space Invaders wrist and Pac Man elbow. And of course there are psychological swamps into which enthusiasts may sink. Julie Winecoff, 21, an unemployed truck driver from Charlotte, N.C., paid her way to an Atari tournament in Chicago recently, lost ignominiously to Ok-Soo Han, 25, a Korean immigrant from Los Angeles, and dolefully swore off the stuff. "I'm never going to play another game of Centipede as long as I live," she said. "I've been whupped bad. I've been sure 'nuff tore down."

And Steve Juraszek, hero of song and news story? His high school banned him from leaving the school grounds for a few days because he missed afternoon classes on the day he set his record. But his eye remains on distant peaks. "I'm going to pick a weekend," he says. "I'll work out before on those spring things to strengthen my wrists and fingers. Then I'm going to go to sleep right after school on that Thursday and Friday and I'll start on Saturday morning and go the whole weekend."

> . . . *A man ain't nothin' but a*
> *man (plink, plunk)*
> *But before I let that Defender*
> *beat me down,*

> *I'll die with my blaster in my*
> *hand (plink, plunk)*
> *Die with my blaster in my*
> *hand.*

From *Newsday*, March 23, 1982, p. 46.

I. VOCABULARY

proficiently
solid state
ignominiously
ravages

labyrinth
sentient
circuitry
simulator

II. QUESTIONS ON CONTENT

1. Skow uses many American and international examples of the video game craze. What points do the majority of these examples illustrate?
2. What is Bagatelle Place? Is it an example of elite culture?
3. Explain Jeffrey Fiskin's parallel of Pac Man to psychoanalysis.
4. Do you agree that video games appeal more to males of all ages than to females? What is Skow's explanation for this? What is yours?
5. Are video games, like the Empire State Building, symbolic of the values of our civilization? Explain.
6. "The waves of color, shape and sound that crash about the ears of the bedazzled player are really incredibly lavish waves of information." Comment on this quotation with reference to the essays by Sargent and Smith.

III. QUESTIONS ON FORM

1. Do you find an implicit or explicit point of view in this expository essay? Give some supporting examples for your opinion.
2. How would you describe the prevailing tone of this essay? Give three examples of authorial tone used for transitions.
3. How do the many humorous anecdotes in the essay function?

IV. SUGGESTIONS FOR WRITING

1. Describe your favorite or least favorite video game. Explain how it is played.
2. Write a persuasive essay on the economic advantages or disadvantages of video games.
3. Defend or attack video games as a pastime. Consider such aspects as sexism, coordination, aggression, and challenge.

> A noted historian and author, **Barbara W. Tuchman** won Pulitzer prizes for *The Guns of August* (1962) and *Stilwell and the American Experience in China* (1971). Her most recent work is *The March of Folly* (1984).

The Decline of Quality

Barbara W. Tuchman

A question raised by our culture of the last two or three decades is whether quality in product and effort has become a vanishing element of current civilization. The word "quality" has, of course, two meanings: first, the nature or essential characteristic of something, as in "His voice has the quality of command"; second, a condition of excellence implying fine quality as distinct from poor quality. The second, obviously, is my subject.

The discussion that follows is not, except for a few samples, based on documentary or other hard evidence according to usual historical method; rather it represents the personal reflections of an observer with half a century's awareness of and occasional participation in public affairs, supported by the study and writing of history. It offers opinion on a pervasive problem and, as opinion, should and, I hope, may be supplemented by factual studies on special areas of the problem, such as education, labor and merchandising.

In the hope of possibly reducing the hail of censure which is certain to greet this essay (I am thinking of going to Alaska or possibly Patagonia in the week it is published), let me say that quality, as I understand it, means investment of the best skill and effort possible to produce the finest and most admirable result possible. Its presence or absence in some degree, characterizes every man-made object, service, skilled or unskilled labor—laying bricks, painting a picture, ironing shirts, practicing medicine, shoemaking, scholarship, writing a book. You do it well or you do it half-well. Materials are sound and durable or they are sleazy; method is painstaking or whatever is easiest. Quality is achieving or reaching for the highest standard as against being satisfied with the sloppy or fraudulent. It is honesty of purpose as against catering to cheap or sensational sentiment. It does not allow compromise with the second-rate.

When Michelangelo started work on the Sistine Chapel ceiling, five friends who were painters came to assist him and advise him in the techniques of fresco, in which they were practiced and he was not. Finding

Copyright © 1980 by The New York Times Company. Reprinted by permission.

their work not what he desired, he resolved to accomplish the whole task by himself, locked the doors of the chapel until his friends gave up and went home, and through four painful years on a scaffold carried the work to completion, as Vasari tells us, "with the utmost solicitate, labor and study." That is what makes for quality—and its cost—and what helped to make Michelangelo one of the greatest artists, if not, as some think, the greatest, of all time. Creating quality is self-nourishing. Michelangelo, Vasari goes on to say, "became more and more kindled every day by his fervor in the work and encouraged by his growing proficiency and improvement." Genius and effort go together, or if they do not, the genius will be wasted.

Quality, however, can be attained without genius. Art, in any case, is a slippery area for discussion of the problem, because values in the perception of art change radically from one generation to another. Everyone knows how the French Impressionists were scorned when they first exhibited, only in recent decades to reach the peak of repute and honor and what seems to be permanent popularity. Now, in our time, we are confronted by new schools of challenging, not to say puzzling, expression. In some individuals among the moderns, quality is emphatic *because* it is individual: in Louise Nevelson's impressive and innovative work, for example; in the intensity of loneliness in Hopper's mature paintings. With regard to the schools—as distinct from individuals—of Pop Art, Abstract Expressionism, Minimalism, hard-edge, scrawny-edge and whatnot, the two criteria of quality—intensive effort and honesty of purpose—often seem missing. The paintings seem thin, if not empty; one feels nothing behind the surface of the canvas. By contrast, behind the glow and mystery of a Turner, for instance, a whole world of ships and storms and eerie seas and men laboring over mountain passes stretches the imagination far beyond the canvas. It occurs to me to wonder whether museums hang the modern abstracts, and the public crowds to see them, in some vast pretense of seeing something where there is nothing; that in the present state of our culture, many do not know the difference.

Here we must confront the contentious question whether quality is something inherent in a given work or something socially induced—as the ultrafeminists say of sex—in the eye and period-consciousness of the beholder. I unhesitatingly opt for the inherent (as I do for sense of gender in the individual). In architecture there is something inherently right in certain proportions of windows to wall space, or for example in the Double Cube Room at Wilton House in England. One may be an architectural illiterate and still recognize, indeed *feel*, the perfection. Any kind of illiterate will recognize a difference in quality between, let us say, Matisse's exhilarating interiors and hotel art of little waifs with big black eyes, or between Michelangelo's marble Moses or David and that school of sculpture which consists of jigsaw puzzles lying on a museum floor, or, alternatively, the ceramic Snow Whites and Bambis advertised at such fancy prices in The New Yorker.

The difference is not only a matter of artistic skill, but of intent. Although the Moses and David are period pieces, they are timeless, universal, noble. They were intended to be—and they are—supreme. The others fall considerably short of that measure because they are designed for lesser reasons: the ceramic princesses and companions for commercial appeal to cheap sentiment, the floor puzzles for appeal to false sentiment—that is, worship of the avant-garde for its own sake as chic.

These examples represent the posing of extremes in which quality versus nonquality is unmistakable. If I come closer, however, and suggest that quality is inherent in, let us say, the stark, exquisite fiction of Jean Rhys but not in "Princess Daisy," in New England's white-steepled churches but not in Howard Johnson's orange-roofed eateries, in the film "Ninotchka" but not in "Star Wars," in Fred Astaire but not in Johnny Carson, I shall be pelted with accusations of failure to understand that what was once considered quality has given way under a change of social values to appreciation of new qualities and new values; that the admirers of the ceramic dolls and trash fiction and plastic furniture and television talk and entertainment shows with their idiotic laughter find something in these objects and diversions that means quality to *them*—in short, that quality is subjective. Yes, indeed, just as there are men who believe and loudly insist they are sober and who stumble and weave and pass out five minutes later. The judgment is subjective but the condition is not.

Contemporary life undeniably marks many improvements over the past, in freedom and nonconformity and most strikingly in material welfare. Such fine devices as the microchips that govern computer systems, a lifesaving mechanism like the cardiac pacemaker, drip-water techniques that permit arid-zone agriculture and a thousand other developments that have added to human efficiency and well-being may be sited as evidence of modern quality. Nevertheless, these are technological and seem to me to belong to a different scheme of things from the creative components of civilized life.

In two other areas, morals and politics, loss of quality is widely felt, but as I am not sure that the present level in these areas is much lower than at many other periods in history, I shall leave them out of the discussion.

In labor and culture, standards are certainly lower. Everyone is conscious of the prevalence of slipshod performance in clerical, manual and bureaucratic work. Much of it is slow, late, inaccurate, inefficient, either from lack of training or lack of caring or both. Secretaries still exist who care and who produce a perfectly typed letter, but more and more letters appear like one I recently received which contained—whether owed to writer or typist—"parred," for "pared," "deline" for "decline," "in tact" for "intact," and the information that removal of portions of an author's text "eschews his political intentions."

The writer in this case was certainly ignorant of the meaning of the word "eschews," while it is impossible to say whether the other errors represent ignorance or simple slackness. Either way, though only a sample, no more manifest evidence could be had of what has become prevalent in many fields. Even more striking is recognition that no such letter could have been written from a reasonably literate office 10 or 15 years ago. The decline has been precipitate, perhaps as one result of the student movements of the 1960's, when learning skills was renounced in favor of "doing your own thing" or consciousness-raising and other exercises in self-fulfillment. It is good for the self to be fulfilled but better if coping skills are acquired first.

In culture the tides of trash rise a little higher by the week: in fast foods and junky clothes and cute greeting cards, in films devoted nowadays either to sadism or teen-agers and consequently either nasty or boring; in the frantic razzle-dazzle of Bloomingdale's and its proliferating imitators; in endless paperbacks of sex and slaughter, Gothics and westerns; in the advertising of sensation-fiction which presents each book as the ultimate in horror, catastrophe, political plot or world crime, each by an unknown author who is never heard from again—fortunately.

Examining the evidence, one could apply a system of Q and non-Q for quality, on the model of the famous system of U (for upper-class) and non-U in language* sponsored by Nancy Mitford. Her categories were devised to distinguish social class, which brings us to the dangerous problem of the relationship of quality to class.

Quality is undeniably, though not necessarily, related to class, not in its nature but in circumstances. In former times, the princely patron had the resources in wealth and power to commission the finest workmanship, materials and design. Since his motive was generally self-glorification, the result was as beautiful and magnificent as he could command: in crystal and gold and tapestry, in exquisite silks and brocades, in the jeweled and enameled masterpieces of Cellini, the carved staircases of Grinling Gibbons. It is also true that cities and states caused works of equal value to be created not for individual glory but for the good of the whole, as in the Greek temples and theaters, the Colosseum of Rome, the Gothic cathedrals, the public parks of London.

The decline that has since set in has a good historical reason: The age of privilege is over and civilization has passed into the age of the masses. The many exceptions that can be made to this statement do not invalidate it. No change takes place wholly or all at once and many components of privilege and of capitalist control remain functioning parts of society and will, I

---

*Based on Prof. alan S. C. Ross's treatise on language, which Miss Mitford incorporated into an article on the English aristocracy for Encounter magazine, and which she and others later expanded in the anthology "Noblesse Oblige."

expect, continue as such for some time. Nevertheless, the turn has taken place, with the result that our culture has been taken over by commercialism directed to the mass market and necessarily to mass taste. De Tocqueville stated the problem, already appearing in his time, succinctly when he wrote, "When only the wealthy had watches they were very good ones; few are now made that are worth much but everyone has one in his pocket."

In the absence of the princely patron, the public is now the consumer, or if government is the patron, it is answerable to the public. The criterion for the goods and services and arts that society produces is the pleasure and purchasing power of the greatest number, not of the most discerning. Therein lies the history of non-Q. Arts and luxuries may still be directed to the few and most discerning, but when the dominant culture is mass-directed and the rewards in money and celebrity go with it, we have to consider whether popular appeal will become the governing criterion and gradually submerge all but isolated rocks of quality.

Will the tides of trash obey Gresham's law to the effect that bad money drives out good? This means, I am told, that as between two coinages of equal denomination but different intrinsic value in gold or silver content, the one of lesser will drive out the one of higher value. I do not know whether, according to our ever-flexible economists, Gresham's law remains valid, but as regards quality in culture, it has gloomy implications.

Quality cannot be put down altogether. As the would-be philosopher said of cheerfulness, it keeps breaking in, and I suspect always will. It appears in the crafts movement that, in a reaction to floods of the tawdry, has been expanding in the last decade, producing fine hand-woven fabrics and handmade utensils and ornaments of pottery, glass and wood. There are art and design in these and individual skills that make for Q. We come across Q here and there in every field of endeavor, from a symphony orchestra to a well-run grocery and on the covers of the Audubon bimonthly magazine. For all its appearances we are grateful and by them encouraged, yet we have to recognize that the prevailing tendency is non-Q.

This is not confined to the taste of the masses. It reaches into the richer ranks, where purchasing power has outdistanced cultivated judgment. Persons in this difficulty tend to buy purses and scarfs and various garments—even sheets—adorned with the designer's or manufacturer's initials in the illusion that, without risking individual judgment, they are thus acquiring the stamp of Q. In fact, they are merely proclaiming that they lack reliable taste of their own. If I were to adopt the Mitford tone, I would have to say that wearing anything bearing commercial initials is definitely non-Q.

Most of the products of non-Q have the economic excuse that they supply needs to pocketbooks that can afford them. An entire level of society has arisen that can now afford to obtain goods, services and entertainment formerly beyond its means. Consequently these are now produced at a price level attractive to the greatest number of consumers and likewise at a cultural level, or level of taste, that presumably the greatest number wants or will respond to. Whether the merchandiser or advertiser is invariably a good judge of what the public wants is open to doubt. Whereas one used naïvely to believe that, under the infallible test of profit, business knew what it was doing, we have now witnessed the most monumental goof in business history committed by the very king of American enterprise, the auto industry. If Detroit with all its resources errs, can the rest be far behind?

A question that puzzles me is why inexpensive things must be ugly; why walking through the aisles in a discount chain store causes acute discomfort in the esthetic nerve cells. I have heard it suggested that raucous colors and hideous decoration are meant to distract the purchaser's eye from shoddy workmanship, but since that only results in a remedy worse than the disease, it cannot be the whole explanation. One had supposed that ugly, oversize packaging obeyed some mysterious law of merchandising, the merchandisers having proved that if the package were neat, discreet and elegant, it would not sell. I wonder if they really know this, based on careful tests, with controls, of consumer response, or whether gratuitous ugliness is not just a presumption of what the public is supposed to like. The automobile companies thought they knew too, and they were so wrong that the taxpayer is now bailing them out in survival loans and unemployment insurance to the workers they had to let go.

I do not see why the presumption cannot be made the other way: that the consumer would respond to good design rather than bad, and to quality insofar as it can be mass-produced, rather than junk. The answer will doubtless be that when this experiment has been tried the mass of consumers fails to respond. For this failure, I believe, two institutions of our culture are largely to blame: education and advertising.

We have some superb schools, public and private, in this country but the dominant tendency, once again, is non-Q. Education for the majority has slipped to a level undemanding of effort, satisfied with the least, lacking respect for its own values, and actually teaching very little. We read in the press that, despite the anxious concern and experiments of educators, college-entrance scores are sinking and the national rate of schoolchildren reading at below-grade levels hovers at 50 percent. The common tendency is to blame television, and while I suppose that the two-minute attention span it fosters, and the passive involvement of the viewer, must negatively affect the learning process, I suspect something more basic is at fault.

That something, I believe, lies in new attitudes toward both teaching and learning. Schoolchildren are not taught to work. Homework is frivolous or absent. The idea has grown that learning must be fun; students must study what they like, therefore courses have largely become elective. Work is left to the highly motivated, and failure for the others does not matter because, owing to certain socially concerned but ill-conceived rules, students in many school systems cannot be flunked. Except by the few who learn because they cannot be stopped, the coping skills society needs are not acquired by the promoted failures, and the gulf between the few and the mass will widen.

Further, one becomes aware through occasional glimpses into curriculums, that subject matter makes increasing concessions to junk. Where are the summer reading lists and book reports of former years? A high-school student of my acquaintance in affluent suburbia was recently assigned by his English teacher, no less, to watch television for a week and keep a record on 3-by-5 index cards of what he had seen. This in the literature of Shakespeare to Mark Twain, Jane Austen to J. D. Salinger! How will the young become acquainted with quality if they are not exposed to it?

The effect appears at the next level. A professor of classics at a major Eastern university told me recently that, in a discussion with his students of the heroes of Greek legend, he tried to elicit their concept of the hero without success, and resorted to asking if anyone could name a hero. Only one student, a girl, raised her hand, and replied "Dustin Hoffman."

I feel sure that Mr. Hoffman, whose real persona is not at stake, will forgive his name being used to illustrate a case of modern know-nothingism. The girl neither knew what a hero was, nor apparently that an actor represents a character without being it. If she could not distinguish between make-believe and real, her school is unlikely to have equipped her to distinguish between quality and vulgarity or fraud, between Q and non-Q. She does not know the difference. Consequently, when the market offers her junk, she and her contemporaries buy it and listen to it and wear it because that is all they know.

Advertising augments the condition. From infancy to adulthood, advertising is the air Americans breathe, the information we absorb, almost without knowing it. It floods our minds with pictures of perfection and goals of happiness easy to attain. Face cream will banish age, decaffeinated coffee will banish nerves, floor wax will bring in neighbors for a cheery bridge game or gossip, grandchildren will love you if your disposition improves with the right laxative, storekeepers and pharmacists overflow with sound avuncular advice, the right beer endows you with hearty masculine identity, and almost anything from deodorants to cigarettes, toothpaste, hair shampoo and lately even antacids will bring on love affairs, usually on horseback or on a beach. Moreover, all the people engaged in these delights are beautiful. Dare I suggest that this is not the true world? We are feeding on foolery, of which a steady diet, for those who feed on little else, cannot help but leave a certain fuzziness of perceptions.

When it comes to standards of labor, the uncomfortable fact must be faced that decline in quality of work is connected with the rise in the security of the worker. No one likes to admit this, because it is depressing and because it does not fit into the sentimental conviction that all's well that is meant well, that good things have only good results. The unhappy fact is that they have mixed results. Work may be a satisfaction to those who can choose their own line of endeavor and who enjoy what they do, but for the majority work is a more or less disagreeable necessity. Therefore, when holding a job no longer depends upon quality of performance but on union rules and bureaucratic protections, the incentive to excellent work is reduced. Like the failing student who cannot be flunked, the inadequate worker cannot be fired, short of some extreme dereliction. If he is laid off or quits for reasons of his own, unemployment insurance provides a temporary substitute for the pay envelope and, in the long run, the various supports of social welfare preclude destitution.

No one this side of the lunatic fringe suggests that these rights and protections of labor should be abandoned or weakened because loss of quality has been part of their price. Gain in one aspect of society generally means loss in another, and social gain in the well-being of the masses has been the major development of the last two centuries. We have put a floor under misery in the West and few would wish it removed because its measures have been abused. The privileged abuse their opportunities too, by monoplies, trusts, graft, bribery, tax evasion, pollution—and with far higher returns. At whatever cost, the working class has obtained access to comforts and pleasures, possessions and vacations that have changed immeasurably not only their lives but the whole of our economy and culture. On balance, this is social progress, but let us not suppose it has been unalloyed.

Other factors have played a part: The alienating nature of the assembly line and mass production is one, but this has been present since the Industrial Revolution. The great change has come with the complacency of—on the whole, in America—a comfortable society (previous to present inflation and recession). As in education, the change has been in attitude. The pressures and needs that once drove us have relaxed. Today's watchword is "Why knock yourself out?" The Asians in our midst—Koreans who put a whole family to work in a grocery of neat, washed, fresh produce, and stay open for 24 hours—exemplify the difference.

What of prognosis? The new egalitarians would like to make the whole question of quality vanish by adopting a flat philosophy of the equality of everything. No fact or event is of greater or less value than any other; no person or thing is superior or inferior to any other. Any reference to quality is instantly castigated as elitism, which seems to inspire in users of the word the sentiments of Jacobins denouncing aristos to the guillotine.

In fact, elitism is the equivalent of quality. Without it, management of everything would be on a par with the United States Postal Service, which, mercifully, is not yet quite the case. Difference in capacity does exist and superiority makes itself felt. It wins the ski race and promotion on the job and admission to the college of its choice. There are A students and D students, and their lives and fortunes will be different. I do not know if egalitarianism applies to horses, but if so how does it account for Seattle Slew and Affirmed sweeping the triple crown; and if all are equal, why do we hold horse races? Given the evidence of daily life, the egalitarian credo must be difficult to maintain and succeeds, I imagine, in deceiving chiefly its advocates.

However, because egalitarianism obviously appeals to those least likely to excel— and they are many—its appeal is wide, and not altogether harmless. It sponsors mediocrity, which, as we learned a few years ago on the occasion of President Nixon's nomination of Judge G. Harrold Carswell to the Supreme Court, has an important constituency in this country. The general criticism of Carswell as mediocre prompted from Senator Roman L. Hruska of Nebraska one of the historic remarks of the century. He did not think Carswell should be disqualified on the grounds of an undistinguished judicial career, because, he said, "Even if he were mediocre, there are a lot of mediocre judges and people and lawyers and they are entitled to a little representation, aren't they?"

The more I ponder this idea of a seat for mediocrity on the Supreme Court, the more it haunts me. The Hruska Principle is only a logical extension, after all, of majority rule, and if carried to its logical conclusion must mean that the mediocre shall inherit the earth. (Carswell was rejected, of course, but for alleged racism, not for mediocrity.)

In the 18th century, Montesquieu saw political egalitarianism as a "dangerous fallacy" that could lead only to incompetence—and, he added, mob control, by which he meant democracy. We are less afraid of democracy than he was because we already have it, but growing incompetence is undoubtedly a feature of contemporary life, although it is not necessarily an attribute of democracy. There never was greater incompetence than in the Bourbon monarchy in the last decade before the French Revolution. It brought the old regime down in ruins, but we need not take that precedent too closely to heart for, despite present appearances, I think our society has built itself more safeguards and a firmer foundation.

I cannot believe we shall founder under the rising tide of incompetence and trash. Perhaps that is merely a matter of temperament; it is difficult to believe in fatality. Although I know we have already grown accustomed to less beauty, less elegance, less excellence—and less hypocrisy, too—yet perversely I have confidence in the opposite of egalitarianism: in the competence and excellence of the best among us.. I meet this often enough, if not quite as often as the reverse, to believe that the urge for the best is an element of humankind as inherent as the heartbeat. It does not command society, and it may be crushed temporarily in a period of heavy non-Q, but it cannot be eliminated. If incompetence does not kill us first, Q will continue the combat against numbers. It will not win, but it will provide a refuge for the trash-beleaguered. It will supply scattered beauty, pride in accomplishment, the charm of fine things—and it will win horse races. As long as people exist, some will always strive for the best; some will attain it.

I. VOCABULARY

inherent	frivolous	avant-garde
exquisite	dereliction	durable
raucous	complacency	avuncular
gratuitous	prognosis	egalitarianism
mediocrity	unalloyed	intrinsic

II. QUESTIONS ON CONTENT

1. What is Tuchman's attitude toward our popular culture? Give three specific examples that she cites.
2. What does Tuchman say has happened to the quality of life in the United States today? Why?
3. What is Gresham's Law? What relevance does it have to this essay?
4. What are some of Tuchman's examples of incompetence? Of complacency?
5. What was Roman Hruska's view on mediocrity? Do you agree with him?
6. Make up your own list of Q and non-Q objects and pastimes in our society.
7. What do you think of the standards of taste in the United States? Is Tuchman correct? Do you agree with her conclusion?

III. QUESTIONS ON FORM

1. What definition is the key to this essay? Why?
2. What is the reason for paragraph two on page 49?
3. List five areas of comparison/contrast within the essay.
4. Tuchman uses only one anecdotal example. Identify and analyze it.
5. What does Tuchman attempt to do in her final paragraph? Is she successful? If so, why? If not, why not?
6. For what audience is this essay written?

IV. SUGGESTIONS FOR WRITING

1. Write an essay explaining how important the concept of quality is for you and your family. How much are you willing to sacrifice to attain quality?
2. Choose two items from your list (question II, 6 above) and write a specific Q, non-Q comparison and contrast.

3. Defend or attack a contemporary piece of music, painting, sculpture, play, film, or dance as either supporting or refuting Tuchman's views.

TOPICS FOR INVESTIGATION

1. Read George Orwell's *1984* and examine his versions of the mass media. How close to reality are they?

2. "You are what you eat," was a line often heard in the 1960s. Investigate the incredible proliferation of the fast-food industry in the last few decades and discuss its impact on American society. Have the effects been beneficial or harmful?

3. Choose a durable trend in recent fashion: the Western look, the gypsy look, the 1930s look, the New Wave/Punk look, and so on; if fashion is a mirror of the times, what do these revivals and forays show us about ourselves?

4. Breakdancing is just the latest of a long history of dance crazes. Popular culture has always included some strain of dance fever. Discuss some of the popular dances of the past, (the Charleston, Peabody, Lindy, Twist, and so on) as characteristic of the epochs in which they flourished.

5. Jeans are perhaps the most popular item in the American wardrobe. Investigate this practical status symbol from its humble beginnings as overalls, through its stages as Levis, dungarees, its French fling, and so on. How did they become our national uniform? Are they here to stay?

3

COMMUNICATIONS

What makes popular or mass culture popular is that it is generally communicated through the mass media. These are systems or vehicles that traditionally employ mechanical or electronic means, such as printing presses and broadcasting equipment, to transmit information or entertainment to large numbers of people.

The essays in this chapter deal with the nature, operations, and impact of mass communications media. The first essay is a general introduction to mass communication. It begins with definitions of key terms—communication, mass media, mass communications—and then discusses the characteristics and functions of mass communication. The focus is on the system of mass communication in the United States and how it differs from systems in other countries.

A vital function of the mass media is to inform the public. Information as a new form of power and its effects on society are the subjects of the next selection. Taking an historical approach to the development of power in Western society, Anthony Smith contends that new electronic devices, especially the computer, are revolutionizing the way information is gathered, stored, and distributed in modern society.

The computer figures prominently in the next two essays. The new electronic information devices to which Smith referred are explored by Stanley Wellborn. The fusion and interaction of such existing technologies as telephones, computers, cellular radio, and satellites, he explains, are bringing about a worldwide telecommunications revolution that will radically transform our lives in the near future. Roger Rosenblatt, in the last essay, is also interested in the practical uses of the computer. Unlike Wellborn, however, his primary concern is not with specific technologies but with the general relationship between the computer and man and what this machine tells us about ourselves as human beings.

Readings

> Journalist, author, and editor, **Peter M. Sandman** is Professor of Environmental Journalism at Cook College, Rutgers University. He is a noted expert on environmental public relations and scientific and technical writing. **David M. Rubin** is Associate Professor of Journalism at New York University at Washington Square and chairman of the department. He is Chairman of the Communications Media Committee of the American Civil Liberties Union and a contributor to academic and literary magazines and newspapers. **David B. Sachsman** is Chairman of the Department of Journalism and Mass Media of Rutgers University. He is a former Fulbright-Hays scholar and a past president of the New Jersey Society of Professional Journalists, Sigma Delta Chi.

American Mass Communication
Peter M. Sandman, David M. Rubin, and David B. Sachsman

Communication

Communication is the process of transmitting a message from a source to an audience via a channel. Consider, for example, a conversation, the most common kind of communication. The person who speaks is the source. The person who listens is the audience. What is transmitted is the message. And the spoken voice carried through the air is the channel.

Now consider a more complicated example, an article in a newspaper. The message is everything the article says, everything it implies, and everything a reader might infer from it. The audience is everybody who reads the article or even glances at it. The source is everybody who contributes in one way or another to the article; this includes the newsmakers who are quoted, the reporter, the editor, and even the proofreaders and printers. The channel is, of course, the printed word, the newspaper itself.

What is a communication *medium?* Strictly speaking, a medium is a channel—the spoken word, the printed word, or whatever. But the term is often used to mean both the channel and the source, and sometimes even

---

Peter M. Sandman, David M. Rubin, and David B. Sachsman, MEDIA: An Introductory Analysis of American Mass Communications, 2nd Ed., copyright © 1976, pp. 1, 3-11. Reprinted by permission of Prentice-Hall, Inc., Englewood Cliffs, N.J.

the message. It includes everything that reaches the audience. When we speak of the "mass media," for example, we usually mean not only the channels of mass communication but also the content of those channels and the behavior of the people who work for them. . . .

Mass Communication

Interpersonal communication is the process of transmitting information, ideas, and attitudes from one person to another. Mass communication is the process of transmitting information, ideas, and attitudes to many people, usually through a machine. There are several important differences between the two.

First, the sources of a mass communication have great difficulty gearing their message to their audience. They may know the demographic statistics of the audience—its average age, its average socioeconomic status, etc.—but they cannot know the individual quirks of each individual reader, listener, and viewer.

Second, mass-communication systems typically include much weaker feedback loops than interpersonal communication systems. When you talk to friends, you can usually tell whether they are listening, whether they understand, whether they agree or disagree, and so forth. All this is impossible in mass communication.

Third, the audience of a mass communication is much more likely than the audience of an interpersonal communication to twist the message through selective attention, perception, and retention. People turn off the TV (literally or figuratively) if they don't like what it's saying. It's a lot harder—though still possible—to turn off someone talking to you.

Fourth, and perhaps most important, mass-communication systems are a lot more complicated than interpersonal communication systems. Each message (an article in a newspaper, for example) may have as many as a dozen sources, with different points of view and different goals for the communication. The channel, too, is typically a complex organization (such as a newspaper), composed of many individuals, whose viewpoints and goals may vary widely. Every mass communication is in a sense a committee product.

All four of these factors tend to lessen the effect of a mass communication on its audience. The power of the mass media is based on the size of their audience, on their ability to reach millions of people in one shot. But in dealing with any individual member of that audience, you'd be a lot more effective if you sat down together for a chat. . . .

American Mass Communication

The American system of mass communication has at least three characteristics that distinguish it from systems in other countries.

1. Pervasive influence.
2. Freedom of the press.
3. Big-business media.

None of these characteristics is unique. There are other countries with powerful media, other countries with free media, other countries with profit-oriented media. But the United States embodies all three traits to an extent unmatched in the rest of the world.

1. Pervasive influence. A fish could no more tell you what it is like to live out of water than an American could tell you what it is like to live without mass communication. As soon as American children are old enough to distinguish between two different makes of midget racing cars or fruit-flavored brands of toothpaste, they are bathed in a constant stream of messages from radio and television. They approach the daily newspaper through the comics or sports section; these lead them to comic books and sporting magazines, and then perhaps to more serious books and magazines.

By the time they enter kindergarten, most American children have already been exposed to hundreds, perhaps thousands of hours of radio and television. They have attended dozens of movies and browsed through scores of children's books. They have cut pictures out of magazines and scowled at the newspaper in unconscious imitation of their parents. All these experiences have taught them something—something about literacy, perhaps, something about violence, something about America. They are in a real sense children of the mass media.

For most adults, meanwhile, the mass media constitute the only advanced education they receive after high school or college. It is obvious that the media offer every American a continuous course in modern world history. But it is not so obvious, perhaps, that the very basics of community living come to us through the media: births, weddings, deaths, weather reports, traffic accidents, crimes, sales, elections.

It is hard to imagine an efficient system of democratic government without an equally efficient system of mass communication. Citizens would learn of new legislation only after it passed, and then only if they visited their representative in Washington. Incumbents would probably serve for life, because no challengers could make themselves known to the electorate. Corruption would go largely unchecked. News of foreign affairs would remain the monopoly of the president and the State Department. And on the local level, mayors would be free to run their cities as personal fiefdoms. Political information is political power. Without the mass media to transmit such information, the American people would be powerless.

Dwarfing even the educational and political roles of the American media is their entertainment function. Television offers a seemingly unending stream of westerns, thrillers, comedies, and star-studded specials. Radio spins records and conversation. Newspapers lighten the weight of the news with puzzles, advice to the lovelorn, comics, sports, and back-fence gossip. Books, magazines, and films supply entertainment packages for more specialized audiences. The Number One source of recreational activity of almost every American is the mass media.

Of course the media are pervasive in other countries as well. Transistor radios are always among the first manufactured products to be imported into any unindustrialized area of the world. Newspapers and government-sponsored radio and TV stations follow soon afterward. Nevertheless, few observers would dispute that Americans are more a product of their media than any other people in the world.

2. Freedom of the press. The American government was founded on a radical political theory: representative democracy. According to this strange notion, the people of a nation should control the government by electing officials to carry out their will. The mass media necessarily play a central role in representative democracy. It is through the media, presumably, that the people get the information they need to decide what they want their officials to do. And it is through the media, presumably, that the people find out if their officials are doing it.

For this reason the First Amendment to the U.S. Constitution forbids the government to make any laws "abridging the freedom of the press." When it was first written, this provision was unprecedented. Other governments had assumed the right of the king to put a stop to any publication he deemed damaging to the nation. The American Constitution denied Congress and the President this fundamental right. The real threat to a democracy, so the argument went, is a mass-media system in chains. As long as every publisher (though not necessarily every reporter) is free to print whatever he or she wants to print, the truth will make itself clear, the people will be informed, and the democracy will flourish.

Today, many foreign governments have copied our First Amendment into their constitutions, and some even practice the freedom they preach. The American government, meanwhile, restrains its media with the laws of libel, obscenity, and privacy, the licensing of broadcast stations, the postal regulations, and so forth.

Despite these limitations, there is no mass-media system in the world today that is more free from government interference than the American system. In recent years, a number of very high officials have attacked the media for "irresponsible" opposition to government policy. Some have interpreted these attacks as attempts to control the press, and so they may be. But it is a testimonial to the almost incredible freedom of the American media that the attacks are limited mostly to speeches, denunciations, and largely futile attempts at intimidation. The government can *do* relatively little. You need only consult the latest news of national politics for fresh evidence of America's freedom of the press.

The purpose of a free press, you will remember, is to insure that the people will be well-informed. Well, we have a free press. Do we have an informed population? Pollster George Gallup often quotes a survey of college graduates which found that only four in ten could name the two senators from their own state; only half could cite a single difference between capitalism and socialism; only half had an accurate idea of the population of the United States; and only one in three could list five of the Soviet Union's satellite countries in Eastern Europe.

The notion that freedom of the press is the basic requirement for an informed population is known as the "libertarian theory." The authors of the First Amendment firmly believed that if every newspaper were free to print precisely what it wanted to print, somehow truth would emerge victorious from its open confrontation with falsehood. The only responsibility of the media was to tell it the way they saw it. The only responsibility of the government was to leave the media alone.

In recent years, many observers have begun to question the libertarian theory. In its place they have proposed a social responsibility theory of the press. That is, they argue that the American mass media must recognize their obligation to serve the public—to be truthful, accurate, and complete; to act as a forum for conflicting viewpoints; to provide meaningful background to the daily news; etc. Social responsibility theorists claim that if the media do not voluntarily live up to their obligations, then they must be forced to do so by the government.

Though the social responsibility theory is gaining in popularity and influence, it is not yet established. The American mass media today are free—free to serve the public or not as they choose.

3. Big-business media. Perhaps the strongest weapon in the arsenal of the social responsibility theorists is the Big Business emphasis in the modern American media. The United States is one of the few countries in the world whose major media are all privately owned. Like General Motors and U.S. Steel, American newspapers, magazines, and broadcast stations spend much of their time worrying about stockholders, dividends, and profits. They may have too little time left for worrying about service to the public.

Like every business, the mass media have a product to sell. In the case of the book and film industries, the product is the medium itself; part of the price of a book or movie ticket is the manufacturer's profit. For the rest of the mass media, the product is you. Newspapers, magazines, and broadcast stations earn their considerable profits by selling your presence and your attention to advertisers. Articles and programs are just a device to keep you corralled, a come-on for the all-important ads.

The inexorable trend in American business is toward monopoly—toward bigness and fewness. The mass media are no exception. Chains dominate the newspaper and magazine industries. The three networks have an iron grip on television programming. The book business is dominated by a few giant companies on the East Coast, the movie business by a few giant companies on the West Coast. Competing with the biggies in any of these fields is incredibly costly and hazardous.

Several conclusions follow from these facts. First, since the American media are businesses first and foremost, they are likely to choose profit over public service when the two come into conflict. Second, since the media are owned by business-oriented people, they are likely to reflect a business-oriented notion of what's good for the public—which may not be everybody's notion. Third, since the media are close to monopolies, they are likely to offer the audience only a single viewpoint on public affairs, instead of the rich conflict of viewpoints envisioned by the Founding Fathers. And fourth, since the media make competition extremely difficult, they are likely to "black out" positions and groups of which they disapprove.

Pervasive influence, freedom of the press, and the profit motive—this is the combination that makes the American mass media unique. Nowhere else is such a powerful social force so little controlled by government, so much controlled by self-interest.

The Four Functions

The mass media in general, and the American mass media in particular, have at least four basic functions to perform. They are:

1. To serve the economic system.
2. To entertain.
3. To inform.
4. To influence.

We will consider each in turn.

1. To serve the economic system. The fundamental economic purpose of the mass media in the United States is to sell people to advertisers. The articles in your newspaper and the programs on your radio and TV sets are merely "come-ons" to catch and hold your attention. Advertisers buy that attention from the media, and use it to sell you their products and services. In the process, both the media and the advertisers earn substantial profits.

It is possible to conceive of a mass-media system not dedicated to profit through advertising. Such systems exist, in fact, in many countries. The British Broadcasting Corporation (BBC), to give but one example, is financed in part by a special tax on radio and TV sets. It accepts no ads and earns no profits. Even in this country there are nonprofit broadcast stations and publications—not many, but a few. And of course some of the profit-making media, such as books and movies, earn their money directly from the audience. But the most influential media in the United States are fueled by advertising.

This dependence on advertising has many important implications for media content, which is inevitably designed to attract the sort of audience advertisers need in the sort of mood advertisers want. But advertising is also important for its own sake. Through advertising, the mass media bring buyer and seller together. Advertising creates the demand for new goods and increases the demand for old ones. It thus helps keep the engine of industry running. No one knows exactly how much of the U.S. gross national product is the result of advertising in the mass media, but most economists agree that advertising's contribution to the GNP is substantial. Regardless of whether we approve or disapprove of advertising, this service to the economic system is certainly a central function of the American mass media.

2. *To entertain.* Entertainment is by far the biggest service of the American mass media. This is especially true from the viewpoint of the audience. Political scientists may evaluate a television program in terms of how much information it imparts. Advertisers may ask what kind of climate for persuasion it offers. Station owners may wonder how much profit it brings in. But with rare exceptions, viewers want to know only how entertaining it is.

Television is undoubtedly the nation's Number One entertainment medium, but film and radio are not far behind. When the movie *Love Story* opened in December of 1970, it broke the house record in 159 of the 165 theaters in which it was shown. The film grossed over $2,400,000 in its first three days. As for radio, the average American family owns at least two receivers in the home and a third in the car. Why do people go to movies and switch on the radio? To be entertained.

Even the print media succeed or fail largely in terms of their entertainment value. The best-seller lists for hardback and paperback books usually include a few works of significance and value. But the bulk of every list is always pure entertainment, and even the "important" books must be entertaining to succeed. Magazines, too, must season their informational content with a heavy dose of fun and games. The least entertaining of the mass media is undoubtedly the newspaper. Yet even that offers the reader dozens of comics, humor and gossip columns, and human-interest features in every issue.

Because the public demands entertainment from its media, the media owner who wants to succeed has no choice but to try to be entertaining. Many critics have deplored this fact, complaining that mere entertainment was a waste and a degradation of media potential. Such an attitude ignores the important social role played by entertainment—the transmission of culture, the enlargement of perspectives, the encouragement of imagination, etc. And even the most virulent opponents of media entertainment must admit that the opportunity to relax and unwind is vital. Entertainment is not merely an economic necessity for media owners; it is an integral, essential function of the media.

But that is far from the whole story. The media have other functions besides entertainment. Moreover, the media *choose* the kinds of entertainment they wish to use. They are subject to criticism for their choices.

It is extremely difficult to come up with a clear-cut standard for distinguishing between "good" entertainment and "bad" entertainment. Nonetheless, most observers will agree that in some sense *Harper's* is better than *True Romances*, "Sesame Street" is better than "Bugs Bunny," and Hemingway is better than Erle Stanley Gardner. The media must cater to public tastes, but they also help to mold public tastes. If the media choose violence, or pornography, or the lowest of lowbrow culture, then they must take responsibility for the choice.

3. *To inform.* Entertainment may be what the public wants from its mass media, but information is probably their most important function. No doubt many people read *Time* and *Newsweek*, say, because they find them entertaining; and certainly the newsmagazines try to entertain their readers. But the best newsmagazine is not necessarily the most entertaining one. It is the one that successfully conveys the most information.

The power of the mass media to inform is almost incredible. On November 22, 1963, at 12:30 in the afternoon, President John F. Kennedy was assassinated. Within half an hour, two-thirds of all Americans knew of the event. Ninety percent knew within an hour, and 99.8 percent had heard the story by early evening. Some got the news directly from the mass media; others were told by family, friends, or strangers on the street, who had themselves heard it on the media.

There was an immediate rush to radio and television for more detail. During the days that followed, 166 million Americans tuned in to the assassination story on television. The average TV set was on for roughly eight hours a day.

Most of the news supplied by the mass media is more routine than a presidential assassination. Weather reports, stock listings, and movie timetables are among the best-read features in your daily newspaper—and among the most informative. We tend to dismiss these services not because they are unimportant, but because they are easy to prepare. Similarly, news reports of natural disasters, crimes, accidents, and the like are genuinely useful. Since they are standard fare for the media and difficult to handle poorly, scholars pay them very little attention—perhaps less attention than they deserve.

The more difficult a story is to cover, the less likely the media are to cover it well. The informational problems of the media are many and varied. Is a story so complicated tht no reporter can understand it, much less repeat it? Is it so technical that few readers are likely to enjoy it or finish it? Does it require days of hard-nosed investigative digging among sources who would much rather keep their mouths shut? Might it insult or embarrass an advertiser, an important newsmaker, a friend of the publisher, or even a reader? Such stories may or may not be more important than the easier ones. But because they are difficult to cover, the way they are handled is a good measure of the media's responsibility to their informing function.

Perhaps the most important information of all is information about the government. The purpose of the First Amendment, after all, is to insure that the media will be free to report and criticize the actions of government officials, free to inform the public about public affairs. When a television station carries live the speech of a president, it is performing a valuable public service. When it offers intelligent commentary on the content and meaning of that speech, it is performing a much *more* valuable public service.

It is worth mentioning that everything in the mass media is in some sense informative, whether or not it is intended that way. Even a soap opera tells us something (true or false) about how people live, how they dress and talk and solve problems.

For centuries, Italy was a country with two different populations: the wealthy, cosmopolitan North and the poor, rural South. The two were so different they even spoke different dialects, and were almost completely unable to understand one another. Then, in 1954, nationwide Italian television was introduced. In just a few years, television began to unify the country.

A university professor comments: "Some intellectuals call television the 'opium of the people.' That may be so in a city like Milan or Turin. But can you imagine a modern bathroom appearing on TV screens from Naples southward?" And a historian adds: "There's been more change in Italy's linguistic situation in the past fifteen years than in the century since Rome became the capital."

4. *To influence.* The power of the mass media to change people's minds directly is very limited. People don't like to have their minds changed, and so they ignore or misinterpret attempts to do so—usually successfully. If influence were limited to changing people's minds, directly, the media would not be particularly influential.

But influence is more subtle than that. When William Randolph Hearst's *New York Journal* championed the war against Spain in 1898, he didn't achieve very many conversions. But through slanted news coverage and sensational writing, the *Journal* did manage to help create a climate of war fever. No doubt most readers viewed Hearst's style of journalism as entertainment and information, not influence. Yet he helped make them go to war.

More than a century before Hearst, Thomas Paine wrote a political pamphlet called *Common Sense,* urging an American Revolution. And about 75 years after Hearst, in 1968, Richard Nixon engineered a series of television advertisements, urging his election as president. Paine didn't convert many Tories, and Nixon didn't win over many Democrats. But Paine did succeed in crystalizing the incoherent resentments of many colonists into a consistent revolutionary ideology. And Nixon succeeded in crystalizing the incoherent frustrations of many Americans into a Republican vote. So Paine got his revolution, and Nixon got the White House. The mass media played a vital role in the success of both men.

The most obvious and prevalent example of mass media influence is advertising. Media ad campaigns have a lot going for them. Through careful intermixture with entertainment and informational content, they gain a captive audience. Through bold colors and imaginative graphics, they make you pay attention. Through catchy slogans and constant repetition, they make you remember. Through irrelevant appeals to sex, snobbism, and the good life, they make you buy.

The very existence of newspapers, magazines, radio, and television testifies to the persuasive power of advertising. For if the ads were unsuccessful, there would be no ads. And if there were no ads, there would be no newspapers, magazines, radios, and television in the form we know them.

Not every media attempt to influence the public is successful, of course. Politicians and manufacturers may spend millions on the media and still lose out to the competition. Editorialists and polemicists may devote page after page to an urgent plea for action, and get no action. Not every revolutionary book foments a revolution; not every TV appeal to voters captures the White House. But it is nearly impossible to foment a revolution without a book, to win the White House without a TV appeal. The persuasive power of the mass media, though limited, is undeniable.

I. VOCABULARY

jargon	denunciation	foment
constraint	inexorable	solace
demographic	virulent	vicarious
quirk	incoherent	catharsis
pervasive		

II. QUESTIONS ON CONTENT

1. What is communication? Mass communication?
2. What are the chief characteristics of the American system of mass media?
3. What basic functions do the mass media perform? Which one do the authors regard as the most important? Do you agree?

4. In what ways do the mass media serve the public needs? What do you use the media for?
5. The authors say that "most Americans . . . are happy with their mass media." Do you agree? If not, what complaints do you have about the mass media?

III. QUESTIONS ON FORM

1. What is the central purpose of this essay?
2. What type of writing is mainly used? Why?
3. For what audience is the essay intended?
4. What pattern of organization is employed?
5. List the methods of development that serve the authors' purpose. Which method predominates? Why?

IV. SUGGESTIONS FOR WRITING

1. Make a formal topic or sentence outline of this essay. Include at least one subheading for each heading.
2. Explain how the mass media serve your personal needs.
3. Discuss some of the chief characteristics of the system of mass communication in another country.
4. How free is the press in the United States?
5. Argue for or against a social responsibility theory of the press.
6. Give examples from your own experience of how your behavior has been modeled by the media.

Since his graduation from Oxford, **Anthony Smith** has written or edited ten books on various aspects of mass communications, including the well-known *Goodbye Gutenberg: The Newspaper Revolution of the 1980's*. Formerly with the BBC, he is a director of Channel 4 Television, London, and a director of the British Film Institute.

The New Form of Power: Information

Anthony Smith

Political science has never quite succeeded in finding an adequate acceptable definition of its own basic raw material—power. Each society in history appears to have run through a set of comparable problems about power

Reprinted by permission of Anthony Smith.

relationships but no two seem to have experienced power in quite the same form. Power in feudal societies is visible through quite different rituals and in different forms from that in commercial and industrial societies, and monarchies and bureaucracies are different again.

We in the West appear now to be entering a new kind of society, or a new phase of capitalist society, in which the creation, storage and distribution of *information* is evidently playing an extraordinarily important role; more and more economists, scientists, technologists and philosophers are employing the phrase "information society" (or one of its equivalents) to describe the phenomenon. Inevitably, power itself is now beginning to seem to depend upon control of the flows of information. Indeed, in the conditions of the late 20th Century it is possible actually to define power in terms of information. To explain this, one must look at what is happening to the actual commodity of information in the conditions of modern technology and modern corporate structures.

In one sense, all societies, past and present, consist of human mechanisms for processing and distributing information, but they have all existed in different physical forms. Religious institutions held their knowledge in manuscripts and in the minds of priests and followers; it was expressed and, in a sense, stored within the practices and imagery of specific faiths. Commercial information has been held in different forms of accounting over the centuries. Political information has been held within courts, administrative systems, bureaucratic structures which collect, sift, select, debate information in precise hierarchies.

Printing changed all of the forms of power after the 15th Century because it became possible to deposit identical stores of information, multiplied almost infinitely in number, across large areas of territory. The central power of princes and governments became capable of being spread far beyond the force of physical or military might as soon as codes of law could be copied through printing limitlessly in identical copies—officials could be dispatched to administer these codes according to fixed constitutional systems.

Modern societies developed largely as a response to the extraordinary capacity of printing. The ability to reproduce information through this mechanical device is the great unconscious assumption that lies at the heart of everything we call "modern." Printing was the watershed separating the medieval from the recognizable world of today.

Now we are experiencing a transformation of the methods for creating and holding text which promises to bring about an equally important shift in the institutions and attitudes that shape societies. The change is widespread and inexorable, simultaneous, complicatedly interdependent between societies and institutions, piecemeal but gigantic, commonplace in outward appearance but massive in implication. It consists at root in the addition of the computer to all of the processes for creating text, from typewriters to newspaper presses. We are already familiar with many of the new devices which are employed by stockbrokers, travel agencies, ticket booking agencies, by lawyers' offices and countless other organizations which employ word processors and video screens to display information. What perhaps we do not consider is the subtle nature of the transformation that lies behind these new contraptions.

The intelligence services provide a good example of a branch of communication and of government that has gone over to the new system fairly comprehensively. Government intelligence services consist of thousands of individuals compiling information about thousands of others. Once this material was held entirely on paper or on cards which entailed extraordinarily complex search methods. By using computer filing systems the whole of civil and military intelligence has gone on line, and an essentially dead system of research has become a live one.

Information can be compared and contrasted simultaneously and input from thousands of sources. Each fresh input makes all existing information more usable, whereas in the past it merely added to the increasing overload. Rather than working file by file through a mound of knowledge, much of it irrelevant, wrong or out of date, the searcher can interrogate what is current and valid.

The computer overcomes overload. Where information once had to be endlessly copied, then physically transported from place to place before the process of mental assimilation could begin, the new process necessitates the existence of only a single "copy" of the material from which each searcher draws merely the required nuggets, the processes of selection, cross-indexing and checking being performed non-physically and, in a sense, non-mentally.

It was the evolution of computer time-sharing in the course of the 1960s which laid the first foundations of the new systems for storing and generating text. Today one industry after another, one living function after another, is being transmuted from the traditional to the computerized mode and, as a result, a number of institutional transformations are gathering pace. Information no longer is obliged to travel through a human system in pyramidal form. The new systems are adept bypassers of traditional hierarchies.

It is easier for someone at the top of a vast bureaucratic pile, over which he or she would previously have found it difficult to maintain authority, to burrow directly through to the information and judgments necessary for decision making. Between the filing clerk and the managing director, there can be far fewer steps than before, so long as both are skilled in the new information techniques and are able to use the new opportunities purposively.

In the rapidly advancing economies of the Far East—Japan in particular—where writing systems have traditionally been nonalphabetic and where, therefore, typewriting in the vernacular has been technically extremely difficult, the 1980s and 1990s will bring about tremendous shakeups within corporate and bureaucratic structures.

Through the new electronic information devices, even Japanese, with its 4,000 common characters, will be written and distributed with the ease of English or French, thereby releasing large numbers of people for different tasks; in many other societies, the changing technologies for producing text will produce social alterations on a comparable scale, as tasks traditionally reserved for women (typing and filing, for example) become merged with the more executive tasks and begin to require more substantial skills (and fewer people).

There exists an enormous "however" poised over the information society. It is turning into an era in which those richest in information skills are best adapted to survive and prosper. That goes for nations as well as individuals. A society which has neither the capacity to launch a communications satellite, nor to work out the methods for scanning its own terrain to assess harvests, mineral deposits or troop movements, nor to process the data which emerges from such operations, will inevitably be susceptible to manipulation by a nation which possesses all such techniques in plenty.

A society which has no news agency of its own will, in the future more than in the past, be dependent upon the news values of societies which do possess skilled news-gathering companies.

A society without adequate computer capacity and trained personnel will depend upon others to operate the booking systems for its airlines, the storage of medical records in its hospitals, the files kept by its police force on its known criminals and suspects, the technologies by which its masses are entertained in their homes, the routes through which its internal mail, its industrial command information, its sea and air defenses maintain internal communication. Those who command and can operate these resources will be kings and princes and those who cannot will live on the perimeter of serfdom, however prosperous they may be at a given moment.

The whole point about the information age is that so many functions and materials can be reduced to the condition of information. The whole point about electronic systems is that they can be highly centralist as well as highly distributive. It is the condition of society and the world as a whole which will determine which way power flows in the information age. If power entails an ability to guarantee previously envisaged ends, then command over information is becoming the chief source of all other forms of power.

I. VOCABULARY

bureaucracy inexorable envisage
hierarchy assess

II. QUESTIONS ON CONTENT

1. How does the author define power today?
2. Why does Smith regard printing as a significant development in Western society?
3. What advantages does the computer have over printing as a source of information?
4. What disadvantages will societies without adequate information skills encounter? Can you suggest any other disadvantages?
5. In what ways do you think computers can be abused? Give some examples from your reading or your experience.

III. QUESTIONS ON FORM

1. The author's thesis appears at the end of the essay rather than, as one might expect, at the beginning. Why?
2. Why does Smith take an historical approach to the topic of power in modern society? What pattern of organization is he using?
3. In what way does the type of writing here differ from that in the previous selection?
4. Point out where the author makes use of the following methods of development: definition, comparison and contrast, and cause and effect.

IV. SUGGESTIONS FOR WRITING

1. In *1984*, by George Orwell, O'Brien, a member of the Inner Party, explains to Winston Smith, his prisoner: "The Party seeks power entirely for its own sake . . . Power is collective. The individual only has power in so far as he ceases to be an individual . . . Power is power over human beings . . . over the mind." Is there still a danger that power, as defined by Smith, can be exploited for the purpose envisioned by Orwell? Explain.
2. Explain how a computer works.
3. If you own or operate a computer, describe the kinds of information you have compiled and explain the uses you have made of this information.
4. Argue for or against the view that deliberate misuse of the computer is a crime that should be severely punished.
5. What kinds of information, if any, do you think should not be made available to the public? Why?

Stanley N. Wellborn is a Senior Editor at *U.S. News & World Report*, where his specialty is science writing. Since joining the magazine in 1972, Wellborn has also covered education, political and social trends, and industry and economics. His articles have won awards from the Westinghouse Science Writing Competition (1983) and the Education Writers Association (1979).

A World of Communications Wonders

Stanley N. Wellborn

A global telecommunications revolution is poised to bring astonishing changes to virtually every American—especially anyone who picks up a telephone, switches on a television set or logs on to a computer.

Growing out of the marriage of communications links with modern computers, the new technologies are spreading lightning fast. Experts say that the upheaval won't end until anyone anywhere can reach out and touch anyone else—instantly and effortlessly—through electronics.

Among the extraordinary possibilities in store for consumers by the end of this century:

- The standard telephone console will become the only computer terminal most people will need. Text and pictures will be viewed on a video screen attached to the phone, and additional data will be delivered as electronically synthesized speech. Phone users also will be able to see who is calling before answering.
- Automobiles will have not only telephones as standard equipment but also satellite navigation devices to pinpoint a vehicle's location and guide the driver to any destination.
- Combining laser optics and computers, three-dimensional holographic images will bring TV features from football games to political debates into living rooms with almost lifelike clarity.
- Automatic-translation devices will allow people to insert a text in English and have it delivered in minutes to a distant point in Japanese, Arabic or one of many other languages.

Such feats, some of which still are in the drawing-board stage, now are considered feasible by scientists who have seen the pace of communications technology move ahead dramatically in recent years.

"We are seeing a technological watershed—a sweeping away of long-established traditions and the opening of enormous business opportunity," says Charles Lecht, chairman of Lecht Sciences, Inc., a communications consulting firm in New York City. "State-of-the-art technology that once would have lasted 30 years is becoming obsolete almost as soon as it is installed."

Already, the conduits of yesterday—copper wires, radio signals, ground antennas and even electricity itself—are giving way to glass fibers, microwaves, satellites, laser beams and the pulsating digital language of computers.

The economic potential of such unprecedented changes in communications technology is practically limitless: Sales of hardware alone reached 60

Reprinted from *U.S. News & World Report* issue of April 9, 1984. Copyright © 1984, U.S. News & World Report, Inc.

billion dollars in 1983, according to estimates by Arthur D. Little, Inc., and will grow to 90 billion annually by 1988.

Added to that will be fees for communications services and software development that will add at least 50 billion dollars a year by the end of the decade.

The international stakes are enormous: Such American giants as AT&T, GTE, MCI Communications and Rolm—plus hundreds of smaller firms and entrepreneurs—are in all-out competition with experienced manufacturers in Japan and Europe.

Like a summer vine that shoots out in every direction without discernible pattern, the telecommunications grid also is spreading uncontrollably. Never before have so many individuals and organizations been able to interact on such a vast scale. By the end of the century, electronic information technology will have transformed American business, manufacturing, school, family, political and home life.

"No one anticipated how fast the demand for communications technology has accelerated in the last three or four years," says William McGowan, chairman of MCI Communications Corporation. "Telecommunications is one business today in which you don't need losers to have winners. There is enough for everybody."

The instruments in this sweeping electronic upheaval—computers, electronic links and video technologies—are the interlocking parts of a communications network undreamed of only a decade ago.

"Even five years ago, I would not have predicted in my wildest imagination how far we would be today," says Howard Anderson, president of the Yankee Group in Boston and a well-known authority in telecommunications research.

Telephones and Computers: Made for Each Other

Within a few years, telephones will be everywhere—in cars, airplane seats, boats, even coat pockets. Also likely: Individuals can have one phone number throughout life that will permit them to be called anytime, no matter where they are. High-tech networks will enable a telephone subscriber in a car in London to communicate by voice, data or facsimile to any other fixed or mobile phone in the world.

Such a network also will allow a variety of interacting banking and retail services, open up access to a wide range of specialized information, provide home-security alarm services and even deliver newspapers and magazines to subscribers through a computer terminal and printer.

Commenting on the trend, one technology analyst notes: "Computers and phones are going to be fused together so tightly that they will be almost indistinguishable."

These possibilities result from the advent of a global linkup known as

ISDN, or integrated-services digital network. Already in operation, the network uses high-capacity optical cables and sophisticated computers to transmit a wide variety of information, including voice, data or graphics, in the same way.

This "supernetwork" converts traditional electrical waves into a stream of on-off pulses, the digital code understood by computers. Once equipment is updated to handle everything in digital form, huge quantities of data can be squeezed onto copper or glass cables or carried by satellites and microwave radio. The result is not only an increase in signal quality but also a dramatic lowering in the cost of sending everything from a simple telephone call to computerized airline reservations and TV pictures across vast distances.

Advocates concede that setting worldwide standards for ISDN will be difficult, comparable to converting the world to the metric system. However, most agree that the economic benefits of a compatible global system will force all nations to get on board quickly.

"We think ISDN will be the biggest hurdle in the communications race," says Warren Falconer, director of the Transmission Network Planning Center at AT&T Bell Laboratories. "But already, business and home users can choose from 150 specialized digital services to customize their communications needs, and more are on the way."

Some companies also see profits in coupling communications lines with powerful computers that could automatically translate spoken or written text into another language. A few systems can make technical translations now, but their creators say it will be many years before a commercial version is widely available.

Another technology on the verge of taking off is cellular radio, a new kind of mobile-phone network that will put full-service telephone in any vehicle on the road.

Car phones have been available for years, but the old transmission severely limited the number of subscribers. Cellular radio uses computers to make better use of radio frequencies, thus opening up thousands of new mobile links.

In Chicago, for example, where the first system is being installed, the existing system allowed fewer than 1,000 mobile users at one time. Using cellular radio, some 20,000 simultaneous conversations could take place.

In designing a system, a local phone company divides a city into cells. Computers track each call and pass it from one low-power transmitter to another as a car travels from one zone to the next, making sure that there is no interruption in the connection. Cellular phones offer more privacy than typical radio links, and calls can be made without the waiting needed when a human operator is involved.

"We think there will be between 1 and 3 million subscribers in the U.S. by the early to mid-1990s," says James Caile, marketing manager for Motorola's cellular operations, a major provider of mobile-radio equipment. Cities expected to be licensed in the next two years include Miami, New York, Los Angeles, Dallas, Washington, Philadelphia, Seattle, Atlanta and Detroit.

The price of a cellular phone now runs about $3,000 for installation, plus a monthly fee of around $100. Initial buyers are expected to be sales personnel and executives, but manufacturers foresee lower prices as demand increases.

"Once people realize how nice it will be to have phones in their cars, the auto manufacturers will begin to offer them as options," says a spokesman for GTE Mobilnet, Inc. "At that point, the prices should come down fast."

Already, Buick is offering cellular phones in some 1984 models, and Ford plans to introduce the devices in 1985.

Fiber Optics: Light Lines to the World

Gossamer strands of ultrapure glass, as thin as human hair, are fast becoming the nerve pathways of the burgeoning telecommunications grid.

Already, a half-inch cable containing 30,000 miles of tiny optical fibers runs between New York and Washington. The link will carry 240,000 simultaneous conversations—twice as many as can be carried by a copper cable as thick as a wrist.

"We are at the start of the light-wave era in long-distance communications," says Robert Kleinert, president of AT&T Communications, which is building an optical-fiber network across the nation. "Light pulses, rather than electrical signals, will be the workhorses of the Information Age."

Optical fibers have greater transmission capacity because they carry tiny staccato pulses of light generated by lasers that can turn on and off 90 million times a second. At such a pace the entire contents of the 2,700-page Webster's Third New International Dictionary could be transmitted over a single fiber in 6 seconds.

Besides major cost benefits, fiber optics offer other advantages, too. They are immune to electrical interference, difficult to wiretap and cheap to produce. A mile-long thread of optical fiber, for instance, can be created from a single tablespoon of raw material.

Experts say the market for fiber optics could reach 3 billion dollars worldwide by 1990. Already, plans are under way to lay 3,500 miles of undersea cable between the U.S. and Europe by 1988, with a cross-Pacific cable later to Japan. Banks and other businesses are building "local-area networks"—intracity optical links to carry all phone and computer data between branch operations. Television and phone links for the 1984 Summer Olympics will be transmitted through a just completed fiber-optics system in Los Angeles.

Meanwhile, technology is bringing even more optical advances. One major step is a lengthening of the distance between the electronic relays that boost light signals before they dim in intensity. Bell Laboratories recently sent 1 billion bits of data—the equivalent of 100 novels—over 75 miles of cable without any electronic boosting.

Although most optical fibers use silicon dioxide, or sand, as their raw material, researchers at Corning Glass Works and elsewhere are experimenting with clearer types of glass. So flawless are some of the new glass compounds that a pane 1 mile thick could be made perfectly transparent.

In time, say researchers, light-wave communications will reach into individual homes and offices, delivering TV and radio entertainment, computer programs, videogames, teletext messages and two-way conduits all through a single optical cable. Such a system also would allow for televised phone conversations with higher quality than the Bell picturephone displayed at the 1964 World's Fair but never put into commercial production because of high cost.

Satellites: High-Flying Birds of High Tech

In a sense, it's not an unusual scene: The boss calls a prospective employe into an office, interviews the person at length and finally announces, "You're hired." The difference is that the boss is 1,000 miles away, and the interview is being carried live and in color between offices by a satellite link.

Communications experts say such electronic conferences soon will be commonplace via satellite. Already, businesses and homeowners are learning to appreciate the services that unmanned orbiters can provide. Mushroom-shaped dish antennas have sprouted atop skyscrapers and in suburban back yards, and new communications satellites are expected to go into orbit at a rate of 200 over the next 10 years in the U.S. alone.

"The fact is, businesses have been bypassing the traditional and more expensive transmission facilities in the U.S. for years," says Robert Hall, president of Satellite Business Systems (SBS), a joint venture of IBM, Comsat and Aetna Insurance. "Satellites have accelerated that trend because they are superb information handlers."

The carrying capacity of the newest satellites has increased more than a hundredfold since the first carriers went into space in the early 1960s. The latest generation of Intelsat VI satellites will carry more than 33,000 simultaneous phone conversations plus two TV channels between the U.S. and Europe.

"Satellites also will eliminate the need for phone lines in most developing nations," notes John Evans, head of Comsat Laboratories. "The smallest, most remote villages will be able to have a satellite phone link."

Businesses have been quick to use this resource, sending vast amounts of computer data from one point on the continent to another in a quarter of a second.

An American Express Company computer center in Phoenix, for example, uses a combination of satellites and phone links to approve 250,000 credit transactions a day from around the world, in an average of 5 seconds or less.

A large insurance company routinely sends computerized material by satellite in 12 minutes that would take 31 hours to transmit by land lines.

A service called Eyesat records new techniques in eye surgery at the St. Louis University School of Medicine, then transmits the video by satellite to physicians elsewhere.

In many cities, businesses are building special satellite-dish fields called teleports to transmit information into space without interference from competing satellite users. One such teleport is being built on Staten Island to alleviate congested airwaves over Manhattan.

Another prospect already being tested in an experimental car produced by Ford: An antenna trained on navigation satellites that display a car's location—within 30 feet—on a video screen mounted in the dashboard.

The newest major use of satellites is teleconferences, in which employes of corporations, educational institutions and government agencies gather around video monitors to hold meetings via satellite linkup around the world. Instead of traveling to meetings, executives can speak to and watch one another without leaving their office buildings.

"Video conferencing is the next best thing to being there," says an official of SBS. "It allows people to see each other on closed-circuit hookups and at fairly reasonable cost."

Conducted on large-screen projectors, video meetings cover questions and discussions by all participants, can be international as well as national and need run only long enough to handle the agenda. Some firms are considering setting up stockholder meetings via satellite links.

Last year, wine critics in France and the U.S. met through satellite to taste and compare notes on recent vintages. The link allowed wine merchants to get expert opinion, but only the wines had to be flown across the ocean.

Atlantic Richfield Company has installed a 17-million-dollar video-teleconference system to connect its Los Angeles headquarters with offices in Philadelphia, Denver, Houston, Dallas and Washington. And the J. C. Penney Company recently set up a laser system linking two New York City skyscrapers to conduct video meetings, and plans to expand the system nationwide.

Despite such efforts, some analysts have doubts about the growth of video conferences. They point out that such companies as SBS have yet to make a profit and note that many people do not like to "perform" on a video monitor.

One breakthrough that would clearly aid all video services would be a higher-resolution television screen that would sharpen the often hazy, dull visual qualities of today's TV screen. "TV's are being used for many more things now—for the computer, VCR, teletext services and video conferences," says a Sony Corporation official. "The U.S. broadcast standard just doesn't allow for the higher resolution that is possible with today's electronics."

Now, scientists at Bell Labs and elsewhere are using digital technology to create a much higher-definition picture. "We can get images that are so crystal clear it's almost like 3-D," says one executive.

CBS and Philips Corporation are developing a high-definition satellite-TV system that would deliver cinema-quality signals to the home screen. Now, the television industry has formed the Advanced Television System Committee to persuade the Federal Communications Commission to write regulations allowing such techniques.

But even advocates of new technology concede that getting consumers to discard old TV sets for new equipment will be a lengthy process, as will convincing government regulators to change existing broadcast standards. "It's not a matter of technology," says a scientist at RCA Corporation, "but of politics and economics."

Telecommunications-industry officials are clearly excited about the potential that new technologies hold out for consumers and business. How fast fiber optics, satellites and computer-enhanced techniques will surpass conventional methods is uncertain, but experts are optimistic that the world will shrink even further by communications advances.

Sums up Anderson of Boston's Yankee Group: "The next five years will surprise us, too. There will be price wars, a vast array of competing technologies and complex choices to be made. Consumers will benefit from the revolution with better service, cheaper prices and more control. Consumers will be the engineers of their own custom-designed communications centers."

I. VOCABULARY

poised (v.)   conduit   advent
upheaval   unprecedented   concede
holographic   discernible   array (n.)

II. QUESTIONS ON CONTENT

1. What is the telecommunications revolution?
2. What are some of the possible future achievements in communications technology? Which one strikes you as the most important or promising? Why?
3. What is cellular radio? What are some advantages of this technology?
4. How will advances in communications technology affect business? The consumer?

84 Popular Writing

5. Would the author of the previous essay, Anthony Smith, welcome the telecommunications revolution? Explain.

III. QUESTIONS ON FORM

1. Locate the thesis in this essay.
2. Unlike Anthony Smith, Wellborn does not speculate on any of the possible adverse effects of the telecommunications revolution. What does this tell you about his aim? His attitude toward his subject?
3. What modes of writing are used to organize the discussion of communications advances?
4. Identify the simile used to describe the growth of the electronic information technology. Why is the essay virtually devoid of such figures of speech?
5. How does the conclusion relate to the thesis? Is the conclusion effective? Why or why not?

IV. SUGGESTIONS FOR WRITING

1. Analyze and evaluate the changes you think electronic information technology will bring about in any one of the following areas of American society: business, manufacturing, school, family, political and social life, or home life.
2. Discuss some of the advantages of having a phone in your car.
3. What possible dangers do you foresee from this forthcoming telecommunications revolution?
4. Describe a development or change in communications technology not mentioned in this essay that you would like to see by the end of the twentieth century. Explain how this achievement will improve life and the world.

An educator and journalist, **Roger Rosenblatt** is an editorial writer and author of a weekly column for the *Washington Post*. He is the author of *Black Fiction* (1974) and a contributor to popular magazines, including *Harper's*, the *Saturday Review*, and *Time*.

The Mind in the Machine

Roger Rosenblatt

The factory robot that crushed a man to death in Japan last year did little to silence the talk that machines are a threat to human pre-eminence. That talk has been alive ever since people first discovered that they could

Copyright © 1982 by Time Inc. All rights reserved. Reprinted by permission from *Time*.

manufacture tools vastly superior to themselves; in Samuel Butler's satire *Erewhon* (1872), the citizens establish a museum of old machines in which they at once deposit and abandon their mechanical inventions, which they believed would swallow up their souls. When machines possess artificial intelligence, like computers, the human fear of being overtaken seems both more urgent and more complex. Science-fiction writers from Capek to Asimov have built much of their genre around robots, androids, computers and their kin—each fairly boring and predictable as characters, but all presenting the same basic paradox: that they will eventually take command of the world, and that a man can beat them every time.

This proposition is not as contradictory as it sounds, since, for one thing, the fact that it takes real (*i.e.*, natural) intelligence to create the artificial kind would seem to give humanity a perpetual edge; and, for another, people are able to hold contraries in their heads simultaneously—a feat that is reassuring in itself, since it is one of the things that distinguishes men from machines. Indeed, man tends to search out the distinctions even as he endows his machines with increasing sophistication, as if to make sure that his evolution is no slower than that of his creations. Still, it is sometimes nerve-racking to read what these boxes can do. Joseph Weizenbaum, of M.I.T., who has recently come to criticize computer education for children as a context for "toy problems," nonetheless got more than a toy gasp out of the public in 1968 when he unveiled his project ELIZA—an IBM 7094 programmed by Weizenbaum to "practice" psychotherapy—and then published a "conversation" between ELIZA and a real patient:

Patient: You are like my father in some ways.
ELIZA: What resemblance do you see?
Patient: You are not very aggressive, but I think you don't want me to notice that.
ELIZA: What makes you think I am not very aggressive?
Patient: You don't argue with me.
ELIZA: Why do you think I don't argue with you?
Patient: You are afraid of me.
ELIZA: Does it please you to believe I am afraid of you?

The elements of parody notwithstanding, it is no joke to see a machine become a man, especially in an era whose main (if somewhat *pro forma*) worry centers on men becoming machines.

A great deal of intellectual effort is therefore spent these days—mostly by the computer scientists themselves—trying to reassure everybody that, as smart as a machine can get, it can never be as intelligent as its progenitor. In part, this effort is made in order to see that the wizened, noncomputer generation—which often regards the younger with the unbridled enthusiasm that the Chinese showed the Mongol hordes—feels that it has a safe and legitimate place in modernity. In part, the effort is made because the proposition is true: a computer cannot possess the full range of human intelligence. Yet in terms of reconciling man and machine, this effort still misses the point. The cultural value of computers does not lie in perceiving what they cannot do, but what they can, and what, in turn their capabilities show about our own. In other words, a computer may not display the whole of human intelligence, but that portion it can display could do a lot more good for man's self-confidence than continuing reassurances that he is in no immediate danger of death by robot.

Essentially, what one wants to know in sorting out this relationship is the answers to two questions: Can computers think (a technical problem)? And, should they think (a moral one)? In order to get at both, it is first necessary to agree on what thinking itself is—what thought means—and that is no quick step. Every period in history has had to deal with at least two main definitions of thought, which mirror the prevailing philosophies of that particular time and are usually in opposition. Moreover, these contending schools change from age to age. On a philosophical level, thought cannot know itself because it cannot step outside itself. Nor is it an activity that can be understood by what it produces (art, science, dreams). To Freud the mind was a house; to Plato a cave. These are fascinating, workable metaphors, but the fact is that in each case an analogy had to be substituted for an equation.

At the same time, certain aspects of thinking can be identified without encompassing the entire process. The ability to comprehend, to conceptualize, to organize and reorganize, to manipulate, to adjust—these are all parts of thought. So are the acts of pondering, rationalizing, worrying, brooding, theorizing, contemplating, criticizing. One thinks when one imagines, hopes, loves, doubts, fantasizes, vacillates, regrets. To experience greed, pride, joy, spite, amusement, shame, suspicion, envy, grief—all these require thought; as do the decisions to take command, or umbrage; to feel loyalty or inhibitions; to ponder ethics, self-sacrifice, cowardice, ambition. So vast is the mind's business that even as one makes such a list, its inadequacy is self-evident—the recognition of inadequacy being but another part of an enormous and varied instrument.

The answer to the first question, then—Can a machine think?—is yes and no. A computer can certainly do some of the above. It can (or will soon be able to) transmit and receive messages, "read" typescript, recognize voices, shapes and patterns, retain facts, send reminders, "talk" or mimic speech, adjust, correct, strategize, make decisions, translate languages. And, of course, it can calculate, that being its specialty. Yet there are hundreds of kinds of thinking that computers cannot come close to. And for those merely intent on regarding the relationship of man to machine as a head-to-artificial-head competition, this fact offers some solace—if not much progress.

For example, the Apollo moon shot in July 1969 relied on computers at practically every stage of the operation. Before taking off, the astronauts used computerized simulations of the flight. The spacecraft was guided by a computer, which stored information about the gravitational fields of the sun and moon, and calculated the craft's position, speed and altitude. This computer, which determined the engines to be fired, and when, and for how long, took part of its own information from another computer on the ground. As the Apollo neared the moon, a computer triggered the firing of a descent rocket, slowed the lunar module, and then signaled Neil Armstrong that he had five seconds to decide whether or not to go ahead with the landing. At 7,200 ft., a computer commanded the jets to tilt the craft almost upright so that Armstrong and Aldrin could take a close look at what the world had been seeking for centuries.

Would one say, then, that computers got men to the moon? Of course not. A machine is merely a means. What got man to the moon was his desire to go there—desire being yet another of those elements that a computer cannot simulate or experience. It was far less interesting, for instance, that Archimedes believed he could move the earth with his lever than that he wanted to try it. Similarly, no machine could have propelled man to the moon had not the moon been in man in the first place.

Thus the second question—Should a machine think?—answers itself. The question is not in fact the moral problem it at first appears, but purely a practical one. Yes, a machine should think as much as it can, because it *can* only think in limited terms. Hubert Dreyfus, a philosophy professor at Berkeley, observes that "all aspects of human thought, including non-formal aspects like moods, sensory-motor skills and long-range self-interpretations, are so interrelated that one cannot substitute an abstract-able web of explicit beliefs for the whole cloth of our concrete everyday practice." Marianne Moore saw the web her own way: "The mind is an enchanting thing,/ is an enchanted thing/ like the glaze on a/ katydid-wing/ subdivided by sun/ till the nettings are legion,/ Like Gieseking playing Scarlatti." In short, human intelligence is too intricate to be replicated. When a computer can smile at an enemy, cheat at cards and pray in church all in the same day, then, perhaps, man will know his like. Until then, no machine can touch us.

For the sake of argument, however, what if Dreyfus, Moore and common sense were all wrong? What if the mind with its legion nettings could in fact be replicated in steel and plastic, and all human befuddlements find their way onto a program—would the battle be lost? Hardly. The moon is always in the man. Even if it were possible to reduce people to box size and have them plonked down before themselves in all their powers, they would still want more. Whatever its source, there is a desire that outdesires desire; otherwise computers would not have come into being. As fast as the mind travels, it somehow manages to travel faster than itself, and people always know, or sense, what they do not know. No machine does that. A computer can *achieve* what it does not know (not knowing that 2 + 2 = 4, it can find out), but it cannot yearn for the answer or even dimly suspect its existence.

If people knew where such suspicions and yearnings came from, they might be able to lock them in silicon. But they do not know what they are; they merely know that they are—just as in the long run they only know that they exist, not what their existence is or what it means. The difference between us and any machine we create is that a machine is an answer, and we are a question.

But is there anything really startling in this? With all the shouting and sweating that go on about machines taking over the world, does anyone but a handful of zealots and hysterics seriously believe that the human mind is genuinely imperiled by devices of its own manufacture? In *Gödel, Escher, Bach* (1979), Douglas R. Hofstadter's dazzling book on minds and machines, a man is described—one Johann Martin Zacharias Dase (1824-61))who was employed by governments because he could do mathematical feats like multiplying two 100-digit numbers in his head, and could calculate at a glance how many sheep were in a field, for example, or how many words in a sentence, up to about 30. (Most people can do this up to about six.) Were Mr. Dase living today, would he be thought a computer? Are computers thought of as men? This is a kind of cultural game people play, a false alarm, a ghost story recited to put one's mind at rest.

The trouble is that "at rest" is a poor place to be in this situation, because such a position encourages no understanding of what these machines can do for life beyond the tricks they perform. Alfred North Whitehead said that "civilization advances by extending the number of important operations which we can perform without thinking about them." In that sense, computers have advanced civilization. But thinking about the computer, as a cultural event or instrument, has so far not advanced civilization one whit. Instead, one hears humanists either fretting about the probability that before the end of the century computers will be able to beat all the world's chess masters, or consoling themselves that a computer cannot be Mozart— the response to the first being, "So what?" and to the second, "Who ever thought so?" The thing to recognize about the computer is not how powerful it is or will become, but that its power is finite. So is that of the mind. The finitudes in both cases are not the same, but the fact that they are comparable may be the most useful news that man's self-evaluation has received in 200 years.

For too long now, generations have been bedeviled with the idea, formally called romanticism, that human knowledge has no limits, that man can become either God or Satan, depending on his inclinations. The rider to this proposition is that some human minds are more limitless than others, and wherever that notion finds its most eager receptacles, one starts out with Bryon and winds up in Dachau. To be fair, that is not all of romanticism, but it is the worst of it, and the worst has done the world a good deal of damage. For the 18th century, man was man-size. For the 19th and 20th, his size has been boundless, which has meant that he has had little sense of his own proportion in relation to everything else—resulting either in exaggerated self-pity or in self-exaltation—and practically no stable appreciation of his own worth.

Now, suddenly, comes a machine that says in effect: This is the size of man insofar as that size may be measured by this machine. It is not the whole size of man, but it is a definable percentage. Other machines show you how fast you can move and how much you can lift. This one shows you how well you can think, in certain areas. It will do as much as you would have it do, so it will demonstrate the extent of your capabilities. But since it can only go as far as you wish it to go, it will also demonstrate the strength of your volition.

Both these functions are statements of limitation. A machine that tells you how much you can know likewise implies how much you cannot. To learn what one can know is important, but to learn what one cannot know is essential to one's well-being. This offers a sense of proportion, and so is thoroughly antiromantic. Yet it is not cold 18th century rationalistic either. The computer simply provides a way of drawing a line between the knowable and the unknowable, between the moon and the moon in man, and it is on that line where people may be able to see their actual size.

Newsday cartoon by Tom Darcy.

90 Popular Writing

Whether the world will look any better for such self-recognition is anybody's guess. The mind, being an enchanted thing, has surprised itself too often to suggest that any discovery about itself will improve economies or governments, much less human nature. On face value, however, the cultural effects of these machines are promising. Every so often in history man makes what he needs. In one sense he made the computer because he needed to think faster. In another, he may have needed to define himself more clearly; he may have sensed a need for intellectual humility. If he needed intellectual humility at this particular time, it may be a sign that he was about to get out of hand again, and so these contraptions, of which he pretends to be so fearful, may in fact be his self-concocted saving grace. The mind is both crafty and mysterious enough to work that way.

I. VOCABULARY

pre-eminence
genre
paradox
progenitor

vacillate
umbrage
replicate
zealot

imperil
fret
volition
enchanted

II. QUESTIONS ON CONTENT

1. Why, according to the article, does man fear the machine? Do you fear machines? Why or why not?
2. What questions does the author ask about computers? What answers does he give to these questions? Do you agree or disagree with these answers? Explain.
3. What difference is there between man and the machine? In what way are they similar?
4. Why is Rosenblatt critical of romanticism? Why does he regard the computer as a valuable corrective to the excess of romanticism?
5. Why did man make the computer? Can you suggest any other reasons for this creation?

III. QUESTIONS ON FORM

1. What is the aim of this essay?
2. What type of reader is the author addressing?
3. Identify the thesis of the essay. Why is it located where it is?
4. What examples are given to show the computer's ability to think? Are these examples effective? Explain.
5. In organizing and developing his material. Rosenblatt uses definition and comparison and contrast. Locate an example of each.
6. What is meant by the statement "The moon is always in the man"?

IV. SUGGESTIONS FOR WRITING

1. Do you own a personal computer? Discuss the reasons that led you to purchase it.
2. If you own or have access to a computer, explain the various uses you make of it.
3. Describe a computer program that you wish someone would write.
4. In 1982 *Time* magazine named the computer Man of the Year for wielding that year's "greatest influence for good or evil." Do you agree with this decision? Why or why not?
5. Defend or attack Joseph Weizenbaum's criticism, in paragraph two, of computer education for children.
6. One of the consequences of the computer revolution has been computer break-ins. In some cases, for example, bright youngsters have broken into nonclassified, public-access computer systems. Analyze the reasons for this activity and explain why you would or would not prosecute youngsters for doing this.
7. Compare and contrast the views of Smith and Rosenblatt on the role of the computer in modern society.
8. Explain how computers have changed your life.

TOPICS FOR INVESTIGATION

1. Examine and evaluate any one of the following indictments of the mass media discussed by Leo Rosten (*Daedalus*, 1960):

   a. "The mass media lack originality."
   b. "The mass media do not give the public enough or adequate information about the serious problems of our time."
   c. The mass media are wary of criticizing Big Business because they themselves are businesses and because they depend upon advertising revenues from the business world for their very existence.
   d. "The aesthetic level of the mass media is appaling: truth is sacrificed to the happy ending, escapism is exalted, romance, violence, melodrama prevail."
   e. "The mass media do not provide an adequate forum for minority views—the dissident and unorthodox."

2. Analyze and evaluate the influential theory of Marshall McLuhan that the medium is the key element in the mass communications process because "the medium is the message."

3. Investigate either the libertarian or social responsibility theory of the mass media with respect to its outlook on the following functions: media ownership, media control and regulation, social and political influence of the media, basic functions of the media, and the responsibility of the individual.

4. Explore the Soviet communist concept of the mass media and explain how it reflects the political philosophy of this country.

5. Consider one or more of the following areas in which the U.S. government restrains its media with laws: libel, obscenity, privacy, and broadcast stations. How fair or effective are these restraints?

6. Research the trend toward concentration of ownership and control in the mass media, and determine the extent to which this trend can be considered dangerous to our society.

7. Investigate the impact of the media on our society in terms of its power to shape and reinforce our attitudes, values, concepts, or lifestyles.

8. Inquire into the changes that have occurred in the past decade in the media's treatment of either women or blacks and other minority groups.

9. Explore the effects of the computer on one of the following:

   a. Newspaper industry
   b. Business world
   c. Educational system
   d. Family life
   e. Privacy and freedom

10. Study the ways in which a change in one mass communications medium affects other media. How, for example, did the advent of television affect film and radio?

11. Using Stanley Wellborn's essay as your starting point, speculate on how our lives in the future may be reshaped by the mass media. Will they, for instance, help to give us more or less control of our lives? Will they help make us more productive and more happy?

12. Probe the discipline known as mass communications research. What is it? What areas does it encompass? What methods does it employ? What kinds of information do communications researchers seek to gain about such subjects as readership, graphics, advertising, public opinion, and the media audience? What job opportunities are available in communications research? What kind of academic training does a mass communications researcher need?

4

NEWS: PRINT AND BROADCAST

The dissemination of information has always been a function of the media. Today, as Anthony Smith pointed out in Chapter Three, more than ever, information is power. It is, then, crucial that our information, our news, be immediate, accurate, and succinctly and professionally communicated. In the last few decades, owing to the accelerated development of electronic technology, that task has been shared by the print and broadcast media: newspapers, radio, and television.

Our knowledge of our immediate environment is influenced by the media's presentation of it, but our knowledge of world affairs, in most cases, is determined by what we read, see, and hear from the media. We must accept the news we receive as the reality of a given situation. Clearly, some examination of the profession that presents this reality to us is necessary. Who are the forces who shape the news, and what are the forces that shape them?

The complexities attendent to news gathering and communication today are tremendous. The essays in this chapter focus on some of the key issues: propaganda versus hard news; individual privacy versus the public right to know; humanitarianism versus professional noninvolvement. Thomas Collins clarifies the differences between television and newspaper journalists for us, while Ronald Steel, writing on political journalism, discusses the temptations of power in two worlds where information definitely is power. Leo and Saltman consider the language of news—"journalese"—while Louis

Lapham employs elegant diction in his exposition and defense of the press and its functions as he sees them. We may see them differently, but that is, after all, one of the messages of this chapter. We must first evaluate how our world view is being affected by the news media before we move on to analyze how we are influenced by the entertainment media.

Readings

> **Donald H. Johnston** worked for many years as a reporter and editor for United Press International and the *New York Times*. The author of *The Bumpy Road to Disarmament* and *Journalism and the Media,* Johnston is Associate Professor of Journalism and Associate Dean for Academic Affairs for the Graduate School of Journalism at Columbia University.

What Is News?

Donald H. Johnston

Every minute, every second, a myriad of events and happenings are taking place across the globe—births, deaths, accidents, natural calamities, fights, strikes, discoveries, meetings, announcements, sports contests, and so on into the endless mechanics of everyday living. Only a tiny fraction of all this is considered by journalists to be news. And only a fraction of the news actually gathered by any one newspaper or broadcast station gets into print or on the air. Whether or not an event or issue is newsworthy is determined by criteria that have evolved among journalists over the years.

Definitions of News

There have been many definitions of news, most of them familiar by now. One dictionary says news is "fresh information concerning something that has recently taken place." Another defines news as "tidings or intelligence of new or hitherto unknown things." A third: "Recent events and happenings, especially those that are unusual or notable."

Various editors have offered their own definitions. All generally recognize that news is intended to interest, inform, and, in some cases, entertain.

Joseph Pulitzer, the nineteenth-century editor and publisher of the *St. Louis Post-Dispatch* and the *New York World,* wanted news stories that were (as he put it) original, distinctive, dramatic, romantic, thrilling, unique, curious, quaint, humorous, odd, and apt to be talked about. Charles A. Dana, editor of the old *New York Sun,* felt that "anything that will make people talk" was news.

One of the most durable, though imprecise, definitions came from

From *Journalism And The Media* by Donald H. Johnston. Copyright © 1979 by Donald H. Johnston. By permission of Harper & Row, Publishers, Inc.

Turner Catledge, former managing editor of the *New York Times,* who called news "anything you can find out today that you didn't know before." And countless editors have merely told their staffs to find stories that would make the readers perk up and say, "Hey, I didn't know that!" All of which has led reporters to a favorite definition: "News is what my editor says it is."

News has been described as both a commodity and a state of mind. Journalism textbooks point out that news is gathered, processed, and packaged by profitmaking news organizations, like any other consumer product. At the same time it is something that stimulates interest in millions of people, often stirring them into action as a result. All news deals in some way with the traditional five W's and H—who, what, when, where, why, and how.

Types of News

Basically there are two kinds of spot, or "live," news: spontaneous and planned. Spontaneous news includes events such as a fire, an earthquake, an accident, a killing, an arrest. Planned news includes prearranged and anticipated events: that is, the news derives from a scheduled meeting, hearing, trial, press conference, speech, statement, demonstration, space launching, and the like. In a sense, a person or group or agency "makes" the planned news, which constitutes a large proportion of any day's news agenda.

Variations in Meaning

No one definition of news is entirely satisfactory for every situation. Perhaps this is because the nature of news changes with the times, and the concept of what is newsworthy is subject to the judgments of both the editor and individuals within his audience.

Effects of time. A half-century ago Charles A. Lindbergh's nonstop solo flight across the Atlantic Ocean was reported in banner headlines. It was a dramatic "first" in aviation, a conquest by man over nature. Measured against this "first," the second and subsequent transoceanic flights declined in newsworthiness. Today such flights by modern jets are common and do not rate public attention; they have been replaced in the news by flights to the moon and robot exploration of the planets.

Effects of judgment. The way journalists look at the news is determined to a large extent by their company's policies, by what they consider to be their audience's principal interests, and by their own backgrounds and personal traits. Studies have shown, for example, that journalists are predominantly male, middle-class, and concentrated in large urban centers and disproportionately in the Northeast. These characteristics generally reflect those of the main body of the news media audience. It is no accident, then, that the media give wide attention to subjects of interest to men, such as sports, to established middle-class institutions, and to urban affairs.

On an individual basis, a journalist's news judgment is influenced by his own prejudices, suspicions, interests, and emotions. For example, an editor who feels that the condition of the environment is particularly important is inclined to emphasize this issue in his selection of news to present to the public.

Similarly, there are disparities among readers in how they view the significance or interest of different kinds of news. A plunge in the stock market may be of vital interest to a businessman, but a bore to a teenager. A woman may be fascinated by the latest Paris fashions; a man probably is not. A farmer wants to know about a new pest threat to crops; an industrial worker is more concerned about factory automation. . . .

Newsworthy Elements

The variables in time and judgments of journalists and readers are critical to the question of what news is. Although the amount and variety of news available to a modern newspaper and broadcast station are as unlimited as life itself, the media's capacity to present the news is rigidly restricted. A newspaper has just so many pages; a radio or television station has just so much air time. Therefore, news editors *must* be selective. They must judge each event and decide whether, in their minds, the event is worth reporting to the public, hoping all the while that the public agrees. Would the event be "interesting" to a large number of people? For every story included, a dozen, a hundred, perhaps a thousand must be excluded. By the same token, these judgments determine whether a selected event rates a long story on the front page or a brief mention buried on an inside page.

In making such judgments, an editor looks for certain elements or qualities that he thinks make some stories more compelling than others at a particular time. The relative value of the elements depends on the nature of the story and the views of the editor. In most stories the elements overlap. There is no set list, but most editors look for one or more of the following qualities:

Timeliness. News has always been a perishable commodity. Few people are interested in yesterday's news, especially now that radio and television provide instantaneous reporting. Therefore, all factors being equal, immediacy probably will give one story the edge over another. Today's fire is likely to get priority over yesterday's robbery—on the assumption that readers and listeners already know about the robbery.

Immediacy applies not only to the time of occurence of an event, but also the time of discovery or disclosure. Such was the case, for example, with the story of the My Lai massacre in the Vietnam War. The incident, in which nearly all Vietnamese civilians in a village were deliberately killed, was kept secret by the United States government until investigative reporters discovered documents in Pentagon files long after the event occurred. The disclosure was front-page news. Similarly, prehistoric bones may lie hidden by time in East Africa; the existence of the bones is not a new happening; but the *discovery* of the bones is news.

Nowadays newspaper editors often pay less attention to the timeliness and more to the significance of a story. This is because the print media, with their production time lag between event and publication, cannot hope to beat the broadcast media in reporting spot news first.

It is not unusual for some newspapers to hold stories until more background details and interpretive material can be added or until the full story can be prepared. Such was the case with the *New York Times* disclosure of the Pentagon Papers about United States involvement in Vietnam. The *Times* did not rush into print as soon as it had most of the 47 volumes of the papers; instead, the editors held back until a special team, in a hushed operation, sifted through the material for six weeks in a rented hotel suite. The chance the *Times* took with the delay, of course, was that none of its competitors would also obtain the material and print it in the meantime.

Proximity. The closer the event, the greater is the interest. People can identify with news if they know the persons, conditions, or localities involved. They are more concerned about an explosion in their own community than an earthquake in another nation. A local election commands more attention than a state election in another part of the country.

An editor is always looking for the "local" angle. An accident in another community has a higher news value if one of the victims was a resident of the paper's town. If the state announces new financial aid to a number of communities, an editor is more likely to run the story if his town is a recipient than if it is not.

Conflict. People have always been interested in wars and other confrontations. There are countless variations: man versus man, man versus animal, man versus nature, nation versus nation.

Prominence. Well-known persons, places, and things always excite the curiosity of readers and listeners. When the governor arrives in town, he rates a story, whereas John Smith on the same plane is ignored. It may be news if a man jumps from a hotel window, but it's bigger news if he jumps from the Washington Monument.

Consequence. Happenings that directly affect the lives of his audience are usually reported by an editor. Examples are a breakdown of waterworks machinery, causing disruption of water flow to local homes; the City Council's passage of a new property tax, and a strike at a plant that employs many town workers. In a broader sense, examples include a scientific breakthrough that will improve the treatment of a common disease, or a problem with the Brazilian coffee crop that will mean more expensive coffee for American consumers. Other factors being equal, the news value is greater if the happening affects 100 percent of the audience than if it affects only 10 percent.

Magnitude. It is human nature that the interest of people seems to increase with the size of the event. Stronger news treatment is given to a traffic accident that kills ten persons than one with a single fatality; to a flood that devastates a ten-square-mile area than one that overruns a city block; to the city's purchase of fifty snow plows than the purchase of two.

Other elements. Among other considerations are oddity (the familiar man-bites-dog concept) and human interest that excites the emotions (sex, helplessness, loneliness, injustice, humor, brutality).

Many studies have been made of news selection patterns, and journalists and readers have generally been found to be in substantial agreement as to their element preferences. Aside from timeliness and proximity, the factors that tend to elicit most interest are consequence and conflict.

Increase in Feature Stories

The rise of broadcast news has led the print media to expand their offerings of feature stories that do not depend for appeal on fast-breaking developments. In a rapidly changing world, the print media see a new job to be done, and the premise is that newspapers and magazines can perform this job better than the broadcast media can. The features are current, but not necessarily immediate, and can be read at the reader's leisure. As so often happens in the competitive news business, the success of features in the print media has led to more features in the broadcast media. The result is that the definition of newsworthiness has been broadened.

Human interest. One class of feature getting increasing attention is the human-interest story. It exploits the old journalism axiom that people make news. Now commonplace, for instance, are tales about a day in the life of a hospital worker and new careers for retired people. Sections devoted to culture, sports, family and leisure activities, and how-to tips have been enlarged by most newspapers.

The interest in personalities has led to gossipy new magazines such as *People* and *Us,* "people" columns in newspapers, and expanded talk shows on radio and television. This same interest assured front-page play for such stories as Representative Wayne Hays's dalliance with a Capitol Hill office worker. All of which prompted the *Columbia Journalism Review* to observe about news judgment that the 1970s were slightly reminiscent of the 1920s era of "ballyhoo" journalism.

"Sidebars." Another newer type of feature includes the interpretive article, the backgrounder, and the person-in-the-news biography that usually supplements a breaking story. The main spot story provides an overall picture of a situation, touching at least briefly on many aspects of the story; the feature, called a "sidebar," goes into detail about one aspect considered especially important by the editors. Sidebars are intended to provide judgment and balance to the news, to give the reader deeper insight to the forces acting on the breaking news.

One example of a sidebar is an expert's analysis of various political groups involved in a revolt in South America. It explains the philosophies, goals, and strengths of the groups, describes the groups' leaders, and puts the current revolt into historical perspective. While these points likely would be noted in the main story, there would not be enough room for details.

Another example is a short biography of a new Secretary of the Treasury. The main story would report the announcement by the President, a few major facts about the appointee, the circumstances that led to the appointment, and some indication of whether the appointment might lead to change in Treasury Department policies. The sidebar would produce a word picture of the appointee: personal appearance, professional experience, age and education, family and hobbies, likes and dislikes, views on his new job.

Sidebar features often are the result of weeks of investigation by teams of reporters. Editors sometimes anticipate news developments, assign investigative reporters to explore conditions expected to provoke the development, and then hold the sidebar until the breaking news actually comes. Or the procedure may be reversed. After the news development, the editor assigns the reporters to explore the conditions that led to the event.

Not surprisingly, broadcast stations have followed suit with their own efforts at interpretation. These efforts take the form of short supplementary material aired with the report on a breaking news story, or long documentaries on such subjects as hunger or migrant workers.

Crusades. Long a staple of newspapers, the crusade story (or series of stories) in the name of community service continues to be popular. These stories usually are not pegged to spot news, but they are newsworthy in that they describe and explain conditions that the newspaper believes should get attention. In a sense, the newspaper "makes" the news. The goal may be almost anything, from better housing or a new school to a crime-prevention program or antipollution measures.

Criticism of News Selection

A longstanding criticism of the media is that they carry too much bad news at the expense of the good. Critics say—and some newspeople agree—that the media fill their pages and air time with stories of crime, corruption, violence, disaster, war, unemployment, and tax increases and that they pay insufficient attention to achievements and triumphs. The criticism was particularly loud during the 1960s and early '70s, a period that included Vietnam, the youth revolt, and Watergate.

Many answers have been suggested. The media merely mirror society. It is a matter of perspective, and whether news is good or bad is in the eye of the beholder. The media *do* report much good news—such as scientific discoveries, space triumphs, cultural events, educational progress, environmental cleanup, success stories, and the routine of weddings, sports, and social activities. The trend toward "soft" service features and consumer guides in the "living" sections has added more "news" of a positive nature.

Perhaps the easiest, and most honest, answer is that the average reader and listener seem to be more interested in bad news than good. They want to know about events that deviate from the norm, that disrupt the stability of daily living. Obeying the law and living free of disaster are the norm for the majority of people; disobeying the law and getting hurt in an accident or a storm or demonstration are not. Some newspapers and television stations have experimented with special emphasis on "good" news and have found through audience surveys and sales that, in general, the public wasn't really interested.

I. VOCABULARY

criteria	proximity	elicit
calamities	sidebar	prominence
spontaneous	crusade	deviate
disparities	oddity	ballyhoo

II. QUESTIONS ON CONTENT

1. Which of the definitions of news given in the first paragraph of the essay do you prefer? Why?
2. Cite examples of the two kinds of news.
3. Explain some of the factors that affect the nature of news.
4. List the eight different newsworthy elements mentioned. Which are the most important? Why?
5. What opinions does Goldsmith voice about newsworthy elements in her essay on celebrity in Chapter Two?
6. What is a feature story? A sidebar?

7. Why have feature stories become more prominent in print?
8. Do you think that people are more interested in bad news than good?

III. QUESTIONS ON FORM

1. This is intended as an essay of definition. Are the definitions clear, memorable?
2. Is the author's tone objective throughout? Consider paragraph nine, page 99 on the effects of judgment in this light.
3. Consider paragraph two, page 99 on news selection. Explain why it is expository writing. How could it become persuasive writing?

IV. SUGGESTIONS FOR WRITING

1. Create a news story fulfilling most of the newsworthy elements cited.
2. Write a feature story related to your news story.
3. Write an objective profile of an individual of whom you approve or disapprove.

A Statement of Principles

American Society of Newspaper Editors

Preamble

The First Amendment, protecting freedom of expression from abridgment by any law, guarantees to the people through their press a constitutional right, and thereby places on newspaper people a particular responsibility.

Thus journalism demands of its practitioners not only industry and knowledge but also the pursuit of a standard of integrity proportionate to the journalist's singular obligation.

To this end the American Society of Newspaper Editors sets forth this Statement of Principles as a standard encouraging the highest ethical and professional performance.

Article I—Responsibility

The primary purpose of gathering and distributing news and opinion is to serve the general welfare by informing the people and enabling them to make judgments on the issues of the time. Newspapermen and women who abuse the power of their professional role for selfish motives or unworthy purposes are faithless to that public trust.

Reprinted by permission of the American Society of Newspaper Editors.

The American press was made free not just to inform or just to serve as a forum for debate but also to bring an independent scrutiny to bear on the forces of power in the society, including the conduct of official power at all levels of government.

Article II—Freedom of the Press

Freedom of the press belongs to the people. It must be defended against encroachment or assault from any quarter, public or private.

Journalists must be constantly alert to see that the public's business is conducted in public. They must be vigilant against all who would exploit the press for selfish purposes.

Article III—Independence

Journalists must avoid impropriety and the appearance of impropriety as well as any conflict of interest or the appearance of conflict. They should neither accept anything nor pursue any activity that might compromise or seem to compromise their integrity.

Article IV—Truth and Accuracy

Good faith with the reader is the foundation of good journalism. Every effort must be made to assure that the news content is accurate, free from bias and in context, and that all sides are presented fairly. Editorials, analytical articles and commentary should be held to the same standards of accuracy with respect to facts as news reports.

Significant errors of fact, as well as errors of omission, should be corrected promptly and prominently.

Article V—Impartiality

To be impartial does not require the press to be unquestioning or to refrain from editorial expression. Sound practice, however, demands a clear distinction for the reader between news reports and opinion. Articles that contain opinion or personal interpretation should be clearly identified.

Article VI—Fair Play

Journalists should respect the rights of people involved in the news, observe the common standards of decency and stand accountable to the public for the fairness and accuracy of their news reports.

Persons publicly accused should be given the earliest opportunity to respond.

Pledges of confidentiality to news sources must be honored at all costs, and therefore should not be given lightly. Unless there is clear and pressing need to maintain confidences, sources of information should be identified.

These principles are intended to preserve, protect and strengthen the bond of trust and respect between American journalists and the American people, a bond that is essential to sustain the grant of freedom entrusted to both by the nation's founders.

Adopted by the ASNE Board of Directors, Oct. 23, 1975

How To Detect Propaganda

The Institute for Propaganda Analysis

If American citizens are to have clear understanding of present-day conditions and what to do about them, they must be able to recognize propaganda, to analyze it, and to appraise it.

But what is propaganda?

As generally understood, *propaganda is expression of opinion or action by individuals or groups deliberately designed to influence opinions or actions of other individuals or groups with reference to predetermined ends.* Thus propaganda differs from scientific analysis. The propagandist is trying to "put something across," good or bad, whereas the scientist is trying to discover truth and fact. Often the propagandist does not want careful scrutiny and criticism; he wants to bring about a specific action. Because the action may be socially beneficial or socially harmful to millions of people, it is necessary to focus upon the propagandist and his activities the searchlight of scientific scrutiny. Socially desirable propaganda will not suffer from such examination, but the opposite type will be detected and revealed for what it is.

We are fooled by propaganda chiefly because we don't recognize it when we see it. It may be fun to be fooled but, as the cigarette ads used to say, it is more fun to know. We can more easily recognize propaganda when we see it if we are familiar with the seven common propaganda devices. These are:

1. The Name Calling Device
2. The Glittering Generalities Device
3. The Transfer Device
4. The Testimonial Device
5. The Plain Folks Device
6. The Card Stacking Device
7. The Band Wagon Device

Why are we fooled by these devices? Because they appeal to our emotions rather than to our reason. They make us believe and do something we would not believe or do if we thought about it calmly, dispassionately. In examining these devices, note that they work most effectively at those times when we are too lazy to think for ourselves; also, they tie into emotions which sway us to be "for" or "against" nations, races, religions, ideals, economic and political policies and practices, and so on through automobiles, cigarettes, radios, toothpastes, presidents, and wars. With our emotions stirred, it may be fun to be fooled by these propaganda devices, but it is more fun and infinitely more to our own interests to know how they work.

Lincoln must have had in mind citizens who could balance their emotions with intelligence when he made his remark: ". . . but you can't fool all of the people all of the time."

Name Calling

"Name Calling" is a device to make us form a judgment without examining the evidence on which it should be based. Here the propagandist appeals to our hate and fear. He does this by giving "bad names" to those individuals, groups, nations, races, policies, practices, beliefs, and ideals which he would have us condemn and reject. For centuries the name "heretic" was bad. Thousands were oppressed, tortured, or put to death as heretics. Anybody who dissented from popular or group belief or practice was in danger of being called a heretic. In the light of today's knowledge, some heresies were bad and some were good. Many of the pioneers of modern science were called heretics; witness the cases of Copernicus, Galileo, Bruno. Today's bad names include: Fascist, demagogue, dictator, Red, financial oligarchy, Communist, muckraker, alien, outside agitator, economic royalist, Utopian, rabble-rouser, trouble-maker, Tory, Constitution-wrecker.

"Al" Smith called Roosevelt a Communist by implication when he said in his Liberty League speech, "There can be only one capital, Washington or Moscow." When "Al" Smith was running for the presidency many called him a tool of the Pope, saying in effect, "We must choose between Washington and Rome." That implied that Mr. Smith, if elected President, would take his orders from the Pope. Likewise Mr. Justice Hugo Black has been associated with a bad name, Ku Klux Klan. In these cases some propagandists have tried to make us form judgments without examining essential evidence and implications. "Al Smith is a Catholic. He must never be President." "Roosevelt is a Red. Defeat his program." "Hugo Black is or was a Klansman. Take him out of the Supreme Court."

Use of "bad names" without presentation of their essential meaning, without all their pertinent implications, comprises perhaps the most common of all propaganda devices. Those who want to *maintain* the *status quo* apply bad names to those who would change it. . . . Those who want to *change the status quo* apply bad names to those who would maintain it. For example, the *Daily Worker* and the *American Guardian* apply bad names to conservative Republicans and Democrats.

Glittering Generalities

"Glittering Generalities" is a device by which the propagandist identifies his program with virtue by use of "virtue words." Here he appeals to our emotions of love, generosity, and brotherhood. He uses words like truth, freedom, honor, liberty, social justice, public service, the right to work, loyalty, progress, democracy, the American way, Constitution-defender. These words suggest shining ideals. All persons of good will believe in these ideals. Hence the propagandist, by identifying his individual group, nation, race, policy, practice, or belief with such ideals, seeks to win us to his cause. As Name Calling is a device to make us form a judgment to *reject and condemn* without examining the evidence, Glittering Generalities is a device to make us *accept and approve* without examining the evidence.

For example, use of the phrases, "the right to work" and "social justice," may be a device to make us accept programs for meeting labor-capital problems, which, if we examined them critically, we would not accept at all.

In the Name Calling and Glittering Generalities devices, words are used to stir up our emotions and to befog our thinking. In one device "bad words" are used to make us mad; in the other "good words" are used to make us glad.

The propagandist is most effective in the use of these devices when his words make us create devils to fight or gods to adore. By his use of the "bad words," we personify as a "devil" some nation, race, group, individual, policy, practice, or ideal; we are made fighting mad to destroy it. By use of "good words," we personify as a godlike idol some nation, race, group, etc. Words which are "bad" to some are "good" to others, or may be made so. Thus, to some the New Deal is "a prophecy of social salvation" while to others it is "an omen of social disaster."

From consideration of names, "bad" and "good," we pass to institutions and symbols, also "bad" and "good." We see these in the next device.

Transfer

"Transfer" is a device by which the propagandist carries over the authority, sanction, and prestige of something we respect and revere to something he would have us accept. For example, most of us respect and revere our church and our nation. If the propagandist succeeds in getting church or nation to approve a campaign in behalf of some program, he thereby transfers its authority, sanction, and prestige to that program. Thus we may accept something which otherwise we might reject.

In the Transfer device, symbols are constantly used. The cross represents the Christian Church. The flag represents the nation. Cartoons like Uncle Sam represent a consensus of public opinion. Those symbols stir emotions. At their very sight, with the speed of light, is aroused the whole complex of feelings we have with respect to church or nation. A cartoonist by having Uncle Sam disapprove a budget for unemployment relief would have us feel that the whole United States disapproves relief costs. By drawing an Uncle Sam who approves the same budget, the cartoonist would have us feel that the American people approve it. Thus the Transfer device is used both for and against causes and ideas.

Testimonial

The "Testimonial" is a device to make us accept anything from a patent medicine or a cigarette to a program of national policy. In this device the propagandist makes use of testimonials. "When I feel tired, I smoke a Camel and get the grandest 'lift.'" "We believe the John L. Lewis plan of labor organization is splendid; C.I.O. should be supported." This device works in reverse also; counter-testimonials may be employed. Seldom are these used against commercial products like patent medicines and cigarettes, but they are constantly employed in social, economic, and political issues. "We believe that the John L. Lewis plan of labor organization is bad; C.I.O. should not be supported."

Plain Folks

"Plain Folks" is a device used by politicians, labor leaders, businessmen, and even by ministers and educators to win our confidence by appearing to be people like ourselves—"just plain folks among the neighbors." In election years especially do candidates show their devotion to little children and the common, homey things of life. They have front porch campaigns. For the newspaper men they raid the kitchen cupboard, finding some of the good wife's apple pie. They go to country picnics; they attend service at the old frame church; they pitch hay and go fishing; they show their belief in home and mother. In short, they would win our votes by showing that they're just as common as the rest of us—"just plain folks"—and, therefore, wise and good. Business men often are "plain folks" with the factory hands. Even distillers use the device. "It's our family's whiskey, neighbor; and neighbor, it's your price."

Card Stacking

"Card Stacking" is a device in which the propagandist employs all the arts of deception to win our support for himself, his group, nation, race, policy, practice, belief, or ideal. He stacks the cards against the truth. He uses under-emphasis and over-emphasis to dodge issues and evade facts. He resorts to lies, censorship, and distortion. He omits facts. He offers false testimony. He creates a smoke screen of clamor by raising a new issue when he wants an embarrassing matter forgotten. He draws a red herring across the trail to confuse and divert those in quest of facts he does not want revealed. He makes the unreal appear real and the real appear unreal. He lets half-truth masquerade as truth. By the Card Stacking device, a mediocre candidate, through the "build-up," is made to appear an intellectual titan; an ordinary prize fighter, a probable world champion; a worthless patent medicine, a beneficient cure. By means of this device propagandists would convince us that a ruthless war of aggression is a crusade for righteousness. Some member nations of the Non-Intervention Committee send their troops to intervene in Spain. Card Stacking employs sham, hypocrisy, effrontery.

The Band Wagon

The "Band Wagon" is a device to make us follow the crowd, to accept the propagandist's program en masse. Here his theme is: "Everybody's doing it." His techniques range from those of medicine show to dramatic spectacle. He hires a hall, fills a great stadium, marches a million men in parade. He employs symbols, colors, music, movement, all the dramatic arts. He appeals to the desire, common to most of us, to "follow the crowd." Because he wants us to "follow the crowd" in masses, he directs his appeal to groups held together by common ties of nationality, religion, race, environment, sex, vocation. Thus propagandists campaigning for or against a program will appeal to us as Catholics, Protestants, or Jews; as members of the Nordic race or as Negroes; as farmers or as school teachers; as housewives or as miners. All the artifices of flattery are used to harness the fears and hatreds, prejudices, and biases, convictions and ideals common to the group; thus emotion is made to push and pull the group on to the Band Wagon. In newspaper article and in the spoken word this device is also found. "Don't throw your vote away. Vote for our candidate. He's sure to win." Nearly every candidate wins in every election—before the votes are in.

Propaganda and Emotion

Observe that in all these devices our emotion is the stuff with which propagandists work. Without it they are helpless; with it, harnessing it to their purposes, they can make us glow with pride or burn with hatred, they can make us zealots in behalf of the program they espouse. As we said at the beginning, propaganda as generally understood is expression of opinion or action by individuals or groups with reference to predetermined ends. Without the appeal to our emotion—to our fears and to our courage, to our selfishness and unselfishness, to our loves and to our hates—propagandists would influence few opinions and few actions.

To say this is not to condemn emotion, an essential part of life, or to assert that all predetermined ends of propagandists are "bad." What we mean is that the intelligent citizen does not want propagandists to utilize his emotions, even to the attainment of "good" ends, without knowing what is going on. He does not want to be "used" in the attainment of ends he may later consider "bad." He does not want to be gullible. He does not want to be fooled. He does not want to be duped, even in a "good" cause. He wants to know the facts and among these is included the fact of the utilization of his emotions.

Keeping in mind the seven common propaganda devices, turn to today's newspapers and almost immediately you can spot examples of them all. At election time or during any campaign, Plain Folks and Band Wagon are common, Card Stacking is hardest to detect because it is adroitly executed or because we lack the information necessary to nail the lie. A little practice with the daily newspapers in detecting these propaganda devices soon enables us to detect them elsewhere—in radio, news-reel, books, magazines, and in expression of labor unions, business groups, churches, schools, political parties.

I. VOCABULARY

propaganda   status quo   beneficient
scrutiny   clamor   titan
effrontery

II. QUESTIONS ON CONTENT

1. Paraphrase the definition of propaganda given on page 104, paragraph three.
2. What is the purpose of studying propaganda techniques?
3. Is name calling passe as a propaganda threat?
4. What is the connection between Goldsmith's "synthetic personality" and the "glittering generalities" discussed here?
5. Are testimonials, plainfolks devices, and bandwagon techniques always negative? Explain.
6. Propagandists appeal to what target area? Why?

III. QUESTIONS ON FORM

1.-3. This essay utilizes the techniques of definition, classification, and illustration or example. Explain how each one functions.

IV. SUGGESTIONS FOR WRITING

1.-7. Write paragraphs with more timely examples on each of the seven listed propaganda devices.
8. Write a propaganda piece for a public or private cause.

> **Thomas Collins** is a career journalist who joined the Long Island publication *Newsday* as a reporter, became editor, Washington correspondent, and Washington bureau chief, and is now the media columnist for the paper.

TV, Newspaper Journalists Abide By Different Roles

Thomas Collins

For better or worse, there are two different styles of journalism being practiced in the U.S. today—print and television. The differences between them may account in part for the public perception that the news media got what was coming to it in being shut out of Grenada.

The differences go beyond the obvious one of television being active and filled with the sight and sound of the news while newspapers are more or less passive. They involve the way the rules of journalism are interpreted in both media.

Television has evolved into a highly personal medium, with a heavy reliance on individual stars. Newspaper reporters, even the handful among them who have become media celebrities, have remained more or less anonymous.

More important, the emphasis on personality, and the promotion of personalities in television, has resulted, apparently while no one was looking, into a bending of some of the basic rules of good reporting. Objectivity is reinforced by tone, attitude, constant attribution of sources and strict distinctions between straight reporting and commentary. But to a large degree TV news regards these as expendable.

For some reason, television news executives came to the conclusion that once reporters began to appear on camera, such distinctions became less important than the appearance and personality of the journalist and his or her need to project an air of great authority, even omniscience—none of which burdens newspaper people.

Newspaper reporters have a nice, cozy life compared with their television colleagues. They can settle down in front of computer terminals, block out the rest of the world and contemplate only the problems that exist between them and the written word. Moreover, they are conditioned to a dispassionate tone and a neutral frame of mind. The personal voice is avoided, and when it appears it is usually edited out.

This provides a buffer between them and the outside world that is denied the TV reporter. What is little understood by the public is that the pursuit of

Copyright © 1983 by Newsday, Inc. Reprinted by permission.

elusive objectivity by a newspaper reporter is often a satisfying experience. For many, it affords a comfortable shelter against having to choose sides and make judgments on an issue. Except for the byline, the writer can remain private and can take satisfaction from having performed a service for the public good in the form of a report free of personal opinion and ego.

TV reporters, on the other hand, are out on a stage, required by the way television news has evolved to range across many of the categories of newspaper journalism—and be personable at the same time. They are frequently reporters, commentators, interpreters and too often pundits, all within a one-minute news report.

Why they are required—or allowed—by television news to wear so many hats has always been something of a mystery to me, but I strongly suspect that the fact that they do is related to the growing antagonism the public feels toward the news media, and its perception that reporters have become self-indulgent, arrogant, unfair and anti-government.

That does not say that television news does not strive for objectivity, but that it strives for it within a different framework from newspapers, using different rules. What began as a desire to throw in some interpretation of a news event seems to have evolved into television reporters becoming needlessly assertive and challenging, particularly among some who patrol the White House.

Aside from personalities, there is the coverage itself, particularly war coverage. One of the recurring themes in letters to the editor about the Grenada coverage is that television simply wanted to get its pictures of soldiers fighting in Grenada, with little respect paid to TV's wanting to genuinely inform the public as to what was going on—which may be the legacy of Vietnam, El Salvador and a preoccupation with "bang-bang."

Readers also objected to the grisly sights of war as portrayed on television, which offends them and is interpreted as an insensitivity to the dead, the wounded—and their relatives back home. "I don't believe that anyone wants to see their loved one mangled or disfigured," wrote one woman. "Was this your son? Was this my brother? . . . Reporters should be more aware of how their news affects the emotions of the viewers."

That is the kind of argument that is easily dismissed by TV news executives. For one thing, they would point out, the really bloody footage is usually edited out, and for another, you can't cover a war without showing what it is. Granted that both are true, they still leave open the questions of how much is enough and when do the dead and the "bang-bang" become ends in themselves. Apparently, there is a strong feeling on the part of the public that wars exist mainly for the media to exploit.

What is most troubling is that the Reagan administration has read the public well, as seen in the almost serene way it went about locking the door in Grenada. Would it have felt as confident if it knew that the media—particularly television news—had the confidence of the public? And is the public wrong simply because it does not think like journalists?

112 Popular Writing

ZIGGY

Copyright © 1983 Universal Press Syndicate.

I. VOCABULARY

expendable   dispassionate   objectivity
elusive   pundits   attribution
omniscience   grisly

II. QUESTIONS ON CONTENT

1. What is the obvious difference between print and television journalism?
2. What does Collins include as some of the effects of personality emphasis on television?
3. Do you agree with Collins's views on television journalists? Name some supporting examples. Name some exceptions.
4. Collins never explicitly lists his titular "rules." What are some that he implies in his essay?

III. QUESTIONS ON FORM

1. This is a comparison/contrast essay; do an outline of its structure.
2. Why does Collins compare and contrast personality before coverage?
3. Evaluate Collins's conclusion. Does he take a position? Does the organization of the essay lead to his conclusion?

IV. SUGGESTIONS FOR WRITING

1. Outline and/or write a comparison/contrast paper on two popular journalists—print and broadcast.

Author of several books, **Ronald Steel** won numerous awards for *Walter Lippmann and the American Century* (1980). He has also contributed to *Harper's*, the *New York Review of Books*, and the *New Republic*.

How Politicians Seduce Journalists
Ronald Steel

Journalists and politicians don't make strange bedfellows. They just get into bed for different reasons. And each, oddly enough, thinks he is seducing the other.

"Put not your trust in princes," the late Walter Lippmann sternly warned his fellow journalists shortly before he retired a dozen years ago. "Only the very rarest of princes can endure even a little criticism, and few of them can put up with even a pause in the adulation."

He was one to know what he was talking about. As the most celebrated journalist of the age—with a career that stretched back all the way to before World War I—he had seen many a political prince come and go. With his reputation as an incorrigible Jove who hurled thunderbolts from Olympus, and his influence over an enormous audience of faithful readers, Lippmann was a power in his own right.

He was also a journalist who had been burned. More than once he dropped his guard and drew too close to the men who sat on or near the throne of power. More than once during his long career he thought he had at last found a prince worthy of his trust. What he sought was a leader both farsighted and practical: one worthy of his fullest admiration. Each time he was disappointed. Yet when a new prince succeeded to the throne, he would be tempted to try—just one more time.

Lippmann's was not a unique story. He suffered no more than most political journalists from the need to be around the great. He was merely somewhat more aware of the pitfalls of the trade.

Journalists and politicians have a special affinity for one another. Each depends on what the other can provide. Politicians, or high-level officials, need the journalist to get their views across and to find out, from their dangerously insulated Washington cocoon, what the outside world is thinking. They also need the press to promote their policies—or themselves.

Copyright © 1981 by Newsday, Inc. Reprinted by permission.

Without press coverage, the politician has no voice. Except for the rare person whose power rests within the hierarchy, like the chairman of a congressional committee, or the head of a quasi-secret organization like the FBI, the politician can hardly be said to exist if he or she is not officially noticed by the press.

For journalists the need is no less than for politicians. They require access to the information that officials have. Power in Washington, or even in a state capital, is measured not by income—a used-car dealer in Hempstead or Hartford no doubt makes a good deal more than the chief justice or the president's national security adviser—but by the ability to make critical decisions. Journalists need access to decision-makers the way plants need light. It allows them to transform air into energy.

People who make decisions know they have something to sell. It is information. Grown men and women will tear each other apart to be the first to get it. Newspapers and networks pride themselves on being the first to know. The effort is constant, and privileged access is not easily surrendered once secured.

Politicians and officials have learned how to manipulate the journalist's insatiable need to be in the know. Henry Kissinger was a master of the art. He used to dole out tidbits of information like grains of salt to a mooing cow. Journalists in his favor—that is, those who wrote nice things about him and never asked embarrassing questions—were rewarded with "leaks" ("A high official today revealed that . . .") and were invited to roam around the world with him on an opulently appointed Air Force jet. Kissinger was not unique in knowing how to massage—or punish—the press through his control over information. He was just better at it than most.

The need for access to politicians and officials poses problems for the journalist—problems that involve very subtle forms of corruption. Most journalists scrupulously reject the most obvious forms of bribery. As professionals go, they are far more honest than most. By they can be drawn into a politician's web without quite realizing it. Powerful people can dispense many kinds of favor and privilege. They may grant a private interview or dispense a judicious tip. They may flatter the journalist by seeking his help in a common (and always worthy) cause. Or, even more flatteringly, by asking his advice.

Temptations come in a variety of guises. The most important forms of corruption in the modern journalist's world, as Lippmann once told his colleagues, are the "many guises and disguises of social climbing on the pyramids of power." Even the most conscientious journalist could fall prey to such temptations without the consciousness of yielding. Only a constant awareness could provide protection. Sometimes not even awareness protects.

Few are those—the most jaded political columnist included—who can resist the call from the White House, the dinner invitation from the secretary of state, the private briefing at the Pentagon. Journalists, too, have their vanity. Such overtures reassure them that there really is something to this business about the press being the Fourth Estate. And if there is, are they not the barons, since they have been asked to sup with the king?

If a dinner invitation from a prominent official is not a delicate form of corruption, it is at least a powerful temptation. A journalist receiving such special favor is loath to offend the person granting it. This means "understanding" the problems the official has to cope with, and not unnecessarily embarrassing him or her in print. This is most human. But journalists who allow themselves to be drawn into a personal relationship with a public official may be tempted to pull their punches.

This is particularly true if the official pays them the great compliment of asking the journalists' advice. We are all flattered by such requests. They make us think better not only of ourselves, but of the person seeking the advice. Journalists are more trusting than people give them credit for. They tend to take such requests seriously. This makes them feel they should work with the politician to find a solution. The journalist, instead of being an adversary, or at least a critical observer, begins to think of the official as a kind of colleague. Naturally journalists want to cooperate in serving the public good. And naturally they cease to be fully objective. They have, to one degree or another, entered into an implicit collusion with the politician.

Coziness with a politician may make for a good social life, but bad journalism. A journalist's job, after all, is to ferret out the news and report it. A politician's is to keep secrets and to act on privileged information. The problem comes when the journalist is persuaded to accept the politician's definition of what the public has a right to know.

A dramatic example of this occurred during the Bay of Pigs landing in Cuba in 1961. A few leading papers were on to the story weeks before the landing took place. They knew of the secret training camps in Florida and Central America; they had talked with some of the Cubans the CIA was arming to overthrow the Castro government. Normally, they would have reported the story. But high U.S. government officials persuaded them to suppress it in the name of national security. With some misgivings they did suppress it, taking the officials' word that the story should not be revealed to the public.

They made a mistake. They should have followed their professional rule of full disclosure. The invasion was a fiasco, embarrassing the Kennedy administration and the United States. It should never have been allowed to take place. The press had been co-opted into collusion with the administration, but it had done no service either to journalism or to the nation. Later, President John F. Kennedy said he wished the press had divulged plans for the landing before it took place because then it wouldn't have happened.

There can be several kinds of collusion. One, just described, is to keep a secret from the public. Another occurs when the journalist and the politician seek a common goal and work together to win over the public. An example from Lippmann's career will illustrate the point. In 1940 the administration of Franklin D. Roosevelt wanted to overcome isolationist sentiment and lend a beleaguered Britain 50 over-age American destroyers. Officials approached Lippmann, who then endorsed the objective, and worked behind the scenes with the administration to sell the plan to Congress and the public.

The third kind of collusion occurs when a politician succeeds in deceiving a journalist as to his true intentions. In this way, the politician can have a favorable press and pursue one course while seeming to pursue another.

Distance is harder for some journalists to maintain than for others. Some naturally gravitate to the king's court, others are happy only in opposition. This is a question of temperament as much as of training. The adversary role is a difficult and often lonely one. Few journalists try it, and even fewer succeed.

Among the great practitioners in our time are Robert Strout, I.F. Stone and Robert Sherrill. These men have made distinguished careers and performed a great public service by standing apart and observing the scene with somewhat jaundiced eyes. They lunch at the Capitol cafeteria rather than the Metropolitan Club, and they know that the truth is not necessarily to be found by rubbing together the shoulders of two $600 suits.

But such people are rare. Far more common is the political columnist who lets us wander with him through the mind of some great man or woman who was canny enough to invite him to dinner the night before and to ply him with brandy and flattery. Not many journalists resist the treatment, which is why most political columns are a blend of "I was there" self-promotion and windy musings about the responsibilities of power.

The real temptation is not bribery but co-option, of being drawn into policymakers' nets and accepting their assumptions. There is no hard and fast rule about how to handle such dangers, but the journalist should at least be aware of it as his host is pouring the second brandy. More than one good columnist has been ruined by letting a policymaker persuade him that he should behave like a quasi-public official. After a few months of writing about the "cruel responsibilities of power," the journalist might as well take a job in the government.

More than one actually has. For example, four years ago the Pentagon correspondent of The New York Times left the paper to take an important job in an agency he covered. This January, with a change of administration, his replacement at the paper then replaced him at the Pentagon. And to make it all symmetrical, the first man replaced his replacement and went back to his old job at the Times. This is not to say that the arrangement was fishy. They are both honorable men. But even the most honorable man may be hesitant to embarrass a potential employer when he is angling for a job. The situation is potentially a compromising one.

Media people unquestionably have to work with officials. But if they are to do their job decently and honestly, they have to keep a discreet distance. Lippmann, who often failed to follow his own advice, described the situation well.

"Newsmen cannot be the cronies of great men," he once said. "There always has to be a certain distance between high public officials and newsmen. I wouldn't say a wall or a fence, but an air space." The hard part of that advice is making sure that the air space is neither so wide as to be a chasm, nor so narrow as to lack protection.

It is not particularly remarkable that some journalists grow too close to politicians and end up sounding like public officials themselves. What is striking is that so many manage to resist the temptation and retain their independence and integrity.

Perhaps the greatest danger facing journalists is not the possibility of giving in to one or another form of temptation on the "pyramids of power," but of muting their voices out of timidity. If cronyism is a curse of journalists, so is caution.

"The truth is that you're afraid to be wrong," Lippmann mused of himself and his fellows early in his career. "And so you put on these airs and use these established phrases, knowing that they will sound familiar and will be respected. But this fear of being wrong is a disease. You cover and qualify and elucidate, you speak vaguely, you mumble because you are afraid of the sound of your own voice."

Journalists are often more afraid of their own voices than their readers might imagine. Too many—the most eminent among them—wonder whether policymakers will consider them "sound" and "responsible." But journalists rarely persuade policymakers by the wisdom of their argument. They persuade by the fact that they have influence over the public. A journalist's strength is in his readers—and his credibility with those readers. He would have little fear of being seduced if he treated the mighty with skepticism and behaved as a public inquirer, not as a guest aiming to please.

I. VOCABULARY

collusion	fiasco	opulently
ferret	beleaguered	jaundiced
elucidate	insatiable	cronyism

II. QUESTIONS ON CONTENT

1. How do politicians depend on journalists?
2. Why is the opposite also true?
3. Explain the relationship between power and information.
4. Are Steel's views like Anthony Smith's in Chapter Three?

5. Describe the three kinds of collusion that occur between politicians and journalists.
6. What does Steel envision as the journalist's role in society?

III. QUESTIONS ON FORM

1. Why does Steel continue Lippmann's metaphor of the Prince?
2. Lippmann's metaphor is found in an earlier classic work. Identify it and its author. Briefly, discuss its content and impact.
3. Steel's essay utilizes the rhetorical techniques of process analysis and cause and effect. Discuss how each is developed.

IV. SUGGESTIONS FOR WRITING

1. Review a book, film, or television show that you have read or seen that deals with the issue of political/journalistic corruption.
2. Does familiarity, as the proverb goes, always breed contempt? Write an essay using your own experiences to support your views.

For the past decade **Lewis H. Lapham** has been the editor of *Harper's*. Prior to that, he was a reporter for newspapers such as the *New York Herald Tribune* and for magazines such as the *Saturday Evening Post* and *Life*.

Sculptures in Snow: Notes on the Uses of the Press

Lewis H. Lapham

Over the next few years the press undoubtedly will come under heavy criticism, most of it arising from the romantic misconceptions of people who expect the daily papers to furnish them, at a cost of twenty-five cents or less, with wisdom, statesmanship, and truth. Against the baying of the familiar hounds—among them the corporate buyers of public opinion and politicians with no other issue at their command—I have begun to collect notes for the defense.

Relatively few people like to make the argument on behalf of the press, because the virtues of the profession consist in its raucousness, its incoherence, and its gall. Honest praise sounds so much like criticism that it offends not only the laity in search of oracles but also the clerks and scribes who construe themselves as an aristocracy of conscience.

Copyright © 1981 by Harper's Magazine Foundation. All rights reserved. Reprinted from the August 1981 issue by special permission.

At random intervals in the nation's history one or another of the liberal occupations attracts a claque of admirers eager for simple answers. In the 1950s it was thought that psychoanalysis could resolve the enigma of human nature; in the 1960s it was the physicists who were going to steal the fires of heaven and the lawyers who were going to reform the laws and manage the nation's foreign policy; the most recent surge of hyperbole has placed the mantle of omniscience on the profession of journalism. For the last fifteen years journalists have enjoyed a reputation for knowing how the world works. This is silly. Reporters tend to show up at the scenes of crimes and accidents, and they take an imbecile's delight in catastrophe. Few of them know enough about the subject under discussion—whether politics, music, or the structure of DNA—to render a definitive opinion about anything other than the menu at the nearest Marriott Inn. But to concede the shallowness and ignorance of the press does nothing to diminish its usefulness or importance. Even the most mean-spirited criticisms fail to answer the question as to why anybody would bother to read or write the news. Why not wait a hundred years, until the archives have been opened and the historians have had time to arrange events in an orderly and patriotic sequence?

Any plausible defense of journalism rests on a modest presumption of what it provides. As follows:

1. If the writing of history resembles architecture, journalism bears comparison to a tent show. The impresarios of the press drag into their tents whatever freaks and wonders might astonish a crowd; the next day they move their exhibit to another edition instead of to another town four miles farther west. Their subject matter is the flux of human affairs, and they achieve their most spectacular effects by reason of their artlessness and lack of sentiment.

Years ago I formed the habit of collecting newspaper items in file folders organized under such rubrics as "mullahs," "absurdity," "campaign promises," "sensational crimes," "allies," "weapons," "scientific discoveries," "the end of the world." Maybe I expected the accumulation of news to achieve critical mass, or that the particles would combine into a coherent organism. This has yet to happen, and I doubt it ever will. Journalism is the data of experience, a substance comparable to the immense population of primeval elements out of which the higher forms of thought evolve. It is the best that can be done at short notice. The antagonists of the press like to pretend that some other intellectual agency (the social sciences, say, or the White House Press Office) could perform the task as well, but this also is a delusion.

When I read through the scraps of crumbling paper in the file folders, some of them long since gone yellow in the light, I notice that it is always the seemingly inconsequential stories that retain their life. The front-page news about treaties signed and generals traveling to China has been superseded by other treaties and other journeys of state; most of the editorial opinion has been proved wrong, and the melodramatic generalization turns out to have missed the point. But the stories toward the back of the paper, about a lost child or a woman paying alimony or the New York City police catching stray madmen in nets, lose nothing with the passage of time.

The press makes sculptures in snow; its truth dwells in the concrete fact and the fleeting sound of the human voice.

2. Two years ago the publishers of Dr. Henry Kissinger's memoir, *White House Years,* publicized the book with the claim that "for eight years, the story of his life was the history of our times." This sort of inflated rhetoric has kept par value with inflation of the currency, but there remains something grotesquely comic about it. Carr Van Anda, the first great editor of *The New York Times* in the twentieth century, was once asked why he didn't decorate the paper's news accounts with the reporter's byline. *"The Times,"* said Mr. Van Anda, "is not running an employment agency for journalists."

What would he have said about the wreaths of celebrity placed on the heads of men who read news bulletins into television cameras? In the United States at this moment there are men and women whose names will live as long as the history of Western civilization—the Nobel laureates sifting the strands of genetic sequence or imagining the inner processes of the stars. Their names remain the property of only a few of their peers, and they dwindle into rushlights when compared with the radiance of Dolly Parton or John Chancellor. It is as if the audience of a Greek tragedy had confused the names of the protagonists with those of the messengers.

3. Journalists hire themselves out as journeymen, not as immortal artists. It would be fair to compare them to a troupe of medieval stonemasons traveling the circuit of unfinished cathedrals with a repertoire of conventional forms. They can carve figures of the saints fifty feet above the nave, but nobody would expect them to impart expression to the face.

Or, to take a metaphor more likely to recommend itself to the Republicans now in Washington, journalists possess the social graces of Pony Express riders—resolution, ingenuity, punctuality. They bring the news from Ghent or California, and they do their readers no favor if they try to shape it into a work of literature. Maybe this is why the books that journalists feel compelled to write, about the war in Algeria or last year's election campaign, so often read like a definitive study of a formation of clouds.

4. The critics of the press complain about its pessimism, its cynicism, its unwillingness to recommend a program of political advancement. Every now and then a reader of *Harper's* writes to say that the magazine should publish sermons. "Be more positive," says a correspondent in Oklahoma. "Imagine that you have been proclaimed king," says a correspondent in Florida, "and submit your blueprint for Utopia."

They send their requests to the wrong address. The reader in hope of inspiration can study the collected works of St. Augustine or Bishop Paul Moore; he can listen to Billy Graham defy the foul fiend or sit in rapturous contemplation of an elm tree or a whale.

William Randolph Hearst once complained to Dorothy Parker that her stories were too sad. To this objection (not very different from the admonitions circulated by vice presidents in charge of public relations), Miss Parker replied:

"Mr. Hearst, there are two billion people on the face of the earth, and the story of not one of them will have a happy ending."

If a man drinks too much and his doctor tells him that one of these days he will fall down dead in the club car on the way to Westport, is the doctor a pessimist? Is Israel a pessimistic nation because it bombs the Iraqi nuclear installation southeast of Baghdad, or is it an optimistic nation because it accepts the conditions of its existence? Is it pessimism to say that the theories of supply-side economics have little basis in fact, or that American novelists don't write very good novels?

Journalism, like history, has no therapeutic value; it is better able to diagnose than to cure, and it provides society with a primitive means of psychoanalysis that allows the patient to judge the distance between fantasy and reality.

5. Why is it that people demand a tone of optimism when discussing the large and safely abstract questions of national policy—what was thought to be the splendid little war in Vietnam, for example, or the incalculable benefit certain to derive from an economic policy that places an intolerable burden on the weak, the old, the poor, the ignorant, the young, and the sick? If somebody advised the same people about their own prospects in so blithe a tone of voice they would think they were talking to a child or a fool.

The question is never one of optimism or pessimism. It is a question of trying to tell the truth, of the emotions required of the teller and of the emotions the attempt calls forth in the reader. If the news, no matter how bad, evokes in the reader a sense of energy and hope, then it has done as much as can be said for it. The unctuous recitation of platitudes usually achieves the opposite effect, instilling in the reader a feeling of passivity and despair.

Great power constitutes its own argument, and it never has much trouble drumming up friends, applause, sympathetic exegesis, and a band. In his commencement address at West Point last May, President Reagan was pleased to announce that the American "era of self-doubt" had come to a satisfactory end. The rest of his speech could have been accompanied by a fanfare of trumpets and drums.

But a democracy stands in need of as much self-doubt as it can muster and as many arguments as possible that run counter to the governing body of opinion. The press exerts the pressure of dissent on officials otherwise inclined to rest content with the congratulations of their retainers. From the point of view of the Soviet authorities the Soviet press is admirably optimistic; the era of self-doubt ended with the revolution of 1917.

6. The press in its multiple voices argues that the world of men and events can eventually be understood. Not yet, perhaps, not in time for tomorrow's deadline, but sooner or later, when enough people with access to better

information have had an opportunity to expand the spheres of reference. This is an immensely hopeful and optimistic assumption. Defined as means rather than an end, journalism defends the future against the past.

7. The media offer for sale every conceivable fact or opinion. Most of these objects possess a dubious value, but it isn't the business of the journalist to distinguish between the significant and the worthless.

During World War II British raiding units pressed far behind German lines in the North African desert in search of stray pieces of metal. The patrols collected anything that came to hand—a shell casing, a broken axle, a button torn from the uniform of a dead corporal. The objects were sent to Cairo for analysis, and by this means British intelligence guessed at the state of German industry.

So also with journalism. The data are always fugitive and insufficient. To treat even the most respectable political ideas as if they were the offspring of pure reason would be to assign them, in Lewis Namier's phrase, "a parentage about as mythological as that of Pallas Athene."

8. Without an audience, the media would cease to exist. Even if people don't read the same papers and periodicals, the media provide the connective tissue holding together the federation of contradictory interests that goes by the name of democracy. How else except through the instruments of the media could the surgeon and the labor leader, the ballerina and the stock-car driver form even a distorted image of one another? The media present a spectacle infinitely more crowded than Balzac's *Comédie Humaine*—the rumors of war on page one, followed, in random succession, by reports of strange crimes, political intrigues, anomalous discoveries in the sciences, the hazard of new fortunes.

Just as every nation supposedly gets "the government it deserves," so also it makes of the press whatever it chooses to imagine as its self-portrait. If the covers of all the nation's magazines could be displayed in a gallery, and if the majority of the images reflected dreams of wealth or sexual delight, a wandering Arab might be forgiven for thinking that the United States had confused itself with the Moslem vision of paradise.

The newspapers yield only as much as the reader brings to his reading. If the reader doesn't also study foreign affairs, or follow the money markets, or keep up his practice of foreign languages, then what can he expect to learn from the papers?

I. VOCABULARY

unctuous	platitudes	hyperbole
cynicism	laity	artlessness
misconception	oracles	mullahs
gall	claque	primeval

II. QUESTIONS ON CONTENT

1. Explain the meaning of Lapham's title.
2. What is Lapham's view of journalists? Why does he liken them to messengers and not protagonists in Greek tragedy?
3. Discuss Lapham's remarks about the "media as spectacle." Do you agree?
4. Do you agree that every nation makes its self-portrait in the press? Give some examples.

III. QUESTIONS ON FORM

1. Lapham's title is but one of the many metaphors he employs. Cite two others and explain their application.
2. To what does the phrase on page 119, paragraph one "steal the fires of heaven" allude? What is its reference here?
3. What are the associations of the "tent show" metaphor Lapham uses for journalism.

IV. SUGGESTIONS FOR WRITING

1. Write an essay describing the self-portrait of your local newspaper.
2. This is a persuasive essay presenting an eight-point defense of the author's subject. Outline the eight points and comment on the pattern of organization.
3. Choose a topic and write about it in figurative language, that is, using two very different metaphors.

John Leo is a New York writer who was once New York City's Assistant Commissioner of the Environmental Protection Agency during the John Lindsay mayoral administration. He has been a reporter for the *New York Times*, and a columnist in the *Village Voice* and has written and edited for *Discover* and *New York Times* magazines.

Journalese as a Second Tongue

John Leo

As a cub reporter, Columnist Richard Cohen of the Washington *Post* rushed out one day to interview a lawyer described in many newspaper reports as "ruddy-faced." The man was woozily abusive and lurched about with such

Copyright ©1984 by Time Inc. All rights reserved. Reprinted by permission from *Time*.

abandon that young Cohen instantly realized that the real meaning of ruddy-faced is drunk. This was his introduction to journalese, the fascinating second tongue acquired by most reporters as effortlessly as an Iranian toddler learns Farsi or a Marin County child learns psychobabble.

Fluency in journalese means knowing all about "the right stuff," "gender gap," "life in the fast lane" and the vexing dilemma of being caught "between a rock and a hard place," the current Scylla-Charybdis image. The Middle East is "strife-torn," except during those inexplicable moments when peace breaks out. Then it is always "much troubled." Kuwait is located just east of the adjective "oil-rich," and the Irish Republican Army always lurks right behind the word "outlawed." The hyphenated modifier is the meat and potatoes of journalese. Who can forget "the break-away province of Biafra," "the mop-top quartet" (the mandatory second reference to the Beatles) and the "ill-fated Korean jetliner," not to be confused with the "ill-fitting red wig" of Watergate fame. Murderers on death row are often saved by "eleventh-hour" reprieves, which would be somewhere between 10 and 11 p.m. in English but shortly before midnight in journalese.

Much of the difficulty in mastering journalese comes from its slight overlap with English. "Imposing," for instance, when used to describe a male, retains its customary English meaning, but when used in reference to a female, it always means battle-ax. "Feisty" refers to a person whom the journalist deems too short and too easily enraged, though many in the journalese-speaking fraternity believe it is simply the adjective of choice for any male under 5 ft. 6 in. who is not legally dead. This usage reflects the continual surprise among tall journalists that short people have any energy at all. Women are not often feisty, though they are usually short enough to qualify. No journalist in America has ever referred to a 6-ft. male as feisty. At that height, men are simply "outspoken" (*i.e.*, abusive).

In general, adjectives in journalese are as misleading as olive sizes. Most news consumers know enough to translate "developing nations" and "disadvantaged nations" back into English, but far smaller numbers know that "militant" means fanatic, and "steadfast" means pigheaded. "Controversial" introduces someone or something the writer finds appalling, as in "the controversial Miss Fonda," and "prestigious" heralds the imminent arrival of a noun nobody cares about, as in "the prestigious Jean Hersholt Humanitarian Award."

Television anchorpersons add interest to their monologues by accenting a few syllables chosen at random. Since print journalists cannot do this, except when reading aloud to spouse and children, they strive for a similar effect by using words like crisis and revolution. Crisis means any kind of trouble at all, and revolution means any kind of change at all, as in "the revolution in meat packing." "Street value" lends excitement to any drug-bust story, without bearing any financial relationship to the actual value of drugs being busted. Many meaningless adjectives, preferably hyphenated for proper rhythm, are permanently welded to certain nouns: blue-ribbon panel, fact-finding mission, devout Catholic, and rock-ribbed Republican. In journalese there are no devout Protestants or Jews, and no Democrats with strong or stony ribs.

Historians of journalese will agree that the first flowering of the language occurred in the sexist descriptions of women by splashy tabloids during the '30s and '40s. In contrast to Pentagonese, which favors oxymorons (Peacekeeper missiles, build-down), the tabloids relied on synecdoche (leggy brunette, bosomy blonde, full-figured redhead). Full-figured, of course, meant fat, and "well-endowed" did not refer to Ford Foundation funding. "Statuesque" (too large, mooselike) and "petite" (too small, mouselike) were adjectives of last resort, meaning that the woman under discussion had no bodily parts that interested the writer. A plain, short woman was invariably "pert." For years, masters of this prose cast about for a nonlibelous euphemism for "mistress." The winning entry, "great and good friend," used to describe Marion Davies' relationship to William Randolph Hearst, was pioneered, as it happens, by a non-Hearst publication, TIME magazine. "Constant companion" evolved later, and gave way to such clunking modernisms as "roommate" and "live-in lover." Nowadays, the only sexuality about which journalese is coy tends to be homosexuality, and that is adequately covered by "he has no close female friends" or "he is not about to settle down."

In political campaigns, underdogs fight uphill battles and hope for shifts of momentum and coattail effects, all leading to rising tides that will enable the favorite to snatch defeat from the jaws of victory. A politician who has no idea about what is going on can be described as one who prefers "to leave details to subordinates." A gangster who runs a foreign country will be referred to as "strongman" until his death, and dictator thereafter. Strongman, like many terms in journalese, has no true correlative. "Nicaraguan Strongman Somoza" is not balanced with "Cambodian Weakman Prince Sihanouk."

What to say about a public figure who is clearly bonkers? Since it is unsporting and possibly libelous to write: "Representative Forbush, the well-known raving psychopath," journalese has evolved the code words difficult, intense and driven. If an article says, "like many of us, Forbush has his ups and downs," the writer is wigwagging a manic-depressive.

Political journalese, of course, requires a knowledge of sources. An unnamed analyst or observer can often be presumed to be the writer of the article. The popular plural "observers," or "analysts," refers to the writer and his cronies. Insiders, unlike observer-analysts, sometimes exist in the real world outside the newsroom. This, however, is never true of quotable chestnut vendors in Paris, Greenwich Village bartenders and other colorful folk conjured up on deadline to lend dash to a story.

Almost all sources, like most trial balloonists, live in or around Washington. In order of ascending rectitude, they are: informants, usually reliable sources, informed sources, authoritative sources, sources in high places and unimpeachable sources. Informants are low-level operatives, whose beans are normally spilled to police rather than to reporters. Informed sources, because of their informed nature, are consulted most often by savvy journalists. An unimpeachable source is almost always the President, with the obvious exception of Richard Nixon, who was not unimpeachable.

Journalese is controversial but prestigious, and observers are steadfast in averring that it has the right stuff.

David Saltman is a producer and writer for CBS News.

No Verbs Tonight. The Reasons. The Consequences

David Saltman

"The best writing," confided one of New York's top TV newsmen, "contains no verbs."

The veteran political reporter had clearly fallen under the influence of the evergrowing "three-dot" school of telespeech. In commercials, in dialogue and especially in news, this powerful language lobby is teaching your television how to talk.

As if to illustrate his point, this same reporter recently began a story thus: "The book of condolences for President Anwar Sadat. The signers . . . and their thoughts."

Admirers of this writing style believe there is no such thing as a story that is too short; the fewer words, the better. All writers must be thrifty with words, of course, but it took real genius to figure out that you could actually omit the verbs and still be understood.

The inventor of three-dot, verbless writing is unknown. He may have been an advertising man back in the "Golden Age of Television," when cars first began to "handle" and cigarettes "traveled and gentled" smoke.

The verb, in its heyday, was thought to be the very essence of language. But television, in its desire to be at once conversational, brief and breathless, now encourages such "sentences" as: "Tonight . . . disaster. A man . . . his wife and child . . . an accident." It doesn't sound too terrible when spoken by professionals.

David Saltman, "No Verbs Tonight . . . The Reasons . . . The Consequences," *TV Guide*, December 12, 1981. Reprinted by permission of the author.

As you might gather, in the verbless, three-dot school, punctuation marks are also regarded as unnecessary: three dots replace the comma, colon, semicolon and parenthesis. At WABC-TV News in New York, for instance, the typewriters do not even contain those symbols. Nor are WABC's writers allowed to use apostrophes or question marks: the typewriters have no punctuation but the dot and the dash. Presumably that makes one's writing more "telegraphic."

TV journalists defend this system by maintaining that "writing for the ear is different from writing for the eye." Possibly they never got earfuls of such conversational writers as Dante, Boccaccio and Chaucer, whose words (including verbs) seem to ring in the head just behind the eardrums. Even if he were working for WNBC-TV, would Chaucer have written: "New York's career men and women. Young . . . unmarried . . . and a world of adventure waiting"?

There are, in fact, a number of languages, like Russian and Arabic, which do without the verb "to be" in the present tense. Now, Anchorese is among them.

Not among them . . . English. (That . . . and this . . . examples of favorite verbless, three-dot constructions.)

John Chancellor pronounces many verbless "sentences" on the news. The other night, while talking about the President's Cabinet, he said: "Not among them . . . Budget Director David Stockman . . . who, etc."

Chancellor probably thinks it makes him sound more laconic to start off a story by saying: "Lots of talk about the President's budget today."

Or: "No new reports of PLO fighting tonight."

That last bulletin is an example of verbless three-dottiness mixed with the notorious "tonight lead." Nowadays, you can't listen to a newscast without the anchorman saying the word "tonight" in every story.

"Under indictment tonight in Brooklyn district court . . . five people . . . including a former college basketball star." Of course, the actual indicting happened during the day. But the "tonight lead" is calculated to make the viewer believe he's getting the very latest updated news. So it's never "Two people died today," but always: "Two people dead tonight. It's only a baby step from there to *Saturday Night Live's* "Franco . . . still dead tonight."

No wonder that, after watching an entire newscast in this unknown language, one often feels he's been listening to frogs croaking before a storm.

Admiring this type of writing is one thing; learning to write this way is quite another. "It reminds me of learning to take care of a burro," says one writer at a New York network flagship station. "First, you whack him over the head with a 2-by-4. That gets his attention. Then, you feed him less and less every day."

First, this writer says, you take out all the adjectives. Conscientious

128 Popular Writing

writers know adjectives should be used sparingly at best. So not using them at all is no great loss.

Then come the adverbs. Same as with adjectives. Three-dotters need only one adverb per story: "tonight."

Adjust all verbs to present tense and active voice. This facilitates taking them out completely later on.

Shake out all extraneous words like gerunds, participles and any phrases in the form of superfluous background, no matter how interesting or amusing.

You are left, like the burro, with the bony skeleton of nouns and verbs.

"For many centuries," this writer says, "nouns and verbs were the mainstay of journalism, not to mention all other types of writing. But now, I suppose because they need more time for commercials, they still tell us "the fewer words the better."

"With the removal of verbs," he says, "the language, like the burro down to one grain of rice a day, keels over and dies.

"It's a pity," this writer continues, "because if we had just a little more time, we could have gotten it down to no words—and no food—at all!"

I. VOCABULARY

oxymorons   rectitude   euphemism
synecdoche   extraneous   laconic

II. QUESTIONS ON CONTENT

1. Were you aware of "journalese" before reading Leo's essay?
2. Do you use it in speech and/or in writing? Recount some instances.
3. How much, if at all, do you think journalese affects the credibility of what is reported?
4. Can it be argued that Leo's journalese is really a negative rendering of the old fashioned virtues of tact and discretion?

III. QUESTIONS ON FORM

1. In this piece Saltman examines "Anchorese," an extreme form of broadcast journalese. He focuses on the decline of grammatical structure. How conscious are you of grammar when you speak? When you write?
2. Do you know what a gerund is? A participle?
3. "With the removal of verbs . . . the language . . . keels over and dies." Identify the verbs in the first five paragraphs of this piece.
4. Do you usually speak in the present tense regardless of its accuracy? Do you consider this tendency part of today's slang?

5. Has journalese contributed to the current popularity of the "eternal present"?

IV. SUGGESTIONS FOR WRITING

1. Leo's humorous essay employs both definition and illustration. Choose three words from the following list and write definitions and examples for each in standard English and in journalese.

   sophisticated   integrity
   feisty   class
   insidious   banality

2. Take a story in journalese from a popular newspaper and "paraphrase" it into more formal English.

Jonathan Friendly currently covers educational issues for the *New York Times*. He came to the *Times* following stints as a reporter in Raleigh, North Carolina, and Minneapolis, and has worked as a press reporter, night metropolitan editor, and regional editor before moving to his present position.

Drawing a Privacy Line Inside Publicity's Glare

Jonathan Friendly

To Richard V. Allen, it was the television crew that pursued his daughter to nursery school. To Louisa Kennedy, it was the 5 a.m. telephone call from a reporter seeking her reaction to the death of the Shah of Iran. To Jacqueline Kennedy Onassis, it was the photographer who sprang in front of her as she came out of a Manhattan movie theater.

In each of these recent cases, the subject of the intensive coverage has raised an issue that reporters say troubles them as well: where and how to draw the line between a legitimate interest in a public figure and the improper invasion of that person's privacy. The journalists, while defending their right and obligation to pursue information, say that even public figures have some rights to privacy, and they are worried that the instances of harassment, real or apparent, could undercut public support for news gathering.

Copyright © 1981 by the New York Times Company. Reprinted by permission.

"It isn't helpful to us," said Michael J. O'Neill, the president of the American Society of Newspaper Editors, to diminish "the public's sense of our being fair and humane in the way we behave."

Mr. Allen, who went on leave as the national security adviser to President Reagan while an inquiry into a $1,000 gift from Japanese journalists was pursued, said the line had been crossed repeatedly by reporters who gathered outside his house as early as 5:30 a.m. day after day last month. The idling motors of the television trucks awoke his neighbors, he said, and one reporter climbed a tree to look in his window.

Mishap From TV Blindness

He said he came home around 11 o'clock one night from a formal dinner and, walking from his car, was blinded by the lights of the television crews. That was when he stepped into the garbage left by a camera crew that had eaten dinner while waiting for him to return.

The most striking thing to him, he said, "was the offensiveness of the video offense." Television coverage was not concerned with getting his serious answers to important questions, he said, but rather seemed to be an effort "to create a scene of confusion and chaos, to provoke a quick response."

Many reporters say that such stakeouts usually produce little hard information from a person who does not want to talk. But one of the reporters who kept watch on Mr. Allen's lawn, Mike Von Fremd of ABC-TV, said that it had proved worthwhile because on several occasions Mr. Allen had paused to talk to the reporters.

"He could have ducked us each and every morning," Mr. Von Fremd, a White House correspondent, said, adding that Mr. Allen had conceded that "none of this would have happened if he had been open with us from the beginning."

Freed from his duties, Mr. Allen actively used television appearances and other interviews to express his side of the issue, insisting that the television appearances be live rather than taped because "you can't beat Mr. Voice Over."

On the other hand, Ernest Schultz, executive vice president of the Radio and Television News Directors Association, suggested that Mr. Allen might be attacking reporters to divert attention from the more crucial issue of his own conduct.

The most notable recent stakeout was the one last summer outside the home of Wayne Williams, who was eventually charged with the murders of two of the 28 slain young blacks in Atlanta. Even as the stakeout was under way, reporters and editors debated whether they should even report Mr. Williams's name, since he was not formally a suspect.

Bill Rose, the Atlanta reporter for The Miami Herald, recalled being part of a crowd of up to 50 reporters at the Williams house and leaving after a few minutes, "halfway grossed out." The Williams family, he said, "were virtually prisoners in their own home."

Stakeout Called 'Repellent'

Jeff Greenfield, the media critic for the CBS network, said he had recently reviewed the footage of the Williams stakeout and found it "repellent." Most such surveillance, he said, is "shabby journalism" that does not produce useful information.

Earlier this month, a smaller stakeout, the subject of which was Chief Justice Warren E. Burger, outside a hotel in Lincoln, Neb., produced no information on the charges by John D. Ehrlichman that in the Nixon Administration the Chief Justice had talked to President Nixon about pending cases. But it did lead to a minor scuffle with a television cameraman.

A CBS producer and camera crew followed Chief Justice Burger into an elevator car, trying to get him to talk, and he knocked the camera to the floor. He said he was reacting to being struck on the chin by the camera lens, but the film showed no such contact.

Reporters said the effort to get a response in that situation was journalistically valid. Chief Justice Burger rarely makes public appearances and had consistently been refusing to discuss a matter of substantial public interest. They disagreed, however, on whether the television crew, having taped his lack of response, had anything to gain by getting into the elevator.

Going 'Too Far' Sometimes

Richard M. Brown, the Chicago bureau manager who assigned the CBS coverage, said, "There are probably times when we go too far." But, he added, "We have all seen situations where we stopped being aggressive, and somebody else got a good story."

Chief Justice Burger's response to the question of his conversations with Mr. Nixon came later, as he toured the newsroom of The Lincoln Journal. He said Mr. Ehrlichman's allegations were only an effort "to sell a book."

The journalists and public figures agreed that part of the problem of apparent journalistic invasion of privacy stems from the technical demands of television. Unlike a pencil-and-paper reporter, a television reporter is usually accompanied by a producer, a light man, a sound man and, on a stakeout, a relay truck with its protruding antennas.

Arthur R. Miller, a Harvard law professor, said that most laywers advised people not to sue the news media for privacy invasion because there were such strong First Amendment protections for reporters and photographers pursuing a story. Professor Miller noted that there existed no Federal law and few state statutes on privacy.

Examples of Privacy Loss

Even very public events can provide examples of invasion of privacy. Last September, a Florida jury ordered a Cocoa Beach newspaper to pay $10,000 to a woman who had been held captive by her estranged husband. The paper printed a photograph of her fleeing the house, naked except for a hand towel. The editor told the jury the photograph "best capsulized the dramatic and tragic event." Her lawyer contended the picture simply violated "good taste."

Instances of apparent invasion of privacy occur repeatedly. This month, Jacqueline Kennedy Onassis told a Federal court in Manhattan that a freelance photographer, Ron Galella, was continuing to make her life "intolerable" despite court orders that he stay away. Although many editors condemn his work as invasive, Mr. Galella has sold his pictures of Mrs. Onassis and her family to a variety of publications.

Similarly, the new Princess of Wales has been subjected to intensive coverage, with photographers popping out of the bushes when she emerges from her house in Gloucester, England. Two weeks ago, British editors said they would reduce the coverage after Queen Elizabeth II's press secretary told them that the Princess, the former Lady Diana Spencer, "feels totally beleaguered."

Louisa Kennedy, whose husband, Moorhead C. Kennedy Jr., was held hostage in Iran for 444 days, said the hostage families were simply not prepared for the spotlight into which they were thrust. She recalled that when her family was home for Christmas a year ago, "we couldn't get on the phone or walk out the front door without the cameras grinding."

She said she had no "hard feelings" toward most of the individual reporters but was still surprised by "what the media and the public have become." There was no recognition, she said, "of the kind of stress and strain we were under."

And, Mrs. Kennedy added, the intense publicity frequently does "a great disservice to our public figures."

In almost the same words, Mr. O'Neill, the editor of The Daily News in New York, agreed. He said the press should ask itself whether "long-range, does this tremendous glare of public attention, magnified by the TV cameras, scare a lot of good public officials away from government?"

Mr. Von Fremd of ABC said that a CBS cameraman outside the Allen home had shown that same doubt. The cameraman carried a sign announcing: "Mr. Allen, I'm only here because my company is making me."

I. VOCABULARY

offensiveness   beleaguered
crucial   stake out

II. QUESTIONS ON CONTENT

1. Has the issue of privacy ever occurred to you after watching a television news story? Describe the instance.
2. What is Friendly's attitude toward his subject?
3. What are your views on privacy? Is it a right or a privilege? A necessity or a luxury?
4. Do you admire "private people?" Do you trust them? Would you classify yourself as a private person?
5. Have you ever felt your privacy was invaded? Recount the circumstances.

III. QUESTIONS ON FORM

1. This article was published in the *New York Times*. Is it a news story or a feature story? Explain.
2. What devices does Friendly use in his introduction and conclusion? Are they effective?
3. Make a list of the examples Friendly cites. Do you see any strategy in the chronology?

IV. SUGGESTIONS FOR WRITING

1. Write a persuasive essay supporting either individual privacy or the public right to know. Choose your examples from one or a combination of the following categories: celebrities, public officials, and private citizens.
2. Describe an invasion of privacy you witnessed in person or on television.

Howard Polskin is a staff writer for the New York bureau of *TV Guide*. He has written articles about television for newspapers and magazines since 1976.

Save a Life or Get the Story?

Howard Polskin

Cecil Andrews holds the lighted match to his leg and waits for his body to become engulfed in fire. A small flame dances to life on his left knee.

WHMA-TV cameraman Ron Simmons and Gary Harris, his 18-year-old assistant, stare at Andrews in disbelief as their camera rolls. A stab of fear

Reprinted with permission from *TV Guide*® magazine. Copyright © 1983 by Triangle Publications, Inc., Radnor, Pennsylvania.

ripples through Simmons' belly: what if the police don't appear? Earlier that evening, after Andrews had repeatedly called the small Alabama television station threatening to set himself on fire to protest unemployment, Simmons had repeatedly notified the police. He thought that they would apprehend Andrews.

As the flame spreads up Andrews' leg, Simmons tells Harris to put the fire out. Just as Harris approaches Andrews, the front of his shirt, which has been doused in lighter fluid, bursts into flame. Andrews rolls on the ground, his entire body encased in the blaze. He staggers to his feet and runs across the quiet Jacksonville, Ala., town square as his fiery clothing falls behind him. Moments later, he is hosed down by a fireman.

Simmons keeps his camera rolling and records the entire incident. It has been just 82 seconds since he first turned on his camera.

That night, Simmons and Harris go to bed with clear consciences, never suspecting that what they did—and more importantly, what they didn't do—might be severely criticized. It is only in the following days and weeks that they find themselves in the midst of a growing controversy centered on one question:

Why didn't they stop Andrews from striking the match?

Several months later, Simmons and Harris, who still are employed by WHMA-TV, maintain that they were only doing their jobs on that night of March 4, 1983. But a larger issue has surfaced that pertains to how deeply TV journalists should get involved in stories they're covering. Should journalists ever help the people involved in those events? When the values of good journalism and humanitarianism collide what should a journalist do?

All three TV networks have written policies that spell out the rules quite clearly: reporters are not to influence the event that they are covering. For instance, the CBS News Standards state, "[News] personnel who are covering a news event must not participate in that event in any way or for whatever reason." From ABC's policy manual: "The responsibility of ABC News is to report and record news events, not to participate in them. We must remain professionally detached in all situations."

Ron Simmons says that he was trying to remain detached on March 4. "I get paid to record events," he says. In his six-year career, he's had to record some rough stuff, like car crashes with burned occupants, and drownings in lakes where little children were pulled out of the water dead amid sobbing relatives. When covering the news, Simmons has drawn a psychological curtain between himself and the event with one goal in mind: keep the camera rolling. That's the key to a cameraman's job, say TV newsmen, no matter how horrible or upsetting the event may be. Says ABC's political and media analyst Jeff Greenfield, "I've heard stories of TV cameramen who take shots of gruesome crashes, develop the film and then throw up." Failure of a cameraman to record an event could result in the loss of a job or, worse yet, the slipping away of an opportunity to film history. For the most part, TV cameramen remain cold observers of the events they cover, even if those events are brutal or life-threatening.

For example, on Feb. 1, 1968, Vo Suu, an NBC cameraman, was prowling Cholon, the Chinese quarter of Saigon, during the height of the Tet Offensive. At the end of his street he spotted a group of South Vietnamese soldiers leading a prisoner, who appeared to have been beaten. As the head of the South Vietnamese National Police, General Loan, approached the prisoner, Suu instinctively began filming the action. Loan walked up to the prisoner, drew his gun without asking any questions and shot him point-blank in the side of the head.

Suu was very calm. His hands did not shake as he kept the camera rolling and zoomed into the side of the dead man's head where blood spurted like a fountain. He slowly panned to the general, who said, "I think Buddha will forgive me." The film, later shipped to New York and shown on NBC, joltingly brought home the barbarities of the war, and thereby helped change American attitudes. For Vo Suu, covering the murder was only a small part of a large chain of horrors that he personally recorded during his 10 years as a network cameraman in Vietnam. His professional philosophy was simple. "I always disregarded the events that I was covering," he says today from his home in Maryland. "I was there just to record events, not to think about them."

Walter James, a free-lance network cameraman with extensive experience, agrees. "You have to remove your feelings as a human being when you're shooting something gruesome," says James, who once covered a plane crash in the swamps surrounding Miami, where he saw alligators carrying away pieces of bodies. "You have to psyche yourself up to cover the news and turn off your personal feelings."

His partner, free-lance sound technician Tom Cosgrove, feels the same way. "If a guy wanted to set himself on fire and I tried to talk him out of it, I'd cover it. But I wouldn't hand him the match," says Cosgrove who's worked for 20 years for all three networks, covering news like the 1968 riots in Chicago, the Kent State shootings and the march on Selma, Ala. But therein lies the controversy. How aloof should a TV journalist be? When should journalists drop their commitment to a story and help a fellow human being?

When President Reagan was shot in 1981, no reporters rushed to aid him or the three other people who were wounded by Hinckley's bullets. Says NBC White House correspondent Judy Woodruff, who covered the incident: "We simply weren't needed. And Reagan's people kept yelling to the press to get back to clear a path for medical personnel. We would have added to the confusion if we'd tried to help." However, Woodruff maintains that she's not callous to the needs of people involved in events she's covering. "If I was working and I came across someone who was lying hurt and alone in the street, there's no question that I would help that person," says Woodruff.

"There are times when a journalist's first duty is as a citizen," notes Jeff Greenfield. "But no one expects a journalist to stop a war or go to Selma to stop the police dogs."

"Journalists are observers, not participants," says George Watson, vice president of ABC News. "But where life is at stake, there may be an exception."

Adds Tom Wicker, an associate editor and political columnist of The New York Times who acted as a mediator for prisoners during the 1971 Attica uprising: "I have always maintained that the journalist owes his duty to humanity. When there's a conflict between being a journalist and a human being, I'll always hope I'll be a human being. It's a grave error for reporters to set themselves aside from humanity."

At times, network TV journalists have dropped their roles as observers and helped shape the news they were covering. In 1977, NBC correspondent Brian Ross was in Buffalo covering the fierce blizzard that struck the city. As he and his crew rode through the empty, snow-covered streets on the back of a huge fire engine, it got stuck in a deep snow bank. In the distance Ross could see the orange glow of a burning building where the firemen were heading. The image of the firetruck trapped in the snowbank while a building burned summed up in one shot the paralysis that gripped the city. But Ross decided against the shot and instead he and his cameramen dropped their equipment and helped push the truck out of the snow. "I decided that it was more important that they get to the fire than NBC get that picture," says Ross.

In 1978, for a CBS documentary on the boat people at Southeast Asia, correspondent Ed Bradley waded into the foaming surf off the coast of Malaysia to help a boatload of refugees make it to shore safely. ABC News correspondent Geraldo Rivera periodically gets physically and emotionally involved in stories he's covering. In a 1974 story on New York's welfare hotels, Rivera was filmed during an interview with a security guard that turned into a bloody fistfight.

But network journalists who get involved are generally exceptions to the rule. That's not the case, however, for some local TV reporters. "Local TV reporters always get more involved than network reporters," observes Jeff Greenfield.

Arnold Diaz, an investigative reporter for New York's WCBS-TV, specializes in involvement. Of the several hundred stories that Diaz has reported on in the past 10 years, one particularly stands out in his mind. More than a year ago, he began working on a story about two elderly couples who were being evicted from their apartment in Brooklyn where they had been living for decades. The story had all the ingredients that Diaz looks for before he gets involved: drama, conflict, humanity and a clear-cut tale of the powerless against the powerful. His crew filmed the two couples in their cramped apartments, capturing their fear and desperation. Diaz followed their plight for months and eventually covered their victory over the landlord, brought about substantially because of his tenacity. Diaz was filmed in their apartment as they ripped up their eviction notices. Diaz murmured "All right!" on camera. Back in the studio Diaz added to the audience, "It's one of the things that makes this job worthwhile." For his crusading reports, Diaz has been given a nickname by a newsroom buddy: Saint Arnold.

But reporting like that, with the intense involvement of the reporter, has its critics. "It's bush-league reporting," charges Fred Friendly, former president of CBS News and Edward R. Murrow Emeritus Professor at Columbia University's Graduate School of Journalism. "You don't show your tripod. In other words, you don't become part of the story. The sense of fairness is threatened. If the viewer knows how the reporter feels, he may feel that facts have been changed. It's much more dramatic in television than in print. It's more personal and graphic. By being a good Samaritan, we get in the way of our lenses. It makes it impossible for us to do our job well. We blur the image of the job we're trying to do: explain complex issues."

Still, Friendly believes that the two technicians in Jacksonville should have stopped Andrews, who was eventually released from the hospital after an eight-week stay. "It had no news value that a poor man would set himself on fire," Friendly maintains. Journalists will probably analyze the 82 seconds in Jacksonville for years, debating whether the story was newsworthy, whether Andrews would have set himself on fire if the camera hadn't been there and what the responsibilities of the technicians were that night.

But there's little debate that objectivity and noninvolvement are cornerstones of the journalism profession. And most professionals tend to agree that there are no hard rules to unusual circumstances that might develop in the course of an assignment. Fred Friendly has one tip, though. "Whenever a journalist has a tough call," says Friendly, "he should ask himself, 'Is it important for the public to see it?' In other words, a lot may boil down to plain common sense and careful on-the-spot news judgment tempered by years of experience.

But even veterans sit on the fence when it comes to the incident in Jacksonville. "It's hard to say exactly what I would've done that night," explains Walter James, who's been covering the South for the past five years as a cameraman for all three networks. "I think Harris and Simmons were just doing their jobs. If I was in a situation where I could aid someone, I think I would . . . as long as I had enough good footage beforehand."

I. VOCABULARY

humanitarianism   bush-league   callous
tempered   tenacity   aloof

II. QUESTIONS ON CONTENT

1. Does Polskin answer his title question?
2. Professional journalism requires noninvolvement. What are the factors that make the Jacksonville incident so disturbing?
3. Do you think it was a "newsworthy" event?
4. Compare and contrast the views of Fred Friendly and Tom Wicker. With whom do you agree?

III. QUESTIONS ON FORM

1. Outline the presentation of argument in this piece. Does the ordering of views influence the reader's opinion?
2. What is the impact of using the President as an example?
3. Discuss Polskin's description of the event on pages 133–134. Would you call it expository or descriptive writing? Is it also persuasive writing? Note some emotionally charged words and phrases.

IV. SUGGESTIONS FOR WRITING

1. Write a persuasive essay supporting either humanitarian duty or journalistic ethics.

TOPICS FOR INVESTIGATION

1. Read some biographies of famous newspapermen: for example, Greeley, Pulitzer, Hearst, and Murdoch and discuss the impact of a dominant personality on journalism.

2. Using films: *All the President's Men, Absence of Malice,* and so on, and television: "the Mary Tyler Moore Show," "Lou Grant," and so on, discuss the image of the press in the other media.

3. Investigate the concept of privacy in other societies. Compare and contrast American views with European, Arabic, Asian.

4. Investigate some news stories about a celebrated event in our past: for example, the Lindbergh flight or kidnapping, the Scopes trial, or the Sacco-Vanzetti trial and determine if press coverage was more or less objective then than now.

5. Explore the possibilities of Lapham's sixth point: "Defined as means rather than an end, journalism defends the future against the past."

5

POPULAR PRINT: MAGAZINES AND BOOKS

The print media encompass not only newspapers but also magazines and books. Like newspapers, therefore, they communicate their messages by words and pictures arranged primarily in a linear and sequential format that appeals to the sense of sight. Like newspapers, moreover, magazines and books serve to inform, entertain, and influence the attitudes of a mass audience. There are, however, some important differences among them.

First, the magazine is more durable than the newspaper but less permanent than the book because its cover and bound pages give it a semipermanence that the newspaper lacks. The magazine, like the book, is also more flexible than the newspaper with regard to the size, shape, or dimension of its package. Second, the magazine is less timely than the newspaper but more timely than the book. The typical newspaper has the pressure of daily deadlines, while the typical book takes up to a year to be published. However, the typical weekly or monthly magazine has enough lead time to be able to probe more deeply into issues than the newspaper usually does and do a better job of analyzing and interpreting these issues or problems. Books surpass magazines in these areas, and because of their permanence they also serve as the repository of our culture, the basis for our eductional system, and the source of much of our knowledge of ourselves and the world in which we live. One of the unique services of magazines, as Sandman, Rubin, and Sachsman point out, is that they are "the only mass medium that is both timely and permanent, quick and deep."

Third, in regard to their respective audiences, the magazine once again stands midway between the other two. The traditional daily newspaper, like the *New York Times* and the *Washington Post,* appeals to a wide general audience, while the book is an individual medium because the person has considerable control over when, how, and at what speed he or she wishes to read and reread the book or a portion of it. By contrast, the mass circulation magazine today, such as *Time, Rolling Stone, People,* or *Cosmopolitan,* usually aims at a specific audience, a single special-interest group with common interests and values.

The first section of this chapter on popular print deals with magazines. The opening essay provides a general introduction to the mass circulation magazine. John Bittner traces its historical development, decline, and reintroduction, and he ends with an analysis and classification of magazines in terms of their characteristics and types. The author contends that the success of the magazine today depends upon its ability to restrict its aim and scope in order to reach existing specialized audiences and new target audiences.

The brief comment by Bittner on the successful reintroduction of *Life* magazine provides the background for Beverly Beyette's account of *Life*'s struggle, in 1978, to reestablish itself as a general-interest magazine at a time when magazines are becoming increasingly specialized in topic and audience appeal. The last article in this section is issue oriented because it implicitly raises questions about the responsibility of the print media to society and about government censorship of the mass media in the national interest. Who decides what the media should and should not do?

The second section of this chapter on popular print focuses on books, chiefly works of fiction, and on three problems relating to them: plagiarism, censorship, and illiteracy. Alfred Kazin surveys current popular writing in relation to American life and sadly concludes that our literary culture is in disarray. Commercialism, factionalism, and transitoriness prevail, he contends, because we lack credible goals, an historical sense, and the imagination to deal with the impact of technology on our psychic lives.

The economic status of the writer is the subject of the next essay. Despite Kazin's complaint about the commercialization of popular writing, especially prose fiction, Herbert Mitgang informs us that best selling authors are scarce; the average American author cannot earn a living solely from his or her writings. Where financial success is achieved, it is clearly related to the type of writing done. Genre fiction, Mitgang reports, is the most lucrative. The erotic historical romance is the specific popular genre that is examined by Carol Thurston and Barbara Dosher. Like Kazin, these authors view popular writing as a reflection of American society. Their analysis of the changes in the heroines of romantic mass-market paperbacks leads them to conclude that these books embody and teach many of the values of one segment of this society, the feminist movement. Another way for a popular writer to achieve financial success, according to the next selection, is to get the help of television. Rod Townley discusses the increasing dependency of publishing and television on each other, to the profit of both.

The remaining three essays treat specific and persistent problems relating to the print media in general and popular writing in particular. One such problem is plagiarism. Elizabeth Peer illustrates a recent case of professional plagiarism and reports on some of the possible reasons why writers would risk their reputations and sales to engage in this objectionable practice. Another generally objectionable but more debatable practice is censorship. In her essay, Rita Ciolli limits this problem to the contents of textbooks. She investigates the increasing attacks on school-book publishers by conservative special-interest groups that accuse them of bias or distortion and demand changes in content or focus that the publishers are often reluctant to make. The final selection deals with a continuing issue that may make discussion of plagiarism and censorship academic because it threatens the very life of the print media. This is the alarming increase of adult illiteracy in the United States. Bill McGowan Jr. explores the crisis in terms of its impact on family, business, and industry and what is being done to solve this problem.

142 Popular Writing

Readings

> **John R. Bittner** Ph.D., Purdue University, is professor and chairperson of the Department of Radio, Television, and Motion Pictures at The University of North Carolina at Chapel Hill. Along with *Mass Communication: An Introduction*, he has authored such texts as *Broadcasting and Telecommunication*, 2nd ed.; *Broadcast Law and Regulation*; *Professional Broadcasting: A Brief Introduction*; *Fundamentals of Communication*; *Each Other: An Introduction to Interpersonal Communication*; and *Radio Journalism* (co-authored with Denise A. Bittner), all published by Prentice-Hall, Inc.

Magazines

John R. Bittner

Finding an Audience

As the nation prospered, a growing audience began to yearn for entertainment, entertainment that took the form of magazines. Entrepreneurs immediately realized that if they could provide light, diversionary reading at nominal prices, they could capture this mass audience. And they did. The magazine publishing boom began. Between 1865 and 1885 the number of periodicals jumped from 700 to 3300.

As competition developed, so did trends in pricing and content. The name of the game was circulation. Circulation lured advertisers who could pay to reach a mass audience. The price was high enough to allow a decrease in subscription prices, making magazines still more attractive to the public. Distribution also became more efficient, as the rails spread their network into hitherto inaccessible rural areas. Many magazines specifically sought a mass audience, just the opposite of what happened fifty years later.

Prosperity and Transition

America's phenomenal industrial growth during the early twentieth century also helped spur the magazine publishing industry. The era saw major strides in corporate expansion and the ability to produce mass goods for the consumer. With that ability came the need to make the consumer

John R. Bittner, *Mass Communication: An Introduction*, 3rd ed., copyright © 1983, pp. 64–70. Reprinted by permission of Prentice-Hall, Inc., Englewood Cliffs, N.J.

aware of these goods and of the various brand names of the products on grocery shelves, in new car showrooms, on clothes racks, and in furniture stores. Magazines filled the bill, and advertisements filled magazines. Although there were ups and downs, many of the publications achieved wide national acclaim. Among them were *Life, Look,* and the *Saturday Evening Post.* The classic issue of prosperity was the *Saturday Evening Post* of December 7, 1929. "Weighing nearly two pounds, the 272-page magazine kept the average reader occupied for twenty hours and twenty minutes. From the 214 national advertisers appearing in it, the Curtis Publishing Company took in revenues estimated at $1,512,000.

For the mass circulation magazine, the glory of that era did not survive. Television already loomed on the horizon. It signaled the growth of specialized magazines and the decline of mass circulation publications.

The exact time of this turning point is debatable. The mass national magazines survived the golden era of radio and at first seemed to hold their own with television. Advertising revenues for *Life* increased in the early 1960s. "A single issue of *Life* in October, 1960 carried $5,000,000 worth; another in November, 1961 had revenues of $5,202,000. But the figures were deceiving. A period followed in which many industry spokespersons argued that television was making gains on the magazine publishers; magazine publishers countered that more than ever was being spent on advertising—magazines were not only holding their own, but gaining. To some extent, both arguments were correct. Magazines in general were still experiencing a period of growth, but television and skyrocketing postal rates finally dealt a fatal blow to the mass circulation magazines.

Inability to direct themselves to a specialized audience was another reason for the demise of such well-known magazines as *Look* and *Life.* These were magazines in the true sense of the word *mass,* having something within their pages that was of interest to everyone. With the advent of television, however, advertisers could reach the same mass audience as *Look* and *Life* did, but more cheaply and more efficiently. In addition, television offered visual messages on a mass scale with both motion and sound accompaniment. With increased operating costs, mass circulation magazines folded. The *Saturday Evening Post* shared the fate of the other mass circulation magazines.

Reintroducing Familiar Publications

After reading the last paragraph, you may stop and say, "Wait a minute. I just saw the *Saturday Evening Post* on the newsstand." You are right. In the past few years you probably have spotted some of these magazines, such as *Life* and *Country Gentleman.* Each represents an unusual trend in publishing that applied to a select few of some of the biggest titles to grace magazine history. But do not be deceived into thinking those editions are reaching the same mass audience they did thirty years ago. They are not. What publishers have done is to purchase the names of the major publications and then reintroduce them into the marketplace, but to a much more specialized audience. What has been created instead are specialty magazines with familiar titles.

For example, after the *Saturday Evening Post* folded, it was purchased by the Ser Vaas family of Indianapolis. The new Curtis Publishing Company, operating out of a different city and with a different staff, introduced a new edition of the *Saturday Evening Post*, with quality articles and top illustrators. Instead of trying to reach the mass audience of the former publication, the new *Post* is directed at a more conservative element of American life and contains many of the same sort of illustrations that its predecessor had. Its secret is that it has been able to control its circulation and distribution systems. Had the old *Post* been able to accomplish this same feat early enough, it might never have disappeared from the scene. But most of the circulation magazines persisted too long in trying to reach a mass audience so that they were unable to make the drastic shift to a specialized audience in time to avoid insolvency.

The *Saturday Evening Post* was not the only magazine revived by the Curtis Publishing Company. A very shrewd gamble paid off when the company reintroduced *Country Gentleman* magazine. Initial circulation had reached more than 100,000 before the new magazine ever left the printer. That continued to swell to more than 300,000 as *Country Gentleman* effectively reached the "gentleman farmer" of the 1970s and 1980s. Advertisers of such products as building supplies for home repair and remodeling, lawn seed, and other suburban homeowner products found the *Country Gentleman* the ideal medium to reach this specialized audience.

In 1978 Time-Life brought back *Life* magazine. Based on the experience of other popular publications such as *People*, the new *Life* was designed for the more contemporary life style and the affluent reader than its mass circulation predecessor was. Advancements in printing and photojournalism permitted the new *Life* to be even more "picture-oriented" than the old *Life* was.

Still famous magazine titles like *Collier's* remain to be reintroduced. But the potential is there, so do not be surprised if you happen to spot them at the newsstand someday.

Modern Magazine Publishing: The Specialized Audience

Not all publications were destined for the fate of the old mass circulation periodicals. Many made the necessary changes to reach the highly specialized audiences that modern magazine publishing demands. For example, *Business Week* offers advertisers a select group of management-level readers by regularly refusing to take subscriptions from nonmanagement-level readers. Even living in a certain section of the country may determine if you qualify for a specialized magazine subscription. *Sunset* magazine, called "the magazine of Western living," is directed to readers in the Pacific coast states and Nevada, Arizona, Idaho, and Utah. If you want to subscribe to the publication but do not live in the West, you have to pay more. As a result, advertisers know that by purchasing an ad in *Sunset,* they can concentrate on this western audience and will not be paying for circulation to other parts of the country that might not be as interested in their advertising. The same is true for *Southern Living* magazine for the southern audience.

Special editions. Many magazines publish numerous special editions to reach those specialized audiences. What may appear to be one nationally distributed magazine is actually several specialized publications under the same cover. For example, *Time* magazine publishes both demographic and regional editions. An advertiser wanting to reach college students can advertise in the *Time* which is distributed primarily to college students, or *Time* offers its *Time Z* and *Time A +* editions. *Time Z* stands for "zip codes." Time Z is directed to subscribers in 1414 of the United States's most affluent zip code areas within metropolitan markets. Thus if you were an advertiser with a product appealing to high-income buyers, the *Time Z* edition might be a good place to put your advertisement. An even more elite audience can be reached through the *Time A +* edition. The A + edition is directed at business and professional people, 600,000 of them.

Another example of specialized editions is *Sports Illustrated.* Not only does the magazine publish four regional editions—East, West, South, and Midwest—but it also publishes a "homeowners edition," limited to 640,000 subscribers in zip code areas that show the highest concentration of homeowners. In addition, it offers special "insert editions" to advertisers, with such special insert features as the U.S. Tennis Open and the Grand Slam of Golf. A manufacturer of tennis rackets, for instance, might find the U.S. Tennis Open insert edition an excellent place to advertise.

Regional editions. We mentioned the regional editions of *Sports Illustrated.* Other publications are realizing the advertising appeal of regional editions. *Playboy* has eastern, central, western, southeastern, southwestern, New York metropolitan, Chicago metropolitan, Los Angeles metropolitan, San Francisco metropolitan, and urban market editions. The centerfold is the same in the New York metropolitan edition as in the Los Angeles metropolitan edition, but an advertiser wanting to reach only the New York audience can do so by buying advertising space in just the New York metropolitan edition.

International editions. *Playboy,* along with its regional editions in the United States, is also among those magazines that publish international editions. Along with its overseas military edition, *Playboy* publishes foreign editions for France, Italy, Germany, Japan, Mexico, and Brazil, but this time different centerfolds do appear in certain foreign editions because some countries prohibit the bold displays used in the United States. The magazine also has different titles, being called *Caballero* in Mexico and *Homen* in Brazil.

Two other familiar publications with international editions are *Cosmopolitan* and *Good Housekeeping*. Both have Spanish-language editions which Spanish and American advertisers find ideal for reaching Spanish-speaking audiences both inside and outside the United States. *Cosmopolitan's* Spanish edition looks much like the English-language edition. The front cover is identical, but a closer look reveals the Spanish-language subtitles. The *Good Housekeeping* version is titled *Buenhogar* and is independently edited. It stresses family life, children, and self-improvement and is sold in 22 countries.

New target audiences: new publications. The magazine industry is much more than a series of specialized editions. New publications are cropping up which are devoted entirely to very select audiences.

Perhaps nowhere is this trend more evident than in magazines directed toward today's changing woman, following her every mood from sports to professions. One of the first of these publications was *Ms* magazine, followed by *City Woman* published for professional women living and working in the city, *Professional Women,* and *Woman. Essence* appeals to an even more select audience—black professional women.

Business executives have always been a prime *target audience* for magazines. These individuals usually make major buying decisions and have higher than average incomes. Reaching this audience is the first aim of another specialized magazine, *Chicago Business.* Published by Crain Communications, *Chicago Business* is an example of a magazine appealing not only to the specialized audience of business people but also refining that even further to reach business people in Chicago. Geared to more general audiences are the many city magazines that have appeared in recent years.

Magazines devoted to audiences in a particular state are becoming prevalent. Features on tourist attractions, politics, and business and industry are commonly found in these publications which may be published by private enterprise or by agency of the state government. While the state magazine itself reaches a specialized audience, other publications reach specialized audiences within the state. One example in the state category is *Texas Sports.*

We discussed *Time's* ability to reach college students through a specialized edition, but one of the more novel examples of reaching college students is the *Directory of Classes* for selected colleges published by University Communications. The college supplies the company with its class schedule, and the company, in turn, sells advertising in the *Directory.* Reaching the college student is a difficult media problem since media attention habits change at that time. The hometown newspaper may no longer be available, the hometown radio station may not be within range, and loyalty to other media may vary since class schedules and different living conditions can intervene.

Characteristics and Types of Magazines

Magazines are of four principal types—*farm, business, consumer,* and *religious.* Each has subcategories. For example, farm publications consist mainly of *state* and *vocational* publications. State publications are directed toward a particular geographic area, such as the *Montana Farmer-Stockman* and *The Pennsylvania Farmer.* Vocational farm publications, on the other hand, are directed toward a particular type of farmer and include such magazines as the *Citrus and Vegetable Magazine* and *Dairy Herd Management* or *Beef.*

Business publications include *professional magazines* such as those pertaining to law, medicine, or education. Here the publisher may be a professional organization such as the American Dental Association. *The Quill,* official publication of the Society of Professional Journalists—Sigma Delta Chi, is an example of a professional magazine. Another subcategory of business publications includes *trade magazines* for specific businesses, such as the *Hardware Retailer* and *Today's Office.*

A third subcategory consists of *industrial publications.* Edited for specific industries, they can include magazines directed to specific processes, for example, manufacturing or communication. Two examples of industrial publications of the printing and broadcasting industries, respectively, are the *Printing News* and *Broadcast Management and Engineering. Institutional business magazines* also abound, such as *Hotel-Motel News.* Publications that are sent to a group of people belonging to an organization are usually termed *house organs.* Copies of house organs may be sent to the news media for public relations purposes. The content of the house organ is usually information of special interest to its select readers.

In addition to these major categories of business publications, you should understand the difference between *vertical* and *horizontal publications.* Vertical publications reach people of a given profession at different levels in that profession. For instance, a major vertical publication of the radio and television industry is *Broadcasting.* Its content is geared to every person working or interested in the broadcasting industry, whether it be the television camera operator, the radio station manager, or even the advertising executive who needs to know about new FCC regulations affecting broadcast commercials. Horizontal magazines, on the other hand, are aimed at a certain managerial level but cut across several different industries. *Business Week,* for example, is directed at management-level personnel in many different facets of the business world. Two other examples of magazines directed at management include *Forbes* and *Fortune.*

Consumer magazines are usually of two types: specialized and general. Magazines directed at audiences with an interest in a special area, such as

Sailing or the *Model Railroader,* are *specialized* magazines. *General* magazines are directed to people with more varied interests.

Religious publications also have various subdivisions, usually based on specific religious denominations. Typical religious publications include *The Catholic Voice, The Jewish News, The Episcopalian, The Lutheran,* and many more regional publications that deal with specific denominations within a city.

I. VOCABULARY

entrepreneur	phenomenal	affluent
diversionary	acclaim	elite
inaccessible	demise	demographic

II. QUESTIONS ON CONTENT

1. Do we today, as in the late nineteenth century, still look to magazines for entertainment, for "light, diversionary reading"? Why or why not?
2. What development in late nineteenth and early twentieth century America led to the rise and prosperity of the mass circulation magazine?
3. What caused the decline of mass circulation publications and the growth of specialized magazines? Can you mention any other causes?
4. How were famous defunct magazines like the *Saturday Evening Post* able to reintroduce themselves to the public?
5. What methods do magazines today have to reach specialized audiences?
6. What, according to the essay, are some of the new target audiences that have led to new publications? What other such audiences and publications can you identify?
7. What are the four main types of magazines? Can you suggest any other way of classifying magazines?

III. QUESTIONS ON FORM

1. Does this essay have a thesis? If so, where is it?
2. What modes does the author use to unify the first three paragraphs? Why does he use these modes?
3. Although Bittner is the sole author of this selection, he uses the plural pronoun "We" twice. How do you account for this choice of point of view?
4. Explain the role of example and illustration in the essay. Are they abundant and specific? Do they interest the reader, clarify the major points, and persuade you of the truth of the author's generalizations?
5. Since this essay is an excerpt from a chapter in a textbook, it lacks an introduction. What do you think would be a suitable introduction?

IV. SUGGESTIONS FOR WRITING

1. Discuss the basic functions of a magazine.
2. Describe the main characteristics of your favorite magazine and explain why you like it or need it.
3. Agree or disagree with the proposition that magazines are more valuable and useful than newspapers.
4. Analyze the reasons for the popularity, as judged by total advertising and circulation revenues, of any one of the following mass circulation magazines: *Reader's Digest, TV Guide, Time, People, Sports Illustrated,* and the *National Enquirer.*
5. Periodicals intended for the woman reader, such as *Family Circle, Woman's Day,* the *Ladies' Home Journal, Good Housekeeping,* and *Ms.,* are one of the two most popular kinds of magazines in the modern era. Analyze the reasons for this phenomenon.

A former writer and editor for *The San Diego Union,* **Beverly Beyette** is a staff writer for the *Los Angeles Times* View Section. She was twice a winner of the California-Nevada Associated Press annual award for enterprise reporting.

He Moves in Close to Bring the Big Stories Vividly to Life

Beverly Beyette

Jackie O was gracing the cover of an issue of People, and Richard Stolley, the man who had guided the magazine from its infancy to the 2 million circulation mark, was puzzled.

"I can't understand," he said. "She's not exactly on everybody's tongues." In short, Jacqueline Kennedy Onassis is what Stolley terms "a B personality."

But then Stolley, who switched two years ago from the managing editorship of People to that of Time-Life's rather more respectable sister magazine, Life, is the first to admit he does not always guess right.

Take the penguins, for example—no fewer than seven pages on the penguins of the Pampas that graced Life's cover in April. "A particularly nasty breed of penguins," said Stolley. He had considered them a sure-fire follow-up to a smashingly successful Life cover on national parks in peril,

Copyright © 1984 by the *Los Angeles Times.* Reprinted by permission.

figuring, "Aha! If they liked national parks, they're going to love penguins." But penguins bombed.

Stolley moved to Life from the gossipy People after eight years as founding managing editor in March, 1982, 3½ years after Life, once a venerable weekly American institution, was resurrected as a monthly with a start-up circulation of 700,000.

His first task, he said, was "assuring everybody in extravagant terms that I was not going to turn Life magazine into a big page People.. And I don't think that has happened, even though Life is doing more stories on personalities."

But there's a big difference between People people and Life people, explained Stolley, who last year went to Monaco for an exclusive interview with Prince Rainier about the death of Princess Grace and its impact on their daughter, Princess Stephanie.

"Life can take only the A personalities," said Stolley. "Every week, People has 15 to 25 people stories, whereas Life, a monthly, will have one or two each issue—the top-of-the-line show business personalities or terrifically interesting, productive and substantial people . . . We're more selective. We can afford to hold out for the A list."

What Life wants of Robert Redford, for example, is "to go home with him, go up in the mountains with him," he said. And, he added, "I think we'll get him."

Whereas People will settle for "one terrific picture of a personality in the bathtub," accompanied by some sprightly text, Stolley said. "We have to live with these folks for awhile. A Life photographer and Life reporter really move in."

Stolley says he thinks "there's some real hope for general-interest magazines," after seeing Life double in circulation since 1978 to its current 1.4 million. At the same time, he does not underestimate the competition from the special-interest publications: "Take Computer World. You have to lift it with your knees, it's so heavy," he said.

Stolley had spent 20 years on the staff of the weekly Life when it suspended publication in December, 1972, covering such diverse stories as the Vietnam peace negotiations and an anthropological expedition seeking the origins of man in Kenya. He said magazines had learned a very important lesson since the first Life folded: "To price themselves realistically. The buyer is willing to bear more of the cost of production."

He noted that when Life folded as a weekly, then 50 cents a copy, "we were convinced we couldn't get any more." Current newsstand price: $2 (The Olympic issue is $2.95).

Life has learned something else, said Stolley. "The old Life was competing with TV for time and in its editorial mission. Life still felt it had to cover the news. By the time we got out there with the news, everybody had seen it, in color, with sound."

He sees as a good sign for the new Life the public's "tremendous appetite for photographs. The baby boom generation is very sophisticated visually. Part of the success of People has been this strong visual sense. A whole generation of Americans is rediscovering the still picture."

The new Life's best-selling issue, its look at John F. Kennedy 20 years later, was a sentimental journey of sorts for Stolley, who covered the assassination in Dallas for the weekly Life. He said of the issue, "Boy, that tapped something in people."

But Life is in general wary of "looking back" stories. Stolley explained, "Life is sold 60 percent by subscription, and the median age of subscribers is 40. For the 40 percent sold at newsstands, the median age is 30. When I took over, I decided to head it for the younger group, figuring 40-year-olds will read a magazine edited for 30-year-olds, but the reverse is probably not true."

To a degree, Stolley said, the new Life's biggest competitor is the old Life. There has been "some disappointment" among older readers who expect Life to be a bit more, well, Life-like. Said Stolley, "I get lots of letters—'Why don't you tell us what happened to so-and-so you did a story on back in 1968?' But half our readers couldn't care less."

While insisting that Life will never be a big-page People, Stolley acknowledges that People (circulation 2.75 million) has had "an impact on American journalism that we're just beginning to understand."

He interprets the direction of the new Life as a return to the Life of the '50s and '60s, with copious photos and "text kept to a minimum." And he insisted, "I cast People in the mold of the earlier Life . . . Am I making a copy of a copy of a copy? I don't know."

While ruffling a few feathers, Stolley said, People gave birth to a new kind of journalism—USA Today, television's Entertainment Tonight—and also influenced traditional newspapers. "The gossip column has been reinvented," he noted, "and there's a far greater pictorial approach to news" in today's newspapers.

None of this distresses Stolley particularly. "People magazine took advantage of a shrinking attention span," he said, "but you can't blame this all on television." There are so many things for people to choose from today—leisure, sports, entertainment—"reading was inevitably going to suffer. But I don't think journalism has suffered," he said.

"People started a huge wave of personality journalism. I was very proud of its success."

I. VOCABULARY

venerable   acknowledge
extravagant   ruffle feathers
wary   distress

152 Popular Writing

II. QUESTIONS ON CONTENT

1. Why is Richard Stolley highly qualified to discuss *People* and *Life* magazines?
2. What, according to Stolley, are some important differences between these two magazines? Which do you think he prefers to manage?
3. Stolley also discusses some differences between the old and new *Life*. What are they?
4. How does Stolley explain the folding of the old *Life?* The success of *People?*
5. Why is Stolley hopeful about the future of general-interest magazines like *People* and *Life?*
6. What, according to Stolley, is personality journalism? How do you think it has influenced television programming and traditional newspapers?

III. QUESTIONS ON FORM

1. Why is the title appealing?
2. This essay takes the form of an interview. Does Beyette present the interview in an informative and interesting manner? Would some other method of presenting the subject be more effective? Explain.
3. The primary mode of organization in this essay is comparison and contrast. Locate at least two examples of this mode. What other modes are used?
4. What transitional word is used to indicate contrasts between *People* and *Life?*
5. This selection contains a large number of short paragraphs, some as short as one sentence. Find some of them and explain what purpose they serve.

IV. SUGGESTIONS FOR WRITING

1. Define and compare, using specific examples or illustrations, the A and B personality in public life.
2. If, you were managing editor of *Life,* which A personality would you most want to feature? How would you present this personality?
3. Compare and contrast two general-interest magazines, other than *People* and *Life,* with respect to their presentation of the lives of celebrities.
4. If you read *People* or *Life,* explain why this magazine appeals to you.
5. Agree or disagree with Stolley's opinion that today's young people have a renewed interest in and appreciation of the visual, particularly in photography.
6. Defend or criticize Stolley's opinion that the traditional newspaper today, with its emphasis on hard-news coverage, has not suffered from personality journalism.

Magazine Runs Hydrogen Bomb Diagram

Associated Press
9/17/80

A diagram and explanation of how a hydrogen, or thermonuclear, bomb is detonated will appear in the October issue of *Fusion* magazine.

The author of the article, entitled "The MIRV Concept and the Neutron Bomb," is Nevada physicist Friedwardt Winterberg, according to the *Peninsula Times Tribune* of Palo Alto, Calif. The newspaper article did not explain the connection between the neutron weapon and hydrogen bombs.

The newspaper obtained subscription copies of the 175,000-circulation magazine from area readers. Winterberg, a professor of physics at the Desert Research Institute of the University of Nevada at Reno, is a pioneer in research on nuclear fusion, in which two lightweight atoms are forced to combine, producing one heavier atom and energy. In addition to weapons use, scientists are attempting to harness the process to provide a cheap and nonpolluting source of electrical power.

"I have never been exposed to any scientific 'secrets' and reject any claims that there are such secrets known only to a few chosen people," Winterberg says in the article. "The public should know the basic principles underlying these concepts without which a rational disarmament discussion is impossible."

Winterberg pointed out that the article doesn't explain how "the fusion trigger is assembled. . . ,"although diagrams for an H-bomb and a neutron weapon accompany the Winterberg article.

A neutron weapon is designed to produce energy mainly as radiation rather than blast. The government has proposed it as a means of stopping a possible Soviet invasion of Europe without causing excessive property damage to non-Communist territory.

Robert Duff, director of the office of classification for the Department of Energy in Washington, D.C., told the newspaper he had not seen the article. But he said the DOE would have no comment on how important the information in the article might be. "Our policy is not to comment on things like this for publication."

Publication of the article comes one year after the publication in the *Peninsula Times Tribune* and elsewhere of an article by local computer programmer Charles Hansen on how a nuclear, or atomic, bomb functions.

The federal government attempted to stop publication of a similar article in the *Progressive,* a monthly based in Madison, Wisc., but later dropped a court case when Hansen's material was published.

Reprinted by permission of The Associated Press.

I. VOCABULARY

detonate
rational

II. QUESTIONS ON CONTENT

1. Why did Winterberg write an article on the hydrogen bomb? Do you agree with the reasons he gave? Why or why not?
2. Why do you think *Fusion* magazine published the article and diagrams? Was their decision, in your opinion, justified?
3. Why did DOE refuse to comment on Winterberg's article? What do you think is their reason for this policy?
4. Do you share the opinion of The Associated Press that the intended publication of Winterberg's article is newsworthy? Explain.

III. QUESTIONS ON FORM

1. What is Winterberg's aim in writing on the hydrogen bomb? What general form of discourse reflects this aim?
2. What mode is mainly used to unify this news story?
3. Winterberg was not interviewed about his forthcoming article. Should he have been? By whom?
4. Why do you think Winterberg decided to publish his article in a magazine rather than in a newspaper?

IV. SUGGESTIONS FOR WRITING

1. Defend or attack Winterberg's decision to publish his article in order to encourage rational disarmament discussion.
2. Define the term "scientific secret" and develop your definition by examples and illustrations of scientific knowledge that you believe should be kept top secret.
3. Agree or disagree with the position that the federal government has the right to halt publication of scientific or other writing that is or may be harmful to the national interest.
4. Write your own explanation of how a hydrogen bomb is exploded.
5. Compare and contrast the hydrogen and neutron bombs.

> Distinguished Professor of English at Hunter College, CUNY, since 1979, **Alfred Kazin** is a writer, anthology editor, and prominent literary critic. His works include the influential *On Native Grounds* (1942) *A Walker in the City* (1951), and *New York Jew* (1978). His most read book is *An American Procession* (Knopf, 1984).

American Writing Now

Alfred Kazin

Well over 40,000 books were published in the United States last year. No one can blame the *New York Times Book Review*, *The New Republic*, the *New York Review of Books*, certainly not the fragmentary book supplements indifferently included by Sunday newspapers in Chicago, Washington, San Francisco, for commenting on few of these books and for listing just a handful. Editors and reviewers have their own tastes; New York sophisticates are not more likely to see, much less to discuss, a book of western history published by the University of Montana Press than *Penthouse, Hustler, Screw*, etc. are to publish a serious review of some new edition of Sigmund Freud.

Like so much in American life, the book world is big, busy, commercial, driven; not likely to be too aware of its compulsiveness, special interests, many blinders. If complaints are made adjacent to the publishing world, they are made by a few writers and still independent publishers about the increasing domination of the trade by toy companies and the margarine trust. If complaints are made about the state of American writing, they are usually aired in small academic quarterlies by "experimental" writers whose most notable trait, as Edmund Wilson said of Cyril Connolly, is "that whether it's peace or war, Cyril complains it keeps him from writing."

So much in American cultural life now depends on money from the government, the conglomerates, the foundations, that I could reel off examples of commercialization and stop in perfect satisfaction. In good populist fashion I could locate in the big money the prime reason why there are so few real bookstores left even in New York that the Columbia University bookstore is now another Barnes and Noble supermarket featuring paperbacks and best sellers. Nor can we forget the unequaled oppression suffered by upper-bourgeois and professional women with tenured husbands who have rallied to the support of Marilyn French's *The*

Alfred Kazin, "American Writing Now," the *New Republic,* October 18, 1980. Reprinted by permission of the author.

Woman's Room (2.7 million in paperback), and Judy Blume's *Wifey* (3.5 million). Judith Krantz three months before the March 9 publication of *Princess Daisy* earned nearly five million dollars. I open a press release about Erich Segal's new blockbuster," 10 years after *Love Story, Man, Woman and Child,* to learn the publication plans for this story of a loving marriage on the brink of tragedy; 200,000 copies on the first printing, $200,000 initial advertising budget. The book is already a Literary Guild alternate, a Doubleday Book Club selection, a Reader's Digest Condensed Book Club selection, a Family Circle excerpt. Foreign language rights have been sold for "record figures" to France, Germany, Italy, Denmark, Portugal, Spain.

Which goes to show you—what? Nothing we do not already know about "the feminine readers who control the destinies of so many novels," as *Harper's* noted on declining *Sister Carrie* in 1900, nothing new about the lure of the big buck in publishing as in academia, the meat business, the David Merrick business. Do any of these stray items explain why you will almost never see a grown-up man in business carrying even a best seller? Why college students are obliged to "explicate" James Joyce and Ezra Pound without knowing where a sentence should end—or begin? Why American publishers are so ruthless about remaindering their books? Why the paperback industry, pulping books the second they cease to be blockbusters," resembles nothing so much as the meat factory in Upton Sinclair's *The Jungle?*

The million-dollar advances and earnings, the money-mindedness that leaves its grease stain on every discussion of a "popular" book (and of a markedly unpopular one)—these, along with the widespread contempt for politics, the breakdown of intellectual authority that gives every sexual and ethnic faction the brief authority of anger, are not just symptoms of some profound cultural malaise—they are the malaise. The malaise is the new book supermarkets that will give no earnest young reader a chance to discover anything unexpected; the magazines and book supplements that accept "cultural comment" only when written in a snappy prose whose function is to startle the reader rather than to inform him; the English departments featuring the triumph of "deconstructionism" over some helpless poem—and this to captive audiences of graduate students whose only chance to get an assistantship at Upper Wyoming State and to mark 300 themes a week is to imitate this fictitious superiority of "creative" critics over the poems they discuss.

Our literary culture is in the same disarray as our politics, or rather our lack of politics and its replacement by mob-mindedness. Factionalism rules the roost; the most desperate ignorance and cruelty have to be heard out with respect; ideologies are as rampant as cancer cures. New wars of religion are upon us, and intolerance rules. This country is going through the profound inner crisis that Marx and Henry Adams foretold: the technology of the future is already here and has outrun our existing social and economic relations. "The history of an epoch," said Einstein, "is the history of its instruments." Frightened of our instruments, yet increasingly dependent on them, we live intellectually from crisis to crisis, hand to mouth. We have no believable goals for our society or for ourselves. If books are more and more produced simply as commodities, just like movies, it is because books even for the minuscule number of Americans that regularly buy them tend to be diet books, self-help books, information manuals, almanacs, thrillers.

Of course film has largely usurped the inevitability of narrative that used to belong to the novel. But as that peculiarly incisive novelist, V. S. Nipaul, says in a wonderful essay on Conrad,

> More and more today, writers' myths are about the writers themselves: the work has become less obtrusive. The great societies that produced the great novels of the past have cracked. . . . The novel as a form no longer carries conviction. Experimentation, not aimed at the real difficulties, has corrupted response. The novelist, like the painter, no longer recognizes his interpretive function; he seeks to go beyond it; and his audience diminishes. And so the world we inhabit, which is always new, goes by unexamined, made ordinary by the camera, unmeditated on; and there is no one to awaken us to a sense of true wonder.

To be sure, there are many good and even valuable books that sell—even by scholars who seek to define our crises and awkwardly chart the inhuman future. Scholarly university presses can at least overlook some, not all, of the terrors of the marketplace and have written a bright chapter in our book history. More good and bad books are published than ever; there are more real and quack publishers; as there are more readers, more "successful" personalities to celebrate in our popular magazines, more facts on file.

When I think of the influence on American life of our two greatest literary periods—the 1850s and the 1920s—of Emerson, Thoreau, Twain, Dreiser, Mencken, Hemingway, Fitzgerald, Faulkner, Edmund Wilson—my complaint is not just that the good books have so little lasting reverberation, but that our many splendid talents don't have the scope in which to exercise influence. They seem to be part of the drift instead of exercising some mastery.

What is ominous about our literary state is that so much is accepted as ad hoc, temporary, spasmodic—and so has to be "sensational" in order to show some effect. American writing, featuring so many "generation crises," leaping off the front pages with personality stars who are such for a month, fiction written from any sexual or ethnic complaint, resembles a parade in the rain. Nothing lasts. I am not so foolhardy as to pretend that I know what lasts—that I can analyze to the depths what has no depth. Scott Fitzgerald, as his friend Edmund Wilson laughed, couldn't spell. Fitzgerald has lasted. He predicted it, for "the stamp that goes into my books so that people can read it blind like Braille." Whatever the stamp is that made *Gatsby* last for all its plotfulness, *An American Tragedy* for all its barbaric epithets, *The Sound and the Fury* for all its obsessive family matter, Frost for all his sententiousness, Stevens for all his contemplative coldness, I am quite sure that most of our leading novelists and poets just now do not have it.

One reason may be the inability to imagine the full impact of the technological storm on our mental life. Tom Wolfe is a very clever journalist, as audience-minded as a strip teaser, and has written his most serious book, about the astronauts, in *The Right Stuff*. I am properly impressed with all his research, his sense of what is new and urgent about the condition of being an astronaut; I recognize the effort of his highly pepped-up prose to convey the danger, the thrill, above all the science, of being an astronaut. Wolfe knows what is going on in the remotest air fields and space stations; his style captures the rassmatazz, the "spritz," as stand-up comics used to call it, the frenetic flow and delirium of a special way of flying, talking, living.

But from the title down, all *The Right Stuff* says about the inner world of astronauts is that they have to show the "right stuff"—to be the super elite that so few can join. Wolfe is satisfied to show how the men—and their wives—respond to this unusual pressure, to show some extra manliness. Even when we grant that this world is entirely new to everyone, especially to the astronauts, the psychology of the book is military. We suspect that human beings in solitude and danger are more complex than this, and above all less chatty. Wolfe is an understandably conceited fellow with this big story and we respond to his assurance. But the only motivations he can explore are those that the astronauts officially know.

The rocket world, like everything excessive and super-mechanical laid on us just now, may be too serious a subject for journalists to dress up as literature. Wolfe can hardly be blamed if he thinks "literature" is old-fashioned. Only a journalist has the drive, the obstinacy, the encouragement from his publisher to do a book like *The Right Stuff*. The most ambitious imaginative work to deal with technology in our lives, Thomas Pynchon's *Gravity's Rainbow*, significantly became just another item in the academic department of "absurdity." Pynchon, unlike most literary fellows, at least majored in science, which may be why, like the cultural historian Jacques Barzun, he looks on science as "the great entertainment." Pynchon may just be a promising candidate for immortality because he is able to infuriate American big shots incapable of thinking an inch beyond their personal importance. The writer's advisory committee to the Pulitzer Prizes, which recommended *Gravity's Rainbow* for the fiction prize in 1974, was overruled rudely by a *Wall Street Journal* editor higher up on the Pulitzer totem pole; no fiction prize was awarded that year. He explained, with some irritation, that he couldn't even read the damned thing.

We are reminded of the glorious days when *Moby Dick* was proclaimed a book "for bedlam," *Huckleberry Finn* "fit only for the slums," *The Waste Land* "a hoax." After all, John S. Sumner and the Society for the Suppression of Vice managed to make even Dreiser's *The Genius* interesting by suppressing it. Nothing is now suppressible or censorable. Our literary thinking is so much geared to the hourly crisis that vulgarities like Joseph Heller's *Good As Gold* are indulged because *Catch-22* became a byword for our anxious belief that nothing works. All is irrational. The fatalism of the man in the street, that perennial victim, has at last been matched by the cynicism of what are called "top intellectuals." So much alienation from American life is understandable—after all, what is a system for if not to satisfy us without limit? But when our precious alienation becomes abrasive at the expense of every bourgeois but ourselves, it becomes just another piece of American claptrap.

Since the future is plainly here, and we cannot understand all it is doing to us—even that may not be the point that some far-off generation will know about us—it may just be the mysticism of knowledge that so much nescience confronts us with. "It is because so much happens," Joe Christmas's grandmother lamented in *Light in August*. "Too much happens." We are no longer sure just where all this is happening. So a whole dimension of present literature is occupied by nostalgia.

Although there is a marked decline in history courses, in the sense of the past, history has become the sense of crisis, of a civilization in decline, of what one might well call the evaporation of history. Too many zigzag lines on our historical graphs lead on the one hand to instant history, on the other to the idealization of the frontier, the John Wayne syndrome so weepily exploited by Joan Didion in nicely simple books like *Slouching Towards Bethlehem*. Nothing historical exists now for its own sake. Our sense of history is entirely contemporary, as witness Barbara Tuchman's *A Distant Mirror*, which is not about the distant Middle Ages but about the chain of wars that along with technology as a form of aggression rushing out of two terrible wars has so clearly subdued our minds.

The writer's problem is that we are locked into "today"—conceptually, superconsciously. We cannot see beyond the whirlwind of change in which we spin round and round like the lovers in Dante's hell whose greatest pain was to remember past happiness, and so could not blame their temptation. We are waiting on history to carry us to some next stage of consciousness as once people waited on God to accomplish just that. But books are not written by history. You have to be strong in the legs to write, said Henry Thoreau. That was spiritual self-confidence.

Yet there is no country in the world with the buoyancy, the inborn sense of freedom, the explosive amount of universal material that we present to the world as the great modern experiment—and feel in ourselves. It is our very disorder and factionalism, the fact that so many Americans have nothing in common but their living on this continent, even the violence and insecurity endemic in our shifting American lives, that in the past produced

160 Popular Writing

writers who were famous—for having nothing in common with each other. American disorder is our strength as well as our dismay. But what we never felt before, never, never! was the sense that nothing is so real to us as ourselves, that there is so little to respect, that we have so few dreams.

I. VOCABULARY

conglomerates	factionalism	reverberation	alienation
commercialization	ideology	spasmodic	bourgeois
academia	rampant	epithet	nescience
blockbuster	usurped	sententiousness	syndrome
malaise	incisive	frenetic	endemic
disarray		obstinacy	

II. QUESTIONS ON CONTENT

1. How does the publishing world reflect American life?
2. What signs are provided that American cultural life is declining? Can you suggest any others?
3. What reasons does Kazin give for the confusion in American literary culture? Why does this situation disturb him?
4. Why does the author refer to American literature of the 1850s and the 1920s? Which of these authors have you read?
5. What fault does the writer find with Tom Wolfe's *The Right Stuff?* Why does he praise Thomas Pynchon's *Gravity's Rainbow?*
6. What problem does the writer face today? What solution, if any, does Kazin provide to this problem?

III. QUESTIONS ON FORM

1. What does the comment on literary taste in the opening paragraph on page 155 tell you about the relationship between a writer and his audience?
2. What evidence is provided in paragraph three on page 155 to support the opinion that the book world is highly commercial? Is this evidence convincing?
3. On page 156, paragraph two Kazin describes the "profound cultural malaise" in America today, but he does not elaborate on any of its indications. Why?
4. What is the topic sentence of paragraph three, page 156?
5. Comment on the meaning and effectiveness of the following phrases: "grease stain" (page 156, paragraph two), "as audience-minded as a strip teaser" (page 158, paragraph one), "Pulitzer totem pole" (page 158, paragraph three).

6. What is the tone of the essay? Kazin uses many difficult words; how does his diction contribute to this tone?
7. On page 158, paragraph one Kazin describes Tom Wolfe's style of writing. How would you describe Kazin's style? How does this style reflect his tone?
8. This is a persuasive essay. Has the author succeeded in persuading you of his central idea? Why or why not?

IV. SUGGESTIONS FOR WRITING

1. Describe your reading habits.
2. Define the term "popular" book or "best seller" and explain fully why a a particular work of prose fiction you have read was or is a popular book.
3. Choose a fictional work you have read by one of the nineteenth or twentieth century American authors mentioned on page 157, paragraph three and discuss the reasons for its lasting value.
4. Discuss some of the ways in which publishers promote books as commodities.
5. On page 156, paragraph three the author declares that "We have no believable goals for our society or for ourselves." Agree or disagree.
6. Analyze the main reasons why people read popular fiction. Consider such motives as pleasure, the desire to rise in society, the need for moral guidance, the search for personal meaning, and the need to reinforce beliefs already held.

Herbert Mitgang is a journalist and author. In the 1960s and 1970s he was a reporter, editorial writer, and member of the editorial board of the *New York Times*. In addition, he is a lecturer, writer, and producer of film documentaries, as well as author of several novels and nonfiction works.

Average U.S. Author's Writings Bring In Less Than $5,000 a Year

Herbert Mitgang

Despite the big movie and paperback deals that convey an impression of glamour and prosperity, the average author in the United States doesn't live on Easy Street. He or she earns less than $5,000 a year from writing, and has to make ends meet with the help of other jobs—or a working spouse. These

Copyright © 1981 by The New York Times Company. Reprinted by permission.

are among the results reported in a major pioneering study to be issued today by Columbia University's Center for the Social Sciences about the economics, and frustrations, of professional authors in this country.

"On the average," the social scientists say, "writing yields little economic return."

Based on responses from 2,239 authors producing books in every field of fact and fiction, who were pledged anonymity, "The Columbia University Survey of American Authors" is a 150-page document that is the most detailed account ever made of how writers earn a living, or don't, and yet survive. For analytical purposes, an author was defined as a contemporary American writer who had had at least one book published.

While generally gloomy, the survey also notes that there is a great gulf—there are writers living on the poverty level and in the top 10 percent, making $45,000 or more a year, and the top five percent, with incomes of $80,000 or beyond.

"It is plain that the average authors of published books eke out a modest income from their writing, approximately $4,775 a year, or about two-thirds of the maximum amount paid to individuals on Social Security," said Robert K. Merton, special service professor and university professor emeritus, who collaborated on the study with Dr. Paul W. Kingston and Prof. Jonathan R. Cole. It was prepared for the Authors Guild Foundation, a nonprofit group, and has been in the works for nearly two years.

These are the main income findings:

¶ The representative (that is, median) author in the 1979 sample year had an hourly writing income of $4.90—and half of the authors had hourly incomes less than this amount.

¶ Professional authors survived because almost half of them held paid jobs in addition to working on their writing. Those holding jobs had writing incomes of about $2,600 a year, which they attributed to a lack of adequate—and preferred—freelance time.

¶ Of full-time authors (defined as those who held no other jobs and devoted at least 25 hours a week to writing), 31 percent made less than $5,000 from writing; two-thirds of the full-time authors did not reach $20,000.

¶ Of recently published authors (whose books appeared between 1977 and 1980), half earned less than $5,000 in 1979.

¶ Incomes fluctuate greatly from year to year. In 1979, 5 percent of the authors earned about 10 times as much from their writing as in the year before, while another 5 percent earned only one-fifth as much as the year before. A quarter of the authors earned five times as much from writing in their "best year" in the past as in 1979.

The "average" earnings figure was pulled up by the writing income of those authors in the very top percentiles who made high five-figure amounts from their book royalties and subsidiary income.

Fair Incomes, Other Sources

The total economic picture changed sharply for most authors when their other personal and family incomes were added to their writing incomes. While only one of 10 authors made a fair living from writing, nevertheless the majority did well because "they are deployed in non-writing jobs which produce substantially higher incomes."

Thus, authors reported median personal incomes from all other sources of $27,000. Such total income came from writing plus professional payments, salaries, return from investments (including those jointly held with a spouse), pensions and Social Security. The median family total for all authors was $38,000. This represented the total of personal income plus a spouse's personal income.

Half of the authors in the survey had spouses holding down jobs. The big gap between total personal and total family income reflected the contributions of husbands or wives. Authors' husbands had median incomes of $28,000; authors' wives had median incomes of just under $4,000.

What types of authors are there in the United States? The social scientists broke them down into five categories:

1. Committed full-timer. These authors spend at least 25 hours a week on writing and don't hold any other paid job (though in some cases they earn related income from editing, translation and the like). Thirty-five percent of all authors are such full-timers.

2. Limited full-timer. These authors report spending no more than 25 hours a week at writing and also hold no other regular paid job. Eighteen percent in the survey are here.

3. Committed part-timer. These authors (another 13 percent) hold paid jobs other than freelance writing, yet average 25 or more hours a week writing. In effect, these authors maintain two jobs.

4. Intermittent part-timer. Members of this group (22 percent) hold paid jobs other than freelance writing, and devote a smaller but still considerable number of hours each week to their writing.

5. Marginal part-timer. These authors (12 percent) hold other paid jobs unconnected with the writing craft and put in fewer than 10 hours a week on writing.

No Judgment on Seriousness

"This categorization is only intended to indicate a rough sense of the extent to which authors are devoted to the occupation of book writing," the survey notes. "It does not imply that the authors who give relatively little time to writing are any less serious about writing as an artistic, creative endeavor."

These categories are not rigid, and authors float both ways. One author commented on the questionnaire filled out in the survey, "I work (that is, hold another job) only when I have to." Just a few months earlier, he would have been considered a full-timer; when the survey was made, he had become a part-timer. Change from part-time to full-time status was common.

The scientists stressed that writing was an "occupation" in which a large majority of authors—70 percent—were actively engaged in some other paid work. What kind of other jobs do these active part-time authors hold?

The largest number—38 percent—taught in universities. "This is not surprising because colleges provide a congenial environment," the survey found, "including flexible hours, time off between semesters, library and other research facilities and, sometimes, collegial encouragement."

A Group Called 'Professionals'

About 20 percent fell into a disparate group called "professional," which included lawyers, doctors and clergy. The combined groupings of editor-publisher, public relations and journalist came to 21 percent (journalists accounted for only 5 percent of this total, disputing the notion that many are writing books at night).

How do authors feel about the jobs they hold to sustain their writing careers? Asked, "If you could at least match your present total income by writing full-time, would you drop your other work?," almost half (46 percent) responded "yes," and 22 percent replied, "possibly." In short, they'd rather support themselves by writing on their own.

The authors did not agree about the value of outside jobs. Two novelists of wide reputation expressed opposite views. One said, "Writers should have a job; writing isn't a job." She believes that work on her job helps to keep her mentally sharp and in touch with how others think. However, she adds, her particular job leaves her a good deal of writing time. A second novelist says, "Other work is death to writing; a writer needs to be obsessive." Most part-time writers agreed with the second novelist.

The survey disclosed a fairly clear relationship between financial success and types of writing. Genre fiction (such as romance, detective, western, Gothic—as distinct from general adult fiction) turned out to be the most lucrative. At the successful extreme, 20 percent of genre fiction writers earned incomes over $50,000; yet, some 40 percent earned under $5,000.

Focusing on those authors who earned less than $2,500 in 1979 from writing, the survey found that 55 percent were poets or academically oriented nonfiction writers. In the median range of about $5,000 a year could be found authors of adult nonfiction, how-to books, general adult fiction and children's books.

Other factors were examined in the nationwide survey.

"Some might suppose that authors who live and work in New York, the publishing capital of the United States, would do better financially, but this is not the case," the survey disclosed. No matter where situated, "most authors earn very little indeed." It was found that among the small group of authors earning upward of $50,000, more Californians turned up than those from any other region.

Although income was unrelated to the social origins or educational achievement, women authors earned a median of $4,000 as against $5,000 for men. In the higher brackets, too, men had a slight edge of about 6 percent more income.

A Look at Best Sellers

The Columbia sociologists also looked at the "few percent" of authors who had a book reach one of the top 15 positions on The New York Times Book Review best-seller lists in either 1978 or 1979. Here is where "the few" sometimes reached the $100,000 mark "though not commonly the million-dollar deals which receive so much publicity."

Most best-selling authors did not emerge suddenly. The great majority had a considerable record of publications—70 percent had at least five books to their credit. About half of the authors on the best-seller lists had been on one of the lists in the past. The great majority of best-selling authors are full-timers (80 percent). A similar majority (85 percent) write at least 20 hours a week on average, and 40 percent write at least 40 hours a week. With one exception in the survey, all expect to continue writing.

Peter S. Prescott, president of the Authors Guild Foundation, an offshoot of the 6,000-member Authors Guild, said that the foundation-backed study served as a corrective to "misapprehensions" by the public and, for the first time, showed how the majority of hard-pressed authors in America really survived.

I. VOCABULARY

Easy Street	subsidiary	dispute
anonymity	intermittent	sustain
eke	marginal	obsessive
freelance	categorization	genre
royalties	lucrative	misapprehension

II. QUESTIONS ON CONTENT

1. Why is this study of the average author in the United States important?
2. What major conclusion does the survey present? Did this surprise you? Explain.

3. On what sources, other than earnings from writing, do most authors depend for their income?
4. How did the two reputable novelists disagree about the value of holding a job while writing? Which one do you agree with? Why?
5. Which type of writing did the survey find to be most profitable financially? Why do you think this is so?

III. QUESTIONS ON FORM

1. What indications are there that this selection is a straight news story rather than an essay? Consider aim, audience, tone, and style.
2. Statistics are used throughout the selection as evidence to support the chief conclusions about the economic status of writers. How effective are these figures? Do they detract from the reader's interest?
3. In elaborating on the findings of the study, Mitgang follows its collaborators by using illustration, definition, and classification. Give one example of each of these modes.

IV. SUGGESTIONS FOR WRITING

1. Explore the reasons why most American authors, despite their low personal income from writing, continue to write.
2. Do you want to be a professional writer? Why or why not?
3. Discuss the traits or qualities that you believe are needed to become a serious writer of fiction.
4. Should professional writers be subsidized?
5. Several recent surveys of the American book reading public have revealed that people read about twice as much fiction as nonfiction. Explain why.

A former professor in the School of Communications at the University of Houston, **Carol Thurston** is a public relations and market research consultant. She is currently at work on a book on popular romances. **Barbara Doscher** is Associate Professor of Voice in the College of Music at the University of Colorado at Boulder. She is presently writing a textbook on anatomy and acoustics for teachers of singing.

Supermarket Erotica:
'Bodice-Busters' put Romantic Myths to Bed

Carol Thurston and Barbara Doscher

Much comment on paperback romances has appeared in the popular press of late. Critics on the culture beat alternately call the books the marketing success of the decade for the troubled publishing business or deride them as either "bodice rippers" or "virtuous virginals." Successful or sleazy, the books accounted for almost 40 percent of the mass-market paperbacks printed in the United States in 1980, bringing publishers an estimated $250 million.

The bodice rippers, or busters, depending on the whimsy of the critic-writer, get their labels either from the bodice-ripping sexual encounters they portray or the hyperventilation readers are said to suffer while reading about them. In stark contrast, the virtuous virginals generally feature saccharine-sweet, submissive heroines, chaste unto their inevitable marriages when, in a euphemism for sexual intercourse, the heroes transport them "up to the stars."

No one knows for sure what share of the lucrative market each type controls today, but throughout the 1970s, the erotic historical romance—the bodice ripper—was the unquestioned queen of the supermarket and newsstand. So much so, editors admit, that some of the tasteless tomes now on the stands were acquired about three years ago, when the market was so hot they were buying every manuscript they could get their hands on. And they agree that these inferior books may have contributed to the recent decline in bodice-buster sales.

Critics, especially feminist critics, tend to lump all paperback romances together and take great delight in aiming potshots at the archetypal submissive-pure heroine and macho-stud hero or in attacking the whole bunch as soft porn. At the same time, they dismiss readers of such drivel as mindless drones living in a fantasy world. But we recently looked at more than fifty erotic historical romances published between 1964 and 1981, and came to a different conclusion.

We found not simpering acquiescence but vehement protest against unequal treatment. The heroine of Lynn Bartlett's *Courtly Love* rails, "A woman has as much pride, as much honor as a man, but she is treated as if she had none." Over and over, we saw a drive for personal independence so strong that marriage seemed too compromising. "Ye may have my love, my

Copyright © 1982, The Progressive, Inc. Reprinted by permission from *The Progressive,* Madison, Wisconsin.

body, my undivided attention . . . even my money!" says Scotswoman Janet Leslie in Bertrice Small's *The Kadin*. "But I'll nae wed again! It's extremely pleasant being your mistress, but 'tis even more pleasant being my own mistress." In short, we found that most of the books we looked at did not fit the mold—did not portray submissive women or focus only on degrading sexual acts. And the readers we queried appreciated the difference.

Recently asked to summarize the advances made by the women's movement in the last decade, Gloria Steinem responded, "We've come to understand that it is the power to choose that is important, not what we choose." Jeanne Williams, writing as Megan Castell, says much the same thing in *Queen of a Lonely Country*, a story set in Fifteenth Century Wales:

"Till now there has not been an hour in all these passing years, Cerri, when I would not have gladly made you my wife and mistress of Heriot. You know that very well!"

"As I know there has not been one moment when you would have left me my own person."

"Yes," he said, mocking, "You must be queen. Even if it is a lonely country where beasts and birds are your subjects along with those who serve you. . . ."

Cerridwen stood quiet and straight, unmoved by his attack. "Sir Rhys, my old friend-enemy, you have forgotten the loneliest country of all."

"What?" he challenged.

"The country of the self." She smiled and watched him with her sea-variable eyes until he scowled and looked away. "And there I will rule. If the price of that is living lonely, then I will live alone."

"Rubbish!"

"There have always been women who ruled themselves," she returned equably. "Men forced them to be goddesses, saints, or witches, or they took refuge on islands or in nunneries. Men have never known whether to worship or destroy them, and so have done both." She laughed and turned to Gillian. "But I have hope, my dear. Perhaps you, or at least your daughters, can love a man and be yourselves, too. Perhaps you won't have to rule to keep from being devoured or broken."

"It is not in nature," Rhys growled.

"Nor is it in nature—except in man's—to clip the wings of swans to bind them to earth and your territory."

Historical settings seem to give authors a chance to send messages about contemporary women's issues, and also to imply that the drive for individual dignity and respect has motivated women for hundreds of years.

The determination to be accepted in one's own right, not defined by sex, marriage, or family lineage, is a common theme in erotic historical romances, as in Marilyn Harris's *Women of Eden:* "What have you always wanted, from the very beginning, John, even when you were a little boy?"

Failing to elicit a response, she provided him with one. "Freedom, dignity, the right to pursue your own destiny, the opportunity to make those decisions that affect and influence your spirit and soul and body." She paused. "We are not different from you, John. Oh, our physiology is different, but that's all. And the difference does nothing to alter our hearts or our minds or our needs. For years, centuries, we've tried to convince each other that it does. But it doesn't, not in any fundamental or profound way."

Another cornerstone of the feminist movement, the belief that women must have control over their own bodies, also crops up again and again. Historical romances have a mixed record on the issue, but we did find many attempts to come up with a successful contraceptive, from the special herbs of harem women in the Middle East to the sponges of the brothel ladies in the old American West. All were attempts to escape physical domination by men.

In Bertrice Small's *Skye O'Malley,* a Catholic nun mounts an especially strong attack against sexual dependence. She acts as midwife to her sister (Skye) twice in ten months and then tells her she must take an herb potion to regulate her fertility. "But doesn't the Church forbid such wicked practices?" she is asked. The nun responds, "The Church has not seen innocent babies dying of starvation because there are too many mouths in the family to feed. What do the well-fed priests and bishops, snug in their stone houses on this snowy night, know of these poor souls and their endless torments? The innocent and superstitious poor I offer a 'tonic' to help them regain their strength. If they knew what I offer them they would not take it because they truly believe the Church's threat of eternal damnation. You, sister, are not so foolish."

The bodice rippers, as expected, vend fairly explicit sex, but always in romanticized language, as in male author Elizabeth Bright's description of multiple orgasm in *Passion Heirs:* "The flames burst inward and upward. She gasped and clutched his arms, hearing him say, 'Godalmighty, what a woman you are,' just before she again erupted, harder and longer than the other times. . . . There were times after that when she wished that glowing spot, the ember of her passion, would go out. But it would not. As long as he remained hard within her and she could move her hips against him, she continued to erupt into flames which lit her inner explosions."

Heroines in bodice busters know they have sexual needs as strong as their lovers', and they are not ashamed to seek satisfaction. Oral sex came up in almost half of the books we read; the heroine had intercourse before marriage in two-thirds of the stories, and with more than one man in almost half. She married more than once in a third of the books and was sexually enterprising outside her marriage in one out of five.

All this sexual activity by the protagonists smacks more of contemporary society than of Victorian England, in which so many of the books are set. Such behavior is so common, in fact, that the stories seem to be telling readers that it is to be expected, and normal, and not in conflict with the roles of good wife and mother assumed later on.

It would be easy to fit all sexually descriptive passages into some category of pornography. But if erotica is a "celebration of the body" (Gloria Steinem) and pornography is degrading to females, many of these books are both.

Still, erotica always wins the day because the heroine overcomes degradation and finds a partner with whom she can "celebrate." That is the overall impression the reader is left with—that women who insist on self-determination, independence, and respect are "winners." Rather than the abductions, rapes, and betrayals common to the genre, it is the overcoming of these misadventures that is the central focus of the stories.

Rapes did occur in about half the books we examined, but in most of those, the hero expressed today's view that rape is a physical and emotional assault, not a sexual act, and certainly not the fault of the woman. To call the readers of these books sick is far from fair, in our opinion. Such episodes portray the kinds of bodily and psychological threats that women, and especially feminists, now decry. Women's rage at their perceived vulnerability is echoed in the experiences and responses of the heroines of these stories.

In probably the most militantly feminist story we found, Michelle de Winter's *Janine*, the heroine is the captain of a pirate ship who accedes to a captured captain's plea for mercy by demanding that he satisfy her sexually or take his chances with her crew. In the events that follow, she turns the tables on the usual male-dominance scene. He found some difficulty performing under the circumstances: "His face became bathed in perspiration, and trickles rolled down his neck. 'The—the circumstances make it difficult for me. The atmosphere isn't—well, it isn't right for making love. Please be reasonable.'

"Janine looked him up and down slowly, making him even more conscious of his nudity. 'I assume you've been intimate with a number of women on many occasions over the years. Am I correct?'" He had no idea where her question might lead, but was forced to nod agreement. "Surely you never stopped to wonder whether the circumstances were appropriate for the lady. You were interested only in your own pleasure and didn't think of her.' 'But that was different—' 'Nonsense,' she declared, her voice sharp. 'A man has such vanity that he believes a woman will be receptive to him at any time and under any circumstances. Now you begin to know better.'"

In spite of cover illustrations and blurbs, heroes in these books are gentle and sensitive, or if they are not in the beginning, they change as they come to admire and desire the woman of independence and integrity. The macho male patterned after the Steve Morgan of Rosemary Rogers' books has fallen out of favor and now is more likely to be the villain of the piece. Heroes are not ashamed to reveal emotions or admit to limitations. They do not need to dominate; they have a desire to control events, yes (as do the heroines), but a sense of fairness, sexual security, and understanding usually lets them compromise. They admire the high-spirited heroines above all other women, prizing them as sexual partners, as friends, and even as business partners, whether in privateering or cattle ranching.

Since both the heroes and heroines are much more androgynous than romance story stereotypes would suggest, if these portrayals do have any influence on readers' thinking or behavior, it is probably through the redefinition of "masculinity" and "feminity" that pervades the interactions of the characters. The central message in the erotic historical romances rings loud and clear: Macho males and saccharine ingenues are the losers in society.

These stories also suggest that freedom and responsibility are prerequisites for a complete and fulfilling life, regardless of gender. And while the majority of the books we studied conform to a generalized romance story formula, in focusing on the male-female relationship and in portraying the love of the hero as the most important motivation in the heroine's life, the fundamental power relationships between men and women have begun to be changed or at least challenged. The hero's love for the heroine is also the most important element in *his* life, and he often is heard to say that he is not "whole" or complete without her.

Such changes probably have been helped along by the many women authors and editors of romances whose own social views are "feminist" in character. Star Helmer, editor-in-chief at Richard Gallen Books, says, "The reason I got into [editing these kinds of romances] in the first place was because I hoped to achieve some subtle brainwashing for the women's movement. And most of the authors I have worked with have had strong feminist attitudes."

How do these books function for the estimated twenty million women who read them? (Unsubstantiated reports from publishers describe typical readers as women between eighteen and sixty, most in their mid-thirties, with some college education and annual incomes of $20,000 and up.) Psychologists say "nonvisual relationships"—what comes across on the printed page—are more sexually stimulating to women than men. A 1971 study at Purdue University found that women are more aroused than men by erotic writing, especially when the story is removed from reality, in the sense that a fairy tale is. "What seems to be critical in this male-female difference is the extent to which mental processes beyond the purely sensory are engaged," says Glenn Wilson of the University of London Institute of Psychiatry. "The more that imagination is activated by an erotic stimulus, the more it is women who respond." The Purdue researchers concluded that if imagination is such a simple, powerful sexual stimulant, "individual differences in sexuality, such as sex drive and preferred frequency of orgasm, may largely be due to the way we learn to use sexual fantasies."

Certainly there is little doubt that avid readers of erotic historical romances are encountering lots of sexual fantasy. Easy access to these books in supermarkets and drugstores allows many women for the first time to "legitimately" obtain material that is sexually stimulating and informative, and for many this may be their first opportunity to "learn to use sexual fantasy."

Now publishers of the short so-called "category" books report that even their readers want "more sex." (Category books are constructed around highly specific publishers' formulas. Because of both plot and length restrictions, these stories are generally unimaginative and repetitive.) Silhouette Romances editor Karen Solem told writers attending the Romance Writers of America meeting in Houston last June that Silhouette would come out with two new lines: Rendezvous Romances would be short but sexier and Special Editions (which reached bookstores this January) would be longer and sexier. But not too sexy. The author's tipsheet for Rendezvous Romances advises writers that "Sexual encounters—which may include nudity and lovemaking even when the protagonists are not married—should concentrate on highly erotic sensations aroused by the hero's kisses and caresses rather than the mechanics of sex." (Such specifications often leave little for a writer to "create," as with the admonition that, "The hero and heroine meet early in the book and are never apart for more than ten pages. Their involvement with other characters is only for the purpose of moving the story forward.")

The profile we drew of the bodice-ripper heroines was that of the independent "total" woman: passionate lover, wife-confidante, devoted mother, astute businesswoman, and social worker. She merges the virtues of the Gothic heroine and her sexy, "bad-girl" counterpart, with the independence and career expectations of contemporary heroines in mainstream fiction. She reminded us of the women Betty Friedan (in her new book, *The Second Stage*) says the first stage of the feminist movement has produced.

For too long, women who should know better have assumed that the gender-free concepts of equality of opportunity, responsibility, and respect were the exclusive property of a highly educated, liberated minority. Surely the new-era bodice rippers, with or without artistic defects, have helped spread these ideas throughout society. Whether knowingly or not, these books and the feminist movement have been moving toward the same end. Only their audiences have been different.

I. VOCABULARY

romance	sleazy	euphemism	erotic
deride	saccharine	macho	fantasy
bodice	submissive	drivel	acquiesence

rail (v)	cornerstone	stereotype	astute
scowl	protagonist	ingenues	Gothic
equably	androgynous	archetypal	

II. QUESTIONS ON CONTENT

1. What are the "bodice rippers?" The "virtuous virginals"? How are they similar? How do they differ?
2. Why have critics, especially feminist critics, attacked these paperback romances? Do you think these attacks are justified? Explain.
3. What were the heroines of romantic mass-market paperbacks like in the past? How have these heroines changed in the last two decades?
4. What fundamental beliefs of the feminist movement are expressed in recent erotic historical romances? What contribution have these romances made to the movement?
5. What change has taken place in the portrayal of heroes in these romances? How would you explain this change? Do you approve of it? Why or why not?
6. Is there evidence of androgny today in popular arts other than romantic fiction? (Consider, for instance, pop music and such recent entertainers as Boy George, Michael Jackson, Annie Lenox, and Grace Jones.) What does "gender-blending" tell you about our society?

III. QUESTIONS ON FORM

1. What is the thesis of this essay? Where is it stated?
2. What is the function of the first paragraph beyond merely introducing the essay?
3. What modes or patterns of organization are used in paragraph two, page 167? What transitional words signal one of these?
4. What is the purpose of the long quotation from *Queen of a Lonely Country*?
5. Analyze the organization of this essay by identifying the main parts of the essay and indicating how they are related to each other.
6. How do the authors connect the last two paragraphs of the essay?

IV. SUGGESTIONS FOR WRITING

1. Define either "masculinity" or "femininity" and extend your definition with examples or illustrations from your own experience.
2. Describe the macho male and explain why he is or is not a "loser" in today's society.
3. Argue for or against the view that erotic historical romances are soft-core pornography.

174 Popular Writing

4. Analyze the reasons why romance fiction has been booming since the early 1970s and why almost all its readers are women.
5. If you have read any erotic historical romances, explain what you liked about them.
6. Why do you think women need so much fantasy in their lives?
7. *Passion's Heirs* and *Relentless Desires* are two titles of actual romance novels. For 15 minutes in class, compose at least three eye-catching, sexy titles for potential romance novels. Be prepared to defend your choices.

A former college professor who published a book of poetry and a critical study of William Carlos Williams, **Rod Townley** has been a free-lance writer for more than a decade. He has contributed to *TV Guide*, the *Village Voice*, and several poetry anthologies.

Wait Till You Read/See the Book/Show

Rod Townley

Mark Greenberg, a vice president at Warner Books, spotted a scientist on *The Merv Griffin Show* not long ago talking animatedly about how to extend one's life span. Greenberg had a tape of the show sent over and circulated among the decision-makers at Warner. Everyone agreed this guy was dynamite. Just the right person to write a book. But what if he couldn't write?

"So what?" says Greenberg. "We get somebody to write it with him."

It turned out that the scientist, Durk Pearson, could write after all (though he has long worked with coauthor Sandy Shaw). His book, "Life Extension," will be published by Warner this June. As for publicity, says Greenberg, "We'll have him go back on *The Merv Griffin Show,* and other network and syndicated shows."

At a time when, according to one survey, published authors in the U.S. are making an average of $4775 per year from their writing, a tiny number of writers are raking in fortunes, usually with the help of TV deals.

Some of these lucky writers were not writers at all before they signed their hundred-thousand-dollar book contracts. Mark Greenberg freely admits: "We do buy books as a result of premeetings with the author" before the book is written. He and his confreres will even conduct mock television interviews to see how a prospective author will handle himself on talk

Reprinted with permission from *TV Guide*® magazine. Copyright © 1982 by Triangle Publications, Inc., Radnor, Pennsylvania.

shows. "If he performs the way we feel he should," says Greenberg, "then certainly we're going to be very interested in the book. If we find that he's a dud, that will influence our decision on whether we want to purchase that book or not."

Sometimes a tongue-tied would-be author can save his book contract by being properly coached. Greenberg and other media mavens might suggest to him "how he should be answering and reacting . . . and coming up with some jokes and levity."

One Warner author who needed very little coaching is Richard Simmons, the diet guru. He had never written a book when the Warner people spotted him as a guest on the soap *General Hospital* (he played himself); but his hyperactive pep talk approach to dieting made him seem a natural author. Sure enough, "Richard Simmons' Never-Say-Diet Book" became a number-one best seller, and Simmons soon had a TV show of his own.

Novelist/priest Andrew Greeley is another Warner author who, says Greenberg, "is tremendous on television and thus is able to help sell a book." Warner executives did pre-interviews with him before deciding to sign him. Greeley had not yet finished writing "The Cardinal Sins," but his TV presence was so strong that the book was sure to be a winner.

Warner's latest literary luminary is Max Leber, who has a syndicated TV show called *The Corner Drugstore*. He's been signed to write his first book—basically a consumer's guide to pharmaceuticals—and when it comes out next fall, he'll be flogging it on the talk shows.

What often happens with such authors, according to Greenberg, is that they get hired to do regular segments on the shows where they've been guests. After Mary Ellen Pinkham chatted up her "Helpful Hints" book on the talk circuit, *Good Morning America* signed her as a regular. Similarly, Pam Young and her sister, Peggy Jones, coauthors of "Sidetracked Home Executives," did so well promoting their book that they, too, have become regulars on *PM/Evening Magazine*. "And then," says Greenberg, "as a result of being television personalities, they're even better as authors the second time around."

Then there are the specials and TV movies, many of them based on books. Fred Klein, the man in charge of movie and TV tie-ins for Bantam Books, recently scanned an in-house list of "properties" optioned for TV. Among them, "believe it or not," he says, is "My Capitol Secrets," by Rita Jenrette, the ex-wife of the former congressman who bared her soul, and more, in Playboy magazine. ABC is working on the TV-movie.

Another project ("Can you imagine?" he interjects) is "The Book of Lists," which Alan Landsburg is turning into four one-hour specials for CBS. "What they're doing, I'll be damned if I know," says Klein.

Bantam, sometimes known as The House that Jackie Built, is still making money off the late Jacqueline Susann, especially now that a five-hour movie has been made from "Valley of the Dolls." It was broadcast last fall on CBS, with the book's cover displayed in the fade-ins and fade-outs whenever the show cut to commercials. Bantam rushed a quarter-million extra copies of the book onto the stands the week of the broadcast and will doubtless do the same this year when the miniseries is rerun.

Perhaps "maxiseries" would be a more appropriate term to apply to ABC's upcoming 16-hour drama based on Herman Wouk's best seller, "The Winds of War." The titanic project involves a huge cast headed up by Robert Mitchum. Wouk, who did the screenplay himself, has described the task of adaptation as a "careful and brutal compression." It's *only* 16 hours, after all. His compensation is said to be well into the seven-figure range, and that's not counting paperback sales of the novel. The miniseries, predicts one publishing executive, "will shoot that book right to the top of the best-seller list."

Perhaps the year's most unlikely best seller is Evelyn Waugh's subtle and problematic novel "Brideshead Revisited." The miniseries based on it prompted Little, Brown and Company to reissue "Brideshead" and Waugh's other works in snappy new paperbacks, and masses of people have been buying them.

Not always does the course of TV tie-ins run smooth. A couple of years ago, ABC bought a treatment (a several-page summary) of a proposed TV-movie about a newspaper's handling of a homicide story. An editor at Dell liked the idea and hired a writer to turn it into a novel, which was subsequently published in hard cover under the title "Panic on Page One." Another writer, meanwhile, was working up a screenplay, but ABC's producers didn't care for it, so they called in the novelizer Linda Stewart to try, in her words, "to make the screenplay more like the book"—the book that had been based on a TV "treatment" to begin with.

The TV-movie, when it ran, didn't help book sales, partly because, in the view of Chuck Adams, managing editor of Dell, a one-night movie "is virtually useless. You really need the momentum of a series, like a *Shogun*, if you expect to sell anything." (It probably also didn't help that the TV-movie came out with a different title: "City in Fear.")

A personable and exceedingly busy young man up to his elbows in million-dollar deals, Chuck Adams has no qualms about hiring novelizers. Richard Woodley is one of them. He's done 15 novelizations, which he regards as "not worth a lot. I certainly don't see them as works of art." Actually, they're worth up to $10,000 apiece plus a 2 per-cent royalty, and they take only three weeks to do. The scripts he works from, he says frankly, "are terrible."

Although the market for novelizations has declined, those scripts continue being turned into books while making wonderful profits for their publishers. Jove, for instance, has printed several "novels" based on the soap opera *All My Children*. Even *That's Incredible!* has been published in some half-dozen Jove paperbacks so far, replete with anecdotes and photos. The show encourages viewers to write in, and as an enticement will send a free copy of one of the books to anyone who does. Jove donates the books gladly. "It's a wonderful advertisement," says the firm's former editorial director, Bill Gross.

More and more, the line between books and TV properties is becoming blurred. Some projects even start as a joint TV/book concept. *Cosmos*, for instance, the popular PBS science show, was conceived as both a book and a TV series, the one product helping to publicize the other. The results have made the perpetually wonderstruck Carl Sagan a very rich man indeed.

A would-be entrepreneur in this area is David Obst, who was president of the short-lived Simon and Schuster Productions, a grafted offshoot of the publishing house and Paramount Pictures. His object, he says, was "to develop ideas in more than one medium"; his method, "to originate ideas in-house," then go out and find good writers to develop them. The first televised product from S&S (farmed-out to Finnegan Associates as producers) was a little thing called "World War III", a four-hour movie. By the time it appeared on NBC this past winter, a novelization was in supermarkets and bookstores around the country.

Obst's main coup in joint development projects seems to have been to corral popular author Allen Drury and get him to write a novel about the Supreme Court. "Based on a story that we developed with Mr. Drury," says Obst, "it has a very strong dramatic potential." By "dramatic" one understands easily convertible into movie or miniseries.

Unfortunately for S&S, the potential was also evident to Drury, and he pulled out of the deal, even though NBC had made an offer before the book was written. Says Obst, "He thought he could get more for it after it was written, rather than what they were offering up front."

If joint TV/book ventures are the wave of the future, what's the likely effect on the way books will be written? Any author who takes pride in his craft, says Obst, "is not going to be thinking about whether a scene he's working on is a good scene for television." He will not, in other words, be writing with one eye on the typewriter and one eye on the tube.

The writers one talks to seem willing to take that risk. "Theoretically," says author Richard Woodley, "there could be some problems of creative control. But I think that really what authors need more than anything else is money to write books." For a struggling writer—one of those who earn the national average of $4775 per annum—a joint TV/book project must seem the dream deal of the future.

Whether all this will result in better books or in better television, especially after the work has passed through the hands of executives, screenwriters and network censors, Woodley declines to predict.

178 Popular Writing

From Auth, *The Philadelphia Inquirer*.

I. VOCABULARY

animatedly   hyperactive   qualms
syndicated   luminary   replete
confrere   interject   enticement
maven   titanic   coup
guru   miniseries

II. QUESTIONS ON CONTENT

1. The survey mentioned on page 174, paragraph four, was discussed in the article by Herbert Mitgang on page 161. To what use does Townley put this survey?
2. What is a television tie-in? A novelization? What disadvantage does each have?
3. Why are publishing and television becoming more dependent on each other? How does this situation benefit both? How does advertising also profit?
4. Should a television program based on a novel be compared with the novel? Why or why not?
5. What is David Obst's opinion of the effect of joint television/book enterprises on authors? Do you agree with him?

6. What does the increasing dependency of publishing and television on each other tell you about the relationship among the mass media? Is this relationship healthy or unhealthy?

III. QUESTIONS ON FORM

1. Where does the author state his thesis?
2. How does the three paragraph introduction about Mark Greenberg capture the reader's attention and interest?
3. What is the topic sentence for paragraphs eleven to fifteen on pages 175-176? How is it developed?
4. Does Townley give his opinion on the effect of joint television/book projects on authors and publishers? If so, where? If not, why not?
5. Describe Townley's tone of voice in this essay. How does his choice of words such as "raking in" (page 174, paragraph four), "mavens" (page 175, paragraph one), "flogging it" (page 175, paragraph four), "up to his elbows" (page 176, paragraph five), contribute to this tone?

IV. SUGGESTIONS FOR WRITING

1. Describe an author on a recent talk show who impressed you.
2. Imagine that you are a struggling writer and that you have just been offered a six figure sum by a producer who is eager to adapt your first novel for a television miniseries. Using specific details, describe your feelings and then explain your decision to accept or reject the offer.
3. If you have read a popular novel and then seen the television miniseries based on it, or vice versa, compare and contrast the two by discussing some of the important changes made in the television version and the reasons why you think these changes were made. Which did you prefer? Why?
4. Argue for or against the view that television versions of novels should never be compared with the novels because the printed page and the television screen are two different worlds.
5. Discuss whether or not joint television/book ventures in the future will result in better books or in better television.

Before her death in 1984, **Elizabeth Peer** was a Senior Writer for *Newsweek*. During her 26 years with the magazine, she covered wars, politics, and popular culture and won several awards for reporting and writing. **George Hackett** is an Associate Editor of *Newsweek* based in New York. A former writer for the Associated Press and London correspondent for *Newsweek*, **Lea Donosky** is the Washington correspondent for the *Chicago Tribune*.

Why Writers Plagiarize

Elizabeth Peer with Lea Donosky and George Hackett

When Jacob Epstein's "Wild Oats," a comic first novel of pubescent pain, appeared in 1979, it spurred admiring critics to conjure up everyone from J. D. Salinger to Woody Allen, and prompted John Gregory Dunne to praise the 23-year-old writer's "wickedly funny" ability to "calibrate every nuance." But Epstein's calibration, it turned out, had been a trifle imprecise. Even as a paperback edition of 110,000 copies hit U.S. bookstores last week, Epstein was denounced for plagiarism by British author Martin Amis, who listed no fewer than 53 "chunks" plundered almost verbatim from his own first novel, "The Rachel Papers."

Epstein pleaded that he was guilty only of "inadvertent use of Mr. Amis's phrases," and far fewer than Amis claimed. But the case sparked a transatlantic plagiarism debate, which gained extra spin from the fact that both authors spring from literary roots. Amis, 31, is the son of famed novelist Kingsley Amis ("Lucky Jim"); his grievance rated no less a forum than the distinguished London Observer. Epstein is the son of Jason Epstein, editorial director of Random House, and Barbara Epstein, who co-edits The New York Review of Books.

Conflicting loyalties sent the publishing establishment scuttling for cover ("If he were my kid I'd horsewhip him," said one top critic, "but for God's sake don't use my name"), while the families themselves took up arms for their offspring. "What my son did was not plagiarism," Epstein père insisted. "It is very common for accidents like this to happen, especially among young writers." Utter flapdoodle, riposted the senior Amis: "This is a flagrant case. It takes one back to the days before copyrights."

Indeed, literary historians accuse Shakespeare, Pope, Keats, Dickens, Kipling, Rabelais, Dumas, Hugo, Melville and even that remorseless old moralist John Milton of borrowing unblushingly from the works of others. More recently, Gail Sheehy settled out of court for filching material that appeared in her best-selling "Passages," and Alex Haley acknowledged lifting modest portions of "Roots"—a lapse that cost him a reported $500,000.

Film critic Penelope Gilliatt was caught appropriating another author's eloquence for a New Yorker magazine profile on Graham Greene, and novelist R. W. Burda was detected (by *Newsweek*'s Walter Clemons) pilfering from W. Somerset Maugham. This week hearings are under way on a suit charging thriller-novelist Ken Follett with swiping "The Key to Rebecca," the nation's No. 1 best seller, from a 1958 nonfiction book. And one of the most distinguished writers on the U.S. scene, John Gardner, was discovered

Copyright © 1980 by Newsweek, Inc. All rights reserved. Reprinted by permission.

to have borrowed lavishly in a 1977 biography of Geoffrey Chaucer. ("Of course I knew what I was doing," Gardner explained. "I'm a popularizer.")

'Shame': Psychiatrists maintain that varied forms of plagiarism are as common as nervous stomach among creative people. To Dr. Wayne Myers, who has a literary practice, deliberate theft is a bid "to get caught and be punished. It derives from lack of confidence, and a feeling that they don't deserve the success they are striving for." Dr. Hariette Kaley sees it as "a desperate attempt to salvage self-esteem. The need for the product becomes more important than the process." Unconscious cribbing is more common, says Dr. Arnold Cooper, the president of the American Psychoanalytic Association, but even that "may denote a need for public punishment. The person, in one way or another, can be inviting shame." Amis had his own Freudian view. Epstein's plagiarism, he asserted, involved not only self-destructiveness but a "death wish" as well.

But Epstein called that "cruel and vindictive." "I've been worrying about this for months," he said last week, his eyes red-rimmed from lack of sleep. As Epstein, a 1978 graduate of Yale, tells it, fifteen blue notebooks catalyzed his misfortune. In them, during a year in London, he scribbled overheard dialogue, ideas, scenes and excerpts from his reading. "I was trying to learn a craft, to learn every trick like a chess player," he explained. Amis was one of his literary heroes, and some of the Englishman's phrases, "which I thought quite wonderful, unconsciously became a kind of scaffolding." It was only after the novel went through four drafts and was in print, Epstein said, that he went back to his "chaotic notebooks," realized his error and discovered that it was too late—a story which his publisher, Little, Brown, corroborates. "There is no similarity of plot or character or setting," Epstein emphasizes. But there are, he admits, echoes of other literary heroes, such as Nabokov, Turgenev and Edmund Wilson, plainly recognizable in "Wild Oats."

Psychiatrist Cooper agrees that "a writer who is learning necessarily borrows a lot. He uses models much the way a beginning painter copies Picassos." Such borrowing signifies both protective bonding with an admired, more established writer and the shoring up of a sense of inadequacy, Cooper says. Even John Updike recalls comfortingly that "my first published novel was very clearly an imitation of Henry James." And Sigmund Freud himself was no stranger to plagiarism; recent biographers charge that he adopted concepts ranging from the id to infantile sexuality from the work of colleagues, without acknowledgment. For the father of psychoanalysis, plagiarism may have been a Freudian slip. Epstein might have had less trouble with a rejection slip.

I. VOCABULARY

pubescent   calibrate   plagiarism
conjure up   nuance   verbatim

inadvertent	flagrant	corroborate
scuttling	remorseless	id
flapdoodle	pilfering	Freudian slip
riposted	vindictive	

II. QUESTIONS ON CONTENT

1. Why did Martin Amis accuse Jacob Epstein of plagiarism?
2. What was Epstein's response to the accusation? Do you believe that he was innocent of plagiarism? Why or why not?
3. Did John Gardner regard himself as a plagiarist in his biography of Chaucer? What do you think of his explanation?
4. Why, according to psychiatrists, do writers plagiarize? Which explanation do you find most meaningful? Can you suggest any other psychological theory to account for plagiarism?
5. What difference, if any, is there between frequent and extensive, almost verbatim borrowing and brief and occasional appropriating of ideas, echoing of phrases from the works of others, or imitating their style?
6. To what extent, if any, do the low earnings of American authors, as reported in the previous selection, explain plagiarism?

III. QUESTIONS ON FORM

1. What is the central idea in this essay? Is it stated anywhere or is it implied?
2. Nowhere does the author give any specific examples of Epstein's presumed plagiarism. Why? Does this omission weaken the effectiveness of the essay?
3. How does Peer convince you that plagiarism is common among professional writers?
4. How would you characterize the tone of this essay? How do such synonyms for plagiarism as filching, lifting, appropriating, pilfering, cribbing contribute to this tone?
5. Examine the last two sentences in the essay. What do they suggest about the author's attitude towards Epstein?

IV. SUGGESTIONS FOR WRITING

1. Formulate your own definition of plagiarism and develop it with illustrations and examples from amateur or professional writing.
2. Using active verbs and dialogue, write a narrative essay about the time you were caught plagiarizing on a school assignment.
3. Agree or disagree with the reasons psychiatrists have given for plagiarism.
4. Defend plagiarism, as you understand it, as a learning process for artists.

Rita Ciolli, lawyer and journalist, has covered legal affairs for *Newsday* since 1977. She received numerous awards for her 1982 series on book censorship including a Page One Award from the Newspaper Guild of New York and the American Bar Association's Silver Gavel Award.

The Textbook Wars

Rita Ciolli

Chapter 25 of "World History, Our Common Heritage" deals with the political and economic effects of the Industrial Revolution. Understandably, a large part of the chapter is devoted to the influence of Karl Marx, but it is illustrated with the pictures of four other people who lived at that time: Florence Nightingale, Elizabeth Fry, Charlotte Bronte and Ludwig van Beethoven.

Marx' impact could not be ignored. But since Marx' socialist message rivals only Darwin's theory of evolution for controversy, his powerful image could be left out to soften the blow.

Beethoven's achievements justified the inclusion of his picture in the chapter, but the publisher ignored Marx in favor of three nonthreatening women. This would have satisfied those feminists who keep tallies of the sex of the people depicted. And it would not have disturbed the Daughters of the American Revolution, either.

A publisher can't get safer than Florence Nightingale.

The textbook, published by Ginn and Co., was not unique among the 11 world history textbooks under consideration this year for use in Texas high schools. Only five of the 11 books contained a picture of Marx. The Ginn textbook was eventually rejected, and that rejection, along with the selection process for all textbooks in Texas, has intimidated many of the nation's book publishers and diluted the content of texts used by public schools throughout the nation.

Ever since the Greeks used Homer's poetry for the first instructional text, textbooks have been the most traditional and enduring way for a society to preserve its cultural heritage. They mirror what society considers acceptable, reflecting national values, goals and priorities. In the United States, textbooks provide a common body of knowledge to a mobile population. They underscore evolving attitudes. They are what we know, and what is important to us. They are controversial and will always remain so, because

Copyright © 1983 by Newsday, Inc. Reprinted by permission.

this is a free society where differences can be expressed, and where local control of education is one of the nation's fundamental underpinnings.

The struggle over the content of textbooks in this country is at least a century old. One of the first complaints against textbooks came from Union Army veterans after the Civil War, who felt history books were not placing enough blame for the conflict on the Confederacy. Southern schools, however, wanted the era of the Confederacy depicted as a time of glory. At the end of the 19th Century, many publishers had two versions of history books, one for the North and the other for the South.

Today, the essence of the dispute remains the same: the charge that vital young minds are being poisoned or weakened. Each textbook critic believes that his view of the facts is the correct one and must be substituted for what is in the books.

Concerns over textbook content manifest themselves in complaints about how big corporations are portrayed, whether women are shown as astronauts or homemakers, how slavery is depicted, and whether the American Indian is described only as scalping settlers or also is credited with having a well-developed civilization. Some issues, such as whether some textbooks are "too soft" on "the Communist menace," are unchanging. Other issues are topical, such as California's ban on pictures of "junk" food.

There has not been much change in who is objecting. The DAR is still there. While the complaints of blacks and feminists are not so strong as in 1973, when congressional hearings determining how educational funds should be used brought new impetus to complaints about racial and sexual stereotypes, they are still being made. The New York City Board of Education rejected a photography book last year because it contained only two photos of blacks: one of a bootblack, the other of a woman leaning against the doorway of a lounge.

What is new is the broad support that many grass-roots groups are now receiving from established conservative forces such as the Moral Majority, Phyllis Schlafly's Eagle Forum and the Heritage Foundation. The support can take the form of funds, information, the backing of evangelical groups and television preachers or the materials churned out by such longtime textbook critics as Mel and Norma Gabler of Longview, Texas.

Education is a cohesive rallying point. Many parents concerned about the quality of education have eagerly joined the "back to basics" movement. Test scores and reading levels have been declining for the last decade, and everyone from the members of PTAs to prestigious national commissions wants to know why Johnny can't read or write. This spectre of illiteracy has enabled many mainline conservative groups to expand their influence and renew support for some of their long-standing crusades for school prayer, an end to busing for integration, anti-abortion legislation and tuition tax credits.

Paul Putnam, a civil rights specialist with the National Education

Association, the largest organization of professional educators, describes the conservative campaign as "an appeal to fear" in order to "take over" the school system.

"They attack books to draw attention, and the next thing you know, they are running for the school board," he says.

These challenges are gaining new force because of their success in Texas, California, Florida and several other large states that have statewide book-adoption policies. Since it is too expensive to publish more than one edition of a text, the decisions made in these states, especially Texas, where most new editions are introduced, largely determine the content of the textbooks used by this country's 39 million elementary and high school students.

Texas, the state with the fourth-largest budget for school books in the country, and other large states that approve textbooks before local schools can purchase them, have become the magnets for challenges to textbook content.

A century ago, an organized purchasing system was merely a way for a state to negotiate a fixed and cheaper price for school books. It also improved the quality of books used in rural areas. Now, such systems are concerned more with ideology.

Although New York State—where local districts spent more than $54 million on textbooks in the last school year—is the second-largest purchaser of textbooks in the nation, it does not have the power to influence content, because the spending is done at the local level. Each school district in New York is free to select any book it wants, so long as the book is in accord with the broad curriculum guidelines issued by the State Education Department. In most Long Island school districts, textbooks are reviewed by faculty committees in the subject areas, and the chairman of the department recommends the book to be purchased to the school board. Although this process appears to give New York great freedom in the selection of textbooks, the choices are limited to the books that are available from the publishers, most of which have been tailored to sell in Texas.

The dilemma of the publisher in trying to meet the needs of so many groups becomes clearer when focused on the continuing controversy over how to depict the ever-changing American family. Many books still depict it traditionally: mother, father, children and dog—each member in traditional roles.

One of "the horrendous problems" for school districts is finding education materials for first- and second-graders that illustrate alternative family concepts, says Richard Ornauer, vice-president-elect of the New York State School Boards Association.

"We have so many single-parent families and those with two working parents that a child finds the books unreal," says Ornauer, a longtime member of the Merrick school board. "Because of the conservative attitudes in states like Texas, publishers are loath to change these books."

In the 22 states where the adoption of textbooks is centralized, critics, organized and otherwise, have a better chance to have their objections heard and, consequently, to have some impact. In Tallahassee, Fla., last year, a major dispute arose over sex education books. Eagle Forum, a group that wants to retain traditional family concepts, took out a full-page newspaper ad and its members arrived en masse with bumper stickers and buttons all bearing the message: "Public Schools—Clean Them Up Or Close Them Down."

An increasing number of states have adopted proclamations specifying what textbooks must contain. Other states set curriculum guidelines that publishers must meet or risk having their books rejected. (In at least 25 states, a science text can't be purchased if it fails to mention alternative theories to evolution.) Selection committees decide which books to buy; through politics, critics can get their supporters named to the committees. Because of the state proclamations, publishers are more likely to alter their books even before they submit them for adoption. This makes it easier for creationists to have their beliefs included in textbooks, and opens the publishers, instead of the critics, to charges of censorship or bias.

The New York City Board of Education last year rejected all three biology texts submitted to it for consideration because they either treated evolution inadequately or supported creationism, says Charlotte Frank, executive director of the Division of Curriculum and Instruction. One of the publishers, Laidlaw Brothers, a division of Doubleday, made no mention of the word "evolution" in its 1981 edition. The publisher offered to provide a supplement with a comprehensive treatment of evolution for New York City, but the board thought this would belittle the subject and rejected the offer, Frank says.

(So great is the pressure on the publishers of biology and other science books that their very integrity is being strained, according to education professor Gerald Skoog of Texas Tech University. In a study presented in July to the National Institutes of Science, Skoog reported that the word "evolution" and the explanation of it as a leading scientific theory has declined. In recently published books, the word "evolution" has all but disappeared from the glossaries and chapter titles.)

Another reason textbook reform groups concentrate their efforts in the large states that control the content of textbooks, such as Texas and California, is the relative ease with which a book can be legally stopped in these states. The chance of stopping a book before it is purchased in these states is much greater than elsewhere. After a book is being used in schools, it is entitled to many First Amendment protections, a challenger must overcome many more procedural obstacles in having his objections heard, and an ultimate victory might affect the use of the book in only one school district.

Publishers don't like to talk about what is happening, but the chances of changing a book are greater when the publisher has million-dollar profits in the balance. "If they back us up against a wall and say, 'You either take it [objectionable material] out or you won't sell the book in Texas,' then we'll take it out," one Doubleday editor says. . . .

Elementary school and high school textbooks are a $1-billion business, according to the Association of American Publishers, but the profits average only 10 per cent of revenues, far less than in some other publishing ventures.

Donald Eklund, vice president of the school division of the publishing group, contends, however, that profits are big enough so that what happens in one state does not make a great deal of difference. "If a book doesn't make the list in Texas, it is not doomed to be an economic failure," he says.

He acknowledges, however, that changes are made in the contents of books to appease critics. "Some will and some won't," he says. "A publisher has to make some conscious decisions, knowing full well that it will sell better in some parts of the country than others."

(Editing a book for the marketplace is not a recent development. Shakespeare's "Othello," for instance, was not included in literature anthologies for decades because the South would not accept the protrayal of miscegenation.)

Like practically everyone else involved in the process, Eklund rejects the label of being a censor. The 23 school textbook publishers that his organization represents are the best example of the free enterprise system, he says.

"Some publishers will choose not to participate [with demands to delete, change and edit] if it is too offensive to them."

The problem with concentrating on who the censors are and what they do ignores the consequence: poor textbooks. Schoolchildren spend 75 to 90 per cent of their time in school and in assignments at home working with textbooks. Are the necessary changing interpretations of history to be made by scholars and academics? Or are they to be made by publishers content with producing salable textbooks that are a bland patchwork of information and pictures not considered offensive to anyone?

On Long Island, many school districts are coping with "inadequate" textbooks by supplementing them with library and research projects, says Ornauer, who is also president of the Nassau Board of Cooperative Educational Services. "These simple texts no longer meet our needs," he says.

The concern about the criteria for textbooks comes at a time when the quality of education has become a national issue. The recent report of the National Commission on Excellence in Education suggests that one way to stop the mediocrity in our schools is to use textbooks that present "rigorous and challenging material clearly."

Another significant report, released in September, found that too much

188 Popular Writing

emphasis is being given to rote memorization and the use of unchallenging and stultifying instructional materials. The study, by noted teacher and education writer John Goodlad, says: "The schools did not appear to be . . . developing all those qualities commonly listed under 'intellectual development': the ability to think rationally, the ability to use, evaluate and accumulate knowledge, a desire for further learning."

The timidity of the current texts about open inquiry and controversial facts has attracted a wide variety of critics and fervent conservatives.

Ernest Lefever is the director of the conservative Washington thinktank Ethics and Public Policy Center, which has published three textbook critiques. "There is perhaps only one way for textbook writers to avoid the slings and arrows of outraged teachers, parents and scholars," Lefever writes. It is "to serve up a bland and balanced diet of contested views which may beguile potential critics but is certain to bewilder pupils."

Another view is from Christopher Pyle, a Mount Holyoke College political science professor, who says good textbooks should force students to defend and, thereby, reconsider ideas that they have accepted uncritically from families, churches, governments and industry.

"Our society purports to value education," says Pyle, "but training is what it usually wants."

I. VOCABULARY

depict   grass-roots
intimidate   ideology
impetus   en masse
spectre   creationism

II. QUESTIONS ON CONTENT

1. Why, according to the author, are textbooks important in any society? In American society in particular?
2. What is the basic reason for the dispute concerning the content of textbooks?
3. Why are national conservative groups especially concerned with attacking textbooks? Do you approve of their motives?
4. What pressures do textbook publishers face as a result of the increasing attack from special-interest groups? How do they often respond to these attacks? Do you respect them for such behavior?
5. How can censorship of textbooks result in poorer rather than better textbooks?
6. Do you feel that established conservative and right-wing groups involved in the censorship of textbooks are simply engaging in reverse indoctrination? Explain.

III. QUESTIONS ON FORM

1. What is Ciolli's purpose in writing?
2. Is this essay intended for a specific or a general audience?
3. The central issue in the textbook controversy is not introduced until page 184, paragraph two. What then is the main function of the first seven paragraphs?
4. What is the function of paragraph three, page 184?
5. We have omitted the middle section of Ciolli's essay. What do you think it deals with? Why?
6. What is the writer's attitude toward the textbook dispute?

IV. SUGGESTIONS FOR WRITING

1. Explain why you think censorship of textbooks, particularly by conservative groups, has increased dramatically in the past five years.
2. During this same period, censorship of school libraries has also increased substantially. Do you feel that this is a greater threat to education and democracy than textbook censorship?
3. Argue for or against the view that the purpose of education is to indoctrinate children with the values of ideas of the majority of the community.
4. Define a poor textbook and give examples from textbooks you have used throughout your schooling.
5. Discuss some of the ways you think the quality of textbooks used in U.S. classrooms can be upgraded in quality.

Bill McGowan, Jr., a former free-lance writer, is now an editor of the *Washington Monthly*.

---

25 Million Americans Can't Read This

Bill McGowan, Jr.

According to a 1979 Ford Foundation Report, nearly 25 million Americans cannot read what you're reading now and another 35 million would probably miss the full meaning.

Afflicting close to 20 per cent of the population, adult illiteracy has become a crisis that is quietly shredding the nation's social, political and

Reprinted by permission of Bill McGowan.

industrial fabric, despite several decades of federal efforts to eradicate the problem.

Whether it's considered for the effect it has on individuals or for the impact it has on society, the fact that 60 million native-born Americans can't read well enough to cope with the routine paperwork of modern life, such as a classified ad or a subway map, is an alarming problem with far-reaching consequences.

Individually, the victims of illiteracy struggle through blighted lives of shame, alienation and underachievement. One illiterate tells how he couldn't complete a job application for custodial work without assistance. Another ruefully explains that he passed up a promotion from laborer to foreman because he couldn't fill out the simple forms and reports that were required by the new job.

But taken together, stories like these add up to more than a sad catalogue of lost opportunity and regrets. When there are more illiterates in the United States than there were people who voted for Ronald Reagan in the last presidential election, the nation's political integrity is sullied. When the levels of literacy in the armed services are so low that officers can't teach their men how to maintain sophisticated weaponry, the nation's defense capabilities suffer.

The illiteracy problem is particularly acute in business and industry—especially in banking, telecommunications and data processing, where competent reading skills are most in demand. As America faces stiffer competition from foreign countries with higher rates of literacy and productivity, such as Japan and West Germany, the literacy crisis will undoubtedly threaten the future strength of the economy.

Though much has been said about why Johnny can't read, very little has been done on the impact of illiteracy on Big Business. Few reports detail how much the adult Johnny's illiteracy costs society in terms of welfare payments when he can't get a job or how much it costs industry in terms of productivity and profits when he messes up in the workplace.

Rampant illiteracy in the United States is creating an underclass of unskilled and unlettered workers that will be locked out of the high-tech economy of the future. One corporate executive asks rhetorically, "Where will the workers come from to operate complicated gear if they already make mistakes with a drill press?"

"Educational mismatching"—the situation where jobs exist but qualified manpower doesn't—has been cited by the Regional Planning Association of New York as the chief problem that business and industry in the metropolitan area will confront through the next two decades. There are an estimated 800,000 illiterates in the metropolitan area, and, according to an executive with the J. Walter Thompson advertising agency who has monitored the scene, banks, insurance companies and city administrators all complain about the enormous problems they face in meeting their clerical needs.

In leading to increased levels of unemployment, illiteracy deepens the disaffection of the underprivileged and aggravates existing social inequities. Black women, the sole breadwinner in many inner-city families and the cornerstone of stability in the ghetto community, are more illiterate as a group than any other in America. As the workplace grows more complex, they will grow more unemployable, and their joblessness will give rise to further urban trouble.

Federal efforts to solve the problem have largely lacked funding and commitment. The Reagan administration wants to cut the $100 million now pledged to literacy programs to $86 million, a figure far short of the $5 billion to $25 billion called for by some literacy activists. "It's a national humiliation for the United States," says Jonathan Kozol, the author of a penetrating study of American illiteracy called "Prisoners of Silence." Kozol and others have given up on government programs in favor of remedies that the private sector may propose in the new spirit of "voluntarism." Their hopes are now pinned on the ability of America's major corporations to see that they have a stake or, as an International Paper Co. executive put it, a "commercial motivation" in developing manpower resources able to read at minimum levels of reading competence.

The impact that illiteracy has on the corporate bottom line is hard to calculate, but it's generally recognized that productivity and profits suffer significantly from the waste and inefficiencies that reading deficiencies generate. Mutual of New York, an insurance firm, estimates that 70 per cent of its dictated correspondence has to be done over at least once because of errors. A steel-mill worker in Pennsylvania cost his company more than a million dollars in disrupted production schedules and inventories when he misordered spare parts from a company warehouse. In 1975, a herd of prime beef cattle was killed accidently when a Chicago feedlot laborer misread a package label and gave the cattle poison instead of food. A Chicago subway motorman, on trial for negligence connected with a fatal accident in 1977, admitted that he had trouble reading his service manual, as did many of his fellow workers.

Everyday across America, sales orders are botched, bank transactions are bungled, messages are mishandled and things by the million are misfiled, all due in some measure to reading incompetence. Just how vital will the much-vaunted "Information Age" really be if people simply can't read. "We must remember," said a General Electric Co. computer executive, "that computers process error at the same bewildering speed at which they process truth."

While the private sector hasn't mounted any serious drive yet to wipe out illiteracy, some companies are doing things in that direction, and some other forces are poised for a coordinated assault. Dow Chemical Co., General Motors Corp. and Philip Morris Inc. are among two dozen or so major businesses that are sponsoring reading improvement programs for their employees or for students in public schools. The National Coalition for

192   Popular Writing

Literacy and the National Advertising Council plan a joint publicity campaign for next year, hoping to draw attention to the problem and to elicit energy and initiatives from various sectors of business and industry.

Because illiteracy cuts deeply into the profits of advertisers, publishers and paper companies, these organizations have been in the vanguard of the attack. Already, J. Walter Thompson and International Paper have been aggressive in their bid to waken their fellow corporate citizens to the situation. Yet so far, not enough major corporations have recognized a dilemma that is casting dark shadows over all quarters of American life and could seriously undermine the country's future economic prospects.

When asked how he managed all his life without being able to read, an illiterate, played by Johnny Cash in the film "The Pride of Jesse Hallam," answered, "You lie a lot, you get cheated some and you fake it." As foreign competition grows stronger, and as the economy evolves into ever more complicated forms, American industry will no longer be able to fake it, and unchecked illiteracy will surely take its toll on social stability, productivity and corporate profits.

I. VOCABULARY

eradicate	sullied	botched
blighted	rampant	elicit
ruefully	disaffection	vanguard

II. QUESTIONS ON CONTENT

1. Why does McGowan regard illiteracy as an alarming problem? Do you agree?
2. According to the article, what effect does illiteracy have on individuals? On society? Can you suggest any other harmful consequences?
3. Why is the author mainly concerned with the impact of illiteracy on the business sector?
4. In what ways does the literacy crisis affect U.S. industry?
5. What actions have some companies taken to attack the problem of illiteracy? Do you think these actions will be effective?

III. QUESTIONS ON FORM

1. Why are the title and opening paragraph effective?
2. Is the author's definition of illiteracy clear and accurate? If not, how would you revise it?
3. What is the function of paragraph five on page 190 in relation to the rest

of the essay? How does the last sentence of the essay relate to this paragraph?
4. The article does not discuss the causes of reading incompetence. Why?
5. How does McGowan persuade you that there is a literacy problem in the United States that must be wiped out?
6. What solution, if any, does the writer propose to eliminate illiteracy? Do you agree with it?

IV. SUGGESTIONS FOR WRITING

1. To be literate, according to Webster's dictionary, means not only to be able to read and write, but also to be well-educated or to have or show extensive knowledge, learning, or culture. On the basis of this definition, would you consider yourself a literate person? Why or why not?
2. Discuss the measures you would take to get rid of illiteracy.
3. Defend the view that literacy is essential for the preservation and growth of democracy in the United States.
4. Assuming you are an illiterate like Jesse Hallam in the film, explain how you would lie and "fake it" to hide your problem.

TOPICS FOR INVESTIGATION

1. Explore the reasons for the death of a major mass circulation magazine, such as *Life, Look, Colliers,* the *Saturday Evening Post, Women's Home Companion,* or the *Saturday Review of Literature.*

2. Investigate the basic similarities and differences among the three major newsweeklies in the United States: *Time, Newsweek,* and *U.S. News and World Report.*

3. Explore some of the magazines that have developed recently to serve changing women's lifestyles. Explain how these magazines, such as *Self, Working Woman,* and *Working Mother,* are different from the more traditional women's service magazines like *Family Circle, Woman's Day,* the *Ladies' Home Journal, McCalls,* and *Good Housekeeping.*

4. Examine personality journalism in newspapers (for example, gossip columns), magazines (for example, *People, National Enquirer*) or on television (for example, "Real People," "PM Magazine," "TV's Bloopers and Practical Jokes") and analyze the reasons for its recent proliferation.

5. Analyze the image of a particular general or special-interest mass magazine with reference to the format and contents of the magazine and the audience to which it appeals. First, consider the following: title and cover, ads, articles, fiction, cartoons, photographs, and such special features as an editorial section and letters to the editor. Next, determine the major purpose

of the magazine, the effect of the magazine on the reader, and the kind of "symbolic world" it creates.

6. Investigate how magazines are marketed.

7. Study the role of the editor in the success of a magazine. Here are some examples:
   Henry R. Luce-*Time, Life,* and *Fortune*
   Hugh Heffner-*Playboy*
   Arnold Gingrich-*Esquire*
   Helen Gurley Brown-*Cosmopolitan*
   Norman Cousins-the *Saturday Review of Literature*

8. Research the national surveys of the adult American reading public conducted by Gallop, Yankelovich, and others in the past decade, and explain what they reveal about America's reading habits. As an alternative, conduct your own survey of people who read fiction and the reasons they do so.

9. Report on one of the bestsellers mentioned by Alfred Kazin, and discuss the reasons for its great commercial success.

10. According to Scot Haller (the *Saturday Review,* March 1981), the world's five best-selling authors are Harold Robbins, Barbara Cartland, Irving Wallace, Louis L'Amour, and Janet Dailey. Choose one of these authors and explore the reasons for his or her great popularity in terms of the messages the author presents and the formula used by the author in writing his or her books.

11. Interview a professional writer. Find out why the writer chose this career and how he or she feels about being a writer.

12. Read an erotic historical romance and determine to what extent, if any, it presents the kind of heroine and message described by Carol Thurston and Barbara Doscher.

13. Compare a popular novel with its subsequent television version. How does the nature of the visual medium affect the various elements of the novel, such as plot, character, theme, and narrative point of view? What is gained in the television adaptation of the novel? What is lost?

14. Describe a recent well-publicized case of plagiarism and decide whether or not the author was guilty of wrongdoing.

15. Inquire into the increase in censorship of school libraries by scrutinizing the Island Trees book-banning case. The case, referred to as *Pico* v. *Island Trees,* was decided by the United States Supreme Court on June 26, 1982, five years after a Long Island school board ordered the removal of nine books from the high school library shelves.

16. Define functional illiteracy and then consider the part played by the U.S. eduction system in contributing to the increase in functional illiteracy.

6

ADVERTISING

Advertising in several respects is unique among the popular arts. Its sheer quantity makes it the most visible. Since we live in a media environment, it is possible for a person to be exposed to several hundred advertisements every day. This makes advertising the most pervasive of the popular arts. Advertising is able to utilize both print and broadcast channels to transmit messages through advertisements in newspapers and magazines and on television and radio, as well as by other means such as billboards, direct mail, and specialty items like ballpoint pens. Advertising is also the most powerful and influential of the popular arts. As Sandman, Rubin, and Sachsman explain in "American Mass Communication," it is powerful because it fuels the mass media. In the past year, for example, advertisers spent more than $60 billion in the mass media. The mass media in turn serve the economic system because they provide jobs and stimulate consumer demand for goods and services, thereby keeping the economy going. Thus the mass media and big business could not exist without advertising. Advertising is also influential because it skillfully uses the art of persuasion to sell goods, services, and ideas to the consumer, and all of us are potential consumers. Advertising is therefore able to affect our attitudes and behavior, if not our very lifestyles.

Finally, perhaps because it is so visible, pervasive, and influential, advertising is the most controversial of the popular arts. On the one hand, it has been praised for helping to do the following: support the mass media, lower the costs of goods and services, keep the media independent by the diversity of advertisers, provide useful information to the consumer, and stimulate the economy. On the other hand, advertising has been criticized for its negative effects. These include: creating false needs and encouraging materialistic standards, exploiting our emotions rather than appealing to our intellect, dehumanizing the consumer by treating him or her only as a commodity, influencing the decisions of big business, lowering the quality of the content of the popular arts such as radio and television programs, engaging in deceitful and fraudulent advertising, and, finally, creating advertisements that are either unduly repetitious, vulgar, or irritating. Whether we approve or disapprove of advertising, one conclusion is inescapable; we cannot ignore it.

Since advertising is so much a part of our lives, we the consumers would do well to understand how it persuades us. In the first essay in this chapter, Marjorie Burns analyzes the various methods and techniques that advertisers use to influence our behavior. These "tricks," as Burns calls them, are employed in the two basic types of ads: the hard sell and the soft sell. Rod Townley concentrates on those elements that make a television ad campaign effective and finds that there is a move toward the soft sell, that is, toward more emotional and sensitive ads with strong images.

In addition to choosing the proper type of ad, the advertiser must also pay careful attention to the package as a persuader and communicator. The design of the package or container and its close tie-in with user imagery is the subject of the next essay. Bob Wiemer is particularly disturbed by what he regards as the obvious and gross use of sexual symbolism to sell deodorant products to males by appealing to their macho image.

Rod Townley's brief comment on the evolution of the Federal Express commercial can be better understood in light of "The Fizz Biz," an article on the new Alka-Seltzer commercials. By exploring the reasons for this product's new look in terms of the history of the Alka-Seltzer ad campaign and recent developments in American society, Bernice Kanner reaffirms the dictum that advertising is a mirror of social change.

Despite the creativity and artistry that often go into the making of advertisements, such as those for Federal Express and Alka-Seltzer, the plain fact is that ads can be a nuisance, especially when they disturb the television shows we are watching by appearing at inappropriate times and with inappropriate messages. John Cheever, the distinguished author, provides a novel solution to this recurring viewer complaint; in his first television drama he wrote his own ads to comment indirectly on the action.

The last two selections are substantive arguments on the roles of language and ethics in advertising. Henryk Skolimowski is concerned with language and how it influences our behavior and our attitudes. He analyzes the linguistic level of ads in order to persuade us that admen manipulate the semantic environment we all inhabit by distorting language, violating logic, and corrupting values. John Crichton, on the other hand, is an advocate for advertising. He defends its standards against the familiar charges that advertising is devoid of morals and ethics because it is biased, inaccurate, and acquisitive.

Readings

> Formerly the editor of Scholastic *Voice*, **Marjorie Burns** now works as an editor in the text division. She has been at Scholastic since 1960.

The Advertiser's Bag of Tricks

Marjorie Burns

Ask the average man or woman on the street what he or she thinks of advertising and you'll probably hear, "Oh, that stuff! I never pay any attention to it." But don't you believe it. People not only pay attention to advertising, they let it influence their behavior. That's because the creators of ads know many subtle tricks for outflanking a person's intellectual resistance and getting their sales messages into his skull.

Here is a bagful of those tricks. For convenience, we've divided them into three categories: Claims, Appeals, and Techniques. Claims focus attention on the products and what they can do for you, the buyer; they are, or appear to be, rational. Appeals zero in on your emotions; they hit you where you are the weakest—in your fears, desires, and cherished beliefs. Techniques are specific ways of expressing or presenting claims and appeals in printed advertisements and in radio and television commercials.

The three compartments aren't watertight. For instance, you may find that some of the Claims seem to be leaking in among the Appeals. But that's not important. The important thing is for you to have a variety of advertising methods to choose from so you can do a good job for your client. If the public is able to recognize these Claims, Appeals, and Techniques, they will become more intelligent consumers.

One note of warning: Some of these tricks are really tricky. That is, they're on the borderline between honesty and dishonesty. However, we do not label any of them "ethical" or "unethical." All of them are widely used in the advertising industry. Whether or not they should be used is for the ad agency and the consumer to decide.

From Scholastic *Voice*, November 8, 1973. Copyright © 1973 by Scholastic Inc. Reprinted with the permission of the publisher.

Claims

C-1 product benefit. The first thing an ad man looks for in the product he's trying to sell is some definite benefit to the consumer. Perhaps it gets dishes clean without water-spotting, helps to prevent tooth decay, or makes the buyer's work easier. If it offers any kind of concrete advantage, the ad man's troubles aren't over, but at least he has something to start with. He can say:

> *Trident sugarless gum. The gum most dentists recommend for their patients who chew gum.*
> *Bounty—the quicker picker-upper (paper towels).*

Of course, he won't stop with the concrete product benefit; he'll try to combine it with some kind of emotional appeal. Have you seen the recent TV commercials for the two products mentioned above? After you read the section on Appeals, you should be able to tell how each tries to involve the viewer's feelings as well as his reason.

The ad man's dream is the product that's first, or among the first, of its kind. When detergents first came on the market, one claim was enough: "Detergent cleans better than soap." (Of course, detergent also pollutes better than soap, but we didn't find that out until later.)

C-2 new, improved. If your product isn't the first in its category, maybe the manufacturer can do something to change it. Then you can claim that it's "new." If the change makes it better, you can even claim it's "improved."

But be careful how you toss that word "new" around. The Federal Trade Commission, which sets standards for truth-in-advertising, says that for an old product to become legally "new," it has to undergo a "material functional change." Don't ask what that means, exactly; the meaning differs from case to case.

Suppose you decide that you can't honestly or legally claim your product is new. Never mind; there are ways you can imply newness. You can "introduce" or "announce" the product. You can say "Now," or "Meet," or "Today's Fresh Idea," etc.

> *Introducing No-Fry Doughnuts. Doughnuts that are different from any other kind. Because you don't fry them. You bake them. (With Gold Medal Flour)*
> *Announcing: the end of city skin! (Pond's Creamy Lemon Facial Cleanser)*

C-3 exclusively ours. If your product has a secret ingredient or an important feature that none of its competitors have, you're in luck. But if it doesn't, don't give up yet. Maybe you can invent a claim to exclusivity, or exaggerate a trivial difference.

  a. Single out an ordinary ingredient or feature and give it a special name.

Mobil detergent gasoline *(All petroleum products have cleansing properties.)*
Colgate with MFP *(MFP is a fluoride formula.)*
RCA Accutron *(One-button color tuning is offered by most makers of TV sets.)*

b. Take some feature shared by all products in the category and imply that it's exclusively yours.

Fly the Friendly Skies of United. *(You thought all airlines used the same sky, didn't you?)*

c. Simply state that your product is different and leave it at that. If the difference is too small to mention, don't mention it.

This is color television as only Sylvania makes it.
There are lots of shirts. There's only one Van Heusen.
No other shortening has Crisco's formula.

C-4 tests show. To be convincing, a test must be conducted by someone who is both impartial and an expert in the field. Usually, the ad states that an independent clinic or laboratory has made the test and found that the product is "58 per cent more effective," or "lasts twice as long as the other leading brand," or some such factual-sounding claim.

Occasionally, however, the "test" is a survey of customer reaction. This can be impressive.

In a test *(of 6 color TV's),* 50.1 per cent *(of 2,707 persons participating)* said Zenith had the best picture. *(Only 21.1 per cent voted for the second best, etc.)*

C-5 take it from me. Sometimes a simple assertion, if made firmly and confidently, will convince people that your client's product is good.

You can be sure if it's Westinghouse.
At Zenith, the quality goes in before the name goes on.

Often an assertion of this type is circular. It says, in effect, "This product is what it is."

Savarin—the coffee-er coffee
Coke—the real thing
Peter Pan Peanut Butter is the P-nuttiest.

If your client has been doing business for many years, that may be considered a recommendation.

We know what we're doing at Big Yank. We've been making cotton jeans for America's families for 75 years.

C-6 careful words for careful claims (weasel words). You can't promise positively that your product will cure nasal congestion, or never leave a single spot on glassware—no product is perfect. But you can convince the buyer that it'll do great things for him if you choose your words carefully. You can say, for example, that your product *helps* clear up nasal passages, acts *like* a cyclone to get rid of dirt, *works* to kill *virtually* all dangerous household germs, or *can* give every girl a clearer, smoother complexion. If the shirt you're selling isn't made of silk, you can still say it *looks like* or *has the look of* silk. Your shampoo may not be guaranteed to get rid of dandruff, but you can promise that it'll *fight* dandruff. If your bread has had most of the nutrients processed out of it, but the manufacturer has put some vitamins back in, you can label it *enriched.*

Get the Cascade look . . . virtually spotless. *(dishwasher detergent)*
Helps your hair stay outdoor-fresh *(Breck instant shampoo)*

Speaking of freshness, that's one of those qualities that depend on personal taste and subjective judgment. One person's idea of robust flavor, smart styling, provocative fragrance, or warm, creamy goodness may make another say, "Yechh!" So you can claim as many of these qualities for your product as you want to, and no one will argue.

Appeals

If the product you're trying to sell offers no special benefit to the consumer; or if it is essentially like every other product in its category (a sugar or an airline, for example), you'll have to fall back on some kind of emotional appeal. But even if you can make lots of rational claims for your product's superiority, your pitch will be more effective if you add an emotional appeal. The makers of Pampers (disposable diapers) learned that lesson.

When Pampers were ready to be put on the market, the ad men decided to "play it straight." After all, the product was new, and it offered definite advantages over old-fashioned cloth diapers. So the agency created ads that simply stated the advantages. What happened? Nothing. Nobody bought Pampers. Store owners started calling the supplier and begging him to remove the space-wasting merchandise from their shelves.

Then the agency got busy and created a new ad campaign. This one consisted of a little slice-of-life drama, with some cute gurgling babies, proud mamas, and perhaps an awkward, fumbling papa or two. The ad showed the product as part of a loving family situation—and it sold Pampers by the carload.

A-1 the family. Most Americans regard the close-knit, loving family as the foundation of a healthy society. Therefore, if you can suggest that your product is a part of family life, or can contribute to family life, you may not need to make any further claims.

Since the woman of the house makes most of the buying decisions in this area, your pitch for home and motherhood will be directed at her. You'll suggest that if she cares about her family she'll buy your product.

> You discovered Profile, Mom. *(Father and the children say this gratefully to a beaming mom as they all munch on Profile bread.)*
> Stop Vitamin Shortage in Children! *(St. Joseph's vitamins for children)*
> The boy by Mrs. Whitehead. The boy's shirt by Kaynee. *(The photo shows a woman and her young son posing together, obviously proud of each other.)*

A-2 it's you! (image appeal). This type of appeal focuses on the user instead of on the product. What aspect of the user's personality should you aim for? Motivational researchers suggest that the best place to hit a prospective customer is in his self-image. They say we tend to buy products that harmonize with the way we would like others to see us.

Take, for example, the full-time housewife who thinks of herself as a conscientious homemaker, a fine cook and gracious hostess. You'll have a hard time selling her an instant coffee, or one of those "just-heat-and-serve" dinners. Your job will be to convince her she can have convenience and her self-image too.

> Instant Maxwell House. We tested against perked . . . and we won! *(In other words, if instant coffee pleases people more than "regular" does, a good cook will use it.)*
> Morton. You don't have to cook to care. *(Packaged spaghetti and meat sauce.)*
> It's easier to get where you'd like to be if you dress like you're already there. *(Mavest sportcoats for men. The appeal is to the buyer's wish to be successful.)*
> Live-it up outfit from Bobbie Brooks *(Women's clothing. Aimed at those who see themselves as active, fun-loving, and youthful.)*

A-3 snob appeal. When you say your product is "for the discriminating few," you're using snob appeal. Actually, of course, you'd like those "few" to be as numerous as possible.

> Our $20 an ounce Make-up. Because a beautiful face is priceless. *(Countess Isserlyn Make-Up)*
> Town & Travel. It looks a little more expensive. It is. *(Ladies' suede coat)*
> Our 'British Clubs'. They don't run with the rest of the crowd. *(Neckties by Rooster. Notice that even the punctuation is British style.)*

A-4 bandwagon. This is the exact opposite of A-3. Here you tell the customer, "Don't be left out. Everybody else is using this product, so you should, too."

> Would millions of women use it if it didn't work? *(One-Wipe Dust Cloths)*

A-5 youth.   In this country, it sometimes seems that everybody would like to have eternal youth. That's impossible, of course, but it gives you the chance to offer the next best thing; eternal (or at least life-long) youthfulness. Perhaps your product will help the user to feel or appear youthful. If it's not that kind of product, then simply try to associate it with youthful people and activities.

A little Morgan's pomade every day/Turns your hair back from gray.
Would your husband like a younger-looking wife? *(Oil of Olay. Note the appeal to fear, too)*
It's Pepsi, for those who think young.

A-6 love.   Here the trick is to suggest that anyone who uses your product will instantly become more attractive to the opposite sex.

Brush up your sex appeal with Ultra Brite. *(Toothpaste)*
Arrow introduces the shirt women love to touch.

A-7 patriotism.   Sometimes you can make a little of the customer's love-of-country rub off on your product.

Chevrolet: Building a better way to see the USA.
The great American wool *(Burlington Woolens)*

A-8 good citizenship.   If you can show that your client is a generous contributor to charities or is working to improve the environment, you will enhance his "institutional image" in the public eye. Eventually some of this approval will probably be transferred to the client's product or service.

Techniques

T-1 straight delivery.   The most direct way to approach the customer is to say, "You should use Product X because. . . ."

T-2 drama.   But if you'll remember, the direct approach didn't work for Pampers, while the dramatic approach did. On radio and TV you'll find many examples of commercial drama. Notice that sometimes there's a "tag" at the end—a statement by the announcer that repeats the name of the product and perhaps the reason people should buy it. In other cases, the "sell" is worked into the drama itself, or delivered along with the drama by a voice-over commentator.

T-3 personification.   You can dramatize your pitch in another way by turning the product into a human or partly human character. Examples are the SOS soap pad, the Jolly Green Giant, the Wonder Bread Fresh Guys, and Rice Krispies' Snap, Crackle, and Pop.

T-4 demonstration. One advantage of TV is that it gives you a chance to show your product in action. For example, watch Josephine the Plumber get a sink clean with Comet. Notice that Josephine combines Drama and Demonstration.

T-5 testimonials and endorsements. This technique can be divided into several sub-types. There's the Expert Testimonial, in which medical men, engineers, laboratory scientists, or other knowledgeable persons say that the product really works. However, since there are rules against in-person endorsements by medical professionals, such endorsements have to be worded carefully. You can't say, "Dr. So-and-so prescribes our pain-reliever for all his patients." But you can say, "Our product contains more of the pain-relieving ingredient that most doctors recommend."

> Dentists want to save teeth, not pull them. That's why a dentist designed the PY-CO-PAY brush.
> 1,694 hospitals use Pampers.

Then there's the Celebrity Testimonial. Find an athlete, actress, or other accomplished and well-known person who will say in public that he uses and likes your product. Then hope the audience will follow his example.

Customer Testimonials can also be very effective. You set up interviews with a number of ordinary citizens who've used your product, and then publicize the comments of those who say they like it. Naturally, you ignore those who say it's terrible.

Finally, there's the Employee Testimonial. This involves identifying some of the workers who make the product or offer the service you're advertising. You present them as interesting, friendly human beings with whom it's a pleasure to do business. Thus you suggest to the customer that if X Company has all these nice people working for it, it must be reliable.

> Come to Gramercy Park *(a men's clothing store in N. Y. C.).* Rosie-with-the-cigar or Flatbush Phil will be glad to help you.
> We don't have to work for Pan Am—but we want to. *(The accompanying photo shows smiling crew and office personnel.)*

T-6 names, slogans, and jingles. Some years ago, National Biscuit Company introduced a cookie called Snickerdoodles. With that name, it just crumbled away from old age on grocery shelves. Then the company changed the name to Cinnamon Sugar Cookies, and sales rocketed past $4 million.

Probably you won't get a chance to name the product; your job will be to make an already established name a household word. To do this, mention it often in your ad copy, perhaps making it part of a memorable slogan or musical jingle.

One observer has called advertising catch-phrases "a good old American substitute for the facts." Yet no one can deny that they stick in the mind. And, after all, getting into the customer's skull is what these Claims, Appeals, and Techniques are all about.

Try it—you'll like it. *(Alka-Seltzer)*
I can be *very* friendly. *(Sunoco service stations)*
We go to a lot of pains. *(Bayer Aspirin)*

I. VOCABULARY

| cherished | robust | gracious |
| exclusivity | provocative | personification |

II. QUESTIONS ON CONTENT

1. According to the author, what is the main purpose of advertising? Do you agree?
2. What are Claims? What are Appeals? How do they differ? Why are they often used together?
3. Which of the advertising techniques cited would be most suitable for newspapers and magazines? For radio? For television?
4. The section on Appeals refers to basic human emotions that advertising manipulates. What are they? Can you suggest any other fears, desires, beliefs, and so on to which advertising appeals?
5. In your opinion, which, if any, of the tricks discussed are on the borderline between honesty and dishonesty? Would you consider any of them unethical? Why or why not?
6. Do you think this article will make you a more independent and intelligent consumer?
7. How does the American system of mass communication, as discussed in the essay on p. 62 both depend upon advertising and enhance its influence upon us?
8. Advertising is like propaganda because both aim to reach a large and defined audience through specified mass media for the specific purpose of persuading this audience. Reread "How To Detect Propaganda" (p. 104) and point out those propaganda devices used by advertisers to develop and reinforce the tricks discussed in the selection.

III. QUESTIONS ON FORM

1. What is Burns' purpose in writing this essay? How does this purpose determine her aim, audience, and tone?
2. In view of her purpose, what mode of organization is used? Is this mode a suitable choice? What other modes are used to develop the primary one? Are they effective?
3. What does the word "trick" in the title imply? Do you think this is the correct word for what ads try to do? If not, what word would you consider right or more appropriate?
4. What is the level of language in the essay? Is it appropriate to the author's purpose and audience?
5. This essay lacks a conclusion. Does this omission make the essay any less meaningful or interesting?

IV. SUGGESTIONS FOR WRITING

1. Describe in detail an ad that relies chiefly or entirely upon either Claims or Appeals to sell its product. Analyze and evaluate the types of claims or appeals used and their effectiveness.
2. Update this essay by providing one recent example for either each of the six claims, each of the eight appeals, or each of the six techniques.
3. Describe in detail an ad that you believe is dishonest or unethical and give reasons for your belief.
4. Tell of a time in your life when you bought products that you felt would harmonize with or enhance your self-image at this time.
5. If you are one of the few who are not influenced by advertising, explain how you are able to screen or block out the attempts to persuade you to buy a particular product.

So Long, Ring Around the Collar! Welcome, Paper Blob!

Rod Townley

It's coming."

A stunned executive looks up from his desk.

"It's taking over in offices coast to coast."

Alarmed woman at file drawer. Aghast junior accountant. Shuddering senior veep.

"It's . . . The Paper Blob!!"

Reprinted with permission from *TV Guide* ® magazine. Copyright © 1982 by Triangle Publications, Inc., Radnor, Pennsylvania.

In a wacky takeoff on all those great old horror movies, a huge mass of paper comes burgeoning down the corridor, overwhelming everyone in its path. The 30-second drama ends with a rescue by the hero, Federal Express, and its ringing slogan: "When it absolutely, positively has to be there overnight."

Created by the Ally and Gargano agency, recent Federal Express commercials have won a Clio award for the best national TV campaign and the American Marketing Association's Effie award for effectiveness. Even competitors like Pat Cunningham, creative director at the NW Ayer agency, willingly concede that Ally and Gargano has done "a tremendous job with Federal Express. They've kept to one simple message and they've executed it beautifully. Everything in there is perfect: casting, cinematography, the voice-over."

And one thing more: the bottom line. In December 1974, the first year of the advertising blitz, Federal Express was moving 11,000 packages per night. By September '81, it was moving 122,000 per night, more than any other company in the field.

What elements make a TV ad campaign effective? And are they the same elements that seemed to guarantee effectiveness in the past?

The answer, of course, is that there are never any guarantees. The ingredients are volatile, and what worked last year may not work today, although it will probably be imitated. One minimum requirement is that people should remember having seen the ad. To find out if they do, research departments put new ads through a battery of tests, among them the "day-after recall," or D.A.R. Assorted people are telephoned the day after a commercial is shown, and are asked if they remember seeing it. An average acceptable score is 22 per cent; anything much below that sends the ad back to the drawing board or into the trash. In many agencies, this leads to understandable friction between the creative and research departments.

But clearly there's more to judging the quality and effectiveness of a commercial than reading off the results of a day-after recall test. "Recall is not a religion," declares Fred Posner, executive director of marketing services and research at NW Ayer. If a commercial is offensive enough, he thinks, high recall can actually hurt, because "the offensiveness may carry over onto the product."

Thus, while some agencies are concentrating heavily on "intrusiveness," or getting the attention of the viewer at all costs, other agencies such as Ayer see the trend of the future as a "softer, more emotional sell; strong images; a greater sensitivity to the possible offensiveness of the commercial."

What many advertisers are finding is that the softer, emotional ads can actually make more of an impression than the old hit-'em-over-the-head commercials that promise "fast, fast, fast relief" from headaches or freedom from the dreaded "ring around the collar." Even here there is disagreement. Pat Stokes, vice president of creative services at the Jordan, Case & McGrath agency, thinks that heavy repetition is fine for certain kinds of products, such as Anacin. "A headache is a droning, repetitive thing. The commercial is reminding you psychologically of what your headache is." Others, like Scott Miller of McCann-Erickson, question the wisdom of a campaign that induces the condition the product is supposed to cure.

For the softer-selling, high-emotion commercials, NW Ayer is the agency one thinks of first. Some of their campaigns are orgies of emotion. "Reach out and touch someone," urges Ayer's ads for AT&T Long Lines. Kids and grandmoms, mothers and long-lost relations fight back tears of joy as they share poignant moments over the phone.

Then there are Ayer's ads for 7UP. What soft drinks have to do with the emotions of fatherhood is never made clear, but there on the TV we see champ Sugar Ray Leonard and his cute little boy sharing a touching father-son moment over a frosty bottle of 7UP. As with the AT&T commercials, a chorus of larklike voices bursts into exhilarating song to emphasize the true human wonderfulness of the product.

Indeed, the use of music seems to be increasing in commercials of all kinds. Geri Warren of Batten, Barton, Durstine & Osborn sees it as a real trend. People are bursting into song these days at the drop of a hat, the churn of a wash load, the whiff of a perfume—yes, even at the sight of TV GUIDE.

Emotion-laden ads may never completely supplant the fast pitches and knock-down-drag-out comparison tests that we still endure daily. In fact, with some products in some markets, a hard sell may still be the best approach. This is particularly true with package goods; advertisers struggle to differentiate their soap or salad dressing from the select of similar products. If they can isolate one clear "benefit"—something that their competition cannot claim—they'll flog it.

In the early days when Federal Express was just getting off the ground, its ads made hard-hitting comparisons with Emery, at that time the leader of the air courier industry. A couple of years later, Federal became the leader and the comparison ads were dropped. Efforts were put into expanding the market rather than clobbering the competition. Sly humor was introduced, evoking sympathy, for the common office worker. Clever 30-second playlets showed underdog workers saving their bosses' hides with a timely call to Federal.

Amil Gargano of the Ally and Gargano agency sees an evolution here from simple hard sell to complex humorous sell, but he is not willing to say that the second kind of ad is better than the first. Early in a company's history, hard comparison ads may be necessary. Later, greater complexity and playfulness may be appropriate.

Sometimes a company may use different kinds of ads at the same time.

Coca-Cola, which has always used an upbeat, emotional "image" campaign as its main thrust, has also undertaken a parallel campaign—a much harder sell—using Bill Cosby to beat back "The Pepsi Challenge."

Using famous personalities to flog products is not a new idea, of course, although it's often done more subtly than in the past. Presenters like Karl Malden (for American Express) and Robert Morley (for British Airways) seem to embody the qualities of the products they push. They're not merely famous persons standing up there telling you what to do. The important thing, says Peter Whitelam of the Parkson Agency, is for the product to have a distinct personality of its own.

"The Polaroid OneStep camera," he opines, "doesn't have its own brand personality. It's known as the thing James Garner does."

Such judgments tend to be subjective, and in fact one of the Polaroid ads was ranked seventh among the "most outstanding" commercials of last year, according to a survey by Video Storyboard Tests. Yet the man who conducted that survey, Dave Vadehra, says that as popular as the ad was, many respondents thought it was for Kodak, not Polaroid. The same confusion, says Vadehra, occurs between Coke and Pepsi.

What usually happens when one brand is mistaken for another, he says, is that "the brand leader takes the lot. Today anybody who makes a light-beer commercial has a half-and-half chance that people will think it's a Miller Lite commercial." A year or two ago, Natural Light came up with a campaign using sports figures who at one time had done ads for Miller. They were saying that they'd now switched to Natural Light. "The net result was that people who saw them thought they were Miller Lite commercials anyway. That was one of the sillier stories of the year."

The moral seems to be that if you're not the brand leader in a given market, try to be as different as you can from the guy who is. Dr. Pepper, says Vadehra, is never confused with any other soft drink. Its "brand personality" is very strong.

The truth is, no one really knows what makes a person go out and buy a product. There's more research being done now. There's a move toward more emotional, "image" advertising. And Geri Warren of BBDO thinks "there's a real trend toward personalizing and humanizing even the hard-sell kind of advertising." (Bill Cosby for Coke would be an example of this.) But no one can say just how that trigger mechanism in the brain works that suddenly lights up the "Buy" sign and makes us open our wallets.

"Despite what people say about this business," says Amil Gargano, "it is not by any means a science."

We live in an age of video clutter, assaulted by some 2500 commercials per month, most of which we pay as little attention to as possible. In such an environment, says Dave Vadehra, maybe the best thing a commercial can accomplish is merely "to leave a nice feeling for the corporation." Vadehra

210 Popular Writing

thinks that the image advertisements for Coke are a good example. "They never say: Go and buy Coke. Or Coke is cheaper. They just make you smile about yourself and about the world. Make you feel that advertisers are not such a terrible bunch after all."

GRIN AND BEAR IT by Lichty & Wagner

"Well, I think ring-around-the-collar ranks right up there with the worst of our problems."

GRIN AND BEAR IT by Lichty & Wagner, copyright © by and permission of News America Syndicate.

I. VOCABULARY

aghast
burgeoning
cinematography
volatile

poignant
exhilarating
flog
opine

II. QUESTIONS ON CONTENT

1. Explain the meaning of the title.
2. According to the article, what elements make a television ad campaign effective? Can you think of any others?
3. What is a hard-sell ad? A soft-sell ad? How do they differ? When should each be used?
4. How and why did Federal Express gradually change its ad campaign?
5. What is "brand personality"? Describe the identity created for Dr. Pepper and explain how it inspires brand loyalty.
6. Do you see any evidence of the trend toward softer, mor emotional ads? Toward the increased use of music in commercials? Do you approve of these trends? Explain.
7. What tricks of advertising in the previous essay does Townley mention? Does he provide any additional insights into these tricks?
8. Do you agree with the statement that "no one really knows what makes a person go out and buy a product"?

III. QUESTIONS ON FORM

1. Why and how is the introduction effective?
2. Where in the essay does the author restrict or limit his subject? How?
3. How is the discussion of ads organized? Is this organization similar to that used by Marjorie Burns in "The Advertiser's Bag of Tricks"?
4. Why does Townley focus on Federal Express commercials?
5. How does the author persuade you that there is a move toward more emotional, "image" advertising?

IV. SUGGESTIONS FOR WRITING

1. Describe a recent commercial ad that takes the soft-sell approach and explain the techniques employed to persuade the consumer.
2. Analyze the reasons for the current trend toward soft-sell commercials. To what extent is this trend a reflection of the 1970s that has sometimes been described as the "Me Decade"—self-centered, self-indulgent, and self-gratifying?
3. Examine the brand personality that ad people have created for a particular product, such as automobiles, beer, cigarettes, soft drinks, and so on. Cite specific tricks or propaganda devices used to create this personality.
4. Locate and describe two different kinds of ads that a company is using at the same time. Which one do you think is more effective? Why?
5. In an article in *Mother Jones* for December 1981, Ron Rosenbaum argued that "The early '80s have witnessed the return of the Hard Sell, or what

212 Popular Writing

might be called the 'no more Mr. Nice Guy' school of commercial strategy. Support this argument with examples and explore some of the changes in personal and social life that you think have led to the revival of the hard sell.

Bob Wiemer is an editorial writer and a reviewer for the Sunday book section of *Newsday*. He was a recipient of a first prize for distinguished editorial writing awarded by the New York State Publishers Association, and has been during his career a reporter, news editor, and United Nations correspondent.

Those Packages Aren't Just Selling Deodorant

Bob Wiemer

Is the time at hand to start assigning G, PG, R and X ratings to supermarket aisles?

Vance Packard's book, "The Hidden Persuaders," explored the way careful and very expensive motivational research shaped packaging decisions.

That was apparently a valuable selling tool, but lately some packages seen on the shelves suggest the process has gone too far. The symbolism used in at least one contemporary merchandising war is so gross, clumsy and obvious that it's ludicrous.

The October issue of National Lampoon contains an advertisement for Faberge's Brut 33 Roller-Ball antiperspirant. "Have a Real Ball!" says the headline, and the copy goes on to say: "The big ball gives you man-sized protection . . ."

The accompanying illustration, however, hints the ad is a Lampoon satire. The phallic-shaped deodorant container is stylized, but there is no chance that the symbolism is accidental. The container was obviously deliberately shaped to make the most basic macho statement its designers could conceptualize. They succeeded. The rendering, in fact, is so blatant it's funny.

It's usually possible to sort out Lampoon satire. It tends toward the sophomoric. But in this case, the question raised by the ad requires a visit to a supermarket. There, among the deodorants and the colognes, it quickly becomes apparent that truth is funnier than fiction.

The National Lampoon wasn't kidding around. That was a real ad. Brut 33

Copyright © 1980 by Newsday, Inc. Reprinted by permission.

Roller-Ball antiperspirant is right there on the shelf. What's more, there's no question why the Faberge people went as far as they did: A Freudian war is in progress. Merchandisers, apparently, have discovered that such symbolism sells. The shelves are crammed with gross macho imagery.

The leader of the pack is the Bristol-Myers Co., which puts out Tickle, a deodorant, in an assortment of pastel-colored containers, all appropriately shaped to tickle the buyer's Freudian sensibilities. The firm also puts out Ban Super Solid, Ultra Ban, Ban Basic and Vitalis in both pump-spray and aerosol containers.

The design brings to mind either the round-domed silos of the Middle West or those cylindrical aluminum cigar containers, which perhaps initiated the packaging trend. Pierre Cardin men's cologne, Mitchum deodorant and Gillette hair spray are similarly packaged.

The male emphasis in deodorant packaging and advertising is a relatively new phenomenon.

The subject was reviewed 16 years ago by Ernest Dichter, the president of the Institute for Motivational Research. He devoted a section of his "Handbook of Consumer Motivation" to deodorants. But he didn't have much to say about packaging, and he said nothing at all about the sort of symbolism that now dominates the market.

He noted that there was a type of individual who suffers from "body-centered" social anxiety, explaining that while such persons might not be any more anxious than anyone else, they tended to translate their anxiety into a concern about cleanliness.

Said Dichter: "The body-centered, socially anxious individual has been strongly and effectively appealed to by old-fashioned, hard-hitting, scare-psychology deodorant type of advertising."

But he added that the products had since come of age. "They have advanced from the role of somewhat painful necessities to become an important toilet article, almost a cosmetic . . . Gone is the appeal to help guard the 'ugly secret;' deodorants are now symbols of femininity and an integral part of a refined woman's toilette, allied to cosmetics, beauty products and expendable luxuries."

Considering the heavy feminine overtones the product carried as recently as 1964, it's not hard to understand how the manufacturers got so deeply involved in masculine symbolic overkill in the years since then.

Another possible reason that the manufacturers found it necessary to get so silly about the packaging may have been a need to overcome what Dichter called "routinization." This refers to the consumer practice of buying the same brand time after time as a sort of ritual.

Dichter saw razor blades as a routinized product, and he predicted deodorants were moving into that category.

"The reason that 75 per cent of the razor-using people still buy Gillette razor blades is anchored in the fact that shaving is one of the slightly unpleasant activities of the modern male," said Dichter. "He doesn't want to have to think about each decision; he simply reaches for the same brand."

So the new X-rated packaging may be only a variation on the way muleskinners started a training session. They whacked the beast with a club to get its attention.

I. VOCABULARY

symbolism macho sensibilities
ludicrous blatant phenomenon
phallic sophomoric toilette

II. QUESTIONS ON CONTENT

1. What, according to the article, are deodorant packages selling besides deodorant? Do you agree with this view?
2. What is motivational research? How is it related to the tricks employed by advertisers to persuade us to buy a product? To their use of the soft and hard sell?
3. What is the Freudian war that is in progress? What is the reason for it?
4. Should any phallic-shaped product or package automatically be considered a deliberate use of masculine symbolism? Are there not times when, as Freud himself once said, a cigar is just a cigar?
5. Why does the author think that the male emphasis in deodorant packaging is excessive and foolish? Do you share his opinion?
6. What is "routinization"? What products do you buy because of this practice?
7. Why do you think deodorant products are much more popular today than in the past?

III. QUESTIONS ON FORM

1. Did the introductory paragraph surprise you? Why or why not?
2. What does the author mean by "macho"? Is his definition clear and accurate?
3. How would you characterize the language in the copy for the Brut antiperspirant?
4. Is the Brut ad a good choice of example to support Wiemer's argument? Should he have given other examples?
5. Why does Wiemer devote so much space to the opinions of Ernest Dichter? Should he have consulted other authorities and more recent literature on the subject?

6. This article contains numerous short sentences and short paragraphs. How does this stylistic trait contribute to the tone of the essay? Does it give you a clue as to the specific mass media for which the article was written?
7. Explain the last paragraph. Is it an effective conclusion?

IV. SUGGESTIONS FOR WRITING

1. Explore some of the reasons for the increasing prominence of the package in advertising.
2. Argue for or against the view that packaging sells products.
3. Imitating Wiemer's treatment of the Brut antiperspirant ad, describe an ad for a product whose package and copy contain masculine or feminine symbolism, explicit or implicit, and decide whether or not you think the ad is in good taste.
4. Describe one or more old-fashioned, hard-sell deodorant type of ads noted by Dichter.
5. Choose a personal-care product such as shampoo, lipstick, perfume, cologne, and so on. Next, write ad copy for it that gives the consumer the feeling of sexual reassurance by choosing words that suggest masculine and feminine images (for example, "handsome" and "beautiful").
6. If you use a deodorant or antiperspirant, explain why you need to use this product. Is it, perhaps, because you are the type of individual described by Dichter?

A senior editor for *New York* magazine, **Bernice Kanner** writes the weekly "On Madison Ave." column on advertising.

The Fizz Biz: Tiny Bubbles

Bernice Kanner

The fact is, Americans just aren't overeating, overdrinking, and overindulging in general the way they used to. And while that may spell relief to millions of heads and stomachs, it has spelled only trouble for Alka-Seltzer. The well-known aid for gluttons, bingers, and all-purpose overdoers had become synonymous with a hangover cure in the public's mind, and therefore almost obsolete in the temperate 1980s. What would make today's

Copyright © 1984 by News Group Publications, Inc. Reprinted with the permission of *New York* Magazine.

consumers reach for the familiar blue-and-white packet, plop its two subway-token-size tablets in water, and wait for the fizz?

To find out, Miles Laboratories, the unit of A. G. Bayer that makes Alka-Seltzer, turned to McCann-Erickson, the advertising agency, last September. McCann came up with the strategy of presenting Alka-Seltzer as an upbeat product, a remedy for all the symptoms of stress that come with success—and a product with almost universal appeal. After all, who does not, as the new campaign states, suffer "the anxious upset stomach that comes with a thumping headache or the thumping headache that comes with an upset stomach"?

According to McCann's research, about 30 percent of the population uses antacids. But who are they? Very middle-American but extremely upwardly mobile types. "They're highly susceptible to advertising and believe literally the claims products make," says Paula Drillman, the agency's research director. "In no other category I've examined do consumers respond like this."

The research also revealed that people who used to pop Alka-Seltzer twenty times a year had begun taking other remedies that addressed more contemporary ailments, such as nervous tension. Furthermore, says Michael Sennott, senior vice-president and management representative at McCann, "people had stopped identifying with the shlumpy characters in the Alka-Seltzer commercials." Interview subjects asked to draw an Alka-Seltzer user invariably penned someone potbellied and tieless. Other antacid users sketched were well groomed. "We had captured the hearts and minds of people—but our message was no longer relevant," says Sennott.

The characters in those spots weren't up to the marketing task at hand. Remember the spicy-meatball man and the stupefied glutton who "can't believe" he "ate the whole thing"? They didn't speak to the masses yearning for success, and their message was more apropos to the permissive, pill-popping 1960s and 1970s than to the all-things-in-moderation 1980s. "The executive lunch that began with a couple of martinis is as much a relic as the weekly hangover," says Drillman. "Many business people don't even order wine at lunch anymore—it's spritzers and Perrier. If you position to the mind-set of overindulgence today, you're dead."

Alka-Seltzer's new commercials, which make their debut this week, may not have the hilarious situations and absurd characters that were long its trademark—and that made the spots part of America's pop-cultural heritage. But they do have drama and style. Where they once leaned toward the ridiculous, they now seem headed for the sublime.

In one almost surrealistic spot, a piano tinkles an Erik Satie melody as the camera focuses on two tablets, bobbing in slow motion in a watercooler, that look more like sculpture than medication. A soothing voice-over salutes the junior executive who has vowed to become a vice-president by the end of the fiscal year, the vice-president who has vowed to become senior vice-president by the time she is 39, and the board chairman who must ultimately face the shareholders. Then the voice delivers the pitch "for the symptoms of stress that can come with success" as the tablets are released—they seem to float—into a glass of water and a sea of bubbles explodes. And in another spot, dedicated to the class of '84, a mortarboard is lofted into Magritte-type clouds, where it spins slowly.

Alka-Seltzer's new look has come to an old product. Miles Labs concocted the first—and only—product combining aspirin and an antacid in 1929. Hub Beardsley, then president of Miles, located in Elkhart, Indiana, had visited the local newspaper during a flu epidemic that mysteriously bypassed the paper's employees. Everyone credited the editor's home presciption—a dose of aspirin and bicarbonate of soda—and Beardsley asked Miles's chemists to imitate the formula. He then distributed Alka-Seltzer to fellow passengers on a Mediterranean cruise who had the flu, and in 1931 began promoting it on the radio, eventually sponsoring shows including *The Saturday Night Barn Dance* and *The Quiz Kids.* The product became associated with relieving hangovers, and in 1933, when Prohibition ended, its sales spurted.

Alka-Seltzer continued to grow through the 1940s and 1950s, when Speedy, the three-dimensional animated figure and precursor of the Pillsbury Doughboy, charmed TV audiences with "relief is just [pause] a swallow away [*ping*]." "Speedy was an unthreatening character who established the brand with viewers," says Bruce Nelson, executive vice-president of McCann. "He didn't dish out any parental stuff. Rather, his style was 'Oh boy, you've done it again, wink, wink.'" Adds executive vice-president Ira Madris, "To have a salesman liked is a wonderful foot in the door for a product. Speedy was a well-liked salesman."

His successor, in the early 1960s, was an animated talking stomach. A cartoon man sat in one chair while his irate little (though bloated) stomach sat in another and took him to task for all his pepperoni binges. About the same time, Alka-Seltzer aired what Miles Labs figures is its most remembered commercial: the stomach montage. The camera panned a universe of assorted abdomens, then, 55 seconds into the spot, a voice-over said, "No matter what shape your stomach is in, when it gets out of shape, take Alka-Seltzer."

The late 1960s were Alka-Seltzer's heyday. Americans guffawed as poor Jack suffered through 59 takes of a "commercial" for those spicy meatballs. They laughed as a waiter urged a hapless diner to "try it—you'll like it." And they so enjoyed the glassy-eyed, rumpled Ralph's lament, "I can't believe I ate the whole thing," that they made it part of the vernacular.

Those glory days for Alka-Seltzer and advertising came to a halt in late 1972 when the Food and Drug Administration, spurred by Ralph Nader, undertook a major regulatory review of over-the-counter drugs. Alka-Seltzer came in for a lot of negative publicity about aspirin's effects on the stomach, and "we could no longer promote it for upset stomachs alone," says Stephen Reim, brand manager for Alka-Seltzer.

Miles Labs defended Alka-Seltzer's formula in the scientific community, but introduced Alka-Seltzer Gold, a nonaspirin product just for stomachs. It has not caught on. The company also cut back on advertising the original Alka-Seltzer, and from 1973 through 1978 tried a slew of different campaigns. Sammy Davis Jr. crooned for the brand, and there was a series of dull testimonials. "We tried to show our critics we were living up to the F.D.A. regulations," explains Reim. But none of the campaigns clicked until Wells Rich Greene came up with "plop, plop, fizz, fizz—oh, what a relief it is" in 1976. That ran for three years.

In 1981, Miles's research confirmed that the public was still skeptical about the government review and Ralph Nader's attacks. "We had to tell more of a reassurance story," says Reim. The company's answer: America's Home Remedy, a campaign in which a disheveled-looking binger groped his way down a long corridor, or pawed through the medicine cabinet panic-stricken that the Alka-Seltzer wasn't there. Those spots worked briefly, but the field was growing increasingly more competitive. In 1982, antacid advertisers spent approximately $70 million, though most of their spots are the heavy-handed, claim-cluttered, comparative kind. (Sales for the upset-stomach-remedy category climbed 9.1 percent to $638 million last year. Liquids are the largest segment, followed by chewables. Alka-Seltzer remains the leader of the effervescents—a relatively small segment that also includes Bromo Seltzer and the regional brand Brioschi—and with a 14 percent share of the overall antacid market trails just Maalox liquid and chewables combined, which have a 15 percent share, and edges out Mylanta [13 percent], Pepto Bismol liquid and chewables combined [13 percent], Rolaids [12.5 percent], and Tums [7 percent], according to A. C. Nielsen figures.)

Alka-Seltzer, which spends about $15-million a year on advertising, stopped being a maverick in 1982 by coming out with its own comparative commercial. In Big Relief, a dyspeptic fisherman rejected offers of Rolaids and Tums before finally finding what he wanted in his hat: Alka-Seltzer, of course.

It was when that campaign also fizzled that Miles started looking around for another approach. Whether the arty new commercials will bring relief to Alka-Seltzer—and prove as memorable as some of their predecessors—remains to be seen. Meanwhile, I admit I was moved after previewing them to try the stuff for the first time. It tastes a lot like regular seltzer, except sharper. It's an acquired taste, they tell me.

I. VOCABULARY

glutton	stupefied	montage	disheveled
temperate	sublime	heyday	maverick
antacid	surrealistic	guffaw	dyspeptic
shlumpy	concoct	hapless	
invariably	irate	slew (n.)	

II. QUESTIONS ON CONTENT

1. What is the brand personality or image that Alka-Seltzer had created for itself from the 1930s through the 1970s? Why was this image appropriate to the period?
2. According to research by the McCann-Erickson advertising agency, why has Alka-Seltzer lost much of its appeal in the 1980s?
3. What is the new commercial campaign that Alka-Seltzer plans to launch? How will the new image of this product differ from the established image? Do you think the new strategy will work?
4. What specific advertising tricks do the new Alka-Seltzer commercials use? How are these tricks or techniques different from previous ones? Do the new commercials rely more on the soft sell than the hard sell? Why?
5. The author says the new Alka-Seltzer commercials have "drama and style." Do you agree with her? Would these ads encourage you, as they did her, to try the product for the first time?
6. What basic assumption about the relationship between advertising and society underlies Alka-Seltzer's plan to change its established trademark?

III. QUESTIONS ON FORM

1. How does the title catch your attention?
2. Identify the thesis in the essay.
3. What evidence does the author give to convince you that Alka-Seltzer is less popular today than it used to be?
4. How does Kanner develop her statement about Alka-Seltzer's "arty" new commercials?
5. Why does the writer discuss the origin and development of Alka-Seltzer and its brand personality? What rhetorical mode is used to organize this discussion? Is this mode appropriate to her intention?
6. Can you describe a "Magritte-type cloud" (page 217, paragraph 1)? Do you think this comparison should have been employed? Explain.
7. In the last paragraph the author introduces personal experience. Why? Does this make the conclusion more effective?

IV. SUGGESTIONS FOR WRITING

1. Commercials are always targeted for specific audiences. Select any two ads for the same product, describe each ad in detail, and then deduce from the ads the intended audience.
2. Using your knowledge of advertising tricks and propaganda devices, formulate your own ad campaign for Alka-Seltzer.
3. Comment on the strategy proposed by the McCann-Erickson ad agency for a new Alka-Seltzer campaign. Is the agency's analysis of the changing times and Alka-Seltzer's failure to adapt to it valid? Do you think this ad campaign will succeed?

4. As the Alka-Seltzer "Big Relief" ad suggests, a recent development in advertising has been the comparative commercial. For example, soft-drink giants like Coca-Cola and Pepsi-Cola and hamburger corporations like Burger King, McDonald's, and Wendy's have spent millions of dollars in ad campaigns that attack their chief competitors. Do you approve or disapprove of this practice of creating ads that make offensive comparisons with competitive products? Provide specific examples of such ads to support your opinion.
5. Select a new type of ad for an established product and compare and contrast it with older ads for this product. Why do you think the company has changed its advertising strategy?
6. Compare and contrast the changes in the ad campaigns of Alka-Seltzer and Federal Express (see "So Long, Ring Around The Collar! Welcome, Paper Blob!"). Give reasons for these changes.

John Cheever, who died in 1982, was a celebrated novelist and short story writer. Author of *The Wapshot Chronicle* (1957), *The Wapshot Scandal* (1964), *Bullet Park* (1969), *Falconer* (1977), as well as television scripts, Cheever was awarded a Pulitzer prize in fiction in 1977, for *The Stories of John Cheever*.

Don't Leave the Room During the Commercials

John Cheever

A few years ago, Dick Cavett asked me, on one of the three shows we taped, if it was true that I answered all of my mail without cards, form letters or the assistance of a secretary. I said, enthusiastically, that this was true. The mail this reply provoked was bulky and various but distinguished by its high quality. The mail one receives after a *Time* or a *Newsweek* cover is voluminous and gratifying but the mail I received from the Cavett show seemed to me exceptionally discerning. The TV audience, in computer surveys, is often described as a mass of cretins with an unmanageable addiction to the plugin drug. On the evidence of the Cavett mail, the TV audience includes a vast number of mature and amiable men and women. One does not write for an audience, of course, but, this late in my career, I have come to think of writing much more as a conversation than discourse. To succeed as a writer depends greatly upon the intelligence of the reader, and here on TV was a huge, responsive and intelligent popuation.

Reprinted by permission of International Creative Management as agents for the Estate of John Cheever.

When the circulation of The New Yorker was under half a million, and when I was a very young man, the response to stories published there was exciting. The magazine was on the newsstands on Wednesday and you could usually count on the beginnings of an enthusiastic response by the Saturday-afternoon mail. It was not that one had been able to ingratiate or charm the reader—it was that one had been able to communicate with responsive adults on such arcane matters as romance, hopefulness and despair. The first canon of aesthetics is, of course, interest; and within this canon lies the fact that serious writing is our most intimate and acute means of communication. The Dick Cavett mail came from cities, but it also came from low-digit P.O. boxes on very low-digit postal routes in places like North Dakota, Florida, the West Coast and that snow belt near the Canadian border. These letters were distinguished by their intelligence and now and then by that keen loneliness with which most thoughtful men and women are familiar. With the exception of two proposals of marriage and two proposed assignations, the letters were all friendly and high-minded.

At about this time, Jac Venza, an executive producer at New York's public-television station WNET, asked me to lunch to discuss adapting some of my stories for television. To adapt fiction to another medium is something I regard unenthusiastically but I agreed to the adaptation of three stories by other playwrights if Jac Venza would be interested in my writing a one-hour original. He would. (The three adaptations, under the title *3 Cheever Stories*, appeared, during the 1979-80 season.)

I have often been invited to write for TV but I have always regretted these invitations since none of them promised me the independence that is imperative to my life as a writer. I had experienced this at first hand. Some years ago CBS had asked another writer and me to write a pilot for "Life with Father." We produced a script for a one-hour show that was received by everyone with great enthusiasm. A company of eight then met for lunch and settled down for our first story conference. My colleague and I said nothing for an hour while we listened to captious observations on the fall of a line, the possibility of cretinous misunderstanding and a good deal of personal reminiscence. I don't recall whether or not the two of us exchanged notes but we certainly exchanged glances and at the end of an hour we stood and said—in unison—that to adapt Clarence Day's memoirs to accommodate eight vastly dissimilar interpretations of the book was a project we did not wish to undertake. We left, slamming the door. So ended my experience with commercial TV.

Jac Venza offered me the independence I find necessary for writing, and the arrangement was settled with a shake of the hand. It is very apparent to me that I am not a playwright. TV is a new medium and one that might accommodate my inexperience and allow me to dissemble my clumsiness in this genre. It was in any case a one-shot and all I hoped was to address those who watch TV and who are conspicuously intelligent.

My screenplay is a comedy of errors revolving around the supposed abduction of the youngest member of the Wooster family. "The Shady Hill Kidnapping" unfolds in the suburbs of the Northeast. This is a world in which I have lived much of my life, and a world that has always seemed to be exceptionally rich and various. My intent has never been to judge the suburbs—they involve an improvised way of life—and when I see a housewife hanging out her clothes *and* and her marijuana I am fascinated. A lucky cross section of suburban life on a summer Saturday afternoon will produce lovers, spiritual pioneers, relics from the past and an astonishing amount of common sense and affection. I chose the importance of a child's life as a catalyst for the scene, and for the villain I settled for that level of bureaucracy one encounters at a motorvehicle bureau.

I am not an aesthetician, but in my opinion any art form or means of communication enjoys a continuous process of growth and change, rather like something organic, and one must be responsible to one's beginnings. There is a sort of highly artistic TV documentary that seems so alien to the true nature of the medium that it is rather like expecting Bucky Dent to do a scarf dance in Fenway Park. Before I wrote my screenplay I watched a great deal of television, timed the scenes and tried to observe the interest span of my wife and my friends.

Commercials seem to me terribly important. To cut from a sinking lifeboat filled with women and children to a decorous woman asking her druggist if he has anything for hemorrhoids is some deep part of the TV experience. It seems to me highly pretentious to compare TV commercials to the chorus in Greek tragedy, but commercials do bring a dimension to TV that completely transcends their merchandising usefulness. The commercials for my screenplay are for a fictitious tonic called Elixircol and they are meant to comment indirectly on the action of the screenplay.

We went into production last summer with Paul Bogart as director and Ann Blumenthal producing. Ann got together a first-rate cast with George Grizzard and Polly Holliday playing the parents of a suburban family in the throes of a *maladie du temps*. In a field of endeavor characterized by its high prices, it is interesting to observe that all our contributions came at basic minimum or less. I have among my dear friends a number of soap-opera millionaires who consider this shocking. Simply by owning the characters in a daytime serial they enjoy indoor tennis courts, art collections and private jets; but isn't it true that a certain amount of financial insouciance is of the first importance in keeping a new means of communication open-ended? Whatever would have become of the serious novel, marathon running or epic poetry if these pure forms of expressiveness had been intercut with commercials that cost half a million dollars a minute? We hope to be concerned with the enormous importance of TV as a means of communication and with the maturity and intelligence its audience possesses. My soap-opera friends tell me this is foolish; but then I tell them money isn't everything, even when you get it locked into old masters and tax-free, short-term municipals.

I. VOCABULARY

voluminous	ingratiate	assignation	bureaucracy
gratifying	arcane	imperative	pretentious
discerning	canon	captious	maladie du temps
cretin	aesthetics	dissemble	insouciance

II. QUESTIONS ON CONTENT

1. How does Cheever's estimate of the television audience differ from that usually found in surveys? Which opinion do you think is more accurate?
2. Why was the author wary of writing for television? Why did he change his mind?
3. Why does Cheever regard commercials as very important? How did he embody this belief in his screenplay? How does he justify artistically this unique conception of the function of commercials on television?
4. Why did Cheever's rich soap-opera friends disapprove of what he did in his first television drama? Do you also disapprove? Explain.
5. What, according to the author, is "serious" writing? How does it differ from writing for commercial television? From the kind of writing you do in your English composition courses?

III. QUESTIONS ON FORM

1. Where is the central idea stated most clearly? Why is it located where it is?
2. Explain how Cheever uses personal experience in the essay. Does he overuse the pronoun "I"?
3. What is the author's attitude toward commercial television? Toward the use of advertising to sell products? Does this, in your opinion, make him seem snobbish? idealistic? foolish?
4. Examine Cheever's diction in this essay. Does it indicate that he is a renowned writer of prose fiction? Explain.
5. Examine the sentence structure in the essay. How does it reflect the author's view of writing as much more a conversation than a discourse?

IV. SUGGESTIONS FOR WRITING

1. Like Cheever, you are probably annoyed at times by commercials that interrupt an exciting moment in a television program you are watching. Write an essay, combining narration and description, about one such event.

2. Discuss some of the ways in which writing commercials for television is different from writing commercials for newspapers and magazines.
3. Write an essay in which you give your own opinion of the television audience.
4. Write an essay in which you explain why you agree or disagree with Cheever's opinion that television commercials should assume a role that goes far beyond their merchandising usefulness.
5. Write an essay offering your own views on serious writing—its nature, aim, audience, and so on.

Author of *Polish Analytic Philosophy* (1967), **Henryk Skolimowski** has taught at a number of institutions of higher learning in the United States, including the University of Southern California where he was Associate Professor of Philosophy.

The Semantic Environment in the Age of Advertising

Henryk Skolimowski

David Ogilvy is a very successful advertising man. In addition, Mr. Ogilvy has turned out to be a successful writer. His book, *Confessions of an Advertising Man,* was a best-seller in 1965. His confessions are in fact intimate whisperings of one adman to another. These whisperings, however, turned out to be interesting enough to make his book one of the most readable and lucid stories of advertising ever written. What is so fascinating about this book is not the amount of linguistic contortions which he advocates, but the amount of truth which is expressed there incidentally. There is nothing more comforting than to find truth accidentally expressed by one's adversary. *Confessions of an Advertising Man* provides a wealth of such truths.

Mr. Ogilvy tells us that "the most powerful words you can use in a headline are *Free* and *New.* You can seldom use *Free,*" he continues, "but you can always use *New*—if you try hard enough." It is an empirical fact that these two words have a most powerful influence upon us. This fact has been established by scientific research. Whenever these words appear, they are used deliberately—in order to lull and seduce us.

The word *Free* is especially seductive. Whether we are aware of this or not, it has an almost hypnotic effect on us. Although we all know "nothing is for

---

Reprinted from ETC., Vol. 25, No. 1, by permission of the International Society for General Semantics.

nothing," whenever the word FREE appears, it acts on us as the light of a candle acts on a moth. This is one of the mysteries of our language. And these mysteries are very skillfully exploited by advertising men.

Apart from the words *Free* and *New*, other words and phrases "which make wonders," as Mr. Ogilvy's research has established, are: "*How to, Suddenly, Now, Announcing, Introducing, Important, Development, Amazing, Sensational, Revolutionary, Startling, Miracle, Offer, Quick, Easy, Wanted, Challenge, Advice to, The Truth about, Compare, Bargain, Hurry, Last Chance.*" Should we not be grateful to Mr. Ogilvy for such a splendid collection? Should we not learn these "miraculous" phrases by heart in order to know which particular ones drive us to the marketplace? To this collection I should like to add some of the phrases which I found: *Simple, Save, Convenient, Comfort, Luxury, Special Offer, Distinctive, Different, Rare*.

Having provided his collection, Ogilvy comments upon these words that make wonders (and this comment is most revealing): "Don't turn up your nose at these clichés. They may be shopworn, but they work." Alas! They work on us. What can we do about their merciless grip? Nothing. Language and its workings cannot be controlled or altered through an act of our will. The cumulative process of the development of language used as the instrument of tyranny or as the bridge to God through prayers; as a recorder of everyday trivia or as a clarion trumpet announcing new epochs in human history; as an expression of private feelings of single individuals or as a transmitter of slogans to the masses—this process has endowed some words with incredible subtleties and others with irresistible power. The only thing we can do about the influence of language on us is to become aware of it. This awareness may diminish the grip language has on us.

It is very gratifying to know that nowadays advertising is so punctilious, so systematic, and so scientific in its approach to the customer. Mr. Ogilvy in *Confessions* relentlessly repeats that "research has shown" so and so, "research shows" this and that, "research suggests" that, "research has established" that, etc. This constant reference is not an advertising humbug. It is through systematic research that we are "hooked" more and more thoroughly. With perfect innocence Ogilvy informs us that "Another profitable gambit is to give the reader helpful advice or service. It hooks about [was this a slip of the tongue, or intentional, plain description?] 75 per cent more readers than copy which deals entirely with the product."

Madison Avenue has, above all, established that through words we may be compelled to perform certain acts—acts of buying. This conclusion is not to be found in Ogilvy. Whether it is an historical accident or not, it is a rather striking fact that, independent of semanticists and logicians and linguistic philosophers, advertising men have made some important discoveries about language. And they have utilized these discoveries with amazing success. They are probably not aware of the theoretical significance of their discoveries and are no doubt little interested in such matters.

J.L. Austin, one of the most prominent linguistic philosophers at Oxford during the 1950's, developed a theory of what he called *performative utterances*. He observed that language is systematically employed not only for stating and describing but also for performing actions. Such utterances as "I warn you to . . . " or "I promise you x" are performances rather than descriptions. They function not only on a verbal level, but also as deeds, as concrete performances through words. The discovery and classification of performative utterances is an important extension of ordinary logic—that is, logic concerned with declarative utterances. On the other hand, it is an important finding of the hidden force of language in shaping our social and individual relationships.

Quite independently, advertising men have developed and successfully applied their own theory of performative utterances. They may be oblivious to the logical subtleties involved; however, they are not oblivious to the power of their medium—that is, the verbal utterances through which they induce our acts of buying. Again, there is very little we can do about it. This is the way language works. We can only recognize this fact. But once we recognize it, we acquire some immunity.

Now, we all know that advertising messages are conveyed in words. Usually, there are not only words, but pictures and images which suggest appropriate associations to the person reading the words. The images are projected to be psychologically appealing. Psychologically appealing images are those which appeal to our seven deadly sins: sexual urges, vanity, snobbery, gluttony, greed, etc.

Many analyses of advertising have shown the mechanism of psychological associations built into the ad message. In particular they showed that the level of most of these appeals is that of sheer brutes, of ultimate half-wits whose only desire is to satisfy their most rudimentary biological urges. However, not many analyses of advertising, if any at all, show how frail the link is between the picture set to evoke emotional reactions and the linguistic utterance which, in the final analysis, is the message of the ad. We must remember that it is the verbal message which ultimately draws us to the marketplace. The analysis of this verbal or linguistic level of the ad is our main concern here.

Language is, of course, basically a medium of communication. To be an adequate medium, language must be flexible. But to be flexible is one thing; to be entirely elastic and malleable is another. These other two characteristics, extreme elasticity and malleability, are required from the language which is set to infiltrate people's minds and contaminate their mental habits. It is in this latter capacity that admen want to employ language. And consequently, they do everything conceivable, and sometimes inconceivable, to make language infinitely flexible and as malleable as plasticene.

The point is very simple. If language is made of plasticene, the meaning of concepts is so stretched that words are deprived of their original sense and end up with whatever sense the wild imagination of the admen equips them. Since the language of ads often departs radically from ordinary language, advertisements could in one sense be regarded as pieces of poetry.

A piece of poetry should have a nice ring to its words, pleasant or extraordinary association of ideas, unusual combinations of meanings. The factual content is not important. For communication, as I shall use the term here, the factual content is most important. It is the content that we wish to communicate, and this is conveyed in messages. Consequently, messages must contain factual information. If there is no factual information in the message, the message does not communicate anything. Usually the actual content of the message may be expressed in many different ways. What is important is the content, not the manner of expression. If the manner of expressing a message is more important than its content, then the message does not serve the purpose of communication. It may serve many other purposes, but it does not serve the purpose of conveying factual information.

And this is exactly the case with advertising. The advertising messages are pseudo-messages, not genuine messages. They do not contain factual information. At any rate, this is not their main purpose. Their main purpose is not to inform but to force us to buy. It is clear that if the content of advertising were of any importance, then the same message worded differently would serve the same function; namely, of informing us. This is obviously not the case with advertising: the overwhelming majority of ads would have little effect, if any, if they were phrased differently.

In art, our emotional involvement is the source of our delight. It is the uniqueness of the form that inspires our thoughts and arouses our emotions. The meaning and significance of the work of art hinge upon the uniqueness of its form. Once the form is destroyed or altered, the work of art does not exist any more. If the validity of advertisements depends on preserving their form intact, then they pretend to be pieces of art, but not the carriers of factual information. The trouble is that they *do* pretend to give factual and objective information—but in a rather peculiar way: in such a way that the "information" would force us to acquire the product which is the substance of the message.

Communication is for humans. It is the mark of a rational man to grasp the content of a message irrespective of the form of its presentation—that is, irrespective of its linguistic expression. The nature of any communication in which the actual information conveyed is less significant than the matter of its presentation is, to say the least, illogical. The illogical man is what advertising is after. This is why advertising is so anti-rational; this is why it aims at uprooting not only the rationality of man but his common sense; this is why it indulges in exuberant but deplorable linguistic orgies.

Distortion of language, violation of logic, and corruption of values are about the most common devices through which advertising operates. This is particularly striking in endless perversions of the word FREE. Since this word has such a powerful impact on us, there is no limit to its abuse. In his novel *1984*, George Orwell showed that what is required for establishing a "perfect" dictatorship is perhaps no more than a systematic reform of language. The condition is, however, that the reform must be thorough and complete. "Double-talk" as a possible reality has, since Orwell's novel, been viewed with horror, but not with incredulity. The question is whether doubletalk has not already become part of our reality, has not already been diffused in our blood stream through means different from those Orwell conceived of. Isn't it true that advertising has become a perfect Orwellian institution?

Nowadays there is in operation a doubletalk concept of freedom according to which protecting the public from fraud and deceit and warning people about dangers to their health is but "an erosion of freedom." This concept of freedom is, needless to say, advocated and defended by advertising agencies. In the opinion of admen, "freedom" for people means protecting people from their common sense and ability to think. For many admen "freedom" means freedom to advertise in whatsoever manner is profitable, freedom to force you to buy, freedom to penetrate your subconscious, freedom to dupe you, to hook you, to make a sucker of you, freedom to take away your freedom. Anything else is for them but an "erosion of freedom." Hail Mr. Orwell! Hail doubletalk!

Now to turn to some concrete illustrations:

"Mustang! A Car to Make Weak Men Strong, Strong Men Invincible."

Do not say that we do not believe such obvious blusterings. We do. It seems that the art of magicians—according to which some incantations evoke events, bring rain, heal wounds; some amulets bring good luck, prevent bad luck or illness—has been re-established by contemporary advertising. Motor cars in particular are the amulets of the atomic age. They possess all the miraculous qualities you wish them to possess—from being a substitute for a sweetheart (or mistress, if you prefer) to being a soothing balm to a crushed ego. Dictionaries usually define an automobile as a self-propelled vehicle for transportation of people or goods. The car industry and car dealers are of a quite different opinion. Perhaps lexicographers are outdated in their conception of "automobile."

Roughly speaking, motor cars are advertised to be amulets of two kinds. The first casts spells on us and makes us happy, or builds up our personality, or adds to our strength, or makes us invincible if we are already strong; the second casts spells on others and, while we drive this magic vehicle, makes other people see us as more important, more influential, more irresistible. As yet, there are no cars which, being driven by us, would bring punishment upon our enemies. Perhaps one day this will come to pass. The question is how many of us can really resist the incantations of car dealers and remain impervious to the "magical" qualities allegedly embodied in the modern automobile. How many of us can remain uninfluenced by the continuous flow of messages, in spite of our ability to see the nonsense of each one individually?

Our civilization has often been called the motor-car civilization. But in no less degree, it is the drug civilization; it is also the detergent civilization. Each of these elements is apparently essential to the well-being of our society. But it is by no means only detergents, cars, or drugs that offer us full happiness "at a reasonable price." Nowadays, practically any product can give you happiness.

"Happiness is to Get (or Give) a Bulova"

The only problem is to believe it. Whether Bulova is a yellow canary, a black watch, or a green giraffe, it unfortunately takes a bit more to achieve happiness than getting or giving a Bulova. But of course the counter-argument can go, "happiness' in this ad was not meant literally but only figuratively. Admen today are like poets; we must allow them poetic license. But must we? And how figuratively would they really like to be taken? It seems that they (and the producers of the products they advertise) would be very unhappy if we took all their messages figuratively. On the contrary, they want their messages to be taken as literally as possible. It is precisely their business to convince us about the "loveliness" of soaps, "happiness" in Bulovas, and "delights" of a cigarette puff. The poetic language they use is meant to break our resistance, to produce desirable associations which we usually associate with poetry.

The sad part of the story is that in the process of serving advertising, poetry has gone down the drain. Poetic expressions are poetic so long as they are in the context of poetry; so long as they evoke unusual emotional reactions, serve as a substance of an esthetic experience—the experience of delight. In its exuberant development, advertising has debased almost the entire poetic vocabulary. And advertising seems to be responsible for a decline of the poetic taste and for a considerable indifference, if not hostility, of American youth toward poetry.

The nausea which one experiences on being bombarded by the pseudo-poetry of advertising may recur when one approaches genuine poetry, unless one has developed love for poetry *before* becoming aware of advertising—which is impossible for young people nowadays. It is quite natural that such a reaction would develop. We are not likely to seek nausea deliberately, and so we would rather avoid whatever reminds us of it. It seems that if the process of debasing and abusing language by advertising is carried further, we may discover a new value in absolute simplicity of language. Perhaps one day, when the traditional poetry is completely ruined, we shall count as poetry some simple and concrete descriptions like this: "There is a table in the room. The table is brown. There are three chairs at the table. A man is sitting on one of the chairs."

The main point is more significant. By applying highly charged emotional terms like "lovely" to soaps, and "bold" and "proud" to automobiles, advertising pushes us to consider objects as if they were human beings. Through the language of advertising, we participate in the process of constant personification of objects which we should "love," be "enchanted by," be "delighted with," and "be happy with." Unconsciously we have developed emotional attachments to objects surrounding us. We have become worshippers of objects. Advertising has been a powerful force in this process.

My thesis is that the semantic environment has a more profound influence on our behavior and our attitudes than we are aware. If this thesis is correct, it may throw some light on the phenomenon which we usually attribute to the population explosion and the mechanization of our lives; namely, the depersonalization of human relations. I should like to suggest that perhaps a transfer of attitudes through the change of the semantic environment has taken place. Previously, highly emotional expressions were applied to human beings. Nowadays, they are constantly and massively applied by the admen to objects. We have thus developed loving fondness for objects which we worship. Dehumanizing of human relations seems to be the other part of this process. It is quite natural that when we become more and more emotionally involved with objects, we tend to be less and less involved with people. As a consequence, attitudes traditionally reserved for objects are now displayed toward people. In love, in friendship, and in the multitude of other human relations, detachment, lack of interest, and coldness seem to prevail. Human beings are treated like objects.

To summarize, the success of advertising and our failure to defend ourselves against it result mainly from our obliviousness to some of the functions of language. We think that language is a tool, an indifferent piece of gadgetry which simply serves the process of communication and that the only relation we have to language is that *we use language*. We do indeed use it. But this is only part of the story. The other part, which is usually overlooked, is that *language uses us*—by forming our personal and emotional habits, by forming our attitudes. Language is thus not only our servant; it is also our master. No one knows this better than the adman!

The relation between language and us is more complicated than we usually are prepared to admit. To escape the tyranny of language, we have to recognize the double role of language in human relations, (1) as a carrier of messages we send, and (2) as a shaper of the content of human relations. We cannot reduce or nullify the influence of language on us by simply denying the existence of this influence. The only reasonable thing we can do is to recognize the force of language: its strength, the way it works, its theater of operations. By identifying the traps of language, by identifying the linguistic strategies of the admen and other propagandists, we shall be able to cope with the semantic environment much more effectively than we have done hitherto.

I. VOCABULARY

semantic	relentless	orgy	lexicographer
linguistic	humbug	perversion	invincible
advocate	gambit	incredulity	impervious
empirical	gluttony	dupe	figuratively
cliché	inconceivable	blustering	evoke
trivia	plasticine	incantation	debase
clarion	deplorable	amulet	malleable
punctilious			

II. QUESTIONS ON CONTENT

1. What is the author's opinion of David Ogilvy's *Confessions of an Advertising Man?* Would you want to read this book?
2. Explain the theory of performative utterances. Why do advertising men practice this kind of language?
3. What is Skolimowski's conception of the function of language? How is it different from that of the ad men?
4. Do you agree with the writer that advertising is a kind of bad poetry? Has advertising in any way turned you off to poetry? Explain.
5. According to the article, what devices does advertising usually employ to compel the consumer to buy products? Which tricks in "The Advertiser's Bag of Tricks" (p. 198) are like those mentioned here?
6. What is the typical adman's conception of freedom? Does it differ from your definition? If so, how?
7. What values, in Skolimowski's view, has advertising corrupted? How has it done this? Are there any other values you would include?
8. What is the semantic environment? Why does the author believe that we need to contend with it more now than in the past? How does he propose that this be accomplished? How do you think we should do it?

III QUESTIONS ON FORM

1. What is the rhetorical aim of this essay? expression? exposition? argumentation? How does the aim limit and define the writer's purpose?
2. Why does the writer devote the first page to Ogilvy's book? Does this beginning mislead the reader with regard to Skolimowski's purpose?

3. What is the thesis of the essay? Where is it stated most clearly? How does the author lead up to the thesis? Cite specific passages. Why wasn't the thesis presented much earlier?
4. What is the topic sentence of the last paragraph on page 227? Explain the importance of this paragraph to the structure of the remainder of the essay.
5. What kinds of evidence does Skolimowski provide to develop the topic sentence of the last paragraph on page 227? Do you find the evidence convincing? Explain.
6. Cite illustrations the author gives to demonstrate that admen distort language by stretching it too far.
7. What transitional word does the writer use to indicate the start of his conclusion? How does the conclusion relate to the rest of the essay? Do you find the conclusion effective? Why or why not?
8. Characterize the level of diction in this essay. Is it appropriate to the audience for which it was written? To the author's profession, a professor of philosophy?
9. Examine the sentence structure of the second paragraph on page 225. What variations in the length and type of sentences do you find here? Describe the construction of the third sentence from the end of the paragraph. Is the sentence structure as a whole in keeping with the essay's level of diction?
10. What is the author's attitude toward David Ogilvy? Toward advertising? Does he sound sarcastic? Can you locate some examples of his use of irony?
11. Unlike Kanner and Cheever, Skolimowski does not draw upon personal experience, in the form of narration, to structure his essay. Can you suggest reasons for this omission? Is the essay therefore less well written and less interesting than those by Kanner and Cheever?

IV. SUGGESTIONS FOR WRITING

1. Skolimowski contends that because advertising urges us to worship and possess objects, it has taught us to dehumanize human relations. Agree or disagree with this statement based on your own personal experience and observation of others. Include descriptions of any ads that encourage this process of dehumanization.
2. Discuss some ways in which language has influenced your personal attitudes and emotional habits.
3. Compare and contrast Burns' and Skolimowski's discussion of the devices that admen use to compel us to buy products.
4. Would you like to see advertisements limited exclusively to providing factual information? What would be gained? What would be lost?
5. Locate specific examples of "powerful" and "seductive" words in current ads, and explain how these words stimulate us to purchase objects.

6. At the end of the essay, Skolimowski makes several proposals for weakening the grip language has on us. Discuss these proposals and evaluate their effectiveness in protecting us from the tyranny of language.

Before his death in 1977, **John Crichton** was president of the American Association of Advertising Agencies.

Morals and Ethics in Advertising

John Crichton

The problems of ethics and morality in advertising are partially those of any form of communications, and some are unique to advertising.

Advertising Restrictions

For example, advertising usually works in confined units of space and time. A poster relies on illustration and a minimum of words; the 30-second television commercial will probably have no more than 65 words of copy or dialogue; even the newspaper or magazine page is compressed and pruned to keep the written copy as terse and relevant as possible. In classified advertising, the language may be reduced to short-hand, or agreed-upon symbols, like "wbf" for *wood-burning fireplace*. So advertising tends to be brief, and perhaps alone of communications media is intended for the casual glance, the preoccupied ear, and the inattentive mind.

Further, advertising—with the exception of outdoor advertising and direct mail—usually occupies a subsidiary position to the news and entertainment and information of the medium which carries it. Its position adjacent to, or following, editorial matter presumes that the reader, viewer or listener will transfer some part of his attention to the advertising. Advertising *competes* with the editorial material which surrounds it for the attention of the audience.

It is clear that some advertising is as useful to people served by the medium as the bulk of its editorial material; on the other hand, by circumstance much advertising has to be *injected* into the reading or viewing or listening pattern of the audience. It is either an added benefit, or a burden, depending on one's viewpoint. As an example of the difference, it is an ominous development if a newspaper starts to lose department store

Reprinted by permission of Zula M. Crichton.

advertising, which is an important part of its circulation allure. On the other hand, research suggests that the interruptive quality of television commercials is a major factor in the irritation some viewers report about television advertising.

Again, advertising as communication is preliminary to another transaction, or communication translation. Most advertising—mail order, or direct response advertising, is a notable exception—is premised on a subsequent visit to a supermarket, drug store, hardware store, book store, or gasoline station. As communication, then, it attracts interest and asks for action, but in most cases that action will be beyond the scope of the advertising.

Automobile manufacturers expect the advertising to build traffic in the showrooms, where the automobiles themselves, the sales literature, and the dealer's salesmen will be the convincing factors which lead to the sale. Grocery manufacturers expect that the coupons in their advertisements will be redeemed at the food store. Department stores sometimes offer mail and telephone service on items featured in advertising, while listing which of their branch stores have the items being advertised.

Finally, advertising alone among communication media has both statutory and self-regulatory mechanisms aimed at preserving its truthfulness. Some classifications of advertising are specifically required by law to state various pieces of language relevant to the real estate or financial community. The advertising of some products—cigarettes, for example—is circumscribed by law or self-regulation. Cigarettes were removed by law from broadcast advertising; they carry warning notices in advertising (Warning: "The Surgeon General Has Determined . . . ") and tar and nicotine percentages in advertisements. Liquor advertising, by voluntary agreement, does not appear in broadcast media, and it is customary to clear advertising compaigns with a branch of the Treasury Department. State laws as well deal with liquor advertising, a reflection of the legislation which accompanied the repeal of the Eighteenth Amendment. Automobiles are required to use Environmental Protection Agency figures for gasoline consumption in advertising.

Most broadcast advertising is screened by individual networks, which require substantiation for individual advertisement claims. The National Association of Broadcasters' Code Authority inspects and clears all advertising for toys, premiums, and feminine hygiene products.

All national advertising may be challenged on a truth and accuracy basis through the National Advertising Review Board, an industry apparatus set up by advertising associations to handle complaints about specific advertisements or campaigns.

The federal government is represented by the Federal Trade Commission, which since 1914 has had a mandate to encourage competition by preventing unfair trade practices, of which deceptive advertising is held to be one. Since 1938, it has had specific powers over deceptive, misleading, and unfair advertising. Other government departments and bureaus have powers over specific segments of advertising (e.g., the Civil Aeronautics Board over airline advertising; the Food and Drug Administration over prescription drug advertising; the Department of Housing and Urban Development over some kinds of real estate construction and development).

The point is that advertising as communication operates in a much more circumscribed sense than most of the rest of communications. The circumscription comes in space and time, in its relationship to accompanying editorial or program material, in its prefatory role to a final selling transaction, and in an array of private and governmental bodies which exercise some control over its content and techniques. . . .

Advertising is essentially an economic process. It is not primarily a political or social process, although it has been used for both political and social ends. It is essentially an instrument for sellers trying to reach buyers. . . .

Myths about Advertising

Advertising often symbolizes the impersonality of modern selling. It is received in an atmosphere of curiosity and skepticism. In recent years various occult powers have been imputed to advertising. These are deeply-held concerns about "subliminal" advertising, or "motivational research." The first suggests that advertising can be successful by operating beneath the ordinary level of comprehension; the second suggests that systematic exploration of the psyche can produce advertising which successfully manipulates people because it is directed toward their most susceptible areas of mind and personality.

Alas for the fable! The human mind is remarkable, and eye and memory can be trained to receive and retain and identify messages or objects flicked on for a split-second. The aircraft identification techniques of World War II are a good example. There is no recorded research which testifies in any respect to the successful use of subliminal advertising in selling. It remains in fact one of those hideous nonsense notions which haunt our fear-filled society.

The motivation research story is more complex. Research will reveal that products, services, and institutions have a personality. Their users and non-users have opinions about the products, sometimes from experience, sometimes from conversations with other users (particularly family and friends); there are publications specializing in analysis of products and their performance, like *Consumer Reports;* some magazines and newspapers have analytical columns which test and review new products.

In short, experience with and opinions about products may be formed from many influences other than advertising.

It is, however, a marketing axiom that people buy satisfactions, not products. As Professor Levitt of the Harvard Business School has said, people don't buy quarter-inch drills, they buy quarter-inch holes. By extension, they don't buy soap, they buy cleanliness; they buy not clothing, but appearance. It is both efficient and ethical to study the public's perception of a product, and to try to alter or to reinforce it, and it may frequently lead to product reformulation or improvement in order to effect the desired change in attitude, buying, and satisfaction leading to repurchase.

Three Problem Areas

There remain three areas which are usually items of vehement discussion with regard to advertising, and its morals and ethics.

The first is *advocacy*. Advertising always advocates. It pleads its case in the strongest and most persuasive terms. It is neither objective nor neutral. It makes its case, as dramatically as possible, with the benefit of words, pictures, and music. It asks for attention, absorption, conviction, and action.

This disturbs critics, who feel that advertising ought to be objective, informative, and dispassionate. They wish advertising not to be persuasive, but informative. Their model for advertising is the specification sheet, and they have to some degree confused *advertising*, which must interest large numbers of people, with *labeling*, which is for the instruction of the individual purchaser, and performs a much different function.

If morals and ethics stem from public attitudes, it may be interesting that the public both perceives and appreciates the advocacy of advertising. It understands clearly that "they are trying to sell me something," and their attitude is appropriately intent and skeptical. Typically they are well-informed about the product and its competitors. It is a useful attitude in a democracy.

Research tells us that the public is both interested in and derisive about advertising. It is interested in the products which are being sold. It finds elements of the selling process entertaining. The public is, however, quickly bored and inattentive when the products or the way they are sold are unattractive to them.

The second problem area is *accuracy*, used here instead of "truth" because its elements are somewhat easier to define. Most advertising people believe advertising should be accurate; that is, they believe the product should not be sold as something it is not, nor should promises be made for its performance which it cannot fulfill.

In general, advertising's accuracy is good. The dress one sees advertised in the newspaper is available in the sizes and colors listed, and at the price advertised. The headache remedy will alleviate headache pain. It could hardly have been on the market for five decades if it did not. The orange juice looks and tastes like fresh orange juice. The instant coffee cannot be distinguished in blindfold tests from ground coffee which has been percolated. The anti-perspirant reduces perspiration.

Beyond accuracy, the question is often one of perception. It is true that the dress in the advertisement is available in the sizes, colors and price advertised—but will the dress make the purchaser look like the slim young woman in the ad? Answer, only if the purchaser looks like her already. There is no magic in advertising, and no magic in most products. The satisfaction with that dress cannot be literal, and most research suggests that in the public mind no such literal translation exists. It is not expected that the purchase of the dress will make the purchaser look like the person in the ad.

And while frozen orange juice may look and taste like fresh orange juice, it will not have the pulpy texture of freshly-squeezed juice, and therefore to many people will never be its equivalent. Therefore the purchaser must decide whether the texture means enough to him to squeeze the oranges. But the accuracy is not the question, it is the extended perception of what the words mean, so that accuracy becomes equivalency.

The third area is *acquisitiveness*. It is felt by many critics that advertising is a symbol of the preoccupation of our society with material things, and that preoccupation preempts the most important spiritual values. It is felt by critics that the steady drum-fire of advertising and advertising claims, the constant parade of products and services, serve to bewitch and beguile the viewer and reader, who gradually is corrupted into being either a hedonist or a consumptionist.

Of this criticism, two things should be said. The first is that the more material a society has, the greater its support for matters and institutions of the mind and spirit. It is the affluent societies of history to which one must look for the art, architecture, music, universities, hospitals, and cathedrals.

The second is that man is acquisitive. Plato again, as the Athenian speaks: "Why, Clinias my friend, 'tis but a small section of mankind, a few of exceptional natural parts disciplined by consummate training, who have the resolution to prove true to moderation when they find themselves in the full current of demands and desires; there are not many of us who remain sober when they have the opportunity to grow wealthy, or prefer measure to abundance. The great multitude of men are of a clean contrary temper: what they desire they desire out of all measure; when they have the option of making a reasonable profit, they prefer to make an exorbitant one. . . ."

It is difficult to imagine that without advertising one would have an elevated society, one in which acquisitiveness had gradually disappeared. What one knows about such diverse tribes as the Cheyennes and the Kwakiutl of the Northwest is that both took individual wealth seriously, whether in stolen horses or gifts to be given ostentatiously in a Potlatch. Acquisitiveness is innate, as Plato suggested; what advertising does is to channel it.

Daniel Bell, in "The Cultural Contradictions of Capitalism," argues that advertising is a sociological innovation, pervasive, the mark of material goods, the exemplar of new styles of life, the herald of new values. It emphasizes glamour, and appearance. While Bell concedes that a society in the process of quick change requires a mediating influence, and that advertising performs that role, he also sees that "selling became the most striking activity of contemporary America. Against frugality, selling emphasized prodigality; against asceticism, the lavish display." It is his judgment that "the seduction of the consumer had become total," and he believes that with the abandonment of Puritanism and the Protestant Ethic, capitalism has no moral or transcendental ethic, and he points to the conflict between the workaday habits which require hard work, career orientation, and delayed gratification, and the private life in which (in products and in advertisements) the corporation promotes pleasure, instant joy, relaxing, and letting go. "Straight by day," and a "swinger by night," in Bell's capsule summary.

But Bell also sees " in Aristotle's terms, *wants* replace *needs*—and wants, by their nature, are unlimited and insatiable."

Probably no more haunting problem exists for society than motivating people. The system of motivation and rewards within a society is critical to the kind of society it will ultimately be, and to the welfare and happiness of the people in it. The drive for material goods which characterizes most Western societies may be less admirable than a different kind of reward and motivation set of goals. The fact is that the system works, and that it does both motivate and reward people. If it appears to critics that the motivations are inferior, and that the rewards are vulgar, it must be remembered that at least the people have their own choice of what those rewards will be, and observation tells us that they spend their money quite differently. It is essentially a democratic system, and the freedom of individual choice makes it valuable to the people who do the choosing. One man's color television set is another man's hi-fidelity system; one man's summer cottage is another man's boat; and one man's succession of glittering automobiles is another man's expensive education of his children. In each case, the choice of the distribution of rewards is individual.

Three Important Reservations

Morals and ethics in advertising have engaged the interest of working advertising people as long as there has been an advertising business in this country. Much of the discussion has pivoted around three ideas:

1. While most advertising is accurate because the advertisers, the advertising agencies, and the media insist that it be so, there is a fourth compelling force. Almost all products depend upon repeat purchases for success. It is the experience of the consumer—his or her ultimate satisfaction with the product in relation to its promises in advertising, its packaging,

its price, etc.—which is crucial. A satisfied consumer has future value, a dissatisfied consumer has none.

2. There are some problems associated with particular kinds of products and purchasers. There are people who feel strongly that advertising directed to children takes advantage of a child's trusting nature, and his inability to distinguish advertising from entertainment, and his undiscriminating wish for products simply because they are attractively presented to him. Further, the fact that the child is induced by advertising to bedevil parents to buy him or her products is annoying to parents. There are two solutions: one is to ban advertising to children, presumably still realizing that products will continue to be sold to children, that children will want these products, and that they will continue to cajole their parents for them. The second is to take the view that the child is socialized in the process—that learning about what to buy, learning to evaluate claims, learning to make discriminating decisions, is an important part of growing up, particularly in a free society which offers so many choices, political and social. The second choice seems more sensible.

3. Advertising is a means of influencing the media of communication; it distorts or subverts the publications and broadcast media which carry it. Experience suggests that this is an overblown issue. There have been publications which have foresworn advertising, in the belief that it would make possible a kind of journalism impossible so long as the "interests of the advertisers" had to be taken into account. None of the publications survived; the truth was that their editorial content was not sufficiently different from those which carried advertising to assure their success. There clearly is a problem with the demand of media for large audiences, because large audiences are able to command larger advertising support. But quality and responsiveness of the audience is also important. It is worth remembering that the *New York Times* survived in New York when it was the fourth largest in circulation in a seven-newspaper city.

Summary

Advertising has particular problems of ethics and morality among communications media because it is essentially a method of selling. It has the ethical obligation to be accurate, and it has the unusual circumstance of extensive voluntary and statutory restrictions, some arranged to protect competitors from unfair practice, others to be sure consumers are fairly treated.

Advertising is a weapon of competition, and it suffers from some of the defects of competition. The late General Sarnoff once said that competition brings out the best in products and the worst in men, and advertising's constant competitive effort is often wearing to people who wish for a quieter world.

Nevertheless, that competition is, in some respects, a public safeguard. The need for repeat purchases requires that advertising present the product so that the purchaser finds the product's performance satisfactory. The pressure of different products and services push and pull the public mind in different ways: fly and get there quickly, take the bus and save money; spend your money and go to the Caribbean, buy a savings certificate and earn 8 3/4%; try the newest coffee, switch to tea. What the consumer has is the misery of choice.

I. VOCABULARY

ethics	impute	acquisitiveness	prodigality
subsidiary	subliminal	preoccupation	asceticism
statutory	vehement	preempt	transcendental
circumscribe	derisive	beguile	gratification
mandate	alleviate	hedonist	insatiable
array	lavish	ostentatiously	bedevil
occult	cajole	frugality	

II. QUESTIONS ON CONTENT

1. Why, according to the essay, does advertising have particular problems of morals and ethics? Were you previously aware of any of these problems?
2. What restrictions have been imposed upon advertising? For what reasons?
3. What myths about advertising are presented? Why does the author dismiss the first myth? How does he respond to the second myth?
4. List three areas of advertising that have been criticized and summarize Crichton's answer to each of these criticisms. Can you suggest any other common complaints against advertising?
5. What three ideas about morals and ethics in advertising are discussed? Which ethical problem do you consider the most serious? Why?
6. What observations does Crichton make on the relationship between advertising and materialism? How does his view differ from that of the previous author, Henryk Skolimowski?
7. Explain why Bob Wiemer ("Those Packages Aren't Just Selling Deodorant") would disagree with Crichton's defense of motivational research.

III. QUESTIONS ON FORM

1. What is the author's purpose in writing this essay?
2. For what audience is the essay intended?
3. Why does Crichton begin with a discussion of advertising restrictions?

4. Why is the author concerned to correct certain misconceptions about advertising? Is his response effective?
5. In the previous essay, Henryk Skolimowski attacked advertising for corrupting values by encouraging us to worship objects. Crichton takes up this moral and ethical issue in his remarks on acquisitiveness (p. 237). Do you find his reply convincing? Why or why not?
6. Skolimowski also criticized advertising for distorting language. Why does Crichton ignore this common and important criticism?
7. How does the author use classification and analysis as structural devices?
8. Locate examples of transitional markers in the first six paragraphs. What relationships do these markers show?
9. Comment on the conclusion. Why does the author take three paragraphs instead of the usual one to end his essay?

IV. SUGGESTIONS FOR WRITING

1. Write a persuasive essay in which you analyze and expose one or more myths about advertising not mentioned by the author.
2. Crichton cites the marketing principle that "people buy satisfactions, not products." Discuss some of the satisfactions you have bought, and explain why you have bought them.
3. Most advertising, according to the author, is accurate. Relate an experience you have had with inaccurate advertising.
4. Write an essay in which you argue that some advertising is unnecessary, perhaps even harmful.
5. Explain how you think the new technologies described by Stanley Wellborn in "A World of Communications Wonders" will affect the future of advertising in our lives.

SELECTED ADS
FOR STUDY

Ο ΕΛΛΗΝ. ΓΕΝΕΣΙΣ ΑΝΘΡΩΠΙΣΜΟΥ.*

(*The Greek. Cradle of civilization.) This, fellow citizen, is the newest state of pleasure. The Greek bath by Kohler.

Here, geometry triumphs. The bath is but 4 feet long (fits in the space of a shower) yet its unique 22" depth assures comfort for any man of stature— even one 6'4". Here, fluid conquers fatigue in an arena of enduring acrylic.

Here, adventure dawns. It's a classic soaking whirlpool whose 4 jets and optional vinyl pillow can send any Homer on an Odyssey.

In white, it's priced under $1000. It comes in a variety of colors with a choice of faucets. It's shown in Sequoia with Alterna Onyx faucets.

The Greek. It's the cradle of civilization.

For more information on this and all the Kohler products for kitchen, bath and powder room, visit a Kohler Showroom. (See listing in the Yellow Pages.) For a 40-page color catalog of great ideas send two dollars to Kohler Company, Department APO, Kohler, Wisconsin 53044

THE BOLD LOOK OF **KOHLER**

KOHLER GREEK BATH AD
Questions for Analysis

1. Do the illustration in the center of the ad and the headline below it catch your attention? Why or why not? What is the function of the pictures in the background? Do you think this ad is well designed?
2. Describe the speaker of this ad. Why, for example, is the audience addressed as "fellow citizen"? Why is the phrase "The Greek Cradle of Civilization" repeated and reference made to Homer and an Odyssey? What do these statements tell you about the speaker's relation to the subject and audience and about the level of information or knowledge of the speaker.
3. To whom is the ad addressed? What appeals and claims does the ad make? How effective do you think they are?
4. Examine the description of the Greek bath in the third and fourth paragraphs. What rhetorical devices are used to make the product attractive? How do the language and style here differ from those in the last paragraph? How do you account for these differences?
5. One of the propaganda devices discussed in "How To Detect Propaganda" (page 104) is the transfer. How is this device used to sell the product?
6. Is this a soft-selling or feel-good ad? Explain why or why not. (See Rod Townley, "So Long, Ring Around The Collar! Welcome, Paper Blob!" page 206.)

The West.
It's not just stagecoaches and sagebrush.
It's an image of men who are real and proud. Of the freedom and independence we all would like to feel.

Now, Ralph Lauren has expressed these feelings, in Chaps, his new men's cologne.

Chaps is a cologne a man can put on as naturally as a worn leather jacket or a pair of jeans.

Chaps. It's the West. The West you would like to feel inside of yourself.

Chaps. The new men's cologne by Ralph Lauren.

CHAPS COLOGNE AD

Questions for Analysis

1. To what audience is the ad aimed? Is it the sort of person represented in the photograph? Explain.
2. What appeals does the ad make? Why does it rely more upon appeals than claims?
3. What myth or image of the frontier West does this ad evoke? Is it the same myth exploited in the highly successful ad campaign for Marlboro that features the Marlboro Man? Explain.
4. How does the packaging of the cologne, as illustrated in the ad, contribute to its masculine image?
5. What does the word "naturally" suggest? Is it a weasel word? Why or why not?
6. The copy contains several sentence fragments. What is the effect of this particular structure?
7. The feminist movement is changing the images of men in ads. Do you think that this type of ad will still continue to be used? Why or why not?
8. Compare the exploitation of cultural symbols in this and the previous ad. To what extent does each symbol accurately reflect the culture being evoked?

"POUND FOR POUND, DOLLAR FOR DOLLAR, THIS IS STILL THE BEST LUXURY CAR IN THE WORLD."
TOWN & COUNTRY MAGAZINE

When people are asked to guess the price of a Jaguar Series III they often overestimate by thousands of dollars. That's because, among the very few high performance luxury sedans that might logically be compared to it, the Series III is a magnificent value.

The virtues of this best of all Jaguars are many. The first, we think, is a rare and distinctive beauty. As *Town & Country* puts it "...there is no more beautiful car being made anywhere today." You will not meet its cousins and clones by the score in your country club parking lot. Yet Jaguar owners agree: the car is *most* beautiful in motion. The response is quick. The handling is smooth, confident and precise. The experience is one of pure pleasure.

Powering the Series III is the most advanced version of Jaguar's famous double overhead cam six. It has electronic ignition, electronic fuel injection and a separate electronic cold start fuel enrichment system. This engine is strong, responsive and the most reliable that Jaguar has ever produced.

Jaguar luxury has been a legend for generations and the 1982 Series III advances that beautiful reality. Here are the rich walnut veneers and silky leather that you expect. Here, too, are electronic conveniences such as cruise control, a heating and air conditioning system which adjusts itself automatically, power sunroof, signal scanning AM/FM stereo radio with cassette player and much more. And it is all standard equipment.

Because the Series III is, demonstrably, the best Jaguar in history, it is backed by the best warranty Jaguar has ever offered. For two years or 36,000 miles, whichever comes first, Jaguar will replace or repair virtually any part which proves defective. The Pirelli tires are covered by the tire manufacturer's warranty. Your Jaguar dealer has full details on the 1982 limited warranty.

Come and drive this uncommon luxury car. You will quickly learn that the Series III is the best value in Jaguar history. For the name of the dealer nearest you, call these numbers toll-free: (800) 447-4700, or, in Illinois: (800) 322-4400.

JAGUAR
A BLENDING OF ART AND MACHINE

Jaguar, Leonia, New Jersey 07605

JAGUAR AD

Questions for Analysis

1. To what kind of people is this ad directed? Is this the same audience that would buy the Kohler Greek bath (see page 244)?
2. What claims are made for the Jaguar Series III car? What pattern of organization is used to present these claims? What techniques does the ad use to make the claims? Do you think most people believe the claims? Explain.
3. What appeals does this ad make? Why do the claims outweigh the appeals?
4. Describe the background of the ad. Why is a rural setting used? Do you think this setting is effective? Why or why not?
5. Characterize the diction used in the ad. Is it appropriate to the product being advertised? Is "car," for example, more suitable than "auto," "automobile," or "driving machine"?
6. Compare the sentence and paragraph structure in the ad with those in the two previous ads. What differences are there? How do you account for the differences?

ZENA JEANS.
FIT FOR THE WAY YOU LIVE.
I mounted the Arabian in the stillness of midday, and together we stirred up the wind. Winding through the red hills with their dead cedars and sweeping below the mesa, we made of ourselves one illuminating shadow.
Woosh.
A firefly am I; free from him at last. And this giant beauty submitting his dignity to me would be the last thing I loved today.
Tomorrow to New York for new supplies. Rice paper, new jeans and one more dull luncheon at the Russian Tea Room with smart people.
Then back to the Arabian and the music of solitude.
I am finally growing up.
ZENA
Made in the U.S.A.

ZENA JEANS AD

Questions for Analysis

1. Describe the contents of the room in the picture. What clues do they give you about the identity of the occupant? Why is the picture given such prominence over the copy?
2. Summarize briefly the three experiences that the speaker imagines. How are these experiences organized? How is each one different from the others? What do they have in common?
3. Characterize the speaker in the ad. What kind of person is the speaker? Who is the speaker addressing? What is the speaker's attitude toward her/himself and the audience? How would you describe the sound of the speaker's voice?
4. Examine the diction used in the ad. What do the following words denote: Arabian, cedar, mesa, woosh, rice paper? What do the following words and phrases connote: Arabian, cedar, Russian Tea Room, smart? What does the diction tell you about the speaker's intelligence, level of education, and class status?
5. Identify and explain the following figurative language: "A firefly am I," "This great beauty submitting his dignity to me," "the music of solitude." Is the figurative language appropriate to the speaker? Explain.
6. This ad uses the first person narrative. Do you think this device enhances the appeal of the ad? Explain.
7. Describe the style of the ad. To what extent can it be considered poetic? Can you relate the style of this ad to any other in this section or to any commercials you have seen on television?
8. Does the ad convince you that Zena jeans are "fit for the way you live"? Why or why not?

"My pharmacist told me how to lose weight."

"I recommend Dexatrim."

More pharmacists recommend Dexatrim than any other weight-loss product. That's advice you can trust from someone you trust.

Pharmacists know that Dexatrim® helps you lose weight. They see the success their customers have with the Dexatrim Diet Plan.

The active ingredient in Dexatrim has been proven in seven years of clinical testing conducted by doctors at leading universities and medical centers.

If you want to lose weight, ask your pharmacist about Dexatrim.

Pharmacists' recommendation based on independent nationwide surveys of over 1,500 pharmacists.

More pharmacists recommend Dexatrim than any other weight-loss product.

© 1984 Thompson Medical Co. Inc.

DEXATRIM AD

Questions for Analysis

1. This ad is directed to people who want to lose weight. What anxiety does it assume in its audience? Is this anxiety widespread in America? Explain.
2. Describe the photograph. What feeling does it give you?
3. What popular notion about women does the ad depend upon? Do you think this notion represents a stereotype of women?
4. What claims and appeals does the ad make for its product? What specific technique is used to present these claims and appeals?
5. The copy does not provide any specific information about the clinical testing and independent nationwide surveys. Nor does it identify the "active ingredient" in Dexatrim? Why? Do these omissions make the ad less convincing?
6. Apart from the presumed effectiveness of Dexatrim, are there any other reasons why a pharmacist might recommend this product over competing brands?
7. Do you think medical doctors would approve of this ad? Why or why not?

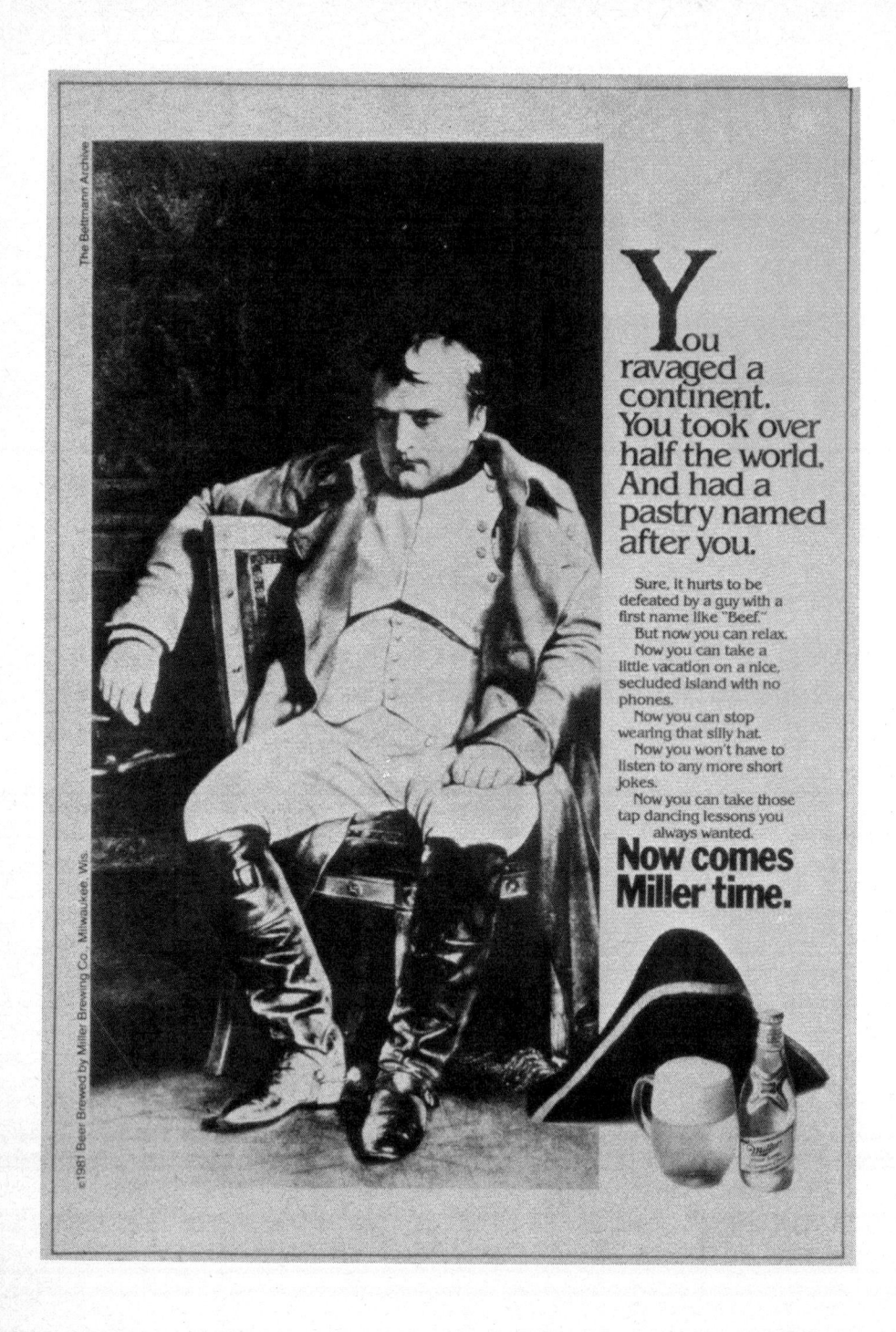

You ravaged a continent. You took over half the world. And had a pastry named after you.

Sure, it hurts to be defeated by a guy with a first name like "Beef."

But now you can relax. Now you can take a little vacation on a nice, secluded island with no phones.

Now you can stop wearing that silly hat.

Now you won't have to listen to any more short jokes.

Now you can take those tap dancing lessons you always wanted.

Now comes Miller time.

MILLER BEER AD

Questions for Analysis

1. Describe Napoleon's mood. Why does he feel this way? How does the illustration convey this feeling?
2. Describe the sound of the speaker's voice in the first three sentences of the ad. Do you notice any change in the speaker's tone of voice in the rest of the ad? If so, how would you explain the reason for the change?
3. Does the speaker expect his audience to be familiar with the references he makes to Napoleon? If so, find examples to support your opinion.
4. To what needs or desires of the audience is the ad meant to appeal? Explain.
5. What rhetorical device is used in the sentences beginning with "How you . . ."? Is this device effective? Why or why not? Find examples of this device in the preceding ads.
6. What image is conveyed by the slogan "Now comes Miller time?" Do you see any connection between this image and that of the West in the Chaps ad (see page 246)?
7. What is a parody? Is this ad, which appeared in *National Lampoon* in November, 1981, a parody of the familiar Miller commercial on television? What is the point of the parody? Why do you think this strategy was used to sell this product?

TOPICS FOR INVESTIGATION

1. In "Morals and Ethics in Advertising, John Crichton refers briefly to subliminal advertising. Find out more about this subject. Exactly what is subliminal advertising? How does it work? What are its advantages and disadvantages? Is its use ethical? A valuable book on this subject is Wilson Bryan Key's *Subliminal Seduction* (1973).

2. Crichton also refers to motivational research. Investigate this subject in the same way as above. A classic study of motivational research that should be consulted is Vance Packard's *The Hidden Persuaders* (1957).

3. Explore the language of advertising. Find examples of ads that effectively use any of the following: repetition, weasel words, connotation, figurative language (similes and metaphors), symbols, personification, rhythm and rhyme, alliteration, and unusual sentence structure and paragraphing.

4. Investigate the role of the Federal Trade Commission in advertising. In what ways does this federal agency control and influence advertising practices? What are the FTC's strengths and limitations?

5. Using Bernice Kanner's "The Fizz Biz" as your model, trace the history of the advertising campaign for a well-known product in relation to changes in American society.

6. Inquire into the aims, structure, and operation of a typical advertising agency. What is the process by which ads develop from ideas into finished products?

7. Explore advocacy ads. What are they? What do they sell? In what ways are these ads similar to product advertising? In what ways are they different? (A good place to begin would be to examine ads by Mobil that express Mobil's viewpoint on economic, social, and political issues.)

8. Using the "tricks" described by Marjorie Burns in "The Advertiser's Bag of Tricks" and the propaganda devices described in "How to Detect Propaganda," create an original print ad for an unusual product or service. This ad will consist of a drawing or picture and supporting copy. On the back of the ad, indicate the specific audience and newspaper or magazine for which you intend the ad. Also, indicate the particular tricks and propaganda devices you used in the ad.

9. Examine all the ads in one issue of a particular magazine. How do these ads suit the image of the magazine?

7

TELEVISION

"Life According to TV"—the title of the article that opens this chapter says it all. How many of our lives and how much of our lives proceed according to television? Social scientists and writers are now coming up with data on the impact of the medium that has, far beyond any of the other mass media, in less than half a century changed our lives and our children's lives irrevocably.

No other medium approaches television in its impact on society. It is found in every home, turned on close to eight hours a day, and watched by everyone, young and old. It communicates our news and our entertainment, influences our political leadership and our economy, changes our lifestyles and our images of ourselves as individuals and as a people. And, as Peter Goodman's article tells us, it has the capability to protect and maintain our homes, do our shopping and banking for us, and monitor our tastes and actions.

The essays in this section explore some of the implications of this staggering power. Some, like those by Jacoby, Hinckley, and Friedman, examine the appeal and problems with specific programming: soaps, sitcoms, and sports. Other authors such as Charren, Alperowicz, and Oppenheim are concerned with the correlations between television and violence. Overall views of the effects of television are presented in the first article where Harry Waters informs us of the results of Dr. George Gerbner's long-range studies of television viewing, and in the last selection where Fred A. Keller writes a searing indictment of the destruction of our intelligence by television.

Whatever our reactions to the individual articles and the chapter, one point is manifestly clear. We must watch out for television as much as we watch it, for it, obviously, is watching us.

Readings

> **Harry F. Waters** is a Senior Writer for *Newsweek* who is responsible for the magazine's television section. In addition, he has written several interpretive cover stories on television and its relation to society.

Life According to TV

Harry F. Waters

The late Paddy Chayefsky, who created Howard Beale, would have loved George Gerbner. In "Network," Chayefsky marshaled a scathing, fictional assault on the values and methods of the people who control the world's most potent communications instrument. In real life, Gerbner, perhaps the nation's foremost authority on the social impact of television, is quietly using the disciplines of behavioral research to construct an equally devastating indictment of the medium's images and messages. More than any spokesman for a pressure group, Gerbner has become the man that television watches. From his cramped, book-lined office at the University of Pennsylvania springs a steady flow of studies that are raising executive blood pressures at the networks' sleek Manhattan command posts.

George Gerbner's work is uniquely important because it transports the scientific examination of television far beyond familiar children-and-violence arguments. Rather than simply studying the link between violence on the tube and crime in the streets, Gerbner is exploring wider and deeper terrain. He has turned his lens on TV's hidden victims—women, the elderly, blacks, blue-collar workers and other groups—to document the ways in which video-entertainment portrayals subliminally condition how we perceive ourselves and how we view those around us. Gerbner's subjects are not merely the impressionable young; they include all the rest of us. And it is his ominous conclusion that heavy watchers of the prime-time mirror are receiving a grossly distorted picture of the real world that they tend to accept more readily than reality itself.

The 63-year-old Gerbner, who is dean of Penn's Annenberg School of Communications, employs a methodology that meshes scholarly observation with mundane legwork. Over the past 15 years, he and a tireless trio of assistants (Larry Gross, Nancy Signorielli and Michael Morgan) videotaped

Copyright © 1982 by Newsweek, Inc. All Rights Reserved. Reprinted by Permission.

and exhaustively analyzed 1,600 prime-time programs involving more than 15,000 characters. They then drew up multiple-choice questionnaires that offered correct answers about the world at large along with answers that reflected what Gerbner perceived to be the misrepresentations and biases of the world according to TV. Finally, these questions were posed to large samples of citizens from all socioeconomic strata. In every survey, the Anneberg team discovered that heavy viewers of television (those watching more than four hours a day), who account for more than 30 percent of the population, almost invariably chose the TV-influenced answers, while light viewers (less than two hours a day), selected the answers corresponding more closely to actual life. Some of the dimensions of television's reality warp:

Sex

Male prime-time characters outnumber females by 3 to 1 and, with a few star-turn exceptions, women are portrayed as weak, passive satellites to powerful, effective men. TV's male population also plays a vast variety of roles, while females generally get typecast as either lovers or mothers. Less than 20 percent of TV's married women with children work outside the home—as compared with more than 50 percent in real life. The tube's distorted depictions of women, concludes Gerbner, reinforce stereotypical attitudes and increase sexism. In one Annenberg survey, heavy viewers were far more likely than light ones to agree with the proposition: "Women should take care of running their homes and leave running the country to men."

Age

People over 65, too, are grossly underrepresented on television. Correspondingly, heavy-viewing Annenberg respondents believe that the elderly are a vanishing breed, that they make up a smaller proportion of the population today than they did 20 years ago. In fact, they form the nation's most rapidly expanding age group. Heavy viewers also believe that old people are less healthy today than they were two decades ago, when quite the opposite is true. As with women, the portrayals of old people transmit negative impressions. In general, they are cast as silly, stubborn, sexually inactive and eccentric. "They're often shown as feeble grandparents bearing cookies," says Gerbner. "You never see the power that real old people often have. The best and possibly only time to learn about growing old with decency and grace is in youth. And young people are the most susceptible to TV's messages."

Race

The problem with the medium's treatment of blacks is more one of image than of visibility. Though a tiny percentage of black characters come across as "unrealistically romanticized," reports Gerbner, the overwhelming majority of them are employed in subservient, supporting roles—such as the white hero's comic sidekick. "When a black child looks at prime time," he says, "most of the people he sees doing interesting and important things are white." That imbalance, he goes on, tends to teach young blacks to accept minority status as naturally inevitable and even deserved. To access the impact of such portrayals on the general audience, the Annenberg survey forms included questions like "Should white people have the right to keep blacks out of their neighborhoods?" and "Should there be laws against marriages between blacks and whites?" The more that viewers watched, the more they answered "Yes" to each question.

Work

Heavy viewers greatly overestimated the proportion of Americans employed as physicians, lawyers, athletes and entertainers, all of whom inhabit prime-time in hordes. A mere 6 to 10 percent of television characters hold blue-collar or service jobs vs. about 60 percent in the real work force. Gerbner sees two dangers in TV's skewed division of labor. On the one hand, the tube so overrepresents and glamorizes the elite occupations that it sets up unrealistic expectations among those who must deal with them in actuality. At the same time, TV largely neglects portraying the occupations that most youngsters will have to enter. "You almost never see the farmer, the factory worker or the small businessman," he notes. "Thus not only do lawyers and other professionals find they cannot measure up to the image TV projects of them, but children's occupational aspirations are channeled in unrealistic directions." The Gerbner team feels this emphasis on high-powered jobs poses problems for adolescent girls, who are also presented with views of women as homebodies. The two conflicting views, Gerbner says, add to the frustration over choices they have to make as adults.

Health

Although video characters exist almost entirely on junk food and quaff alcohol 15 times more often than water, they manage to remain slim, healthy and beautiful. Frequent TV watchers, the Annenberg investigators found, eat more, drink more, exercise less and possess an almost mystical faith in the curative powers of medical science. Concludes Gerbner:

"Television may well be the single most pervasive source of health information. And its overidealized images of medical people, coupled with its complacency about unhealthy life-styles, leaves both patients and doctors vulnerable to disappointment, frustration and even litigation."

Crime

On the small screen, crime rages about 10 times more often than in real life. But while other researchers concentrate on the propensity of TV mayhem to incite aggression, the Annenberg team has studied the hidden side of its imprint: fear of victimization. On television, 55 percent of prime-time characters are involved in violent confrontations once a week; in reality, the figure is less than 1 percent. In all demographic groups in every class of neighborhood, heavy viewers overestimated the statistical chance of violence in their own lives and harbored an exaggerated mistrust of strangers—creating what Gerbner calls a "mean-world syndrome." Forty-six percent of heavy viewers who live in cities rated their fear of crime "very serious" as opposed to 26 percent for light viewers. Such paranoia is especially acute among TV entertainment's most common victims: women, the elderly, nonwhites, foreigners and lower-class citizens.

Video violence, proposes Gerbner, is primarily responsible for imparting lessons in social power: it demonstrates who can do what to whom and get away with it. "Television is saying that those at the bottom of the power scale cannot get away with the same things that a white, middle-class American male can," he says. "It potentially conditions people to think of themselves as victims."

At a quick glance, Gerbner's findings seem to contain a cause-and-effect, chicken-or-the-egg question. Does television make heavy viewers view the world the way they do or do heavy viewers come from the poorer, less experienced segment of the populace that regards the world that way to begin with? In other words, does the tube create or simply confirm the unenlightened attitudes of its most loyal audience? Gerbner, however, was savvy enough to construct a methodology largely immune to such criticism. His samples of heavy viewers cut across all ages, incomes, education levels and ethnic backgrounds—and every category displayed the same tube-induced misconceptions of the world outside.

Needless to say, the networks accept all this as enthusiastically as they would a list of news-coverage complaints from the Ayatollah Khomeini. Even so, their responses tend to be tinged with a singular respect for Gerbner's personal and professional credentials. The man is no ivory-tower recluse. During World War II, the Budapest-born Gerbner parachuted into the mountains of Yugoslavia to join the partisans fighting the Germans.

After the war, he hunted down and personally arrested scores of high Nazi officials. Nor is Gerbner some videophobic vigilante. A Ph.D. in communications, he readily acknowledges TV's beneficial effects, noting that it has abolished parochialism, reduced isolation and loneliness and provided the poorest members of society with cheap, plug-in exposure to experiences they otherwise would not have. Funding for his research is supported by such prestigious bodies as the National Institute of Mental Health, the surgeon general's office and the American Medical Association, and he is called to testify before congressional committees nearly as often as David Stockman.

Mass Entertainment

When challenging Gerbner, network officials focus less on his findings and methods than on what they regard as his own misconceptions of their industry's function. "He's looking at television from the perspective of a social scientist rather than considering what is mass entertainment," says Alfred Schneider, vice president of standards and practices at ABC. "We strive to balance TV's social effects with what will capture an audience's interests. If you showed strong men being victimized as much as women or the elderly, what would comprise the dramatic conflict? If you did a show truly representative of society's total reality, and nobody watched because it wasn't interesting, what have you achieved?"

CBS senior vice president Gene Mater also believes that Gerbner is implicitly asking for the theoretically impossible. "TV is unique in its problems," says Mater. "Everyone wants a piece of the action. Everyone feels that their racial or ethnic group is underrepresented or should be portrayed as they would like the world to perceive them. No popular entertainment form, including this one, can or should be an accurate reflection of society."

On that point, at least, Gerbner is first to agree; he hardly expects television entertainment to serve as a mirror image of absolute truth. But what fascinates him about this communications medium is its marked difference from all others. In other media, customers carefully choose what they want to hear or read: a movie, a magazine, a best seller. In television, notes Gerbner, viewers rarely tune in for a particular program. Instead, most just habitually turn on the set—and watch by the clock rather than for a specific show. "Television viewing fulfills the criteria of a ritual," he says. "It is the only medium that can bring to people things they otherwise would not select." With such unique power, believes Gerbner, comes unique responsibility: "No other medium reaches into every home or has a comparable, cradle-to-grave influence over what a society learns about itself."

Match

In Gerbner's view, virtually all of TV's distortions of reality can be attributed to its obsession with demographics. The viewers that prime-time sponsors most want to reach are white, middle-class, female and between 18 and 49—in short, the audience that purchases most of the consumer products advertised on the tube. Accordingly, notes Gerbner, the demographic portrait of TV's fictional characters largely matches that of its prime commercial targets and largely ignores everyone else. "Television," he concludes, "reproduces a world for its own best customers."

Among TV's more candid executives, that theory draws considerable support. Yet by pointing a finger at the power of demographics, Gerbner appears to contradict one of his major findings. If female viewers are so dear to the hearts of sponsors, why are female characters cast in such unflattering light? "In a basically male-oriented power structure," replies Gerbner, "you can't alienate the male viewer. But you can get away with offending women because most women are pretty well brainwashed to accept it." The Annenberg dean has an equally tidy explanation for another curious fact. Since the corporate world provides network television with all of its financial support, one would expect businessmen on TV to be portrayed primarily as good guys. Quite the contrary. As any fan of "Dallas," "Dynasty" or "Falcon Crest" well knows, the image of the company man is usually that of a mendacious, dirty-dealing rapscallion. Why would TV snap at the hand that feeds it? "Credibility is the way to ratings," proposes Gerbner. "This country has a populist tradition of bias against anything big, including big business. So to retain credibility, TV entertainment shows businessmen in relatively derogatory ways."

In the medium's Hollywood-based creative community, the gospel of Gerbner finds some passionate adherents. Rarely have TV's best and brightest talents viewed their industry with so much frustration and anger. The most sweeping indictment emanates from David Rintels, a two-time Emmy-winning writer and former president of the Writers Guild of America, West. "Gerbner is absolutely correct and it is the people who run the networks who are to blame," says Rintels. "The networks get bombarded with thoughtful, reality-oriented scripts. They simply won't do them. They slam the door on them. They believe that the only way to get ratings is to feed viewers what conforms to their biases or what has limited resemblance to reality. From 8 to 11 o'clock each night, television is one long lie."

Innovative thinkers such as Norman Lear, whose work has been practically driven off the tube, don't fault the networks so much as the climate in which they operate. Says Lear: "All of this country's institutions have become totally fixated on short-term bottom-line thinking. Everyone grabs for what might succeed today and the hell with tomorrow. Television just catches more of the heat because it's more visible." Perhaps the most perceptive assessment of Gerbner's conclusions is offered by one who has worked both sides of the industry street. Deanne Barkley, a former NBC vice president who now helps run an independent production house, reports that the negative depictions of women on TV have made it "nerve-racking" to function as a woman within TV. "No one takes responsibility for the social impact of their shows," says Barkley. "But then how do you decide where it all begins? Do the networks give viewers what they want? Or are the networks conditioning them to think that way?"

Gerbner himself has no simple answer to that conundrum. Neither a McLuhanesque shaman nor a Naderesque crusader, he hesitates to suggest solutions until pressed. Then out pops a pair of provocative notions. Commercial television will never democratize its treatments of daily life, he believes, until it finds a way to broaden its financial base. Coincidentally, Federal Communications Commission chairman Mark Fowler seems to have arrived at much the same conclusion. In exchange for lifting such government restrictions on TV as the fairness doctrine and the equal-time rule, Fowler would impose a modest levy on station owners called a spectrum-use fee. Funds from the fees would be set aside to finance programs aimed at specialized tastes rather than the mass appetite. Gerbner enthusiastically endorses that proposal: "Let the ratings system dominate most of prime time but not every hour of every day. Let some programs carry advisories that warn: 'This is not for all of you. This is for nonwhites, or for religious people or for the aged and the handicapped. Turn it off unless you'd like to eavesdrop.' That would be a very refreshing thing."

Role

In addition, Gerbner would like to see viewers given an active role in steering the overall direction of television instead of being obliged to passively accept whatever the networks offer. In Britain, he points out, political candidates debate the problems of TV as routinely as the issue of crime. In this country, proposes Gerbner, "every political campaign should put television on the public agenda. Candidates talk about schools, they talk about jobs, they talk about social welfare. They're going to have to start discussing this all-pervasive force."

There are no outright villains in this docudrama. Even Gerbner recognizes that network potentates don't set out to proselytize a point of view; they are simply businessmen selling a mass-market product. At the same time, their 90 million nightly customers deserve to know the side effects of the ingredients. By the time the typical American child reaches the age of reason, calculates Gerbner, he or she will have absorbed more than 30,000 electronic "stories." These stories, he suggests, have replaced the socializing role of the preindustrial church: they create a "cultural mythology" that establishes the norms of approved behavior and belief. And all Gerbner's research indicates that this new mythological world, with its warped picture of a sizable portion of society, may soon become the one most of us think we live in.

Who else is telling us that? Howard Beale and his eloquent alarms have faded into offnetwork reruns. At the very least, it is comforting to know that a real-life Beale is very much with us . . . and *really* watching.

ZIGGY

..AND REMEMBER, WE WOULDN'T PROGRAM GARBAGE LIKE THIS IF PEOPLE LIKE YOU DIDN'T WATCH IT ALL THE TIME!

8-16   Tom Wilson
© 1984 Universal Press Syndicate

I. VOCABULARY

subliminally   ominous   eccentric
mundane   warp   demographic
syndrome   paranoia   videophobic
parochialism   mendacious   rapscallion
conundrum   potentates

II. QUESTIONS ON CONTENT

1. What is Gerbner's thesis about television? Do you agree with Waters' description of his views as "ominous?"
2. Do you agree with Gerbner that women "are portrayed as weak, passive satellites" on television? Name some examples. Some exceptions.

3. Do you think old people are "cast as silly, stubborn, sexually inactive, and eccentric" on television? Cite some illustrations. Cite some exceptions.
4. Is there an imbalance in television's treatment of blacks? Are they usually portrayed in subservient roles? How has this affected you personally?
5. Is television unrealistic in its career portrayals? Have you ever formed occupational impressions based on television? Do you think that the workplace situations shown are ever/never/always realistic?
6. Has television changed your attitude toward crime? Cite an example.
7. How does Gerbner say television is different from all other media. List its ritualistic qualities.
8. Explain a "spectrum-use fee."
9. Discuss the advantages and disadvantages of using television as a subject for political debate.
10. Is television the new mythology? What will happen if we live as if the world is similar to what we see on television? Will we change the world or become "vidiots?"

III. QUESTIONS ON FORM

1. Where has Waters placed Gerbner's positive findings about television? How does their location in the essay affect their impact?
2. Where does Waters locate his paragraph on responsibility?
3. Is this a cause and effect essay? Why/why not?
4. What are the implications of the phrase "network's command posts?"
5. What does Waters mean by "McLuhanesque shaman" and "Naderesque crusader?"

IV. SUGGESTIONS FOR WRITING

1. "No other medium reaches into every home or has a comparable cradle-to-grave influence over what a society learns about itself." Write a persuasive essay pro or con this statement.
2. Using your family and friends for subjects, do a sociological study of television use and its impact.
3. Choose one of the areas of Gerbner's research: women, the elderly, blacks, or health, and write an essay applying it specifically to television programming today.

Peggy Charren is president and **Cynthia Alperowicz** is publications director of Action for Children's Television, which has its headquarters in Newtonville, Massachusetts.

TV Violence Breeds Violent Children

Peggy Charren and Cynthia Alperowicz

At last, the belief is officially confirmed: Violence on television can lead to violent behavior in young viewers. "Television and Behavior," a report commissioned by the U.S. Department of Health and Human Services and prepared under the direction of Dr. David Pearl of the National Institute of Mental Health, surveys a decade of research on this controversial subject and concludes that yes, there is "overwhelming" evidence that excessive violence on TV causes aggressiveness in children who watch it.

Any parent who has ever been pulled down an aisle in a supermarket or toy store by a pleading 7-year-old knows how adept TV has been at teaching children to lobby for the sugary foods and expensive toys they see advertised. But broadcasters have been coy in acknowledging that children learn from the messages between the commercials as well, even though a 1972 surgeon general's report tentatively linked TV viewing and aggression.

The new study—issued May 5—stops short of recommending changes in television programing. But NIMH Director Herbert Pardes anticipates that "persons bearing responsibility for policy and for television industry practices would be interested in the findings for use in decision-making." How the television industry will ultimately respond to the government study is anyone's guess, but the whines already heard from the commercial networks make it unlikely that the TV picture is bound to change dramatically. Indeed, NBC plans to release its own study in September, research which, predictably, NBC says, "certainly does not support the overall conclusions about the effect of viewing violence."

However much the networks may quibble over so-called inaccuracies in the NIMH report, however much industry executives would like to shuck responsibility for shaping young minds, children *do* learn from television. The average American who finishes high school has spent 15,000 hours in front of the television set—and only 11,000 hours in front of the blackboard. We know that they learn arithmetic and history during school hours; why is it so hard to accept that what they watch on TV after school also sinks in?

Even if those responsible for television programing policy choose to ignore the study, there are other groups that will no doubt embrace its conclusions for their own purposes—New Right groups such as Morality in Media and the Coalition for Better Television that aim to rid TV of the dual bugaboos, sex and violence.

Peggy Charren and Cynthia Alperowicz, "TV Violence Breeds Violent Children," *Newsday*, May 27, 1982. Reprinted by permission of Peggy Charren.

"How can the networks think that we approve of our children watching programs that teach them how to commit adultery, ransack an apartment, commit murder, or inform them on how to hotwire an automobile?" the Rev. Jerry Falwell shrieked in a recent Moral Majority broadside. The morality watchdogs propose a solution: boycotts and censorship. And to parents concerned about what their children see on the TV screen, that solution may sound tempting.

The problem, as our country has painfully learned from the past, is that a little censorship goes too far toward imposing someone else's arbitrary standards on all of us, toward removing any controversial material from the public eye, toward erasing precious First Amendment freedoms.

What's a parent to do? Even parents who strongly support the *principle* of free speech may be hard pressed to support its *practice* when they are faced with their desire to shield young people from violence and mayhem. But if censorship isn't the answer, what is?

With television, as with most issues in our children's lives, perhaps our most important role is to guide youngsters to make thoughtful choices of their own. Just as we try to teach our children the merits of good nutrition versus a diet of junk food, we can try to help them choose a "nutritious" TV diet, low on "junk" and high on food for thought. We can let them know how we view violence: when we think aggression is justified, when another response is more appropriate. And we can point out the disparities between violence on the screen and violence in the real world, helping them to understand that violence hurts.

For parents who decide that reasoned guidance is not enough, especially for the youngest of TV watchers, there are several devices on the market that give mothers and fathers the option of blocking out programing they deem unsuitable. These range from key-operated safety locks that keep the set off entirely to programmable units that can be set to block selected channels.

The next step is to ensure that these options are available to all who want them, at a cost all can afford. The press has smirked that such parental control devices "take the fun out of being a kid." But television would be a lot less fun for children and adults alike if every show with a shred of controversy were forced off the air by those who want to "clean up" TV.

The brouhaha over violent television content is certain to mount as cable television grows in popularity. Cable will bring us many more program choices, a lot of which will be considered too adult for young viewers. Since each community determines for itself just what comes through the cable, becoming involved in the cable-franchising process is an important means of ensuring that what we want is what we get. We can require cable operators to reserve a number of public-access channels for programs made by the community. We can see to it that detailed program guides are available to all subscribers so that identifying programs for children is easier. And once a contract is signed, we can stay on the alert to make sure that cable operators deliver what they have promised.

Although Action for Children's Television (ACT) believes that the government has no place in *limiting* TV options, the government does have a role to play in *increasing* diversity in programing. The Federal Communications Commission's "Children's Television Report and Policy Statement," published in 1974, emphasizes that "broadcasters have a special obligation to serve children" and "to develop and present programing which will serve the unique needs of the child audience." Yet under the current administration, the FCC is sending broadcasters a message that marketplace economics are what matters, that children's programing needs are not important. And the future of public broadcasting, which has consistently offered an alternative to the kinds of programs children see on commercial stations, is cloudy, with Reagan administration budget cuts threatening to devastate it.

It's an uphill battle, but ACT is fighting federal neglect of children's television and is working to ensure that there are enough program choices to provide alternatives to violent shows and other programing not necessarily suitable for the young. The new government report indicates that this is perhaps the best course.

For "Television and Behavior" does not condemn TV, despite what recent headlines would have us think, nor does it suggest that we force off the air any shows with a message of violence. Instead, it implies that we must increase the number of shows that teach children how to deal with the world in a way that is beneficial—to themselves, to us all.

Mike Oppenheim is a free-lance writer who also practices medicine.

TV Isn't Violent *Enough*

Mike Oppenheim, M.D.

Caught in an ambush, there's no way our hero (Matt Dillon, Eliot Ness, Kojak, Hoss Cartwright . . .) can survive. Yet, visibly weakening, he blazes away, and we suspect he'll pull through. Sure enough, he's around for the final clinch wearing the traditional badge of the honorable but harmless wound: a sling.

As a teen-ager with a budding interest in medicine, I knew this was nonsense and loved to annoy my friends with the facts.

Mike Oppenheim, M.D., "TV Isn't Violent Enough," *TV Guide,* February 11, 1984. Reprinted by permission of the author.

"Aw, the poor guy! He's crippled for life!"

"What do you mean? He's just shot in the shoulder."

"That's the worst place! Vital structures everywhere. There's the blood supply for the arm: axillary artery and vein. One nick and you can bleed to death on the spot."

"So he was lucky."

"OK. If it missed the vessels it hit the brachial plexus: the nerve supply. Paralyzes his arm for life. He's gotta turn in his badge and apply for disability."

"So he's *really* lucky."

"OK. Missed the artery. Missed the vein. Missed the nerves. Just went through the shoulder joint. But joint cartilage doesn't heal so well. A little crease in the bone leaves him with traumatic arthritis. He's in pain the rest of his life—stuffing himself with codeine, spending his money on acupuncture and chiropractors, losing all his friends because he complains all the time. . . . Don't ever get shot in the shoulder. It's the end. . . ."

Today, as a physician, I still sneer at TV violence, though not because of any moral objection. I enjoy a well-done scene of gore and slaughter as well as the next viewer, but "well-done" is something I rarely see on a typical evening in spite of the plethora of shootings, stabbings, muggings and brawls. Who can believe the stuff they show? Anyone who remembers high-school biology knows the human body can't possibly respond to violent trauma as it's usually portrayed.

On a recent episode, Matt Houston is at a fancy resort, on the trail of a vicious killer who specializes in knifing beautiful women in their hotel rooms in broad daylight. The only actual murder sequence was in the best of taste: all the action off screen, the flash of a knife, moans on the sound track.

In two scenes, Matt arrives only minutes too late. The hotel is alerted, but the killer's identity remains a mystery. Absurd! It's impossible to kill someone instantly with a knife thrust—or even render him unconscious. Several minutes of strenuous work are required to cut enough blood vessels so the victim bleeds to death. Tony Perkins in "Psycho" gave an accurate, though abbreviated, demonstration. Furthermore, anyone who has watched an inexperienced farmhand slaughter a pig knows that the resulting mess must be seen to be believed.

If consulted by Matt Houston, I'd have suggested a clue: "Keep your eyes peeled for someone panting with exhaustion and covered with blood. That might be your man."

Many Americans were puzzled at the films of the assassination attempt on President Reagan. Shot in the chest, he did not behave as TV had taught us to expect ("clutch chest, stagger backward, collapse"). Only after he complained of a vague chest pain and was taken to the hospital did he discover his wound. Many viewers assumed Mr. Reagan is some sort of superman. In fact, there was nothing extraordinary about his behavior. A pistol is certainly a deadly weapon, but not predictably so. Unlike a knife wound, one bullet can kill instantly—provided it strikes a small area at the base of the brain. Otherwise, it's no different: a matter of ripping and tearing enough tissue to cause death by bleeding. Professional gangland killers understand the problem. They prefer a shotgun at close range.

The trail of quiet corpses left by TV's good guys, bad guys and assorted ill-tempered gun owners is ridiculously unreal. Firearms reliably produce pain, bleeding and permanent, crippling injury (witness Mr. Reagan's press secretary, James Brady: shot directly in the brain but very much alive). For a quick, clean death, they are no match for Luke Skywalker's light saber.

No less unreal is what happens when T. J. Hooker, Magnum, or a Simon brother meets a bad guy in manly combat. Pow! Our hero's fist crashes into the villain's head. Villain reels backward, tipping over chairs and lamps, finally falling to the floor, unconscious. Handshakes all around. . . . Sheer fantasy! After hitting the villain, our hero would shake no one's hand. He'd be too busy waving his own about wildly, screaming with the pain of a shattered fifth metacarpal (the bone behind the fifth knuckle), an injury so predictable it's called the "boxer's fracture." The human fist is far more delicate than the human skull. In any contest between the two, the fist will lose.

The human skull is tougher than TV writers give it credit. Clunked with a blunt object, such as the traditional pistol butt, most victims would not fall conveniently unconscious for a few minutes. More likely, they'd suffer a nasty scalp laceration, be stunned for a second or two, then be extremely upset. I've sewn up many. A real-life, no-nonsense criminal with a blackjack (a piece of iron weighing several pounds) has a much better success rate. The result is a large number of deaths and permanent damage from brain hemorrhage.

Critics of TV violence claim it teaches children sadism and cruelty. I honestly don't know whether or not TV violence is harmful, but if so the critics have it backward. Children can't learn to enjoy cruelty from the neat, sanitized mayhem on the average series. There isn't any! What they learn is far more malignant: that guns or fists are clean, efficient, exciting ways to deal with a difficult situation. Bang!—you're dead! Bop!—you're unconscious (temporarily)!

"Truth-in-advertising" laws eliminated many absurd commercial claims. I often daydream about what would happen if we had "truth in violence"—if every show had to pass scrutiny by a board of doctors who had no power to censor but could insist that any action scene have at least a vague resemblance to medical reality ("Stop the projector! . . . You have your hero waylaid by three Mafia thugs who beat him brutally before he struggles free. The next day he shows up with this cute little band-aid over his eyebrow. We can't pass that. You'll have to add one eye swollen shut, three missing front teeth, at least 20 stitches over the lips and eyes, and a wired jaw. Got that? Roll 'em . . .").

Seriously, real-life violence is dirty, painful, bloody, disgusting. It causes mutilation and misery, and it doesn't solve problems. It makes them worse. If we're genuinely interested in protecting our children, we should stop campaigning to "clean up" TV violence. It's already too antiseptic. Ironically, the problem with TV violence is: it's not violent enough.

I. VOCABULARY

adept   bugaboo   mayhem
coy   arbitrary   brouhaha
plethora   acupuncture   sadism

II. QUESTIONS ON CONTENT

1. Were you aware of the report "Television and Behavior" before reading this essay? Did its findings surprise you?
2. Cite any evidences of television viewing and aggression that you have witnessed or in which you have participated.
3. Have you spent 15,000 hours in front of the television? How much time do you spend now? (The average American in 1984 spent close to eight hours a day.)
4. What do you think about program blocks and locks for televisions?
5. Has cable television increased the problem of television violence or simply isolated it?
6. What are Charren and Alperowicz's three suggested solutions to the problem of television violence?
7. Dr. Oppenheim offers a different more radical solution. What is it? Do you think it would work?
8. Would you watch more realistic scenes of violence? Would you let children watch them?
9. At what age would you let children watch today's violent television programs? Explain.
10. At what age would you let children watch Oppenheim's version? Explain.

III. QUESTIONS ON FORM

1. Is the title of Charren and Alperowicz's essay consistent with its tone?
2. Explain how theirs is a cause and effect essay.
3. Is it also a process analysis?

4. What is the difference between "censorship" and "reasoned guidance" as used in the essay?
5. Which writing style is more effective—Charren and Alperowicz's or Oppenheim's? Why?
6. How does Oppenheim use description in his examples?
7. Why does Oppenheim begin his conclusion with "seriously?"

IV. SUGGESTIONS FOR WRITING

1. Compare and contrast two television adventure programs, a violent one and a nonviolent one, in terms of style and impact.
2. Write an expository and persuasive paper on your own 15,000 hours. Was it time well spent? Any afterthoughts?
3. Write an essay to an eight-year-old child explaining why you are selecting his/her television programs.

TV Fan, 15, Leaps to His Death

Combined News Services 1979

St. Paul Minn.—Eddie Seidel Jr.'s world was wrapped up in the programs he viewed in his bedroom, on a TV set he had bought. His favorite was "Battlestar Galactica."

The 15-year-old boy filled his room with posters, magazines, plastic models and other paraphernalia about outer space. "They made a lot of money off him," his stepmother, Dawn Seidel, said yesterday, "He bought everything put on the market. He also took tape recordings of all the shows."

In the pre-dawn darkness Wednesday, Eddie, perched on a railing of High Bridge, told police he was upset that the ABC network had canceled "Battlestar Galactica." Then he jumped 200 feet to his death.

"I talked about suing ABC or doing something," Mrs. Seidel said. "But my husband said to just leave things like they are and not make a big hassle out of it. I know it's not their fault because they had the program." Edward Seidel Sr. said that, when his son learned last spring that "Battlestar Galactica" was being canceled, he contacted ABC to ask officials to keep it on. The last rerun of the program was Aug. 5.

On Tuesday, Seidel said, Eddie came home from his job as a supermarket stockboy about 5 PM, apparently in good spirits. He went to his room to watch television.

When his sister, Crystal, 19, passed Eddie's door later, she found a note—his last will and testament, in which he left the space models and posters and

Reprinted by permission of The Associated Press.

the TV to family members, along with the motorbike he rode to the bridge. He told his parents in the note they'd find his body under High Bridge, a half-mile, two-lane link between downtown St. Paul and the suburb of West St. Paul.

The Seidels reached the bridge about 10 minutes after Eddie leaped to rocky ground beside the river, before police could reach him on a cable below the highway.

His father described Eddie as a sometimes brilliant boy. "He has been interested in outer space ever since when 'Star Trek' used to be on," Seidel said. "He got so super-involved in this stuff on outer space, it was his whole world."

Seidel said that when he learned about four years ago that Eddie had been sniffing gas with friends, he sent the boy to a psychiatrist. "The psychiatrist said he was just kind of bored with life, that there was nothing here for him to excel in," Seidel said. "There was no real challenge here on this earth."

Peter Goodman started as "Viewpoints" editor and "Long Island Culture" writer for *Newsday* and is now the paper's music critic.

Orwellian Implications of Two-Way Television

Peter Goodman

Shopping by television; working at home; videodiscs; two-way television: These are just a few of the possibilities offered in the future of video communications.

But roses have thorns, wonder drugs have side effects, and super-sophisticated TVs just might have Big Brothers tagging along.

What if computers linked directly to your home television, besides letting you participate in the shows, tracked your movements, watched your bank accounts, monitored your political preferences and turned off all your appliances?

That's all possible now. In scattered places around the country and the world, in bits and pieces, it's being done. Computers already have vast stores of information about Americans' buying and voting and TV-watching habits. Two-way television offers the viewer a chance to communicate directly with the TV studio and even other viewers. But as it spreads, with

Copyright © 1980 by Newsday, Inc. Reprinted by permission.

centralized computers that keep constant track of viewers' habits and opinions, as it is linked to burglar alarms and political polling and electronic banking, the possibilities of abuse spread with it.

"It's scary stuff. We in the media have a responsibility for what's going to be happening, and I don't know the answer," said Nathaniel Kwit, a marketing executive at United Artists who earlier was involved in developing Warner Amex Communications' QUBE two-way TV system.

"You worry like hell about television in the home, a computer system that can override whatever you do in the home, that can shut off every device in your home," said Howard Anderson, president of The Yankee Group, a Boston-based consulting firm that has prepared a detailed report on the new communications technologies.

Here's what can be done right now on systems already in operation in the United States:

Using a computer that scans more than 30,000 television sets once every six seconds, a two-way TV system can determine what programs each home is watching. Viewers, by pushing a button, can respond to questions asked by studio announcers, and the system has already been used to take political polls. Residents in one suburb have participated in a town meeting.

More than 700 QUBE subscribers in Ohio, residents of a small town in Texas, and about 100 Manitobans have burglar and fire alarm systems hooked from their televisions or phone lines to local police and fire stations. QUBE executives are considering adding an "energy monitoring" system that can turn appliances on and off to control electricity usage. They're planning to add shop-by-TV and electronic fund transfer programs, where you choose a product, order it and pay for it—all over your television set.

A national magazine has used two-way TV to test which of five possible covers were more attractive, and used the best two. An insurance salesman spent 10 minutes talking about insurance on the air, and was deluged with responses afterward.

QUBE's computers are not being used to keep track of individual choices, or to zero in on individual homes in a community roughly the size of Long Beach. The only records QUBE keeps, Warner executives say, are for their own billing purposes. Two-way television doesn't create any problems that don't already exist, according to Gustave Hauser, chairman of Warner-Amex Cable.

"We are a computer-based society," Hauser said. "When you go to the bank, you talk to a computer. A computer routes your phone call.

"There is no privacy issue we are raising that doesn't already exist in every facet of society. Unless you are against the computer, this is just another computer-related activity . . . It's one more way of doing things better; I don't see that as a major issue."

But two-way TV, because it centralizes a lot of computer functions that are currently scattered among banks, pollsters, credit bureaus and other agencies, does raise some very disturbing questions. Consider the picture drawn in a magazine article last year by John Wicklein, currently a news executive with the Corporation for Public Broadcasting and former president of Long Island's WLIW, Ch. 21:

A mayoral candidate in a mythical city, over her television set, orders a book advocating liberalization of laws on sexual activity and then buys an aerosol deodorant, using her computer credit number both times. After she leaves home, her husband, answering a TV poll, votes against letting lesbians work as teachers. Then he watches a pornographic film over a different channel.

His bank flashes a message over the TV: Their credit account is overdrawn. He transfers some money from the savings account, and goes back to his movie.

It's all very convenient and efficient. Pushing those buttons can even be fun. But because all the activities pass through a central computer, a lot of personal information is easily accessible.

A series of clients are buying computer profiles of the family. The incumbent mayor learns that the candidate's husband's opinions differ from hers, and that he watches pornography. The mayor is also observing his opponent's movements through the cable system's burglar alarm system. The family's name goes onto a sex magazine's mailing list. An environmental group studying the candidate's positions is horrified to learn that she uses aerosols, which threaten the ozone layer in the atmosphere. A national credit-rating company notes that the family overdrew its credit account, and also learns the size of its bank balance.

And there are no laws against gathering and distributing that information, Wicklein said.

It would be unfair to focus attention solely on QUBE, for similar computer-TV systems are being tested all over the country, in Canada and elsewhere.

Wicklein, like many others who are following the growth of the new technologies, said he is fascinated by their possibilities for good. But he is also concerned about the chances of abuse. "Big Brother is the danger," he said. "I think it's going to be very valuable, but the public has to think of these things in advance, and know how they are going to use it.

"Suppose you have a system in which you tell this computer what your interests are, and it gives you what you are interested in from its data bank. What happens when the person putting the information in decides to correct some of your thinking by putting things into the system that try to shift your thinking?" Wicklein asked. If education comes through a central computer, whoever controls the computer controls what we learn.

Although executives such as Warner's Hauser and R. E. (Ted) Turner of the Cable News Network play down the potential dangers of two-way systems, others in the industry are aware of the public's fears.

A two-way system being developed by the Manitoba Telephone Co. has been named "Project Ida," after Ida Cates, the phone company's first female operator. In "Project Ida," between 100 and 200 test homes are being hooked up through their TV sets to burglar and fire alarms, computer data banks, cable television and two-way TV systems.

According to a Yankee Group report, Canadian research found that the greatest threat to Manitoba's investment would come from "misunderstandings by various consumer groups. Ida is an attempt to humanize the Orwellian specter and to neutralize the opposition before it forms."

Laurence Wiseman, an executive of the polling firm of Yankelovich, Skelly and White Inc., said recently in Broadcasting magazine that two-way television might run counter to "a deep and growing public concern about privacy." For example, he said, companies could offer video training and public relations programs in their employees' homes, but might run into "tremendous skepticism if not hostility" because of a concern about the power of large corporations in local politics.

Two-way communications offer other possibilities. Utility companies are now being offered "energy load management" devices—so they can control electricity usages by turning home appliances on and off from a central office.

One device being sold by Scientific-Atlanta, a major communications equipment maker, sends an FM signal to switches mounted on air conditioners and water heaters, to distribute the electricity load during times of peak usage. "The homeowner generally would not be aware of what is going on," according to Scientific-Atlanta vice president Jay Levergood.

Described that way, the system sounds just fine. But if appliances can be turned off to regulate energy demand, they can be turned off for other reasons, too.

Computer-controlled burglar alarms that detect an intruder's movements and automatically call the police give the homeowner a warm feeling of security. But motion detectors can also keep track of the legitimate resident's movements, something he or she might not be so happy to reveal.

Ted Turner of the 24-hour Cable News Network and superstation WTBS in Atlanta, scoffs at fears of Big Brother. "The government has pretty deep files on everybody now," he said.

"People don't have to use the two-way system if they don't want to," Turner said. "We are going to see our mobility greatly curtailed, I believe. Two-way can be very valuable for most people; you'll be able to order things electronically, have your bills processed from your home."

Ultimately, no one knows what will come from the vast potential of two-way, computer-controlled television and other communications and entertainment systems. "This is a period of crisis, in the best sense of the word," said Gabriel Samuels, vice president for media research at the J.

Walter Thompson advertising agency. "There is a situation of great flux; a lot of things are happening. Turning points are being reached."

The list of possiblities is as long as the list of fears. How about a low-cost antenna so viewers can get satellite-relayed TV programs right at home, without relying on what their local TV stations offer? Comsat, the Communications Satellite Corp., has been working on plans to develop special satellites with signals anybody could pick up using a $300 receiving "dish" (earth receiving stations used by cable systems currently cost $10,000 and up). Already, enterprising companies are offering satellite dishes for as low as $3,000.

If the Comsat plan comes to pass, it might even wipe out local television stations.

"You want my best projection?" Samuels asked. "For 1985: Some new technology, very major, that we don't even know about—maybe digital, maybe direct-to-home transmission—could eliminate the need for cable and local stations. This is not really science fiction. These are things that are happening today."

I. QUESTIONS ON CONTENT

1. Have you read George Orwell's *1984*? What does Goodman's title mean? Who is Big Brother?
2. Explain the capabilities of the two-way television computer systems in operation today.
3. What aspects of the system appeal most strongly to you?
4. What aspects do you find most frightening?
5. Would you subscribe to QUBE or a similar system?
6. Do you agree with Nathaniel Kwit that "the media have a responsibility for what's going to be happening?"
7. Does it bother you that personal information about you is already in easily accessible files?

II. QUESTIONS ON FORMS

1. Outline the article according to time and argument.
2. How effective is Wicklein's hypothetical example?
3. How does Goodman write about the technological possibilities he raises? Where are they suggested within the piece?
4. What is the tone of his conclusion?

III. SUGGESTIONS FOR WRITING

1. Is the spread of two-way television the first step into an electronic Utopia or an invitation to Oceania (Orwell's mythical state)? Write a persuasive essay.

2. Write an expository essay on the functions of two-way television.
3. Write a process analysis detailing how two-way television can assist you in getting through your day.

Susan Jacoby is a prolific freelance writer. Her weekly *New York Times* column, "Hers," was published as a collection entitled *The Possible She.* Jacoby was a foreign resident in Moscow for several years and produced numerous articles and two books, *Moscow Conversations* and *Inside Soviet Schools* about her experiences there. She is a frequent contributor to magazines, including *Nation* and *McCall's.*

Washing Our Minds Out with Soaps

Susan Jacoby

Today is the 25th anniversary of the first broadcast of "Edge of Night," a member of the founding generation of television soap operas. (I originally typed "foundling generation"—a true Freudian slip in view of the extraordinary number of illegitimate births on the soaps.)

Launched in the 1950s, the survivors of that first batch of soaps have retained a good deal of the public piety of that decade while offering a liberal dose of the divorces, extramarital affairs and horrendous illnesses that are staples of what television bureaucrats prefer to call "daytime drama." On days when I was home from school in the 1950s, I used to sit down with my mother and watch "Edge of Night" along with its contemporaries—"As The World Turns," "The Guiding Light" and "Search For Tomorrow." I liked them all.

Although I am no longer a fan of the first-generation soaps, I am still a devotee of the genre. I prefer the second-generation shows—"Another World," "Days Of Our Lives," "The Doctors"—launched roughly) in the mid-1960s. As Soviet propagandists are fond of saying, this preference is "not by accident." The main characters on the second-generation soaps are in their 30s and 40s. So am I. In my 30s, that is. Soon I will be moving into my 40s, and my favorite characters are having their mid-life crises along with me.

There is also a third generation of soaps, originating (again, roughly) in the mid-1970s. Loyal fans will recognize their names—"All My Children," "The Young and the Restless," "Ryan's Hope." They are very popular with

Copyright © 1981 by Susan Jacoby.

college students, and most of the main characters seem to be in their 20s. All of the soaps have characters of different generations, and all of them make periodic efforts to introduce exotic new types in an effort to capture a larger share of the viewing audience. In spite of these forays into the unknown, each soap bears the stamp of the era in which it was created.

A working person usually feels obliged to offer some rationalization for the time devoted to soaps. When I was writing an article on the soaps some years ago (a good excuse to watch them without guilt), I found that one-fourth of an estimated 20 million viewers were men. When I mentioned this to a man of my acquaintance, he sneered, "Out of a job, I suppose."

Not at all. A great many employed solid citizens—factory workers, airline pilots, college professors—are apt to find themselves at home during the day. My office is at home, and my best writing hours are between 8 AM and 2 PM—when I usually break for lunch in front of my favorite soap, "Another World." When the show ends at 3—around the time editors are returning from their three-white-wine lunches—I begin the phoning-and-negotiating part of my business day.

I suspect that a great many other busy people (including housewives) squeeze a little soap time into their days in the same way. We soap fans do an honest day's work; we don't sit around all day munching the chocolate-covered creams we have bought with food stamps at the taxpayers' expense.

It's easy to explain how a busy person finds time for a soap or two, but the *why* is a more complicated matter. Dan Wakefield, in his novel "Starting Over," (made into a movie starring Jill Clayburgh and Burt Reynolds) has his recently divorced male hero turn on the soaps to get through his first Christmas alone.

"Potter was at first surprised to find he *liked* the soaps, that he found them far more credible than any of the dramatic series on nighttime television; their slow, nagging pace of problems and misunderstandings and high-strung, headache-y conflicts were far more typical of daily life as he knew it and saw it around him than adult evening TV dramas or the quick-image flashings and clean resolutions of the hip new movies . . .

"He sat at the tube engrossed all afternoon, as the real traumas of the holiday were enacted . . . husbands explained to mistresses they had to hurry home to the wife and children, idealistic interns tried to comfort patients whose cases were hopeless and later cried their hearts out to lovesick nurses. Young married couples argued bitterly over whether the in-laws who tried to stop the wedding should be given a day of amnesty on Christmas and forgiven with a visit . . . "

Needless to say, this scene was *not* written into the movie. On film, it would be hard to convey the special pleasure of watching the soaps while your nearest and dearest are squabbling in the kitchen over the preparation of the turkey. My brother and I always head straight for my parents' TV room on Christmas Day. Until I read Wakefield's novel, I thought we were the only ones.

Most "cultural observers" who make snide remarks about the soaps have never actually looked at them. That is why so many critics have drawn silly comparisons between the daytime soaps and prime-time series like "Dallas." The only thing shows like "Dallas" have in common with the daytime soaps is the existence of a continuing story line. With its pat villains and heroes, "Dallas" harks back to the saints-and-sinners formula that characterized daytime soaps in the 1950s.

Even those first-generation soaps, like "Edge Of Night" and "As The World Turns," have long since abandoned their saints and sinners in favor of realistic characters with a combination of good and bad traits. A character like Dallas's dastardly J.R. Ewing would be laughed off the screen on the daytime soaps. Men on the daytime soaps tend to have modest successes and modest failures. Women didn't used to work outside their homes, but they do now. A few of them are doctors and businesswomen but most of them are nurses and secretaries (like their real-life counterparts).

The soaps are not, of course, entirely realistic. There are no fat women on them. And one-time sexual indiscretions cause a truly alarming number of pregnancies. Continuing relationships, on the other hand, produce a remarkably small number of children. Time is . . . elastic. Women with children in their 20s routinely produce new babies. These mothers look like they are in their 30s, and the generations simply don't add up.

In spite of these inconsistencies, the soaps deal with, and always have dealt with, serious individual and social problems in a much more realistic way than prime-time TV.

The list is endless: Sexual boredom in marriage; conflicts between work and love (for both sexes); infertility; impotence; venereal disease; teenage sex; alcoholism; generational conflict; aging. When these topics were first explored in prime time on programs like "The Mary Tyler Moore Show," television critics were totally unaware of the fact that daytime TV had long been dealing with the same subjects.

The only problem that never appears on the soaps is loneliness. Everyone is surrounded by concerned, inquisitive relatives and friends. That may be one of the real secrets of the soaps' appeal: No one is ever alone. And that's the way it is on another world, this side of the edge of night, as the world turns.

I. VOCABULARY

amnesty   exotic
snide   forays

II. QUESTIONS ON CONTENT

1. Do you watch soap operas? a. never b. occasionally c. habitually. Why?
2. Do you agree with Jacoby that soaps are generational? Does that factor influence your viewing?
3. Have you worked soap viewing into your school and work schedule? How many hours? Do you feel guilty about it?
4. Jacoby says soaps are realistic. In what areas? Where are they unrealistic?
5. What does she say about nighttime soaps? Do you agree? Explain.

III. QUESTIONS ON FORM

1. What is Jacoby's opinion on soaps? Identify her thesis statement.
2. What modes does she employ in this persuasive essay?
3. What is the effect of the long quotation from Wakefield's novel?
4. What is her last point? Is it the most compelling one in the article? Why doesn't Jacoby develop it further?

IV. SUGGESTIONS FOR WRITING

1. Write a persuasive essay disagreeing with Jacoby.
2. Write a description of the world of your favorite soap opera.
3. Recount a recent plot episode.

Since 1980 **David Hinckley** has been a feature and entertainment writer for the *New York Daily News*.

It's Nothing to Smile About: The Decline of TV Sit-Coms

David Hinckley

Once upon a time, we could turn on the television set and know what to expect. Seven o'clock? Walter Cronkite. Eleven-thirty? Johnny Carson. In between? Situation comedy.

Life was easy then. Right after Cronkite we could hunker down in our

Reprinted by permission of *New York Daily News*.

favorite chair, wrap a hand around our favorite beverage, send our brain upstairs to get a good night's sleep, and relax, knowing that no matter what else was happening, we were safe at home with situation comedy.

Is this a great country or what?

But that was before everything changed. Cronkite was last seen on Martha's Vineyard. Finding a live Carson show is like finding the Ayatollah Khomeini at a Mets' game. And now they tell us the situation comedy is in more trouble than John DeLorean.

This is no laughing matter.

In the 1983-'84 season, no sitcom finished among the top 10 programs—for the first time since 1950-'51. ("After MASH," "The Jeffersons," and "Newhart" finished 12th, 17th and 20th, respectively.) This is in contrast to say, the 1977-'78 season when seven of the top 10 shows were sitcoms, or 1967-'68, when sitcoms provided four of the top five.

For all practical purposes, the television sitcom was born in 1951, with "I Love Lucy." At the outset, CBS thought so much of the idea it wouldn't put up $5,000 to film the first episode. So Lucille Ball and Arnez did it themselves, creating the "three-camera" technique wherein virtually every scene is shot on the same set, from three different angles. Since then, this is the way sitcoms have been shot.

Actually, "Lucy" wasn't the first sitcom—only the first successful one. "Life of Riley," for instance, began in 1949, with Jackie Gleason as Riley. It lasted only one season; Riley didn't become a star until William Bendix exhumed him in 1953, by which time "Our Miss Brooks," "December Bride" and other sitcoms were also on the scene.

By the mid-'50s the sitcom had vanquished the variety show. By the early '60s it had vanquished the Western. By the mid-'60s it was king, and it remained king for 20 years—which, considering the nature of TV programming and viewer attention spans, is like your pet hamster living to be 50.

But enough history. What's happening now?

- We're getting our laughs elsewhere. "There used to be a clear distinction between comedy and drama" says Jeff Sagansky, NBC senior vice president of programming. "On 'Hawaii Five-O' or 'Streets of San Francisco,' they rarely cracked a smile. But in the last five years, dramas like 'Cagney and Lacey,' 'The Fall Guy,' 'The A-Team' or 'Knight Rider' have developed a great deal of humor."

    "The audiences have gravitated toward light fantasy adventures." says Harvey Shephard, vice president of programing for CBS. "Response to comedy in its traditional form is weak, if you will."

- Consequently, some of the better writers are drifting away from sitcoms. Say you're a scriptwriter and you want to make a living at a time when adventure/dramas are big and sitcoms are small. What are you going to write?

"When writers sense the networks' reluctance to do comedies," says Shephard, "they move toward adventure."

- You can't swear or take your clothes off on TV. "Look what's doing well in the movies," says Sagansky. "Sexy comedies like 'Police Academy' or 'Splash.' TV can't compete with them; we can't do what they do. And won't."

  Cable can, however. The Playboy Channel has produced what it billed as the first adult sitcom, called "4Play."

- The Family Hour has dissipated. Phil Burrell, vice president of TV programing for Dancer Fitzgerald Sample, an ad agency which analyzes TV shows, notes that for years, "There was an unwritten law that the 8–9 p.m. time block would be for family programing, which meant either The Waltons' or comedy. So that in effect guaranteed a certain amount of airtime for comedy. But that law gradually softened, and when 'Magnum P.I.' and then 'The A-Team' came along, the barriers fell apart. Now that time is filled with adventure-comedies."

- Part of the sitcom audience may have peeled away. "Youth was a prime market for shows like 'Happy Days,'" says Sagansky. "Today, some of those kids are playing video games." (Indeed, "Happy Days" was canceled last week, after 11 years.)

- We need a new Archie Bunker. Like any other product, sitcoms need to be invigorated periodically, by the emergence of something new and different.

  The most recent sitcom to qualify was "Mork and Mindy" in 1978–79. That's too many years ago. A couple of subsequent sitcoms have enjoyed modest success—"Cheers," the new "Kate and Allie"—but they haven't set the Nielsens on fire. "Breakthrough comedies aren't the kind of thing you can plan for," says Burrell. "A show like 'Square Pegs' was a blatant attempt to be different; it just didn't catch on. Some people thought Norman Lear's 'a.k.a. Pablo' would do it, but obviously it didn't." (The show was canceled after a brief test run.)

  Sagansky suggests landmark comedies depend as much on personality as content. "The breakthroughs have always had someone unique and funny in the lead, like Archie or Lucy or Fred Sanford. We had hoped Dabney Coleman might be that kind of character in 'Buffalo Bill.' It was a noble attempt even if it turned out to be a miss."

- Today's sitcom may be competing against the ghost of Lucy past. Not everyone agrees, but there are indications that viewers who fill up on reruns of "The Honeymooners," "M*A*S*H" and "Mary Tyler Moore" may be less interested in new product.

Lucille Ball believes that's true, and Sagansky, among others, agrees that "to an extent, we are competing against the reruns." Homes with cable, in particular, have more reruns than ever, since most cable systems pipe in out-of-town independent stations.

On the other hand. CBS' Shephard says he doesn't believe the competition theory "for one minute," and Burrell says that since reruns aren't shown in prime time, "It's like comparing apples and oranges."

In any case, it would be premature to suggest the sitcom has gone the way of the Third Ave. El. First, who ever rejected a laugh? Second, sitcoms can be cost-efficient; Sagansky says two half-hour sitcoms are often cheaper than a one-hour drama.

Truth is, the number of sitcoms starting 1984-85 (18-20) isn't much lower than the number for 1978-79, a golden sitcom year (22). NBC, which announces its '84-85 schedule Thursday, has six sitcoms definitely returning ("Diff'rent Strokes," "Silver Spoons," "Facts of Life," "Cheers," "Family Ties," "Gimme a Break") and should add two or three more, either renewals (the highly praised "Duck Factory," a recent addition, may survive despite low ratings), or new shows (one that's certain, though maybe at midseason, stars Bill Cosby as an obstetrician).

CBS will have five returning sitcoms in '84-'85—"The Jeffersons," "Alice," "Kate and Allie," "Newhart" and "AfterMASH"—joined by the new "E.R." (with Elliot Gould as a doctor) and "Charles in Charge" (with Scott Baio of "Happy Days"). Casualties include "The Four Seasons" (see story below).

At ABC, two sitcoms will start '84-85: the new "Who's the Boss?" with Tony Danza of "Taxi," and "Three's a Crowd," an overhauled "Three's Company" with two new women joining John Ritter.

So TV isn't completely abandoning its old friend the sitcom. "In the '60s, when Fred Silverman was at CBS, comedy was the linchpin of their domination," says Burrell. "Then, when Silverman joined ABC, that network went to the top with comedy."

"I don't think sitcoms are dead at all," adds Sagansky. "It's just that the three-camera living-room set has been around for 30 years, so people are used to it and maybe a little tired of it. Our challenge is to revitalize it by making it look different: more sets, more imaginative camera work, maybe film instead of tape."

There now, Don't we all feel better?

I. VOCABULARY

hunker   dissipated   blatant
vanquish   linchpin

II. QUESTIONS ON CONTENT

1. What is a sit-com?
2. Briefly discuss the history of the sit-com in television.
3. Have you ever watched and/or do you still watch sit-com reruns? Which ones?
4. List your own Top Ten Television Programs. What is the ratio of sit-com to adventure series?
5. Is family entertainment declining in television? What about your family?

III. QUESTIONS ON FORM

1. What is the tone of Hinckley's introduction?
2. Hinckley often uses "one-liners" for transitions. Cite some examples. Are they effective?
3. Outline the organizational structure of the article. Does Hinckley present more reasons for the decline of sit-coms or for their survival? In which order does he present them?
4. Is the article persuasive and if so, for which view?

IV. SUGGESTIONS FOR WRITING

1. Choose one of the "big four": "The Odd Couple," "The Mary Tyler Moore Show," "Happy Days," or "MASH" and write an essay analyzing its phenomenal popularity and endurance.
2. Write an essay analyzing the appeal of what in your opinion is the best sit-com on television today.

A former sports editor of *TV Guide*, **David Friedman** is TV critic for the *Philadelphia Daily News*.

Ball Games or Brawl Games?

David Friedman

In a ruling late last season, National League president Charles (Chub) Feeney fined outfielder Cesar Cedeno, then of the Houston Astros, $5000 for entering the stands to argue with a patron in Atlanta—but terminated Cedeno's "indefinite suspension" after only two days. "The fan's remarks," Feeney explained, "went beyond the realm of decency."

The "realm of decency"? Is that somewhere near Camelot, pray tell? Does it have a king? A round table? A zip code?

No matter what the answers to such queries might be, there's no questioning one fact about Feeney's "realm": it's a small community, getting smaller all the time.

The Phillies' Pete Rose and Reggie Smith of the Dodgers were also involved in altercations with fans last season. Dave Parker of the Pirates dodged batteries hurled from the stands. The Orioles' Dennis Martinez, poor soul, was kabonged by a bottle. Yes, baseball fans are growing wild in

Reprinted by permission of the author.

the seats—and sometimes even out of them, as a disturbing occurrence at Yankee Stadium last year showed all too well.

Angered by what he felt was a bad call during a Brewers-Yankees playoff game, a Yankee fan vaulted onto the field and assaulted umpire Mike Reilly. The Reilly incident, like the others, illuminated the fine line separating fan from fanatic. But it raised other issues as well—for the crime was witnessed not only by the more than 56,000 in the park that night, but by the millions at home watching ABC's telecast of the game.

Should ABC have covered the incident? Or ignored it? How valid is the position, articulated on the air by Howard Cosell, that "we had to show this scene. We wouldn't be journalists if we didn't"?

Does TV coverage imply approval? Does it encourage viewers to mimic what they've seen?

These and similar questions have elicited various—and complex—responses.

One critic of ABC's decision to show all is Tom Villante, director of broadcasting for major league baseball. "By putting the spotlight on these cuckoo birds, you're glorifying them," says Villante. Villante's view is seconded by Rep. Ronald M. Mottl (D-Ohio), sponsor of the Sports Violence Act pending in Congress. If passed, the act would attempt to curb violence among athletes by setting up a special arbitration procedure to assess financial penalties against the teams of the belligerents. (The act does not cover fan violence, however.) "The networks certainly have freedom of speech," says Mottl. "But TV is so pervasive that is has a duty to try to prevent violence in society. Such a duty would be well served by a decision not to cover such incidents."

Ironically, the loudest voice coming to ABC's defense is that of Mike Weisman, who coordinates baseball coverage for rival NBC. "You have to make a distinction between exhibitionists and those people who are violence-prone," he insists. "Exhibitionists *are* encouraged by exposure, so we try to avoid them whenever possible. On the other hand, I'm convinced that violent fans couldn't care less whether they're on TV or not."

Weisman's view is supported by psychiatrist Stanley Cheren of the Boston University School of Medicine, an expert in the field. "There is no conclusive evidence," says Dr. Cheren, "that fan violence is related to the desire to get on TV." Rather, the doctor attributes the rise of fan violence to a number of factors. Among them: the ambivalence of hero worship. "Athletes are admired," says Dr. Cheren, "but they're envied as well."

Nor does Richard Phillips, attorney for the Major League Umpires Association blame television for the current spate of fan violence. "Violent fans," he says, "are encouraged when they see managers like Earl Weaver and Billy Martin bump, push or taunt umpires."

Many social scientists agree with Phillips' assertion that violence or abusive behavior on the playing field triggers violence in the stands. And as proof, they cite the numerous instances of rowdyism that have occurred in the stands at National Football League games, where the mayhem of the field can be considerable. Indeed, during the first five Monday-night games of the past NFL season, more than 100 people were arrested, most of them on assault-and-battery charges.

Many of these incidents, to be sure, were related to alcohol abuse—a problem that certainly is no stranger to baseball. Only a few seasons back, a besotted "Dime Beer Night" crowd in Cleveland ran amok through the stands and onto the field, causing the Indians to forfeit.

It's quite clear than unless something changes, sports fans may soon find themselves left out of the fun altogether—as has already happened on at least one occasion in England.

It seems that when the first of two games in a scheduled home-and-home series between England's West Ham United soccer club and Spain's Castilla of Madrid was marred by excessive fan violence, a ruling was handed down that the second game in the series could go on at West Ham's home field *only if no paying spectators were present.* And so it did, at Upton Grounds (capacity 35,000), before an assortment of team officials and journalists estimated at about 100.

No incidents of fan violence were reported.

I. VOCABULARY

realm   ambivalence   amok

II. QUESTIONS ON CONTENT

1. What is your attitude toward rowdy fans and exhibitionists?
2. Has the problem of fan violence escalated because of television?
3. Should television film those violent incidents or ignore them? Explain your views.
4. What are Richard Philips' views on violence on the field? Do you agree with them?
5. Should alcoholic beverages be allowed at sporting events? What is the impact of televised beer commercials during games?

III. QUESTIONS ON FORM

1. What is the effect of the series of questions in paragraph two, page 287? Comment on the phrase "pray tell."
2. This is a three part essay. What is its aim? Does it answer its title question?

it employ? Cite some examples.
...pact of the conclusion?

SUGGESTIONS FOR WRITING

1. Choose an athlete whose career you are familiar with and commenting on fan ambivalence, write an essay on the athlete as hero.
2. The ethologist Konrad Lorenz wrote that aggression in sport was healthy as it provided a substitute for war. Do you agree? How does television affect this aggression? Write an expository/persuasive essay.
3. Relate the idea of the athlete as hero to Barbara Goldsmith's essay "The Meaning of Celebrity" in Chapter Two.

An educator and pioneer television producer and director at WBEN Inc., Buffalo, New York, **Fred A. Keller** has served as director of communications at Erie Community College and Medaille College, Buffalo.

Television and the Slow Death of the Mind

Fred A. Keller

In recent years the voices of well-meaning, concerned parents and teachers have been raised—with some effect—protesting the content of TV programming and the false promises of advertising, particularly commercials directed to children.

Only lately have we begun to realize that TV as a pernicious influence on the minds of our children may stem from the very act of viewing itself; that it really doesn't matter much if our kids watch "Sesame Street" or "Superman." The basic problem lies in their watching anything.

In order to understand how this could be, it's necessary for us to know something about the construction of the human brain.

First of all, physiologists tell us that what we call the "brain" isn't a single undivided organ at all; in fact, we all possess two brains in our heads or, rather, a cerebral cortex divided into two hemispheres which makes it possible for us to possess two minds differing in content, mode of operation, and, possibly, goals.

Fred A. Keller, excerpt from "Television and the Slow Death of the Mind, *Buffalo News*, July 22, 1979. Reprinted by permission of the author.

Dr. R.W. Sperry, a noted brain researcher, explains that "learning and memory are found to proceed quite independently in each separated hemisphere. Each hemisphere seems to have its own conscious sphere for sensation, perception, ideation, and other mental activities; and the whole inner realm of gnostic experience (knowledge) of the one is cut off from the corresponding experiences of the other. . . .

The left hemisphere controls the movements of the right side of the body and is also predominantly involved with analytic, logical thinking, speech, and basic mathematical calculations. It is the left hemisphere that is responsible for individual survival, our continuation as a species, and for the development of organized culture. Since its operational mode is linear, concerned with sequences of cause and effect and a consciousness of events enduring in time, it enables us to plan for the future and learn from the past.

The right hemisphere controls the movement of the left side of the body and has a limited language capacity. It is responsible for our orientation in space, our ability to recognize faces and distinguish parts of the body, our artistic endeavors, and our ability to appreciate music, pattern, and design. It is also believed to be that part of the brain most concerned with dream and fantasy.

While both hemispheres are necessary to our physical and mental well-being, there is no doubt that dominant to our lives and to our survival as "human" beings is the supremacy of left hemisphere thinking. Without it we would have no coherent speech, limited communication, no science, and no history. Still huddled in our caves we would have only our teeth, hands, and nails to defend ourselves.

When a child is born, one side of his brain cannot be differentiated from the other. It is during the first three years of life that the brain begins to develop special hemispheric functions and that verbal thinking begins to play an increasingly important part in the child's cognitive development.

With the ability to speak, to use language to communicate and to manipulate his environment, the child soon outdistances other animals who must depend on nonverbal forms of thought.

But the child's mastery of self and surroundings is based entirely on the opportunities afforded him to develop and use his language capacity and thereby to order his thoughts. There is overwhelming evidence to prove that this capacity must be developed during the first few years of life or it will never mature at all.

Dr. Burton L. White, the celebrated child specialist, underlines the point when he says, "Let me stress again that language is absolutely central to the development of intelligence and that a child doing well linguistically has a solid asset in his attempts at becoming a well-rounded human being."

What is at stake in these crucial early years is not merely the child's proper acquisition of language but his commitment to language as a means of expression.

Neurological evidence shows that the brain achieves its final state of maturity in terms of structure and specialization at about the age of 12. If left hemisphere development has been neglected or retarded, it is virtually impossible for significant improvement to occur in later life. It appears that certain functions of the brain are locked into place at this early age, particularly the ability to express one's self clearly and eloquently. Missed opportunities for language development and appreciation, and for conceptual thought, are opportunities lost forever.

For example, it has been observed that children who have been heavy viewers of TV do not turn to reading when deprived of television. More time is spent in conversing, playing, and athletics but the printed word, apparently, no longer attracts.

Researcher Arthur Deikman explains, "If the balance of motivational force is very strong in favor of a particular mode (of hemispheric thought), that mode will be quite resistant to change, even if a component (like removing the TV set) is changed."

Numerous studies show that by the age of 3 an almost adult-like fascination with TV has set in. The average child enters kindergarten having spent more time in front of a television set than a college graduate has spent in his classrooms. Preschool American children to the age of 6 spend more time watching television than in pursuit of any other activity except sleeping.

TV affects a child's mental development in certain very specific ways.

First, it's obvious that time spent staring at a picture tube is time not spent in playing, exercising, exploring one's environment, and, most importantly, in communicating with siblings and parents.

Many psychologists have noted the likeness of TV viewers of subjects under hypnosis. Sitting in a semidarkened room, eyes defocused on the flickering light of the television screen, viewers soon are reduced to a conscious level of somnambulism.

TV is a one-way street. It talks at you, not with you. It allows for no interruption, no dialogue, and it communicates largely with pictures—with imagery that acts upon the right hemisphere of the brain while leaving the left hemisphere deprived and dormant.

In effect, information communicated electronically from the TV screen enters our brain while our critical defenses are down and our awareness is dulled.

Dr. Eric Peper of San Francisco State University, who has written extensively on this phenomenon, says: "The horror of television is that the information goes in but we don't react to it. It goes right into our memory pools and perhaps we react to it later but we don't know what we're reacting to. When you watch television you are training yourself not to react and so, later on, you're doing things without knowing why you're doing them and where (the impulses) come from."

In this regard television viewers are very much like the subjects of hypnotists reacting to posthypnotic suggestion.

Television watching is addictive. Like drugs and alcohol, TV allows the participant to blot out the real world and enter into a pleasurable fantasyland where real experiences seem vague and distant and time becomes distorted.

Characteristic of the drug experience is the inability to function without the addictive substance, the need to repeat the experience again and again, and a loss of discrimination toward the object which satisfies the craving. An alcoholic, for example, is not interested in the taste of alcohol nor is the compulsive eater particular about what he eats.

If you think TV is not conducive to addiction, consider these twin facts: (1) the average broken TV set is either repaired or replaced within 48 hours—faster than any other household appliance, including the stove and refrigerator; and (2) between 1950 and 1975 TV watching increased from 4 hours and 25 minutes per day to 6 hours and 8 minutes per day. The average American now spends more time watching TV than any other activity save working and sleeping.

As children become teenagers and problems multiply, the need for a "pleasure fix," for an escape from reality easier and more effective than TV provides, is intensified and TV, unfortunately, has already subliminally planted a solution. After thousands of eye-catching commercials directed to the uncritical mind of the child, the message comes through clearly that drugs and alcohol are swift, sure answers to frustration, anxiety, boredom, and fear.

Violence is another familiar television escape. Day after day our children watch grown men (and sometimes women, too) settle their differences with guns and fists. Fiction is reinforced by fact when the child watches our local newscasts. What are they if not a catalogue of murders, assaults, robberies, rapes, accidents, violence, and war. The "real" world depicted on TV is a world of disaster. With television as his tutor, ought we be surprised that a threatened child's reaction is to strike out? Perferably before the other kid hits first?

What can we do about television? We can't get rid of it; what we so proudly hail as "The American Way of Life" depends on a never-ending, ever-increasing consumption of commodities and TV is the best salesman the world has ever known.

Obviously, the first step is to limit the number of hours our kids spend staring at the tube. In the case of children under 5, reason dictates it would be best to eliminate TV altogether. For those kids already hooked on TV perhaps a frank discussion on what it's doing to us—one in which the entire family participates—might prove a good beginning.

But make sure you're armed with the facts. It's easier to take candy from a baby than to take away TV. Read Marie Winn's *The Plug-In Drug* and Jerry

Mander's *Four Arguments for the Elimination of Television*. Better still, if the kids are old enough, read the books with them and then begin the discussion.

And let's not weaken our moral posture by continuing to slump in front of the set, abjectly indulging our own viewing habits. What's good for the goslings is good for the goose and gander, too; "Do as I say, not as I do" never was much of an argument.

God (and the TV industry) knows your job won't be easy, but what have we to lose? Just the minds and hearts of our children, that's all, and their capacity—their will—to preserve and make true the brave American dream of a free and democratic society.

I. VOCABULARY

pernicious   orientation   ideation
siblings   cognitive   abjectly

II. QUESTIONS ON CONTENT

1. Keller's analysis of the effects of television watching does not focus on programming. Why?
2. Explain briefly the functions of the two hemispheres of the brain.
3. By what age is brain specialization and function achieved? Were you aware of this before reading this essay?
4. List the six specific ways Keller cites that television affects a child's mental development.
5. Do you agree that television is addictive? Is it dangerously addictive?

III. QUESTIONS ON FORM

1. What is the impact of the introductory physiological description of the brain? Is the explanation written clearly?
2. Paragraph one, page 292 opens with the words "Neurological evidence" and proceeds to discuss age and brain function. Is this paragraph situated for optimum effect in the essay? Where else might it be inserted?
3. Outline Keller's arguments. Do you agree with the order of importance?
4. What is the tone of his conclusion?
5. Did this essay persuade you?

IV. SUGGESTIONS FOR WRITING

1. Write a persuasive essay disagreeing with Keller.
2. Describe a case of television addiction you may have witnessed or experienced.

3. Write an expository essay on how television has affected your reading habits.

TOPICS FOR INVESTIGATION

1. Watch the reruns of some old sit-coms still in syndication such as "The Honeymooners," "The Twilight Zone," "The Beverly Hillbillies," and "Leave It to Beaver" and compare and contrast them with today's programming. What is the source of their enduring appeal?

2. Investigate the roots of soap opera in melodrama and grand opera. What are the correlations and the differences?

3. Investigate the development of one of the following areas of television programming: talk shows, children's programming, or variety/entertainment programming. Has the quality improved or declined?

4. Choose a sport you enjoy and investigate the impact television has had on it: the game itself, its development, and its expansion. Have the changes been positive or negative?

5. Take your real television temperature. Turn off the television for one week (that means *off*). Observe and record the effects on you and your family. If violence is imminent—test only yourself. Avoid watching television for a week. Leave the room and so on. Record your reactions.

8

RADIO

Radio is the ubiquitous medium, especially now that "boxes" and Walkmen have made "go anywhere sound" a reality. Radio is so much a part of our lives that we have almost ceased to notice its presence. Most of us wake up to the sound of music and hear with or without consciously listening some combination of music, news, and information throughout a great portion of our day. At bedtime we are lulled to sleep by radio, and some of us sleep more peacefully because our radios play throughout the night.

    This immersion in sound was not always the case. Not too long ago, radio knew hard times. Television, the experts predicted, would spell its end. This demise did not take place, and the reasons why radio not only survived but in Karl Meyer's words was "born again" are the subjects of the articles in this chapter.

    In the first article, Karl Meyer describes the radio's present success and concurrent mood of optimism and experimentation. Kevin Goldman looks at one of radio's very successful experiments, late-night talk shows. Robert Palmer, on the other hand, questions the possible negative effects that a successful experiment in another medium might have on radio's staple Top 40 programming. (Chapter Nine contains Richard Corliss' contrasting views of rock videos.) A more modest but mobile technological development than rock videos are the large portable radios or "boxes" with their "big bucks in big sounds" that Jeff Bailey explores in his article. The final selection is a *New York Times* editorial on one of the most controversial areas in radio—

control of programming. Whether the airwaves should reflect the tastes of a minority of listeners (classical music fans) or respond only to the dictates of the marketplace is very much a live issue, just as radio is a medium very much alive today.

"Radio GaGa," a song by the group Queen, is a tribute in which the band assures radio that "someone still loves you." As these articles indicate and our ears can confirm, that someone is not alone.

Readings

> Karl E. Meyer, who holds a Ph.D. in politics from Princeton University, served on the staff of the *Washington Post* as editorial writer, London bureau chief, and chief New York correspondent. Since 1979 he has been a member of the editorial board of the *New York Times*. Among his books are *The Pleasures of Archaeology*, and *The Plundered Past*.

Radio's Born-Again Serenity
Karl E. Meyer

When television came on strong in the 1950's, it seemed as if radio, dear old radio, had the growth potential of czarist bonds. There was a place for radio, people said, but only as a supplement to television; it was good for news flashes, the odd talk show and, of course, music. To conceive of radio as a vital medium was outlandish, as ridiculous as questioning the future of the American auto industry.

Times change, and a funny thing has happened. As the 1980's begin, it is radio that seems reborn, while television is in a state of shock. Radio's golden age may well be over, but something like a silver age beckons.

The big change in radio is psychological, as the industry sheds its hangdog attitude about television. Indeed, what causes the most panic at television networks—the possible loss of a national mass audience to many-channeled and local cable television—holds no terror for radio programmers.

Most radio is local and small-scale. It programs with a rifle, not a shotgun. The typical small station employs a dozen or so people, and grosses from $200,000 to $300,000 a year. If a station is to turn a profit, it must develop an audience, keep it interested and earn its loyalty. The industry is as competitive now as the newspaper business was before one-paper cities became the rule.

And, the Federal Communications Commission willing, the rivalry will intensify. In an important and controversial proposal, the commission has given approval to the creation of as many as 125 new AM radio stations, a move that clearly would enhance competition, and could provide an opening

---

Karl E. Meyer, "Radio's Born-Again Serenity," *Next* Magazine, January/February 1981. Reprinted by permission of the author.

to minority groups now underrepresented on the broadcast spectrum. The commission is talking about ultimately licensing up to 700 new AM stations.

The initial opening up of the market can come about by ending the "clear channel" rights of stations whose signals are propelled by 50,000 watts. These stations were granted "supersignals" in 1928 to reach remote areas. But the commission has unanimously held that since radio now reaches almost every corner of the country, there is no longer any need for "clear channels." Naturally enough, owners of the 25 superstations don't agree, and they are appealing the ruling.

The move, however, is in tune with changing views about competition and deregulation. The commission is considering whether radio should be exempt from cumbersome public-service performance surveys, from time limits on broadcasting commercials and from the public-service programming requirements. These changes, which are also being contested, stem from a conviction that the marketplace is sufficiently competitive to provide its own controls. The experience of stations that have voluntarily cut down on the number of commercials per hour because incessant huckstering drives listeners away proves that this proposition is tenable.

Radio is also benefiting from satellite transmission, which has just begun to offer multiple feeds at low cost, and with stunning aural quality. Static-free FM is now generally accessible, and has jumped ahead in audience ratings over long-dominant AM. (Twenty years ago, only 8 percent of radios sold in America were AM-FM; in 1979, the figure was 77 percent.)

Listeners and advertisers alike are discovering that radio does many things better than television, and does everything more cheaply. Adweek recently published the telltale figures on the comparative cost-per-million in reaching audiences. Since 1967, radio's cost-per-million has gone up less than any other medium's. The result: Radio led all media in national advertising revenue increases during the 1970's. Projected revenues for 1980 are $3.6 billion, twice what they were a decade ago and 15 percent more than in 1979. Radio has prospered despite—and because of—two recessions.

What has lured advertisers is not just the bargain-basement time rate. No less appealing is the size and loyalty of a steadily expanding audience. Radio is universal: There are at least 450 million sets in America, which comes to about six per household. Radios are in alarm clocks, in the headphones of joggers, in the vast majority of automobiles, in tiny transistor models on the beach and in big Boom Boxes slung on the arms of urban teenagers.

Granted, the picture is not all wine and roses. Most of the country's 8,800 radio stations are hard-core commercial operations whose formats are usually determined by market research as broadcasters seek audiences attractive to advertisers. But that search is leading to new byways, and a decade-old National Public Radio system is poised for a new takeoff. As never before, Americans should have a choice of superior fare: better newscasting, offbeat drama and music reaching well beyond the jukebox repertory.

Innovators who come up with distinctive formats will be rewarded: A case in point is William O'Shaughnessy, owner of WRTN in New Rochelle, New York. Two years ago, he acquired the insolvent 3,000-watt FM station and gambled that there was room for something besides the usual popular-music formats authorized by the "contemporary" market, and known in trade jargon as album contemporary, urban contemporary, beautiful contemporary, adult contemporary and even temporary contemporary.

None of this suited O'Shaughnessy's taste. He guessed that there was an audience for a sophisticated blend of Cole Porter and Billie Holiday, big bands and evergreen show tunes, presented in the emblematic style of Fred Astaire. Though WRTN's signal is weak, the station is in the affluent heart of Westchester County and reaches mid-Manhattan. It quickly found an audience so grateful that some listeners turned up at the station with treasured albums. Advertisers took note, and billings rose so dramatically that within months the 40-year-old O'Shaughnessy was featured on the business page of *The New York Times*.

Radio is *par excellence* an experimental medium, and its potential is just beginning to be tapped. It has immediacy, flexibility, accessibility. Its most formidable strength is in news: There is simply no faster or more economical way to relay information. Morley Safer of CBS-TV's "Sixty Minutes" team remarks: "If there's a coup or an earthquake, all you need is a reporter in a telephone booth. You don't need photographers, camera crews or a platoon of producers." All-news, round-the-clock radio is now being paid the ultimate compliment by Ted Turner's cable-television news network: imitation.

Less obvious is radio's strength as an opinion forum. Television has a horror of "talking heads," a screen showing two people just conversing. By contrast, radio invites strong spoken opinion, such as the counterculture talk shows on the listener-supported Pacifica stations or the commentary by the "Spectrum" team on CBS.

Safer, who contributes a "Notebook" to CBS radio, finds his stint a welcome relief: "Radio is my only outlet for commentary, a chance to speak my own piece, and the listener response is instant." Michael Jackson, a talkshow host on KABC in Los Angeles, whose ratings are the highest in that city, says, "Radio can teach television an enormous amount about conversation. More and more Americans are yearning for information, are becoming news junkies, media freaks. And people want to be kept company. That's why conversational radio, information radio, is growing by leaps and bounds."

Esthetically, however, radio's secret weapon is its most exhilarating distinction: Its picture tube is in the listener's head. Radio drama has a tenacious grip, so much so that in 1938, countless Americans believed that

Martians had landed in a New Jersey meadow when Orson Wells dramatized "War of the Worlds" on CBS. Commercial radio has only tentatively tapped this rich seam, mainly in the form of rebroadcasting vintage mystery and horror shows. But public radio has commissioned first-class plays from established dramatists. Arthur Kopit's "Wings," for example, had its debut on the National Public Radio series "Earplay," which is resurrecting a neglected art form.

Beginning in March, National Public Radio will broadcast a 13-part dramatization of "Star Wars," featuring two of the stars from the blockbuster film—Mark Hamill as Luke Skywalker and Anthony Daniels as the robot C3PO. The story will be an elaborated version of the movie, but the entire series will cost less than $300,000, which is what a single episode would cost on television.

National Public Radio is the creative flagship of American radio, and with any luck, it may reshape the medium during the 1980's. Established 10 years ago, National Public Radio has rapidly evolved into a full-fledged alternative network—partly thanks to the grit and street savvy of its president, Frank Mankiewicz, onetime press secretary to Robert F. Kennedy and campaign strategist for George McGovern in the 1972 presidential campaign. Mankiewicz can wax enthusiastic about the homely wireless: "You know that if something happens that affects your life—a giant snowstorm or hostages being seized or school not meeting tomorrow—the man on the radio will tell you about it. But Mary Tyler Moore isn't going to tell you there's a hurricane coming. She's going to go right on talking about Ted Baxter and Murray."

Under Mankiewicz's leadership, National Public Radio has set up a national production center in Washington. One result has been "All Things Considered," a late afternoon news-magazine program that "towers over the competition on commercial radio and television," in the view of Fred Friendly, former president of CBS News.

"Morning Edition," a wake-up sibling of "All Things," was launched in 1979. It offers two hours of news and features, without commercials or the tiresome repetition of all-news stations. What makes the venture feasible is the new satellite transmission system, which provides an instantaneous linkup with member stations.

When the satellite went into operation last summer, 230 of the 1,036 public stations scraped up the funds to equip themselves to accept program feeds. This means that the stations no longer have to depend on more expensive telephone-line transmission, or the vagaries of the mails, to obtain National Public Radio programming. The cost to the network for a typical live performance via satellite was less than $100 in the first half-year of operation. There are surely few bigger bargains in modern communications. And satellite sound quality is uncannily good, a great plus for music broadcasting.

Satellite transmission should enable all American radio stations, public and commercial, to maximize their advantages: immediacy, economy and verisimilitude. The satellite's rise coincides with the rise of FM broadcasting. As recently as 1962, there were only 983 commercial FM stations, and their future seemed unpromising. Today there are 3,216 stations, and a year ago the turnabout came: FM signals were outdrawing AM. Cheap transistor radios gave FM broadcasters access to a youth audience eager for rock, and the clarity of the signal began to pay off. But not just for hard rock. What the trade calls "good music stations" were also able to reach out for new audiences for classical music.

Some of FM's advantage may be offset by a probable Federal Communications Commission decision to enable AM to duplicate the stereo sound of FM. The commission has five systems to choose from, which, when remaining technical wrinkles are eliminated, would give both bands stereo capability.

There's a lesson in all this. If radio is commercially prosperous and increasingly adventurous in its formats, it's because the industry has learned that the sheer number of listeners counts less than the character of the audience.

The bright outlook for radio in the 1980's is for more stations, a stronger public system and more effective use of a benign technology. Radio cannot supplant television, but it can run nimble circles around the box by playing up the strengths of a rediscovered medium. There is every prospect that an interesting part of the future will belong to radio.

I. VOCABULARY

cumbersome	tenacious	huckstering
vagaries	tenable	

II. QUESTIONS ON CONTENT

1. How has radio recovered from its television slump?
2. What has the FCC role been in this recovery?
3. Explain the correlation between audience and economy in radio.
4. What does the example of WRTN demonstrate about radio?
5. Have you ever listened to drama on radio? Are you familiar with NPR (National Public Radio)?

III. QUESTIONS ON FORM

1. What comments does this essay make about radio's audience? For what audience is this piece written?
2. How is the aim of the piece expository? Is it heuristically developed?

3. How effective is the comparison and contrast between radio and television? Why?

IV. SUGGESTIONS FOR WRITING

1. Develop Meyer's comments on radio's "immediacy, flexibility, and accessibility" into a persuasive essay on radio news.
2. Choose an AM or FM station that you listen to and profile it in terms of format, personnel, and image.
3. "People want to be kept company." Write a persuasive essay, explaining what this need tells us about ourselves.

Kevin L. Goldman is a freelance writer with a particular interest in broadcasting.

Radio's Latest Boom: Late-Night Talk Shows

Kevin L. Goldman

Every night, as millions of Americans are counting sheep, radio executives are busy counting newly found listeners and advertising dollars.

AM radio stations have discovered that there is a wide awake, not to mention highly responsive, audience for late-night call-in talk shows. At the same time, they have realized that there are profits to be made in a time period that, until recently, had not been all that appealing to advertisers.

Tomorrow, the ABC Radio Network will launch TalkRadio, a service available to AM stations nationwide via satellite, providing six hours of phoned-in conversation a night, beginning at 1 a.m., E.S.T. Locally, the shows will be carried on WABC.

TalkRadio, as well as other network overnight programming, is following the lead of Larry King, whose six-hour call-in program has been broadcast nationally for the past four years. His show, which nightly attracts about four million night owls, consists of three hours of interviews with celebrities, authors and politicians, who take calls from Mr. King's listeners. But the most popular feature, audience surveys have shown, is the three-hour portion of the show, "Open Lines," during which listeners call Mr. King and discuss just about anything they wish. The Mutual Broadcasting System broadcasts Mr. King's show live on weekdays, with taped highlights

Copyright © 1982 by The New York Times Company. Reprinted by permission.

from earlier interviews on weekends. It is heard locally at midnight on WOR.

With a sizeable audience to tempt advertisers with, AM radio—to survive the growing popularity of the FM band, with its capability of broadcasting music with a clearer signal and in stereo—has had to look for alternative fare. The trend in most major cities is for music to be on the FM band and for talk, news, sports and information shows to be on AM. Indeed, starting at midnight tonight, the only AM station in New York City that will still be programming popular music will be WNBC.

"Music on AM is doomed," says Rick Sklar, vice president of programming for ABC's radio networks. "Radio always had to adapt itself to changes. When TV came in, radio took a back seat until it realized its entertainment and information potential. Now, AM has to evaluate itself again and see how it can survive without music. Talk and information is the obvious solution."

ABC's TalkRadio programs, which will originate from Los Angeles, feature three hours with Ira Fistell, who is self-described as having a photographic memory and who will be the host of an "anything is up for discussion" call-in show, and three hours with Ray Briem, who will interview individuals currently in the news and will also take calls from listeners.

ABC is not the only network to venture into the late-night call-in program arena, which seems to concentrate heavily on discussions of personal finances and relationships. Last month, WVNJ-AM, a New Jersey-based station that is heard in the New York metropolitan area, began to broadcast TalkNet, a service provided nationally by NBC Radio. It offers three hours of advice from Bruce Williams to listeners who call in with questions about financial problems ranging from mortgages to stock-market investments and three hours of phone discussions about personal problems with Sally Jessy Raphael. While not a trained psychologist, NBC says Miss Raphael dispenses "sensible advice about relationships" to her callers.

The RKO Radio Network has a six-hour call-in show heard nationwide— though not yet in New York City—called "America Overnight," with Ed Busch broadcasting three hours from Dallas and with Bob Dearborn for three hours from Los Angeles. The programs feature interviews with celebrities and authors of financial-advice books.

It was not long after the Larry King show first went on the air nationally in 1978 that the competition recognized there were profits to be made through late-night talk programming: the Mutual Broadcasting System had increased its affiliates by close to 200 stations within six months. According to listener surveys, the average caller to Mr. King's program was 30 years old, a college graduate and listened to the show for more than two-and-a-half hours nightly. Also, the listener anxious to speak with Mr. King on the air had to pay for the opportunity and continues to: While all the other overnight nationwide radio programs have an "800" toll-free telephone number, listeners who want to chat with Mr. King must still pay for the call. This, according to a Mutual Broadcasting System spokesman, cuts down production costs to the network and the affiliates that broadcast the program, as well as discouraging crank phone calls.

Technologically, it is has been the advent of satellite transmission that has made these national call-in programs possible. Someone in San Francisco who is listening to the Larry King show, which is broadcast from Arlington, Va., can phone and, at the same time, speak with Mr. King, his in-studio guest, plus another caller from say, Miami, Fla. This is all done by conference calls facilitated by satellites. An individual station pays a network for use of the satellite and the "dish" that is needed to receive the program from an orbiting satellite.

Signals from the satellite are not the only thing a network affiliate receives. There are financial benefits that both the network and its affiliates gain. NBC Radio, for example, can get "big name" guests that a station in a smaller market couldn't attract on its own. Affiliates are thus persuaded to join the NBC TalkNet in order to boost their own image by being able to advertise a personality on a talk show that their listeners would not otherwise be likely to get a chance to call and speak with. Naturally, the more affiliates a network can boast of to advertisers, the more money it can charge per commercial minute.

An individual station can also reduce its staff when there is network programming during the overnight hours, cutting down even further on expenses.

"With network call-in shows, a station in a small market that does not have that much money might only have to bring in one engineer," says Morrie Trumble, program director of NBC's TalkNet. "That's better than employing a disc jockey and an engineer and a producer."

Indeed, that is one of the reasons WABC, which during the 1960's was the most popular and profitable music station in the country, is switching its 20-year-old format tomorrow morning. The other reason is that radio executives have realized that there is money to be made from appealing to listeners in the 18-to-34 age bracket in ways other than broadcasting rock-and-roll. America is, after all, still in the midst of the "me generation" and listeners to these overnight talk shows are phoning to discuss their individual problems.

"Rarely do people call for any other reason than to discuss what concerns them and not the world at large," says Dr. Judith Kuriansky, a clinical psychologist, whose show has been broadcast on WABC weeknights from 11 p.m. to 1 a.m. for the past five months. "And the age of my listeners even surprised me. I thought, at first, they would all be in their 40's and 50's. But they're actually younger. Some callers are teen-agers."

"We're learning we're not just a companion to old people and 'shut-ins,'" says Jay Clark, operations director at WABC. "We're learning that there is money in late-night talk radio. Now that's something to talk about."

I. QUESTIONS ON CONTENT

1. Do you listen to talk radio? Often? Have you ever participated?
2. Do you agree with Rick Sklar that "music on A.M. is doomed?"
3. Explain the call-in system on the Larry King and other talk shows.
4. What does the phrase "me generation" mean? Is that applicable today?
5. What is the age of the average listener to talk shows?

II. QUESTIONS ON FORM

1. There are two aspects to the topic for this article. Which one does Goldman use to introduce and conclude it?
2. Outline the structure of the article.
3. Cite some examples of comparison/contrast in the piece.

III. SUGGESTIONS FOR WRITING

1. Write a comparison/contrast of talk shows on radio and television.
2. Thousands of people stay up half the night, call total strangers, and air their most personal problems for the edification of all. Does this tell us something about our contemporary culture? Write a persuasive essay.

Robert Palmer is a popular music critic with the New York Times.

Will Video Clips Kill Radio as Maker of Rock's Top 10?

Robert Palmer

"Video Killed the Radio Star" was a modest hit for a duo called Buggles a few years back. It was a pleasant tune, too chirpy and lightweight to be taken seriously. But from today's perspective, "Video Killed the Radio Star" was positively prophetic. Almost overnight, it seems, promotional video clips have become the most effective and highly publicized means of introducing new pop music and new pop artists to the record-buying public.

MTV, the Warner-Amex cable-television channel that plays pop videos 24 hours a day, has been credited with almost singlehandedly boosting

Copyright © 1983 by The New York Times Company. Reprinted by permission.

records by new groups like Men at Work and Duran Duran into the top 10. Last Friday, NBC-TV introduced its own weekly program of pop music clips, "Friday Night Videos," which is being shown nationally and simulcast over radio via the Source network. New York's WABC-TV introduced a black-oriented late-night music video show, "New York Hot Tracks," on July 15. And last week, Russell Mulcahy became the first of the more sought-after pop video directors to announce that from now on he will be working full time in film.

The pop video boom is already beginning to transform the environment; restaurants and bars in New York and other major cities are investing in elaborate video jukeboxes, like the one that is the center of attention at the Century Cafe, on West 43rd Street. And the English language may never be the same. Just when one was beginning to get used to the latest in disk terminology (maxi-single, mini-lp), along comes a whole new category of pop-music celebrity, the V.J., who is to pop-music video what the disk jockey is to radio.

There have been dire predictions that the new emphasis on video will make image and style more important than musical content, and so far most of the new bands that have benefited from extensive video exposure *have* been more original in look than in sound. But overall, the effect of MTV and related phenomena seems salutary.

Video was a staple of the new-wave club and concert circuit from the beginning; when video caught on, a number of new-wave rock groups were ready, with sophisticated clips that won them broad exposure. New-wave video successes have forced the most conservative and formula-bound radio programmers to make room for new performers and new sounds.

Will pop-music video actually "kill the radio star" by becoming as crucial as radio exposure is now, and by leaving recording artists who lack video expertise out in the cold? It could happen, but the medium is still new, and several important details have yet to be ironed out.

As of now, record companies pay for the making of video clips and supply them to MTV and other broadcasters free of charge, as promotional items. But NBC is paying record companies a figure said to be around $1,000 a showing for the clips that it uses on the new "Friday Night Videos," and as the market for these clips expands, other broadcasters will probably follow suit.

As more and more companies and artists enter the rock video competition, the clips become more elaborate, and more expensive to make. In addition, the major record labels are now negotiating with the American Federation of Musicians on a proposal that would pay royalties to musicians whose work is viewed as a video-clip soundtrack. If broadcasters don't follow NBC's lead by offering to pay the record companies for clips, the record companies themselves will probably begin asking for payment; Warner Brothers reportedly has already done so. And as videos become more expensive to make and to air, the newer artists in musical directions that are currently receiving a shot in the arm from pop video could get priced right out of the market. The resolution of these economic issues will determine the nature and extent of video's long-term effect on pop music—that, and the public's reaction once pop videos have been around too long to be considered a novelty. Stay tuned.

ZIGGY

© 1983 Universal Press Syndicate.

I. VOCABULARY

dire   salutary   V.J.

II. QUESTIONS ON CONTENT

1. Does Palmer's article answer its title question?
2. Do you recall videos you have seen when you hear the music on the radio?
3. Do you think that the image will outweigh the music in impact on a song's popularity?

4. Cite some examples where videos have helped performers and where they have hurt.
5. Rock videos have been extremely successful. What about country and mor performers? Have many tried the form? What were the results?
6. Explain the problems with videos and royalties.

III. SUGGESTIONS FOR WRITING

1. Select a song you like and write a storyline for a video.
2. There are video jukeboxes and screens in department stores, restaurants, and so on. Write a persuasive essay on the impact of this assault of sight and sound. Is it a pleasure or an annoyance?

A former reporter at the *Los Angeles Times* and the *Register,* **Jeff Bailey** now works for the Chicago bureau of *The Wall Street Journal.*

Stereo "Box":
Big Bucks in Big Sounds
Jeff Bailey

George Della, a Baltimore city councilman, was sitting on a hill near his home last summer, trying to enjoy the adagios and scherzos of the Baltimore Symphony wafting his way from an outdoor amphitheater below.

But a group of teenagers nearby preferred a different type of music—disco—and the giant radio-cassette players that they were carrying drowned out the symphony's gentler sound.

"It really got out of hand," Della recalls.

The councilman got his revenge last month, when he helped enact a noise ordinance calling for a $25 fine or 30 days in jail for people creating a disturbance with the big portable stereos. Baltimore thus had joined such other cities as New York and San Francisco in using noise ordinances to restrain use of the "boxes," as they are widely known.

The cities face an uphill fight. Portable radio-cassette players are the fastest-growing audio product in the country. From nearly zilch five years ago, their sales have climbed into the millions—8 million last year, twice as

Copyright © 1981 by the *Los Angeles Times.* Reprinted by permission.

many as in 1979, reports the Electronic-Industries Association. And manufacturers say the boom in portable audio equipment sales has only begun.

Consumers' desire for go-anywhere music with sound quality to match that produced by car, and even home, stereos has spawned a generation of expensive portable radios nearly as large as those seen in pre-television days. The boxes weigh from 8 to 12 pounds and have speakers that can blast disco or rock and roll the length of a bus or across a city street.

Some lighter-weight units, such as the Sony Walkman, now come with earphones and no speakers, and hence are not objectionable to people whose music tastes conflict with the radio owner's.

Still, stereo makers' cash registers continue to ring loudest for the boxes. And manufacturers say the market for portable hi-fi is broadening to include more age groups, while spreading out from its initial concentration among inner-city youths.

Indeed, boxes seem to be everywhere, from up and down Third Avenue in New York to the Venice oceanfront walkway in southern California. Their users range from millionaire rock stars to prison inmates. And box makers are adding new lines of portable audio equipment and bigger advertising campaigns, attempting to capture larger shares of the growing market.

The full, rich sound that the new units pump out—in contrast to the tinnier tones of earlier types of portables—has lured many adult buyers.

"It's our yard music," says a dental nurse in southern California, Melissa Hewitt, 28. She and her husband, Mike, a cement-truck driver, listen to rock and roll tapes while lounging in their hot tub.

But the teenage market is the main target of the manufacturers, and Panasonic's advertising campaign featuring Earth Wind and Fire—a black rock group with wide appeal among white and black youths—has been successful. For their eight hours' work in the studio preparing the "Platinum Power" television and magazine ads, the group received about $1 million.

Suggested retail prices for the boxes, which can be heavily discounted by retailers, range from a little over $100 to $500 and beyond.

While boxes priced near the lower end of this range continue to be the big sellers, manufacturers are adding more high-priced models, "with all the bells and whistles," as one stereo retailer refers to features such as "program search" and flashing lights.

In Los Angeles, loud radios have become the No. 1 complaint by bus riders, says Southern California Rapid Transit District police chief Jim Burgess. "In the last few years it seems everybody is walking around carrying one of these things on their shoulders," he says.

When radio-playing passengers persist, Burgess says, a $50 fine can be levied. Although that seldom happens, he says, "we have made some arrests where the radio playing was excessive."

"On commuter lines it's not usually a problem," Burgess says, "but the downtown lines are bad."

In few places have the irritations aroused by the radios reached the extreme registered last summer in New York. There, a 20-year-old man was killed and a transit policeman wounded during a gunfight after transit officers sought to ticket a youth who had been playing his radio loudly in a subway station.

The controversy has produced some cautious reactions from manufacturers. "To disturb the peace is never a good thing to do," says Bob Greenberg, assistant general manager of Panasonic. He notes that how the units are used is "up to the consumer," and suggests that the negative publicity that the big boxes have received in some places may accelerate the trend to units featuring earphones instead of speakers.

But stereo companies are not pulling in their marketing horns because of the complaints and profess not to be intimidated by the effort of various cities to curb use of the big radios. "I think it's good publicity for us," says Harvey Schneider, national sales manager for Sharp Electronics.

Some observers believe that cities may be taking the boxes too seriously. "If you're asking to be recognized by your radio, it's certainly not awful," says New York psychiatrist Robert T. London.

"A very powerful radio is a symbol of power," he says—not too different from other status symbols, except that "the noise level can be distracting."

Owners frequently become very attached to the big new portables, though few so much so as one inmate at the Fort Grant Training Center near Bonita, Ariz.

The minimum security facility, 34 miles from Interstate 10, is surrounded by desert and mountains and the grounds have no outer walls. "We had this one prisoner," says former Fort Grant guard John Hammond. "He was out every day on the jogging track. He was in great shape."

"Well, one day he jogged right off the prison grounds and made a run for it," recalls Hammond. "We caught him about three miles from the highway. He would have made it, except he was trying to lug one of those big radios under his arm while he ran."

I. VOCABULARY

adagios   scherzos   zilch

II. QUESTIONS ON CONTENT

1. What is your view on ordinances restricting noise?
2. Do you or your friends own "boxes" or "Walkmen?" Do you feel they are worth the financial investment required?

3. Are you aware of the documented hearing loss within the last two generations? Does this problem disturb you?
4. Do you see very powerful radios as status symbols? Explain.

III. QUESTIONS ON FORM

1. Bailey begins and ends his piece with anecdotes. How do they differ?
2. What is the aim of this article? The thesis? What mode is used extensively?

IV. SUGGESTIONS FOR WRITING

1. Write a persuasive essay on the individual's right to loudness: the boxes cranked up versus the public's right to quiet.
2. Why has "go anywhere sound" in its various guises become so popular? Are we trying to tune out reality? Explain your views.

Tuning Out Controls on Radio
the New York Times 5/8/81

It hasn't been long since the United States Court of Appeals was routinely insisting that Isaac Stern rather than Dolly Parton appear on some radio programs. The court sought to protect desirable and rare radio formats—those pledged to classical music. It thus instructed the Federal Communications Commission to give special weight, in reviewing station licenses, to a broadcaster's fidelity to any promises about unusual program content. But increasingly, the commission defied the court, arguing that the marketplace was a better judge of listener interest.

Now the Supreme Court has settled this argument, in the commission's favor. And it has done so in a way that may reach far beyond music formats, to other controls on radio and even television. For the Court found reasonable the commission's view that there are now enough radio outlets to serve every significant taste.

If scarcity is no longer a valid justification for regulation, Government's control over any aspect of programming may disappear. Whether the matter can be left at that is a fateful question, which Congress needs to face.

The defeated format doctrine grew out of the so-called public interest standard in the Communications Act of 1934. Congress took the radio

Copyright © 1981 by The New York Times Company. Reprinted by permission.

spectrum to be a limited resource that should not be wholly governed by private interest. It thus allowed the commission to impose program standards—which, over the years, came to include limits on commercials and requirements for public affairs programs. The order to satisfy diverse tastes was later added by the appellate court.

The commission feels, however, that diversity will now take care of itself. And since the Supreme Court agrees, other broadcast regulations are likely to fall, especially as cable channels greatly enlarge the viewer's choice on television screens.

The trend is surely healthy. Any Government control over entertainment or information is an irritant to American values. Even loose standards, like the F.C.C.'s, tread ominously near free-speech rights. And while they exist, they can be tightened as well as relaxed. Within our hearing, there is certainly evidence that a lively competition in radio produces sufficient diversity on the dial.

But there are critics of the trend. Some ask how listeners in areas with only a few stations will get their news if the owners ignore it. They wonder how some audiences would learn about controversial issues and opposing views if station owners had no obligation to be fair or even to bother with political discussions.

There may be factual answers for such doubts. Congress ought to inquire about the number of Americans now receiving a reasonable variety of radio programs. If significant choice is denied in only a few sparsely populated regions, it would surely be ill-advised to perpetuate regulation everywhere.

The Supreme Court gave the F.C.C. the benefit of its faith in the radio spectrum. But it did not finally settle the question of whether the broadcast market as a whole meets plausible public interests. Congress, having created the requirement in the first place, should be the judge of that.

I. QUESTIONS ON CONTENT

1. What is the topic of this editorial?
2. Explain the "free marketplace" position.
3. Explain the "defeated format" position.
4. What is the position of the *New York Times* on this issue?
5. What is your position?
6. Does the broadcast market today meet plausible standards of public interest?
7. How can Congress determine if it does?
8. Could listeners in rural areas receive slanted news or virtually no news?
9. Are classical music afficionados entitled to some air time?
10. What would Barbara Tuchman's answer to question nine be? Why? (See Chapter Two.)

II. SUGGESTIONS FOR WRITING

1. Write an editorial disagreeing with the *New York Times*.
2. Are the airwaves a right or a commodity? Write a persuasive essay.

TOPICS FOR INVESTIGATION

1. Investigate radio's "Golden Age" in one or more of the following areas:

   a. comedy programs
   b. mysteries
   c. adventure series
   d. soap operas
   e. music/variety programs

2. Investigate college radio in your area and in the United States.

3. Investigate the role of radio disc jockeys past and present. Consider individuals like Murray the K, Wolfman Jack, Cousin Brucie, Symphony Sid, Dr. Demento, and so on as star makers, generational spokespersons, and cult figures.

4. Look into radio duos past and present. Research couples like Ed and Pegeen Fitzgerald and/or comedy teams like Klavan and Finch, and Bob and Ray.

5. Listen to Orson Welles' classic Martian Invasion broadcast. Would it work today? Why/why not?

9

POPULAR MUSIC

Popular music is simply music that many of us share. Music itself has always been a medium that occupies a special place. Lance Morrow says, "We organize time and myth with music; we mark our lives by it." Nothing less. We may spend our lives watching television, but the significant moments are not marked by "the tube" but by song.

"Music is the way that our memories sing to us across time," continues Morrow. Because of its universality, music is at once both timely and timeless, our touchstone with the present and the past. If film was the medium of the 1940s, television of the 1950s, then music, since the 1960s, has been the most dynamic art. In today's world of electronic wonders music has become for many of us a barometer of our emotions, sometimes our reality. Music is unquestionably the medium of the young. The youth market dominates the industry, and the tastes of the young have galvanized our society in ways we are just beginning to examine.

Some of the writers who have examined the impact of the music revolution can be found in this chapter. Lionel Tiger, the anthropologist, looks back at the Beatles, while music critic and scholar John Rockwell examines the emergence of country music into the national mainstream and in another piece analyzes a cult favorite of the last decade, Pink Floyd's "Dark Side of the Moon." It is not surprising that popular music has received so much academic attention; it has been the most pervasive force in college cultural life since 1960. Benjamin DeMott of Amherst explores the world of the undergraduate "pop-cult savants," their rock libraries, rock concerts, and personal curriculum and Louis Menand of Princeton speculates on the ascent of the rock musician as symbolic of the suffering culture hero in American society. In the other three articles Wayne Robins offers us a brief but vivid description of "heavy metal," while Daniel Goleman and Richard Corliss discuss two very contemporary and immensely popular phenomena: Michael Jackson and rock videos.

As these writers suggest, popular music has been and is, for many, "where it's at," and whether through technology, performance, or sheer raw emotive power, popular music may lead the way to where it's going.

Readings

> A writer for *Time* for the past 18 years, **Lance Morrow** is currently Senior Writer for the magazine. He is the author of *The Chief* (1985), a memoir of his father Hugh Morrow. In 1981 Mr. Morrow won a National Magazine Award for his essays and criticism.

They're Playing Ur-song
Lance Morrow

The crowd at the Grammy Awards last week looked as if it had just flown in from one of the moons of Saturn: glittering, snorting the intergalactic dust. Touches of the high crass mingled with a sort of metaphysical flash. Stevie Wonder, for example, wore a cumulously quilted white satin tuxedo whose upswept lapels formed great angel wings. The costume had the curious effect of making him look like a Puritan headstone.

The American popular-music industry was having its annual pageant. The program was about to end. Joan Baez walked onstage unannounced. As if she were lost in time, Baez driftingly began to sing Bob Dylan's anthem: "How many roads must a man walk down,/ Before you call him a man. . . ./ The answer, my friend, is blowin' in the wind,/ The answer is blowin' in the wind."

At that instant, a television audience of millions, including much of the baby boom that is now losing its hair, went time-traveling with Baez. Some felt 20 again. Some felt a thousand years old. They swooped back, daydreaming. Tears shot to their eyes. She was playing their song.

It is a fascinating, if familiar, process. When songs have that magic in them, they take on strange powers of recall. Commenting on a Noël Coward song, a character in Coward's *Private Lives* remarks: "Extraordinary how potent cheap music is." Songs eerily consolidate the memory, making obscure chemical connections in the brain. They conjure up moments out of time. They reconstitute things long gone to the point that smells and images and a precise forgotten ache of the heart return hauntingly for a moment. The dramatization that occurs in the mind is intimate and utterly private. One has only to hear a snatch of Simon and Garfunkel's *Mrs. Robinson* ("Where have you gone, Joe DiMaggio?/ A nation turns its lonely eyes to you,/ Woo woo woo") to be again in a rental car chasing Robert Kennedy's

Copyright 1983 Time Inc. All rights reserved. Reprinted by permission from *Time*.

whistle-stop primary campaign across northern Indiana in May of 1968. And other memories cascade down on that.

The conjuring song, in turn, becomes a signature, an act of self-definition. *Blowin' in the Wind,* of course, was only one of a thousand defining anthems of the '60s.

Traditionally, it is couples, not generations, that have their songs. Rick and Ilsa would put themselves in a trance by getting Sam to sing *As Time Goes By* in *Casablanca*. Sometimes we have more than one special song, or a different song for a different mate or a different archaeological layer of our lives.

Among the Tuvinian people of the Soviet Union, an individual can sing two melodies simultaneously. That has wonderful possibilities. Might one cross in the Tuvinian mind two simultaneous numbers, like, say, Bing Crosby's *Mississippi Mud* ("It's a treat to beat your feet . . .") with *Rock the Casbah* by the Clash? Would the Tuvinian stay sane if that happened?

A couple's "our song" presupposes an enduring and developing relationship of which the melody will be the theme. Every year on their anniversary, House Speaker Tip O'Neill sings *I'll Be with You in Apple Blossom Time* to his wife of 41 years, Mildred Anne. It is more difficult to develop a privately meaningful song if you plan to part company in the morning.

There may be an "our song" for a cause *(We Shall Overcome),* for a college ("Bulldog, bulldog, bow wow wow. Eli Yale!"), for a specific event, like the release of the hostages *(Tie a Yellow Ribbon Round the Ole Oak Tree),* and even for an era *(Brother, Can You Spare a Dime?).* Nations have them. But *The Star-Spangled Banner* has never quite become "our song" in the way that the *Marseillaise* utterly and unquestionably belongs to the French. Politicians have their "our songs." John Kennedy may have thought of his Administration in terms of the words and music of *Camelot*. But it is said that once, during a reception at the White House, he heard *Hail to the Chief* and muttered to Jackie, "They're playing our song."

The choice may sometimes be perverse. Abraham Lincoln rather liked *Dixie*. Someone decided that poor Franklin Roosevelt loved *Home on the Range,* so he was condemned to sit through the tune scores of times.

Music is a form of spiritual carbon dating. If one came of age in 1938, then Artie Shaw's version of *Begin the Beguine* might be the signature he went by, the sound that would date his soul like the exact ring on a redwood. A few years earlier, it might have been Hoagy Carmichael doing *Stardust*.

One can never quite imagine people younger than oneself having a plausibly magical song of their own. It is a trick of age and generational perspective. Parents believe that the songs their children cherish, far from amassing rich emotional associations, are merely destroying brain cells. The workings of special songs are necessarily subjective, and they promote a kind of hubris. Still, even allowing for that effect, it is sometimes hard to imagine what private anthems will arise from, say, punk or new wave music. Are there couples now that will for years grow mistily tender when they hear a ditty by Meat Loaf?

But a romantic fallacy may be hidden in such prejudices. What the music stirs in the mind need not be mere sentimentality. The evocative magic worked by songs is essentially mysterious. It doubtless has something to do with the organization of the brain. The musical faculty resides chiefly in the right hemisphere, along with the emotions, the nonlogical, intuitive powers of the mind. Music cohabits in the brain with myth. Says Howard Gardner, a research psychologist at Harvard: "Music mirrors the structure and the range of our emotions. It has the same kind of flow as our emotional life." What is the sound of the right brain singing?

We organize time and myth with music; we mark our lives by it. The death by assassination of John Lennon was an event that mingled music and myth and completed the relationship between the two. Music, as the anthropologist Claude Lévi-Strauss once said, "unites the contrary attributes of being both intelligible and untranslatable."

Music is the way that our memories sing to us across time. The loveliest quality of music involves its modulation upon the theme of time. Songs, playing in the mind, become the subtlest shuttles across years.

But sometimes the music is a weapon, and sometimes it is a trap. For centuries, Celts have given themselves battlefield noise and nerve with bagpipes, making the "our song" of the regiment, the tribe, stirring up the blood. The pipes have their wild rhetoric. It may both stiffen and imprison the spirit. Sometimes people cannot escape from their songs. The Irish gift for the instant ballad that glorifies this afternoon's martyr will ruin a human heart and turn children into killers, the heroes of tomorrow's pub songs.

In the past, some scholars have pursued the idea that there is a universal "our song": the *Ur*-song that is said to run through the imagination of every child in the world, an eerie universal croon. Actually, it need not be eerie. For all we know, the *Ur*-song may turn out to sound like the opening bars of Perry Como doing *Hot Diggity*.

I. VOCABULARY

| crass | carbon dating | modulation |
| cumulously | hubris | |

II. QUESTIONS ON CONTENT

1. Why does Morrow begin with the Grammy Awards? What aspects of the event does he emphasize? Why?
2. How is the term "anthem," as in "Bob Dylan's anthem," used in this piece?

3. Paraphrase the following sentence: "The conjuring song, in turn, becomes a signature, an act of self-definition."
4. What is a romantic fallacy?
5. Morrow, like Keller in the chapter on television, talks about brain function. Are their comments similar?
6. What does Morrow say about music and time?
7. Do you know all the songs Morrow cites?
8. What is *Ur*-Song? Do you think it exists?

III. QUESTIONS ON FORM

1. Paraphrase Lévi-Strauss' definition of music, quoted in the article. Then, consider, can this be an essay of definition?
2. What techniques does Morrow use in his definition of music?
3. Where does Morrow use classification?
4. Where does he employ cause and effect?
5. Comment on Morrow's example of Celtic music. Does his tone change in this section? Are the remarks in keeping with the remainder of the article?

IV. SUGGESTIONS FOR WRITING

1. Write a description that accords with a particular song—your song?
2. Write a satirical piece on some "our songs" you cordially detest.

Lionel Tiger is a social scientist and anthropology consultant. He is the author of works such as the popular *Men in Groups* (1969) and *Optimism: the Biology of Hope.* (1979). This essay appeared in *Rolling Stone* magazine.

Why, It Was Fun!

Lionel Tiger

Sigmund Freud once announced that "sometimes a cigar is just a cigar," and it is unquestionable that a forthright reason for America's response to the Beatles was that they played melodious music avidly and with joy and sang songs that, first of all, you could hear and understand and that, second of all, addressed everyone's real concerns—love and life—with quirky integrity and charming irreverence.

By Lionel Tiger. From ROLLING STONE, February 16, 1984. By Straight Arrow Publishers, Inc. Copyright © 1984. All Rights Reserved. Reprinted by permission.

Also, it was clear from the start that a trove of music was coiled, waiting to emerge, and that these were fellows of labyrinthine resource, creative artists who were wholly unsanctimonious, chaps who connected with a whoop of fun. And for once, the public was right, dead right. The Beatles embraced the world, and the world embraced them back. The anthropologist examining the whole business would have to say their tribe loved them, and they gave something to their tribe that the tribe treasured.

A full generation later, we are entitled to ask, we want to ask: How did they accomplish that? And we are driven to, obliged to, sneak in the *massive* question: How did *we* accomplish that? (Massive because we were happy and, as a community, united. Let's face it, could we ever be so happy again?)

How on earth did it happen?

For starters, try remembering all those high-pitched screams, the swoons, the highly ritualized adoration. Could anyone have ignored those young women? Of course not. They were us, they were our daughters, our sisters, our school chums and girlfriends, our girls next door. And their excited, dramatic reaction was an attention-getting signal to the rest of the community that a powerful force had been unleashed or revealed. By Monday afternoon, the day after the Beatles' first Sullivan show, every girl had chosen a favorite, and he was symbolically taken home to meet Mom and Dad, or at least discussed forcefully with Sue and Jill. It was a primitive response, buried deep in the central nervous system, rather like the response to winning warriors coming home or to a posse of provident hunters.

The reaction of these female adolescents was sweeping because there were millions of them—baby-boomers, born in those three fecund years after World War II when there was an explosion of new life, of happy arias (just as in the six previous years there had been a dread symphony of international murder). Their birth had been an antidote to war, living proof that societies could emerge from holocaust and horror and triumphantly reproduce. And now they were beginning their own reproductive years. They were in their hot teens, they were a swarm of vital energy, and they were healthy and wise enough to love them.

In England, the symbolism was even more dramatic. There, the baby-boomers were products of the Labour government that supplanted Churchill's after the war—remember? They turned him out when his work and war were done—and, for the first time, working-class pregnancies were given extra fruit, extra time and the new care of the national health system. It was the healthiest English working-class generation since the Industrial Revolution.

So in both countries, the Beatles found a willing and able audience of teenage females. The sociosexual demographics were there, and it all clicked—including the male aspects.

One of the enduring themes of human culture is the manner in which men form attachments to each other—I call it "male bonding"—and how male groups relate to one another (take sports teams, for example) and to the rest of the community (take outlaw gangs, for example, or the marines, or the fellows in *West Side Story*). The Beatles were a male group, bonded and precise and exuberant, and the deep energies involved in their work and play were readily communicable at the most basic level of human contact. In the slums of Glasgow and Liverpool, working-class males formed male-bonded groups and often, literally, fought over the symbolic issues of territory and honor. This bellicose high drama of poor young men could be and *was* transformed by music. The male war parties became bands, and the competition was with songs, not shivs, and honor was in a riff, not a rumble. The primitive energy was still there—just refined and amplified.

Of course, only a few of those acned lads whose bands practiced away in garages and basements ever made the spotlight. But for those who did—for John, Paul, George and Ringo—the constituency was waiting, homegrown and learning all the hits. And the eager fans weren't all females.

For even if their girlfriends weirdly screamed and steamed away, young men were not threatened by the Beatles. While women who were Beatle fans might ignore their parents' bewilderment or disapproval of their symbolic loves, better their boyfriends should approve and join in. They did. The Beatles were sexually benign; with their marine-stunning long hair, they were even somewhat androgynous, yet unmistakably heteroactive. While Presley could elicit class fear and confusion with his sullen anger and clearly poor origins, the Beatles somehow caught a wave of classless assertion: Their infectious impudence was rarely cruel, usually direct, almost smilingly amiable.

They had perfect pitch in attitude as well as in music. They lured young women without any sense of decadence, challenged young men without putting them down, teased parents, school principles, recruiting officers and ambassadors without being recognizably political.

In their music, they managed unpretentiously to merge the cool purity of the English folk tradition with the turbulent force of American black rhythms. So what they sang was familiar as well as alien in both English-speaking cultures; they skimmed the best off the top of both. And they made everyone feel better because their musical alloy was lit with sun.

Of course, when they hit town, they were preceded by a skillfully tempting barrage of preparatory publicity. And they had the wholly disproportionate advantage of *The Ed Sullivan Show*—there is nothing now that has the reach, the centrality, the eclecticism or the ability to authenticate an artist that the Sullivan show had. It was the National Show, and the Beatles made the utmost of it. After all the advance work and amid all the ululating fans, when they pounced onstage—happy, vibrant, clear-minded and as tuneful as youthful angels playing hooky in spring—our hearts yielded.

For once, the hype was true: The lads could sing and swing, the energy and affection were real. It was fun. What a shock. The community was in awe of its own ability to enjoy and share with decency and warmth, and while the event was a giant effort of the very mass media, it took private shape through ears and eyes. The music still does.

Inevitably, the claim is made that continued interest in the Beatles is nostalgia, which is nonsense—like suggesting that we listen to Brahms or Telemann out of nostalgia.

Why can't we just admit we enjoyed their music and enjoyed them and that it was all a very fine and colorful time of reassuring fun?

I. VOCABULARY

avidly	trove	unsanctimonious
quirky	labyrinthine	provident
bellicose	shiv	benign
androgynous	eclecticism	ululating

II. QUESTIONS ON CONTENT

1. This article is a retrospective on the Beatles 20 years later. What are your ideas on the era and the group? How did you arrive at those views?
2. Lionel Tiger is a well-known anthropologist. How has he applied his science to this topic? Cite some examples in approach and vocabulary. What is your reaction to this approach?
3. What does Tiger say about the Beatles themselves? What is male bonding?
4. What does he say about their music? Recall some songs that reflect the "cool purity of the English folk tradition" and the "turbulent force of American black rhythm."
5. The Rolling Stones were contemporaries of the Beatles. Does this essay apply to them as well?
6. Who are today's successors to the Beatles?

III. QUESTIONS ON FORM

1. Tiger discusses the Beatles' audience. For what audience is Tiger writing?
2. Explain the phrases "classless assertion" and "infectious impudence."
3. Tiger asks two direct questions: what are they and where in the essay are they located? Does he answer them?
4. Comment on the author's time references in the article. Is he specific? What events does he not mention?

IV. SUGGESTIONS FOR WRITING

1. Write a piece describing your own memories of the Beatles.
2. Write an essay on your reaction and/or the world's reaction to John Lennon's death.
3. Write an article about the surviving former Beatles. What has happened to them?

John Rockwell, Ph.D. Berkeley, joined the *New York Times* in 1974 as a staff music critic, the first staff critic to write about popular music as well as classical. A former Woodrow Wilson Fellow, he taught at Berkeley, Princeton, and Brooklyn College before devoting full time to criticism. He has contributed to numerous magazines and is the author of a book of essays on American composers, *All American Music.*

Country Music Is No Small-Town Affair
John Rockwell

Traditionally, "country music" has been either disparaged or ignored by big-city sophisticates, who found it simpleminded or funny. But today, country music is everywhere, and musically more vital than ever. Sociologically speaking, it is hardly confined either to the country or to the Southeast, almost anywhere you look in the American countryside, you will find a bar or tavern that advertises live country music on weekends. And nearly every big city boasts a country radio station and a country nightclub or two. In 1961, according to figures compiled by the Country Music Association, there were 81 radio stations devoted to country music, nearly all in the Southeast. In 1982, there were 2,014, spread throughout the nation.

Mainstream country music seems to represent the upward social aspirations of a once unqualifiedly unsophisticated class. The audience for country music used to be farmers and small-town folk with only a distant connection to big-city life. Now, in part because the audience itself has spread to more affluent sections of the country, the standard of living of the country-music audience has risen. The Country Music Association asserts that studies show the average country-music fan to have a *higher* than average income.

What kind of music do these fans listen to, and what is it telling them? In order to answer those questions, I decided to make a random sampling based

Copyright © 1983 by The New York Times Company. Reprinted by permission.

on the current Billboard magazine top 10 country LP chart, with sidelong glances at singles and the lower reaches of the LP chart.

Country music today seems to be split between a Nashville-based old guard and a new guard that draws its inspiration from all over the country, and attains its novelty by a paradoxical return to the folk basics of the country style.

The urbanization and gentrification of country music is usually linked with the rise of Nashville as the center of mainstream country music. This centricity came about through the dominance of the Grand Ole Opry radio network and the concentration since World War II of the country record and publishing industries in Nashville. Stylistically, the "Nashville sound" has meant the softening of older-style country-folk music with strings and other city-slicker arranging touches that sound closer to Las Vegas than the Appalachians.

Perhaps the most pervasive characteristic of the Nashville mainstream is the prevalence of drippily sentimental ballads. From Alabama (No. 1 on both the LP and singles charts) to Ronnie Milsap to the Oak Ridge Boys to Lee Greenwood to George Jones (who towers above the rest as a singer) to Kenny Rogers, this is music with a calculated inent to strum the heartstrings.

Country music of this sort is a neon-lighted terrain of weepy despair and drunken carousing. The "road songs" that were popular during the CB-radio craze may have abated, but the melodramatic image of a latter-day cowboy, alone against the world and guarding his innocence in the face of heartless women, a cruel world and his own weaknesses, remains as powerful as ever.

In country's cowboy world, the role of the woman has always been ambivalent. The fact that Shelly West is the only woman in the current top 10 is an accident; usually, these days, there are more. But Miss West admirably epitomizes the female stereotypes that predominate in country music. She alternates between cheery uptempo songs glorifying the good times in bars (her hit is called "Jose Cuervo") and tough but submissive ballads. Country women can be strong, but their strength must be exercised within the confines of a male-dominated world.

The parallel between country ballads and television soap operas is a real one: both deal in basic emotions—love, adultery, betrayal, vengeance—with a cartoon brightness. And yet their simple persistence in recognizing the pain and pleasure of such emotions guarantees both forms a direct connection to life.

Mainstream country music, blending imperceptibly into what is called "middle of the road," has become the successor to the ballads of pre-rock Tin Pan Alley as the principal source of "easy listening" for American adults. This has partly to do with its isolated critical status. Ignored even by most jazz and rock critics, country is a critical stepchild. As such, however, it has been allowed to continue as a purely popular entertainment, almost entirely unfettered by self-consciousness. Its innocence has been preserved—along with, to be sure, an inescapable naivete.

But with the naivete comes an unfortunate aura of calculation and cynicism—as if the singers or their producers were very carefully crafting just what they thought the public might accept, rahter than attempting to express themselves through their music. This is a danger in all commercial music, of course. But with the four-square formulas of country, in which dogged simplicity can so easily lapse into the numbingly predictable, the danger of seeming calculation looms all the larger.

Part of the problem is the very reliance most country singers place on their producers, who pick repertory and shape arrangements, and the hectic recording schedule still favored in Nashville. In country music a business situation akin to the 1940's and 50's prevails. With managers and producers calling the shots, their artists crank out records at a rate of two or three a year. The practice almost assures the continuance of what Nashville likes to think of as "tradition," but which really amounts to a deadening repetition of a few stock harmonic structures, ballad forms and clicheed instrumental licks. With recording schedules like these, only the determined can find time for originality.

Country music used to be called "country and western," lumping Appalachian folk music and cowboy ballads. If Nashville's country music answers the needs of cowboy-western mythology, it does so in faint imitation of the first and still most commercially potent wave of reformist new guard of country music, which came out of Texas a decade ago and articulated the cowboy mythology far more forcefully.

The leader of that movement was and is Willie Nelson, who happens to have the No. 3, 4 and 5 LP's this week. That may be a little unusual, it is not unprecedented. Along with Mr. Jennings, and allied with Mr. Haggard, Mr. Nelson led the fight to toughen up country, to bring it simultaneously closer to rock and to a purer, pre-Nashville style of country folk. (Dolly Parton's latest LP, "Burlap and Satin," should also be mentioned here. At No. 13 and climbing, it is about to enter the top 10, counts as Miss Parton's best, most country-oriented disk in years, and contains a haunting duet with Mr. Nelson.)

There was an irony in this revitalization through antiquarianism. But such a concern for the past by the most vital musical minds within a given style is shared by other kinds of music today: Classical, with its eclectic "new Romanticism"; jazz, with the newfound interest by the best younger black vanguardists in jazz history, and even rock, with the various revivals by hip young new-wavers of rockabilly, blues and psychedelia.

The success of the Texas "outlaws" was salutary for a country mainstream that had been threatening to lose most of its flavorful distinctiveness. Of Mr. Nelson's three LP's in the top 5, the closest to mainstream country is his duet with Mr. Haggard, but even it retains a knotty integrity that the disks of Mr. Milsap, Mr. Rogers and Mr. Greenwood don't even hint at.

The album with Mr. Jennings comes closest to rock on this list, and it is appealingly done, too. Mr. Jennings croaks more than he sings, these days, but he croaks with a gruff authority.

"Tougher Than Leather" is the most unusual of the three, but a disappointment. Eight years ago, Mr. Nelson released an album called "Red Headed Stranger" that raised "country music" to a new level. A gripping cycle of original songs mixed with traditional ballads, the LP told a tale and did so in a way that suggested at the very least a rock "concept album," and more deeply an art-song cycle. This new disk attempts to repeat that success, with its ongoing narrative and its spare, campfire arrangements. But the tale is less moving, the songs less tuneful and the overall effect more repetitious than compelling.

If Mr. Nelson and his Texans represented the first wave of country's reform movement, the circle of Emmylou Harris and Ricky Skaggs counts as country's "new wave." Miss Harris doesn't happen to have a disk in the top 10 just now, but she and her producer-husband, Brian Ahern, remain central to his movement. Based originally in Virginia, the home of a thriving bluegrass scene, Miss Harris amoved to Los Angeles, played a key role in the country-rock fusion led by the late Gram Parsons, and then struck out on her own.

Through her own records and the encouragement she provides to band members and other singers, Miss Harris has helped revitalize a whole tradition of country music that avoids both the fake-sophisticated glitter of Nashville and the gruff manliness of Texas. This style involves harmony singing (also favored by Alabama and the Oak Ridge Boys in the current chart, but subverted by them with poor materials and bathetic arrangements), instrumentation that recalls old-time country music, and inventive new songwriting in this style.

Mr. Skaggs happens to have the No. 11 album in this week's chart, "Highways and Heartaches" (EpicFE 37996); it has been on the chart for 41 weeks. He also has the No. 4 country single—it was No. 1 last week—in "Highway 40 Blues." Best of all, he is the producer of another LP, "Old Familiar Feeling" by The Whites (Warner/Curb23872). This is rapidly climbing the LP chart, already boasts the No. 9 single in "I Wonder Who's Holding My Baby Tonight," and counts as the best disk discussed in this article.

The Whites are a family group—so is Alabama; singing families are another nice country-music tradition—consisting of Buck White and his daughters Sharon, who is Mrs. Skaggs, and Cheryl White Warren. Their album is just delightful—freshly played, truly sung, full of a joy that stops short of raucousness and a sentiment that never lapses into sentimentality.

And this record should not be thought of as something pecking at country music from the outside, from Virginia or Texas or California. It was recorded right in Nashville, as was Mr. Skagg's own record. Which goes to show that what we call "country music," so seemingly conservative, may be as capable of renewal as any other art form in the nation right now.

I. VOCABULARY

disparage   paradoxical   gentrification
epitomize   naivete   antiquarianism
raucousness   bathetic

II. QUESTIONS ON CONTENT

1. What does Rockwell say accounts for the spread of country music since 1960?
2. Do you listen to country music a) ever, b) never, c) always?
3. Are you familiar with the artists and recordings referred to in this article?
4. Do you agree with Rockwell's description of the stereotypes in country music?
5. Why does Rockwell say that "middle-of-the-road music has "an inescapable naivete?"
6. Into what three areas does the author divide country music?
7. What are Rockwell's views on Nashville?
8. What does the author think are the best qualities of country music? What are the worst?

III. QUESTIONS ON FORM

1. Explain how this article is both expository and persuasive.
2. What is Rockwell's attitude toward country music?
3. Rephrase a description like "drippily sentimental" more positively. List some of the other judgmental phrases he uses.

IV. SUGGESTIONS FOR WRITING

1. Listen for a few days to your local radio station with a country format. Which type of country music is played? Write an article on the music and its presentation.
2. Expand (if you agree) on Rockwell's point that country music today is really the nation's middle-of-the-road popular music.

3. Do a comparison/contrast of two artists from differing schools of country music: Dolly Parton/Emmylou Harris, Kenny Rogers/Merle Haggard, and so on.

Benjamin DeMott is Andrew Mellon Professor of the Humanities at Amherst College. An author as well as an educator, he has written two novels and a collection of essays entitled *America in Literature* (1977). Like Leslie Fiedler, he is a prominent commentator on popular culture.

Ordinary Critics: Immanuel Kant and the Talking Heads

Benjamin DeMott

I spend part of my day teaching an undergraduate seminar in popular culture—movies, sitcoms, best sellers, rock music, and the like—at a small liberal-arts college in New England. People differ about whether this is a good idea and I defend it, when pushed, but what's pertinent is that the course exists. It has required reading and listening, a measure of theory, and a critical perspective (how do you distinguish better from worse when dealing with the products of the culture industry?); essays are written and grades are posted at the end of the course. The previous academic performance of those enrolled is above the average of the college—which is itself classified as elite—and the inclass talk is serious. Most of the time, when engaged in interpretive work, the group abides by straight-arrow, commonsense norms.

Most of the time. When treating rock music and films, my students diverge sharply, sometimes a shade troublingly, from those norms. They engage, that is, in several varieties of what was once called Reading In: symbol-hunting, supersubtle motivational analysis, hermeneutic high-rolling in the large. My impression, moreover, is that the incidence of this behavior is increasing. Whither Youth? Who knows?—heavy whithering isn't my beat. I've brooded more than a little, though, about the high-rolling I mention, because of its bearing on other intellectual fronts and, indirectly, on the vitality of popular culture in general.

Let me clarify, using an example—one of a dozen I remember vividly—drawn from a seminar discussion last year of Robert Redford's *Ordinary People*. For those who have forgotten, *Ordinary People* is a film about Cal, a

---

Copyright ©1981 by Harper's Magazine Foundation. All rights reserved. Reprinted from the March, 1981 issue by special permission.

Lake Forest, Illinois, tax accountant, played by Donald Sutherland, and his wife, Beth, played by Mary Tyler Moore; a couple afflicted with exceptional domestic stress. Following their older son's death by drowning in a sailing accident, their guilt-racked younger son tries to kill himself. Efforts by the parents and a therapist to draw him back into normal adolescence exacerbate tensions and lead to the collapse of the family.

The film's scenes of suburban high-school life—turf Hollywood seldom gets right—are well observed. Its disabling defect is its conception, or, rather, lack of a conception, of the parents; their feelings, motivations, movements of mind are nearly incomprehensible throughout. At crises, without explanation, the mother repeatedly rejects her disturbed son's attempts to speak to her from the center of his anguish. Robert Redford, as director, may have assumed that the pervasiveness of contemporary cant about the failure of communication in middle-class family life made it needless to search out reasons for any individual case of unresponsiveness. But that was a dumb assumption and the film is a muddle.

It was, however, regarded with respect by English 80, the course I'm speaking of. (In undergraduate discussion of films, flatly negative comment is rare anyway.) Few students were bewildered by the mother's spurning the attempts of her son to reach toward her. Confidently, thoughtfully, my undergraduate Readers-In created for her, almost from nothing, a coherent set of inner complications: the mother's grief so overwhelms her that the touch of her surviving son's hand, the sound of his voice unbearably return the image of the son she's lost; the mother has an instinctive suspicion that her son, in intimate chats with his therapist, is betraying her through acts of objectification, violating family privacies; the mother, because comparatively unsophisticated, superstitious, and wary of psychotherapy, sees her son—a would-be suicide who's dropped out of school activities that she understands to be healthy—as a freak, and is repelled by his certainty that her love for him has undergone no change; the mother senses that the father and son are in secret collusion against her, accusing her silently of having had an incestuous desire for her elder boy, the drowning casualty; the mother holds the son responsible for the older boy's death, since he survived the accident. On and on, voice after voice accounting fluently, often sensitively for deeds the film itself doesn't account for.

Naturally I didn't lie doggo in the face of this inventiveness. I reviewed scenes and shot sequences up at the board, held out for the superiority of interpretations supportable by gesture, expression, image, and word, condemned offhand novelizing. But the politic acquiescence I finally extracted was clearly superficial. Beneath the students' admission that they might have been Reading In lay the conviction that, really, their inwardness with the figures on the screen was privileged, their access unchallengeable. *You asked us and we told you. What's this scam about evidence? We know, that's all. We simply know.*

Similar behavior surfaces, as I say, on the rock front. Sexual themes predominate in rock lyrics but, as everyone who listens to the music or pauses at his children's door as they listen is aware, the images seem dependent on random and arbitrary association; little contextual guidance, much opacity. But my students are usually unshaken nevertheless. Giving no impression of scrambling improvisation, they summon interpretive proposals for each cunning passage in the albums of the Talking Heads, productions especially dense with impenetrable allusions. Portentously imprecise "symbols" in the music of the late Jim Morrison and the Doors—the monotonous "this is the end" refrain, for instance, on one hallowed cut—are unpacked with a no-hands shrug. Enigmatic, oracular declarations that a "rock literature" has come into being are soberly, extensively glossed. No sweat. We *know*.

One assessment of this knowingness dismisses it as a species of dimwitted self-indulgence, testimony to the school system's inability to inculcate respect for the disciplined pursuit of knowledge, sequential reasoning, and rules of evidence. Another version, farther out, sees it as a sign of the expanding influence of those academicians, impressed by the French critic Derrida, who have taken to arguing that true meanings are illusions; every poem or book is a "textual infinity," and the good critic is by definition a highroller—somebody who's stopped seeing himself as subordinate to the creative writer or filmmaker or lyricist and begun functioning, in his essays, as a poet. (For the record, I looked into the possibility that my student high-rollers are closet undergraduate Derrideans: no way.) Still another idea—attractive to explorers of the unique psyche fabricated in movie-house darkness—is that the acts of interpretation I describe are richly in the cinematic grain: movies legitimize every kind of fantasy, not excluding the fantasy of full explanation.

My own belief is that behind the Reading In lies the contemporary authority problem. Admittedly there's been some effort by faculties over the past decade to reoccupy positions abandoned during the previous decade: stabs at restoring requirements, curricula, and so on. But the overall impact has been slight. Soft options and easy B's are far commoner than hard courses and gratefully accepted C's, and the preceptors at the front of the room nowadays—more likely to be veterans of war protest and marital strife than of wars—aren't a particularly commanding bunch.

Yet, within reasonable limits, the appetite for tricky work—for challenge, as they say—persists, and so too does the interest of smart undergraduates in finding a corner of the brain-world to call their own. Intelligence in youth resembles animal spirits or sexual vitality; it longs for expression somehow, anyhow, and if, owing to an interval of nervous self-hatred, elders seem momentarily diffident about providing arenas for arduous exercise, it will undertake to bring them into being by its own inventive will.

And the desire for ownership—for a personal position in some closely held, intricately problematic stock—is a key element in this equation.

Through many gates left ajar during the epoch of "openness," students glimpse a vision of the Personal Curriculum, a body of knowledge of their own: private, specialized, exempt ordinarily from the tyranny of set questions, due dates, and letter grades. The Personal Curriculum promises a chance to be more definitive and peremptory than conventional authority dares to be on its own ground. All that's essential is to observe the conventions—meaning, you must possess your knowledge with an air of mastery and establish that you're proof against intimidation by interrogation.

Toward that end Reading In is the ticket. It enables you simultaneously to preserve the dignity of your chosen theater of expertise, to reveal your fluency, and to "work out"—push the headpiece, that is, at your own pace toward your own goal. Tell the man up front what Morrison was preaching in "The End," what the Talking Heads are alluding to, what passes through a character's mind as she stares away into the middle distance, oblivious to her heartbroken child—do this and you receive, together with mental exercise, a ticket of admission to the best circles of authority available in an age without Authority, namely those revolving exclusively around you.

Predictably, I have a sentimental worry about differences between them and us, youth and age, in the choice of objects of intellectual desire. It often erupts when I'm asked in to admire an undergraduate rock library. (They're composed of carefully catalogued taped concerts and bootleg prints, as well as of mint-quality standard albums.) I should note that while my college, like others, gives an annual prize to an undergraduate book collection, passion, expertise, and ingenuity—a collector's prime virtues—are better represented by at least two or three individual rock libraries per class than by any recent book collection I've heard of.

Browsing through a rock library, it's hard not to think back on personal aspirations, personal covetousness. It was expertise that *we* wanted back then, all right, people like myself, but our academic elders had managed to make their holdings in the knowledge line glamorous and desirable. What was it we were after? The meaning of the word *faïence*? Not, at any rate, information on what some electric guitarist said about his mother before slamming into "It's My Life" at a 1979 East Coast rock concert. I feel a twinge of self-accusation while listening to the collector across the room running on about the original Presley Sun singles, explaining that it's a pity the reissues of these classics couldn't duplicate the sound of that first, primitive studio. Condescension and self-accusation. How *did* we blow it? How *can* we explain our failure to make the particulars of tradition—academic *bricolage*—consequential to student imaginations?

But this is a sentimental turn of thought. The meaning of *faïence* ranks as no grander a piece of property than knowledge of the sound of Elvis's first Nashville studio. What counts, I repeat, is that the hunger for mastery and the desire to push the mind a bit—somehow, anyhow—are still alive.

The real problem—the potential danger—lies in the damage this sort of mind-pushing does the rock-film sector itself. In the public arena (an often risky scene), rock is the most various popular entertainment in the West. A musical event in one dimension—a display of lyric, melodic, or virtuoso gifts—a first-class rock concert is also by turns a demonstration, a dance, a melodrama, a comedy, an outburst of protest, an occasion for the forging of social solidarities, and an hour or two of responsive reading on the myth of The Rise, the Miracle of Success, and the wild joys of wild sex. The audience consists chiefly of persons hived off, under existing social arrangements, into the ghettos of youth- and student-powerlessness.

But because of the variousness of the entertainment and its capacity to embody contradictions and to draw together segments of the youth population ordinarily socially segregated, the experience provided by a rock concert is remarkably energizing and empowering, managing at moments almost to escape the control of the very culture industry that contrived it. Fantasy released through film is, to be sure, not negligible, although weakened by furtiveness and solitariness. But the rock concert at its best both expresses oppositional force and—by confirming, briefly and artificially yet intensely and publicly, the continuing existence of broadly shared satisfaction in democratic settings—shakes youthful cynicism and despair and recharges the idea of possibility. The undergraduate specialists bent on aestheticizing and academizing rock for ego-building purposes are, in sum, risking the impoverishment of an experience without equal in popular culture elsewhere. They're as remote from the truth of rock as I, as a fancier of the meaning of *faïence,* was from the true core of the humanities.

They've been encouraged to do this, of course, by grown-up "experts," just as undergraduate movie savants have been encouraged in their direction by oversolemn grown-up readers of film—specialists in the "codes" of Keaton, Fields, and the rest. One might have hoped that, grown-up and in less need of pseudo-authority, rock savants would have shed a layer of pretentiousness and dropped the charlatanry. But that's happened too infrequently. The tutors of the present undergraduate high-rollers—my Readers-In—range from respectable music-loving elders who discovered the Beatles in the late Sixties, as that group was producing its most pretentious and least durable work, to the literary commentators who rhapsodize about David Byrne as an "ambitious thinker." There's *The New York Times*'s John Rockwell saluting "artistic breakthrough" in Linda Ronstadt: she "has attempted with sovereign success a song that transcends the humanistic, amorous-psychological basis of her music and moves into the realm of metaphorical abstraction." There's the *Village Voice*'s Ellen Willis doing litcrit about a Velvet Underground album, calling it a *"Pilgrim's Progress* in four movements," and laying down that: "For the Velvets the roots of sin are in this ingrained resistance to facing our deepest, most painful, and most sacred emotions; the essence of grace is the comprehension that our sophistication is a sham, that our deepest, most painful, most sacred desire is to recover a childlike innocence we have never, in our heart of hearts, really lost."

And, most regrettably and depressingly, there's *Rolling Stones*'s Dave Marsh settling in to persuade Bruce Springsteen, who stands among the most vibrant popular entertainers of the age, of his obligation to transform himself into material for scholarly exegesis. In a long interview in the current issue of *Musician,* Marsh harries the creator of "Born to Run" with observations on his concert programs as two-part philosophical disquisitions, and on artistic self-consciousness as a Higher Good. Responding gushingly to a new album called *The River,* Marsh lectures the performer about the development of his oeuvre: "Certain ideas that began with the second and third albums have matured, and a lot of the contrasts and contradictions have been—not resolved—but they've been heightened." And a moment later: "The way [your] stage show is organized is that the first half is about work and struggling; the second half is about joy, release, transcending a lot of things in the first half. Is that conscious?"

Shut up shut up shut up, one thinks as one reads—and then at once the further thought comes that perhaps teaching a course in popular culture itself adds to the pedantry and punditry. Not likely: not a course in the *criticism* of popular culture. It's demonstrable that those now promoting rock and film pedantry in the establishment press didn't learn to do this in popular-culture classes. The *Times*'s John Rockwell has a Berkeley doctorate in European culture, not in the history of pop; in his present field of intellection he's plainly rolling his own.

And, anyway, who's-to-blame and who-can-justify-himself aren't the subjects at hand. We're addressing not the extravagance of rock and film chatter in itself but the question of what it signifies when it's heard on campus. It signifies, I think, that students believe they're in possession of a vital culture of their own (they're roughly right about that), and it also signifies that, out of pride, students enjoy locating the problematic side of their culture and talking about it in professorial tones (it's a mistake in some respects, but they could do worse). Lots of us itch to sound off with appropriate, urgent-voiced warnings—and with invitations, too.

The appropriate invitation is: Come home, come back to the *real* library, come cudgel the brains where the payoff is richer—Kant, Shakespeare, that crowd. The appropriate warning is: Turn Bruce Springsteen into an academic abstraction and you rip yourself off. But my money tends to say, cool it. One can take heart, whatever the look and sound of things, that the pop-cult savants in the student body aren't that far out of the fold; could be all the way back in tomorrow. And there's at least some ground for trusting the toughness of "people's culture." Many times before, it's broken the stranglehold of both the culture industry and of phony erudition. With a little luck— the break I have in mind would do as much for Kant and Shakespeare as for rock and film—it could just bring off that amazing feat again.

I. VOCABULARY

pertinent	exacerbate	collusion
hermeneutic	cant	politic
opacity	enigmatic	oracular
preceptor	faience	bricolage
savants	charlatanry	exegesis
disquisitions	cudgel	erudition

II. QUESTIONS ON CONTENT

1. What message is DeMott conveying in his first paragraph?
2. What does the author mean by "Reading In?"
3. Two cultures are compared and contrasted in this article. Define each.
4. How does this piece comment on Barbara Tuchman's essay in Chapter Two?
5. Explain the "Personal Curriculum."
6. What does DeMott say about his undergraduates and their rock libraries? What positive aims do these reveal?
7. DeMott's view of academics emerges clearly in the article. Explain it and your views on it.
8. Who are the "pop-cult savants?" What are your views on them?
9. How would Kant and Shakespeare benefit from a revival in the "people's culture?"

III. QUESTIONS ON FORM

1. For what audience is DeMott writing? To whom does he refer in the question near the end of part two, "How did we blow it?"
2. Comment on the phrase "Whither Youth? Who Knows." What is the author's perspective here?
3. What is the effect of DeMott's mingling of academic terminology—oeuvre, faience—with idioms like "No Sweat," "No way," "Cool it?"
4. Comment on DeMott's definition and description of a rock concert. Can he himself be accused of Reading In?
5. Analyze the explicit contrasts in diction within one sentence, "Shut up shut up shut up, one thinks as one reads—and then at once the further thought comes that perhaps teaching a course in popular culture itself adds to the pedantry and punditry."

IV. SUGGESTIONS FOR WRITING

1. Write a persuasive essay disagreeing with DeMott's view of the intellectual lightness of popular culture.

2. Write an essay upholding the necessity of a "Personal Curriculum."
3. Write a description applying DeMott's analysis of a rock concert to a specific concert (or concerts) you have attended.

A Pink Floyd Album Marks 10 Years as a Best Seller

John Rockwell

On May 14, a quite remarkable milestone will be reached. In the Billboard magazine issue that goes on sale that day (the actual date of the issue will be May 19), Pink Floyd's progressive-rock album, "Dark Side of the Moon," will have appeared on the magazine's top-200 album chart for 520 weeks. That divides neatly into 10 years.

A full decade! Think of it: The term "pop charts" is almost a metaphor for ephemerality. Classical music is supposed to be timeless, and we are told that while classical recordings may not sell in huge initial bursts, thus qualifiying them for the charts, they have a "shelf life" that insures them a longer-lasting commerciality. Yet here is an LP by a mere British rock band that seems to be with us permanently.

But if Pink Floyd is so dominant, why is it still so marginal as far as truly mass awareness is concerned? Why isn't it as familiar to everyone as the Beatles, the Rolling Stones and Michael Jackson?

Before we try to answer these questions, and address the even more basic issue of why this particular LP has been so popular so long, some more precise statistics may be helpful. "Dark Side of the Moon" entered the chart on March 17, 1973. That means its 520 weeks were not consecutive, but cumulative. The album fell off the chart at Christmastime 1974, and came back in April 1975. It went off again the following February, only to return, and remain, during the 1976 Christmas season.

According to Joel Whitburn's Record Research, a firm which tabulates statistics based on the Billboard charts, "Dark Side of the Moon" tied Carole King's "Tapestry" at 302 weeks as the longest-charted rock record in Billboard's history on March 15, 1980. On Oct. 22, 1983, it matched the longest-charting record of any kind, tying Johnny Mathis's "Greatest Hits" at 490 weeks. Since then, every week it surpasses only its own total. In the most recent issue as of this writing, dated May 5, "Dark Side of the Moon" was at No. 172, up three positions from the previous week, and had been charted for 518 weeks.

Billboard's album chart is assembled strictly on a basis of sales, according to Thomas Noonan, the magazine's associate publisher and director of

Copyright © 1984 by The New York Times Company. Reprinted by permission.

charts. Some of the other charts factor in radio play, as well. In the bottom reaches of the album chart, the precise ordering becomes a little vague; Mr. Noonan says that a given chart position can be as much as 15 positions off the mark, either way.

Capitol Records, which distributes the Harvest label on which "Dark Side of the Moon" appears (SMAS-11163), refuses to divulge sales figures. A company spokesman did say, however, that the album was the biggest-selling LP in the company's history. It should be remembered that another Capitol group was the Beatles. Mr. Noonan, who used to work for Columbia Records, recalls that in the final months on the chart of the Mathis record, it was still selling between 5,000 and 8,000 copies a week in this country alone, and he guesses that "Dark Side of the Moon" today is selling about the same.

That figure does not include international sales, and according to the Capitol spokesman, "Dark Side of the Moon" is very much a sales phenomenon abroad, as well. Domestic figures include eight-track, cassette and compact-disk configurations, as well as LP, but exclude sales of Mobile fidelity Sound Lab's audiophile disk version of the album.

The reason the general public is not instantly aware of Pink Floyd (despite its much-admired tours and film of "The Wall") is that this is the quintessential, larger-than-life cult band. Pink Floyd's cult is not only large, it is unusually loyal. Capitol asserts that a surprising number of copies of "Dark Side of the Moon" are sold to buyers who are replacing worn-out copies. Proof of the disk's cult status—meaning both that it is loved by its fans but that it never made a broadbased, mass impact—is that in 1973 it took seven weeks to reach the No. 1 spot (not so unusual in itself) and only held the top position for one week (it did stay in the top 10 for nearly seven months, however).

No previous Pink Floyd album had come close to No. 1. And while subsequent albums have done well, momentarily boosting the chart status of "Dark Side of the Moon" back into the middle of the top 100, none has come close to equalling its long-range success.

And so, we finally ask, why? What has this album got that still impels 5,000 or more people every week to go out and buy an 11-year-old pop record?

"Dark Side of the Moon" was recorded in the Beatles' Abbey Road studio in London between June 1972 and January 1973, with Alan Parsons as engineer. There are lyrics here and there on the album—musing, distracted ruminations on teen-age boredom, rock-star wealth and, above all, the visions and damage of drugs—plus deftly handled sound effects that establish a sort of audio theater between the songs: pre-visual rock video, perhaps.

But all these extras serve primarily to focus attention on the music, which in a really compelling way manages to look both backward and forward. It is this timelessness probably more than anything else that explains the album's continued popularity: It doesn't sound dated today at all.

Pink Floyd was born as a British psychedelic band in the later 60's; its first record dates from 1967. At that time, its dominant figure was Syd Barrett, who sang, composed and played the guitar. But Mr. Barrett had drug problems (his situation recalls the comparable psychedelic "genius" of the early Beach Boys' Brian Wilson). In 1968 he was first bolstered, then replaced, by Dave Gilmour. The other members are Roger Waters, bass and now principal composer; Nick Mason, drums, and Rick Wright, keyboards, who recently left the group.

The band's "psychedelic" music consisted of long, spacy instrumentals built on distended blues structures, rather like the Grateful Dead in California. To this were added Mr. Wright's sinuously atmospheric keyboard textures (electric organs, synthesizers, etc.), and a nascent sense of aural theater.

This style facilitated an extension of idiom into the sort of British art-rock that took off from some of the Beatles' late-60's experiments and became particularly popular in Britain in the early 70's. The inner space of drugs connected easily with the outer space of science-fiction imagery.

Most British art-rock bands quickly stumbled into the quagmire of symphonic pomposity, born of a desire to imitate, or actually employ, a symphony orchestra. Pink Floyd indulged in a bit of that, as well. But for the most part, the band stuck to the sparer, simpler sound that defined its initial image, and expanded in the direction of increased theatricality rather than increased volume or textural clutter.

By retaining this sonic and stylistic focus, the band managed to survive the new-wave reaction against the sillier excesses of the art-rock movement. Pink Floyd survived in the sense of making new albums ("Wish You Were Here," 1975; "Animals," 1977; "The Wall," 1979, and "The Final Cut," 1983—this last without Mr. Wright, who was missed; they replaced him with orchestral strings).

But the band also survived in the sense that its quintessential sound, as heard on "Dark Side of the Moon," retained a freshness that makes its steady sales less a matter of nostalgia than of ongoing relevance. This is an album that may not sound like the latest dance-rock hits, or rate very high in the estimation of trendier critics. But it still answers the esthetic and emotional needs of a tangible audience. And for all we know, it may continue to answer those needs for years or even decades to come.

I. VOCABULARY

ephemerality	ruminations	psychedelic
quagmire	sinuously	quintessential

II. QUESTIONS ON CONTENT

1. Do you know the album discussed in this article? When did you first hear it? Does its endurance surprise you?
2. To what does Rockwell attribute the album's longevity?
3. What bands might the author be referring to who "stumbled into the quagmire of symphonic pomposity?"
4. How drug oriented do you think this album is? How much do you think this aspect has contributed to its long popularity?
5. How would Benjamin DeMott account for the endurance of "Dark Side of the Moon"—a decade of Reading In or genuine art?
6. In view of its continued elite cult success would Barbara Tuchman consider the album Q or non-Q?

III. QUESTIONS ON FORM

1. How much of the article is exposition?
2. Identify the thesis paragraph.
3. Explain in what way the piece illustrates cause and effect.

IV. SUGGESTIONS FOR WRITING

1. Write an analysis of "Dark Side of the Moon" or "The Wall" as concept albums.
2. Compare and contrast Pink Floyd with one of the following groups: Moody Blues, Yes, Emerson, Lake, and Palmer, Kansas, Styx, or The Grateful Dead.

Wayne Robins writes on the popular music scene, television and movies for *Newsday*. Former editor-in-chief of *Creem* magazine, he has contributed to *Rolling Stone*, the *Village Voice*, *Berkeley Barb*, the English *Melody Maker*, and the Japanese *Music Life*.

Heavy Metal
Wayne Robins

Rock trends come and go, but heavy-metal never dies. In fact, it hardly ever changes. Reviled by many critics, disdained by most rock radio stations, heavy-metal has for more than a dozen years been the music of generations

Copyright © 1983 by Newsday, Inc. Reprinted by permission.

of teenagers. Heavy-metal has proved so resilient that its first generation of fans from the late 1960s are, at least biologically, old enough to be the fathers of today's believers.

Of course, that is unlikely. You don't see a tremendous number of dads taking their sons and daughters to Ozzy Osbourne concerts. Rebellion, or at least sublimated rebellion, is a large part of the appeal of heavy-metal. One would have to assume that if a parent *encouraged* an appreciation of Black Sabbath, Led Zeppelin, and Judas Priest, the frustrated offspring would almost certainly hole up in his or her room, and listen to Frank Sinatra records at modest volume.

How to describe heavy-metal? Consider this appreciation written by the late Lester Bangs, a fan and defender of the music who wrote about it in "The Rolling Stone Illustrated History of Rock and Roll": "As its detractors have always claimed, heavy-metal rock is nothing more than a bunch of noise; it is not music, it's distortion—and that is why its adherents find it appealing. Of all contemporary rock, it is the genre most closely associated with violence and aggression . . . it's a fast train to nowhere, which may be one reason it seems to feel so good and make so much sense to its fans."

Among the conventions shared by most heavy-metal bands are one or two lead guitarists who play furious flurries of demented notes; a drummer whose brute strength and stamina are more important than his ability to keep time; and a bass player capable of sending out reverberations that can shatter human bone, not to mention eardrums. Add a lead singer with long stringy hair, tattoos, and an assortment of bellows, yelps, yowls, profanities and sexual declamations, and you have an accurate caricature of a heavy-metal band.

The optimum situation in which to hear heavy-metal music is in an acoustically imperfect hockey arena among at least 10,000 other members of the teenage tribe. But because of a miraculous invention known as the phonograph record, you can also listen to heavy-metal in the privacy of your own home.

I. QUESTIONS ON CONTENT

1. What does Robins imply with the phrase "at least biologically old enough?"
2. What, according to Robins, is the appeal of heavy metal? Does it appeal to you? Why/why not?
3. Do you agree with the author's comments on distortion?
4. Name some of the better heavy metal bands. Some of the worst.
5. Should Robins have labeled his description of a typical heavy metal group a "caricature?"

II. SUGGESTIONS FOR WRITING

1. Write a persuasive essay espousing Led Zeppelin, Black Sabbath, or Judas Priest as the definitive heavy metal band.
2. Is heavy metal, as Robins suggests, a static form? Who are the new practitioners? Are there improvements?

Louis Menand, Ph.D. Columbia, is an Assistant Professor of English at Princeton University. He has published in *The New Republic* and *Bennington Review,* and his most recent article "Rules of the Game" appeared in *Dissent* magazine.

Transforming Elvis into a Suffering Culture Hero

Louis Menand

The publication last fall of Albert Goldman's biography of Elvis Presley was an important event, not so much because of Goldman's cruelties as because of the enormous response the book provoked.

When serious writers in journals ranging from The Village Voice to the Times Literary Supplement rose to defend Presley's cultural significance, it was clear that "Elvis" had identified a substantial audience of intellectuals with an interest in popular entertainers. It is tempting to speculate on the reasons for this fascination with the heroes of popular culture.

The interest can be attributed in great part to the change the image of the modern artist has undergone in the past 15 or 20 years. Once the symbol of a heroic alternative to the voracious commercialism of modern life, the avant-garde artist has come since the 1960s to look like just another entrepreneur in the business of culture.

An episode recounted in Andy Warhol's memoir of the 1960s, "Popism," provides a neat illustration of what happened. One day in 1960, Warhol, at the time a successful commercial artist who made his living drawing shoes, decorating the windows of fashionable department stores and, on a few occasions, drawing little suns and rain clouds for TV weather maps, showed his friend and mentor Emile de Antonio two paintings he had made. Both were of Coca-Cola bottles: in one, the image was embellished with abstract expressionist drips and hash marks; in the other, the bottle was unadorned.

Reprinted by permission of *The Nation.*

De Antonio told Warhol that one of the paintings was worthless, but he said, "The other is remarkable—it's our society, it's who we are, it's absolutely beautiful and naked, and you ought to destroy the first one and show the other."

It is of course the fondest sort of romanticism to read cultural history in the light of the aesthetic decisions of individual artists; but it would not be indulging in more than the usual critical hyperbole to say that when Warhol threw out the canvas with the drips and hash marks, a major phase in the history of modern culture came to an end.

Those painterly effects were the signature of the special sensibility that guaranteed art. They were the traces of the painter's heroic struggle to transform the everyday into art, to make a statement about his special relation to the world of ordinary experience.

It is perhaps easier to accept the significance of Warhol's decision if we remember that it was not in the ordinary sense an artistic decision but primarily a commercial one. De Antonio may have thought he saw a work of art; Warhol realized he had something that would make him famous.

What Warhol had done was to turn one of the oldest of avant-garde strategies on the avant-garde itself, inverting the conventional relationship between high art and the marketplace and transforming the high-culture art work into a commodity.

Or, to put it in esthetic terms—well, here is Warhol's own gee-whiz prose: "Pop art took the inside and put it outside, took the outside and put it inside. The Pop artists did images that anyone walking down Broadway would recognize in a second—comics, picnic tables, men's trousers, celebrities, shower curtains, refrigerators, Coke bottles—all the great modern things that the abstract expressionists had tried so hard not to notice at all."

"All the great modern things." The collapse of the distinction between high and popular culture that this phrase sums up has seemed to many people to be the defeat of culture. But it is really culture's triumph: it has always been the secret and mastering desire of modern culture to enter into our lives, to be experienced as more than simply a collection of aesthetic artifacts, and now, by some extraordinary but inevitable adjustment of its self-image, it has done so.

The price paid by high culture in this adjustment was the loss of its heroic status. The consequences of Warhol's cynicism—a cynicism so profound it looked like innocence—for the content of modern art were really not as far-reaching as its consequences for the image of the modern artist. "I threw the bottle rack and the urinal in their faces for a challenge," complained the unwilling godfather of pop art, Marcel Duchamp, "and now they admire them for their artistic beauty."

The modern artist had always been the heroic challenger of official culture—of its commodity fetishism, its marketplace morality, its bourgeois notions of art. With the arrival of popism and the emergence of the big money art world of the 1960s and '70s, the avant-garde suddenly seemed to join forces with that part of modern life it had traditionally been understood to despise.

But the need for the culture hero that modern high culture had always filled—the artist whose life and work are the heroic testimony of the modern world's hostility to genius—did not disappear with the institutionalization of the avant-garde. The culture hero was simply rediscovered in another part of the cultural spectrum—in the world of popular culture. Since the spirit of modern art and literature had always been in direct conflict with the notion of art as a form of popular entertainment, this relocation of the culture hero from painting and poetry to rock music makes for one of the lovelier ironies generated by the collapse of the cultural hierarchy.

Looking back, we can see the kind of attraction someone like Presley would have for intellectuals in the modernist version of the myth of the artist as culture hero. Presley's career can be read as the embodiment of one of modern culture's two strategies for dealing with the phenomena of mass society and mass culture. The two strategies were resistance and submission, and both were understood to be heroic because both were understood to entail suffering. The notion that Presley submitted his talent to the inhuman machinery of commercial exploitation, and that he paid in consequence a terrible price, is the basis for his present peculiar stature as both the hero and the victim—the heroic victim—of modern mass culture.

The history of 20th Century culture might accurately be written as the history of the tensions between high and popular culture. The more familiar of high culture's two strategies for dealing with the majority culture was that of resistance. But the modern artist might also submit himself to the experience of the modern world.

One way for the modern artist to represent the experience of life without recourse to the alien language of high culture was to appropriate the forms of popular and commercial art: the prose of journalism, the structure of the detective novel, the typography of advertising, the "found object" from the detritus of the consumer society, the lyrics or the tune of a popular song. Though these things were intended to de-aestheticize the work, their presence had the effect of endowing the familiar objects of popular culture with a kind of artistic resonance.

The notion that readily attached to this "higher" view of popular art is that the popular artist is the purest embodiment of the expense of spirit in the wasteland of modern mass culture; and this is the basis for our present-day inclination to elevate the status of popular artists and entertainers, and to see some of them as culture heroes.

Often it is the popular musician who seems best able to fulfill our requirements for the culture hero. This is in part because the corruption of talent is so much more fascinating to us than its cultivation. It strikes us, in the case of the popular musician especially, as an authentic expression of and response to the predatory commercialism that we like to think of as the peculiar bane of contemporary life. The origins of rock in the efforts of white working-class kids to sound like black singers have made it an especially attractive ground for the generation of culture heroes.

John Lennon is a perfect example. Facing a future as a member of the industrial working class in Liverpool he applied his special talents to the form of expression most readily available to him, both as a mode of protest *and* as a ladder out of the depths of his social position. This was, of course, a contradictory motivation, and one of the reasons Lennon is admired is because he tried to live out that contradiction even in the circumstances of his incredible commercial success—and because he appeared to know that the attempt was bound to be a failure, appeared willing at times to be the victim of his own success.

With Presley, willingness was not an issue. His talent was made to undergo every form of commercial exploitation his manager could invent and his public could consume. His genius was natural, powerful and extremely limited: he was a great interpreter of other people's songs. His eventual disappearance into the saddest depravities of contemporary life is precisely what has given his reputation among intellectuals its heroic cast. He traveled to that foreign land, and it killed him.

This idea of the artist-hero, and even and especially the entertainer-hero, is one of modern culture's myths. We know, I think, that it is a myth, but we still subscribe to it because it allows us to cling to the notion which, as contemporary culture continues to cash in on all the myths of modern high culture with ever-increasing speed and assurance, will come to seem more and more a delusion.

I. VOCABULARY

| voracious | fetishism | depravaties |
| artifacts | detritus | |

II. QUESTIONS ON CONTENT

1. How much of this essay is actually on Elvis Presley?
2. What is Menand's real topic? Explain what he means by "institutionalization of the avant-garde."
3. What, according to Menand, was the price paid by high culture for its new popularity?
4. Why is the elevation of a rock musician to a culture hero so ironic for the author?

5. What two strategies were embodied in Presley's career and why were they heroic?
6. How do you feel about Elvis? Is he still "the King"?
7. What does Menand see as the essential difference between John Lennon and Elvis Presley?
8. Do Goldsmith's ideas on celebrity replacing character (Chapter Two), apply to either Lennon or Presley?
9. What does Menand predict for the musician as culture hero?

III. QUESTIONS ON FORM

1. Count the number of paragraphs in the essay. Then count the number on Elvis Presley.
2. Is this essay difficult to comprehend? Why/why not?
3. What is the aim of the article? Does it succeed?
4. Note uses of the following modes: example, comparison and contrast, and cause and effect in the article.
5. Paraphrase Menand's conclusion. What is the effect of his understated writing?
6. The author calls Andy Warhol's writing "gee-whiz prose." Explain.

IV. SUGGESTIONS FOR WRITING

1. Write a persuasive essay defending Elvis as a genuine culture hero.
2. Write an essay explaining how the rock opera and film "Tommy" by the group The Who illustrates many of Menand's views.

Daniel Goleman, who received his Ph.D. from Harvard University, is a contributing editor to the science department of the *New York Times* and a former senior editor of *Psychology Today*. His recent book is entitled *Vital Lies, Simple Truths: The Psychology of Self-Deception*.

Psychologists Examine Appeal of Michael Jackson

Daniel Goleman

Why such an outpouring of adulation for Michael Jackson?

Admittedly, he's a talented performer, and his popularity undoubtedly stems from his abilities as a singer, songwriter, dancer and performer. But

Copyright © 1984 by The New York Times Company. Reprinted by permission.

as with every entertainer of such mass appeal, part of that popularity can be explained by the image and personality he projects. That image, moreover, is highly unusual and goes against many earlier rock-star stereotypes. But, in the view of many psychologists and observers, it may be the very unconventionality of Mr. Jackson's persona that makes him the star of the moment and accounts for his appeal to contemporary—especially young—audiences.

On stage, Mr. Jackson, who, with his brothers, started a multicity, multimillion dollar concert tour last Friday, is famed for his sexually ambiguous appearance and voice. In that regard, he resembles several other recent rock stars, such as David Bowie and Boy George, the latter of whom was the subject of "Androgyny" a program on "Face the Nation" on CBS yesterday.

But in the view of many psychologists, Mr. Jackson's appeal may go beyond androgyny. In his private life, according to portrayals in the popular press, Mr. Jackson, who is 25 years old, has never touched alcohol or drugs, eats no red meat and is a virgin. A devout Jehovah's Witness, he lives with his parents as a virtual recluse, although he occasionally makes forays in disguise to distribute religious literature.

Mr. Jackson reportedly spends much of his free time watching cartoons from his own large collection, carries on imagined conversations with mannequins as though they were people, and has very few personal friends. One of those friends, Jane Fonda, has said: "Michael reminds me of the walking wounded. He's an extremely fragile person."

That fragility, in the view of many experts interviewed, may be one psychological key to Mr. Jackson's popularity.

"His vulnerability is especially appealing to young and preteens," said Robert Gould, former director of adolescent psychiatry at New York University medical school. "When he makes an appearance in public, he's so shy and inarticulate he looks like he needs someone to take care of him. It brings out protective feelings—he's almost like a pet you want to adopt."

"Jackson's passive shyness is quite unusual in rock stars, as is his cleancut, sweet innocence," Dr. Gould added. "It's particularly attractive to young girls who would be threatened by a macho type. And just those girls—13 and younger—seem to be a core constituency of his."

Mr. Jackson's ambiguous sexuality may also appeal to teenage boys, though for different reasons. "His androgyny holds a fascination for adolescents, particularly boys," said John Munder Ross, a clinical psychologist at Cornell Medical College. "Unconsciously, it's hard to give up the possibility of being both sexes. This ambivalence is more obvious in the early teens, and goes underground around 15 or so. He embodies someone who seems to live out that ambisexual fantasy."

Also, there is the sense of Mr. Jackson living in a "fantasy land," in the view of Dr. David Guttman, professor of psychiatry at Northwestern University.

"Michael Jackson evades the choices of adult identity," Dr. Guttman said. "He embodies the fantasy of being and having everything. He seems to be both sexes, to be sensual and sexy while staying a good boy, to be black and white at the same time. He's forever young, a potent refutation of having to grow up and choose adult responsibilities. That seems to appeal to kids these days, who seem to want to put off considering an adult identity."

'Antidote to Excessive Violence'

The innocence of that perennial youthfulness may be another drawing card of the Jackson persona right now. "With all the violence kids are subject to these days, Jackson's sweet and pure appeal speaks to an inner need," Dr. Guttman said. "He's an antidote to the excessive violence of the times."

Still, Mr. Jackson's audience is a far larger group than teenagers alone. What might be the more general psychological attractiveness? In the view of James Hillman, an eminent Jungian analyst, the appeal of Michael Jackson is in large part as someone who represents the "Puer," a psychological archetype representing an ageless innocence and probably best-known in our culture in the form of Peter Pan.

"It's as though someone like Jackson is an incarnation of some much-desired psychological, mythic element. The stars often embody some crucial psychological characteristic. Elvis Presley, for example, was a Dionysus figure, the seductive man who came to town and stole all the girls. They carry the repressed side of life, the part people are aching for in their own lives."

Mr. Jackson himself once said, "I totally identify with Peter Pan, the lost boy of never-never-land," and in many ways, he bears an uncanny resemblance to descriptions of the Puer. According to Dr. Hillman's description, for example, the Puer is "inspired, effeminate, inventive, passive, fiery and capricious." The Puer also has an "angelic hermaphroditic quality where masculine and feminine are perfectly joined."

The Puer archetype, Dr. Hillman said may have a special appeal to the collective minds of America at this moment in history.

"As much as we are pressed by the harsh and tough economic realities, the world of the bottom line and success and failure, we yearn for the time when life was free of all those pressures. Michael Jackson embodies that innocent boy whose life is unfettered, full of style and beauty without the grit of reality."

I. VOCABULARY

recluse   mannequins   perennial
inarticulate   persona   archetype

II. QUESTIONS ON CONTENT

1. What are your reactions to the persona of Michael Jackson inasmuch as we can ascertain it through the press? Do you accept the account given in paragraphs 4 and 5 on page 346?
2. What seven qualities do the psychologists cite as the key to Jackson's appeal? Do you agree with their views?
3. Does Dr. Guttman's theory about Jackson embodying "the fantasy of being and having everything" seem plausible to you? Is this part of his appeal for you? Is there any other artist about whom that could be said?
4. How is Michael Jackson a hero for today? Explain how his persona conflicts with much of what Barbara Goldsmith and Louis Menand have written.

III. QUESTIONS ON FORM

1. What is the aim of this article? Does it come to any conclusions?
2. Does Goleman himself make any evaluative observations on Jackson?

IV. SUGGESTIONS FOR WRITING

1. Write a descriptive essay on Michael Jackson's unique style as a performer.
2. What happens when Peter Pan grows up? Write an imaginative account of what might occur when Michael Jackson gets older and/or matures.

Richard Corliss has been the editor of *Film Comment* since 1970. The author of several books on film, he has also written extensively on film for many magazines. Currently he is a film and theater critic for *Time*.

The Medium is the Maximum

Richard Corliss

Neil Armstrong hippety-hops in slomo across the surface of the moon to a flag bearing the legend: "MTV Music Television." This non-stop rock video system has the goods—the new right stuff. The television of today from the world of the future for kids who were maybe just born on July 20, 1969. MTV occupies a lunar landscape of strobo-scopic images: an albino-blond

Reprinted by permission of The Film Society of Lincoln Center. Copyright ©1983 by the Film Society of Lincoln Center.

man paints his body red; a silver bullet whizzes through a playing card; young women with lawnmower hairdos and punk-elegant cheekbones prowl toward the screen, rotorized by sexual taunt. Do you, poor anachronistic early-middle-ager, want to live in this world? Doesn't matter, it's here. MTV is a time capsule containing the evidence that, in 1969, everyone went to the moon.

The most pervasive and disturbing aspect of MTV's audio-video mix is that it doesn't quit. Anyone who grew up in the Fifties or Sixties, ear soldered to AM radio, got used to the systole-diastole of Top 40 programming. Fast song, slow song, raver, ballad, uptempo, down mood, the Isley Brothers, the Five Satins. It was like breathing, like life: musical melodrama followed by doo-wop romance. Old movie directors, even the shock masters, worked on the same premise; they knew that a climax had to come from somewhere, from the measured intake of narrative breath. MTV has a different life, a different rhythm. Each MTVideo says: I got three, four minutes, and in that time my sights and sounds are gonna blitz your brain. The next video says the same thing, and the next and the next. MTV doesn't exhale, doesn't allow for relaxation. It's like a 24-hour dance marathon where no one's allowed to drop out.

What MTV does is to mirror and echo the currents of pop culture in the past decade. Movies, especially those made by the British TV-commercials graduates who seem the exemplars of MTVideos, have become image assaults featuring outré folks whose deathly fear is of stasis. When modern art and photography deserted academe to enter the pages of fashion magazines, they easily assumed the glamour of decadence on a fast-moving treadmill. TV commercials, of course, have been compressing conflict and resolution into 30-second spots since the Sixties; and soon after that, educational and entertainment programs were extending those wham-bam commercial effects to 60 minutes *(Laugh-In, Sesame Street)*. Is it causal, or only coincidental, that soon after Broadway shows started advertising on TV in 1975 they turned into machines of perpetual energy, light shows of Manhattan aggression for the tourist trade? *Pippin, A Chorus Line, Dancin', Dreamgirls, Cats* haven't been made into movies; it would be redundant. They have coopted the relentless vigor of the film-art-photography-TV-commercial medium.

So MTV continues the trend. It is all about the death of context; it is the shotgun annulment of character from narrative, the anaesthetizing of violence through chic, the erasing of the past and the triumph of the new. It is also (apocalyptic masticating to the side for one moment) a school for tomorrow's film-making hot shots. Can we take solace from this? Perhaps. Whatever the sins of MTVideacs, they are sins of commission, not hackwork lethargy. And the form can be seen as an adolescent rumble, a chance to purge the spirit of excess before the advent of artistic maturity and its dominatrix of choice, restraint, discipline, the knowledge of when to say no to oneself.

Rock video is but a few years old, an infant art form. Even so sophisticated a "video" as Golden Earring's *Twilight Zone* (*not* the movie) is the MTV equivalent of D. W. Griffith's early one-reelers. Is a rock *Intolerance* in MTV's future? Or just *The Struggle?* Will the medium age decently, or die of rock-star exhaustion? The kids who live with MTV may not care. Why reach for the stars, one can hear them saying, when we already walk on the moon?

I. VOCABULARY

lethargy	slomo	rotorized
dominatrix	stroboscopic	anachronistic
outre	stasis	

II. QUESTIONS ON CONTENT

1. Do you watch MTV or videos often? Is Corliss' description of them accurate?
2. What does Corliss mean by the "systole-diastole of Top 40 programming"? Is this still true of AM or FM?
3. What in your view is an "early-middle-ager"?
4. When Corliss refers to the "film-art-photography-TV-commercial medium" he is implicitly making a point about the arts today. What other essay in this chapter refers to this point?
5. The fourth paragraph on page 349 is central to Corliss' analysis. Discuss videos with reference to
    a. death of context
    b. shotgun annulment of character from narrative
    c. anaesthetizing of violence through chic
    d. the erasing of the past and the triumph of the new

III. QUESTIONS ON FORM

1. What is the author's tone? For what audience is he writing?
2. Comment on the descriptive phrases Corliss employs in his introduction.
3. Why does Corliss write in a truncated style, as in paragraph four on page 349 where he synthesizes major ideas into phrases?
4. Are these phrases self-explanatory or does the article need more development?
5. Why is the phrase (apocalyptic masticating to the side for one moment) in parentheses?
6. Explain the metaphor of going to and walking on the moon. Why does it begin and end the essay?

IV. SUGGESTIONS FOR WRITING

Choose a video that you know well and,
1. Write an evocative description of it.
2. Write an analysis of it, using the points raised in the fourth paragraph, page 349. (See question five on content.)

TOPICS FOR INVESTIGATION

1. Investigate the paradox of the great popularity of country music when its companion genre, the Western, is all but extinct on television and in films.

2. Investigate the legend and concept of the Ur-Song. What scholarly support can you find for its existance?

3. Compile a history of a decade through its songs.

4. Investigate music and myth. Trace the legend of Orpheus, the musician, through the centuries. Use the ideas of Menand where applicable.

5. Investigate the manifestations in music and the other arts of

   a. the Dionysian figure
   b. the Puer

10

FILM

Film is the oldest of the new media. Full length feature films (silent ones) were being shown as early as 1912. The medium expanded rapidly; talkies, color, wide screens, and stereo are some of the many technological developments that made movies the favorite entertainment in the United States until the reign of television. We may have grown up with television, but our parents and some of their parents grew up at the movies.

Hollywood is a place, true; however, it has also come into the language as a description of a state of mind and of a unique kind of glamour, patented by the early makers of the "dream machine." Creator and corruptor of our myths, the movie industry has been a seminal force in our popular culture throughout the century. It has produced great art and artists and destroyed others. The historical impact of film on our society must be examined, but it is too vast to be assessed fully here. Rather, the selections in this chapter elaborate on two central concerns: first, the development of the medium that began as inexpensive entertainment for the masses (movies still fulfill that role) into the art of film with all the complexities attendent to any art form and second, the state of that art and its reflection of our society today.

Tony Pipolo's introductory essay addresses this development from entertainment to art, as he provides a lesson in film analysis for those who have never studied it formally. Focusing on one of the essential elements of film, point of view, he uses the classic films *Psycho* and *E.T.* to educate us to some of the subtleties of the genre. Film, he demonstrates, cannot or certainly should not be watched with the mindless passivity with which much television is viewed.

Roger Ebert is also concerned with point of view in recent horror films and as he analyzes them he suggests their disturbing implications about our society. Janet Maslin, too, is disturbed—by what she *doesn't* see up on the silver screen—realistic contemporary heroes in real, identifiable conflicts. Gerald Clarke finds in the same films entirely different values. For him, the contemporary adventure films (Star Wars and others) are today's electronic version of the ancient myths of the hero being tested, tormented, and finally triumphant.

Marilyn Milloy focuses on the film industry as well as its products, as she examines racial discrimination in hiring and in the films themselves, while Vincent Canby muses on the enduring appeal of 007. Both of these authors look at what, respectively, the images of blacks in film and the continuing popularity of James Bond tell us about ourselves.

Pauline Kael in her article dismisses movies on television; however, as a film critic Kael herself appears occasionally on television, exemplifying "the critic as image maker," the subject of the final essay by Charles Champlin.

These essays indicate that film and filmmakers have grown up. It seems time for us, the audience, to do the same and become critics and students as we analyze and learn from contemporary film, one of the most intellectually and emotionally stimulating of the mass media today.

Readings

> **Tony Pipolo** is Associate Professor at Queensborough Community College where he teaches English and film. He is editor of the new film journal *Persistence of Vision* and assistant editor of *Millennium Film Journal*. His articles have appeared in the *New York Times*, the *Village Voice, Film Reader*, and other publications. He is currently at work on a book about the German director Fassbinder.

"P.O.V., *Psycho*, and E.T."
Tony Pipolo

Few people would deny that movies have an enormous impact on our culture. For many, they have replaced popular fiction and despite the advent of television they remain the most powerful visual means of telling stories, of exciting people's imaginations and affecting their emotions. Yet few people are able to recognize or evaluate the methods and techniques through which movies exert their power. Learning how movie stories are put together and how to perceive their meanings has generally been an assumed talent, but to judge from the way most people—including media critics—talk about movies, it's not a talent in endless supply. A somewhat reckless assumption abounds that anybody can be a movie critic and that one opinion is as good as another.

The same lackadaisical attitude doesn't seem to apply to the more traditional forms of narrative. For example, the usual approach to the study of literature—short stories, novels, plays, and poems—is to instruct students how to identify and appraise important elements of a work. This is not limited to clarifying the plot or the theme, but includes specific attention to the use of language, sentence structure, imagery, poetic devices, symbolism, and so on. Awareness of these features sharpens our perception of the meaning of a work and allows us to understand *how* meanings are produced. Critical judgment of the value of a certain novel or poem is arrived at with some effort and with the help of a well-learned methodology.

Only very recently has similar attention to the "elements of film" become part of the school and college curriculum. Some people still resist the formal study of film. They insist that since we have all grown up with movies, it is

Copyright ©1984 by Tony Pipolo.

either superfluous or presumptuous for someone to teach us how to watch them. But we have also grown up with the language we speak and read, yet this does not guarantee an adequate comprehension of literature, which is a specialized use of language. Such achievements—intelligent comprehension of literature or film—are not part of one's birthrights; they are learned through hard and persistent work, either in formal study or through individual efforts.

In addition, movies are very personal experiences, often bound up with strong emotional and psychological associations from our past or present. We may resent it when an expert intrudes upon this private and close encounter between the screen and our conscious or unconscious fantasies, or when we are told that we have misunderstood a film's meaning or are unduly influenced by a single factor (for example, a particular actor or actress, clever special effects, or a powerful message) that has clouded our judgment. For these reasons movies tend to divide people more sharply than novels or plays. Learning how movies generate intense feelings, how they employ specifically cinematic techniques, how they create and satisfy—or fail to satisfy—audience expectations, may or may not alter our strongest feelings, but such knowledge does make it possible to speak more intelligently about a film's merits or failings. It helps to clarify vague sentiments and inarticulate gut reactions.

Many aspects of film technique and film conventions can be learned by watching movies regularly and attentively, becoming familiar with repeated techniques, styles, and genres. After dozens of horror films about prowling maniacs, it becomes fairly easy to recognize the conventions of the genre. Consequently, when a young woman is seen alone in a house answering the telephone and we hear deep breathing on the other end of the line, we take it as a cue that some dangerous character—an escapee from an asylum, a psychotic killer, or a potential rapist—is about to threaten her life. Subsequently, every scene with a doorway, a window, a corridor, or a darkened street is likely to be infused with the fear and anticipation of this as yet unidentified menace. The repetition and variation of such conventions comprise what we call the standard ingredients of that particular genre.

Grasping the rudiments of a genre is a useful skill and one of the easier things to perceive about films because they are linked to the more literary traditions of deciphering the plot and hunting down themes. But within the familiar structures of plot and theme in any well-made film, there are formal and technical elements that usually go unnoticed and unappreciated by most filmgoers. Far from being mere frills with only a peripheral relation to the more literary aspects, these elements are crucial to a full understanding of the film's themes and the director's attitude towards his material. Whether a filmmaker uses close-ups or not; whether he moves his camera in a certain scene or chooses to shoot the scene from a static viewpoint; whether he allows actions and scenes to evolve without interruption or breaks up the continuity through editing or crosscutting; how decor is used; how scenes are lit; how the actors are employed in relation to the sets and the action—all of these things constitute the very substance of a film. To ignore the role they play in the impression the film creates and in the delineation of its meaning is similar to ignoring the meter, rhyme scheme, choice of language, and imagery in a poem. The fact that most people take such features for granted in movies or remain largely indifferent to the varied options available to a filmmaker is not an indication of the insignificance of the features, but of a lack of awareness in the general audience concerning the specific characteristics of film language.

One essay cannot hope to cover all such elements, but since we have already made certain analogies between literature and film and since most students are somewhat familiar with literary terminology, it might be useful to concentrate on a device important to both forms—the use of "point of view." In everyday speech, this term usually refers to the way people look at things. We say that people have different opinions on a given subject depending on their point of view, the vantage point from which they look at an issue. In literature, the technique has a complicated history, the most sophisticated experiments with it probably to be found in the novels of Henry James. If a novel is written in the first person, for example, this "I" can be the main character emotionally involved in the story, a mere objective bystander of the novel's action, or the novelist himself who claims to be recounting a tale someone has told him. The possibilities are many, but the "I" will always be understood to be the perspective through which the action is witnessed and/or described, the vantage point from which things are seen and/or understood. Almost any conceivable narrative situation is affected by the point of view from which the author tells the story. Imagine a novel about an insane asylum written from the point of view of the chief doctor or a sympathetic member of the staff; then imagine the same events as seen and experienced by one of the inmates, and you can readily see how extreme the difference in point of view can be. Many works of fiction are written in the third person in which the author tells us everything he or she wants us to know and freely enters the minds and thoughts of several characters. Whichever method a novelist selects, the reader is generally clued in to the point of view early and the perspective is continually reinforced by a restricted use of language that holds us within the mind of the controlling voice—a character or the novelist himself.

Point of view in a film narrative, however, is not as easily established and even less easily sustained. There are many reasons for this. First, film images—the visual components that make up a movie—are not the equivalents of words. In a limited number of cases, of course, isolated images can evoke a word; a large close-up of a gun or a knife might be said to trigger the words, "gun," or "knife." But what single word or words come to mind when the entire screen is filled with action or dozens of characters? Furthermore, no individual shot on the screen can represent or refer to or stand in for the pronouns, "I," or "we," or "you." It is true that the term "film language" is often used—as I have used it above—to draw attention to the different mode of communication that films employ, but here the word, "language," is meant figuratively, not literally. The sequence of images on a movie screen is not reducible to the grammar and syntax of written language. Likewise, "point of view" in a movie cannot be equated with its linguistic counterpart. We must look to the specific means that *films* employ to create the sense that a certain point of view is controlling a scene, determining an impression, or governing an entire story.

Of course, many films have attempted to duplicate the linguistic form of point of view by having a story narrated by a character on the sound track *over* the images. This method was commonly practiced in Hollywood films throughout the 1930s and 1940s, but rarely did the screenwriter or the director bother to make sure that what the character was saying on the sound track did not contradict what the audience saw on the screen and what it knew the character could not know. All too often the viewer would see things that the character was in no position to know, or could not have known until much later, and this would weaken the credibility of the narrative structure.

In order to avoid such inaccuracies, some filmmakers resorted to an extreme solution, whereby everything the camera recorded was directly seen by the point-of-view character. This meant that the camera *was* the character and that the flesh and blood actor behind it was virtually nonexistent. Such an experiment was employed in the first part of a Humphrey Bogart movie called *Dark Passage* (1947), in which the character is an escaped convict who undergoes plastic surgery to conceal his identity. Up to the operation, we never see the character—only what *he* sees—but we do hear the familiar Bogart voice. Immediately following the operation, the technique is abandoned and we see the convict's "new" face—Bogart himself. In a detective movie called *Lady in the Lake* (1946), the detective is never seen except via occasional glimpses in mirror reflections so that whenever he questions suspects, they address the camera as if speaking directly to the audience. In other words every move and pan of the camera across a room or from person to person is a direct translation of the detective's activity and attention. The camera's "probes" into the surroundings are *his* probes into the case.

This method, however, is in a special category and has rarely been used with any degree of success. On paper, it may sound like a clever idea, but on the screen it creates an awkwardness difficult to ignore. We might ask, then, how, short of going to such an extreme, can a filmmaker establish and sustain the point of view of a character? Clearly he must do it through the technical means available to him—editing, camera angles, framing devices, and camera movements—but he must carefully construct and organize these techniques so as to reinforce the impression that we are seeing something *as*—or in the manner that—a particular character sees and experiences it. This must be accomplished without sacrificing the presence of the character on the screen and without having to resort to the mixed blessings of voice-over narration. Experience and hundreds of experiments have proven that the most effective way of making a point of view emphatic at any one point is to vary it with alternative points of view in a continual play of perspectives. In what follows, we shall consider a few ways in which a point of view is made manifest by a variety of methods. They range from the simple restricted use of editing to more subtle and pervasive uses of framing, lighting and camera angles.

To some degree, every narrative film depends on point of view in the restricted sense. So basic is it to the comprehension of the action and the connections between shots that we take it for granted. Yet failure to set it up clearly will confuse an audience immeasureably. This restricted sense involves the simple exchange of shots that make it clear that someone's glance in one shot is directed at and/or matches the glance of someone else in a preceding or succeeding shot. This principle makes it possible to follow the action from moment to moment and to perceive the relations between characters and their environment. The breakdown of this simplest type forms an A-B-A' model:

> Shot A: Character x looks towards the left to someone (or something) off screen.
> Shot B: Character y (or object y) is seen at an appropriate angle and in an appropriate position vis-à-vis shot A to indicate unambiguously that he, she (or it) is the object of character x's glance.
> Shot A': Return to character x and a similar look, reinforcing the implications of shots A and B and completing the entire exchange.

We say of shot B—the middle term of this model—that it represents the point of view of character x; and conversely, if the glance is returned by a character, the shots A and A' represent the point of view of character y.

Generally, this is the most easily recognizable form of point of view in films. Yet as simple as it is, the A-B-A' exchange, in the hands of sophisticated filmmakers, can have complex thematic implications. Alfred Hitchcock, for example, used the point-of-view structure in highly intricate ways to engage the spectator in the experience of his most disturbed characters. In doing so, he forces the spectator into the uncomfortable position of these characters themselves by demonstrating that the so-called normal person can share the same obsessions and drives as the so-called abnormal person. In *Psycho* (1960), the viewer peeps at Marion Crane (Janet Leigh) preparing to take her ill-fated shower primarily through the point of view of Norman Bates (Anthony Perkins) who is in the dark spying through a hole in the wall. Shot A shows us a large close-up of Perkins in profile as he looks off screen; shot B shows us the girl undressing, but the image is encircled by darkness to indicate the shape of the peephole through which it is being seen; shot A' shows us Perkins again. In setting up the shot in this way, Hitchcock is not merely establishing the information that Norman is spying on the girl. The large profile close-up of Norman's eye stresses the concealment of the look and the fact that for Norman this is a forbidden sight, one he dare not admit to his "mother" (that is, his repressive conscience). In other words, as viewers, we do not merely look on at what Norman sees, we see it *as* he sees it: a secret, voyeuristic act that—for Norman—must be punished. But of course, Hitchcock counts on the fact that most people are guilty of voyeurism at some time or other and that, in fact, in looking at the same sight that Norman looks at and perhaps enjoying it without the consequences that Norman must face, we *share* his voyeuristic experience. In fact, as spectators in the movie theater, *we* are peeping at forbidden sights and are also concealed in the dark. By thus complicating the relationship between Norman's experience and the spectator's, Hitchcock makes it more difficult for the spectator to quickly condemn Norman's behavior. As it turns out, in fact, after the girl is killed, Norman becomes the main protagonist whose plight the audience follows. It should be obvious that the role played by this simple exchange of point-of-view shots in establishing Norman's psychosis is significant.

This use of point of view is commonly found in narrative films simply because it is such a basic way of establishing and reinforcing the connections between characters on the one hand and action or setting on the other. And, of course, if a film repeatedly ties a particular character to the environment in such specific ways, we can conclude that a large part of the film's story (if not all) is grounded in that character's viewpoint. In *Psycho*, the first half of the movie is primarily seen through Marion Crane's point of view. We see her boss, her co-worker, her lover, policemen, other people, and Norman Bates as she does, so that the guilt, anxiety, and tension Marion goes through after stealing the money from her boss's office is continually underlined by the specific ways the camera frames and lights the views she has of others and, of course, by how the editing cuts from her frightened, nervous looks to the objects of her fear. It is this close identification between the character and her surroundings on all levels of the film's design that creates such a feeling of intimacy. The spectator shares Marion's dilemma and easily recognizes and even identifies (figuratively speaking) with her shifting emotions. It is precisely for this reason that Marion's murder is so shocking. We are startled that the character we have been following so closely and whose fate becomes our prime concern is killed off in the middle of the film—and at just the moment she has decided to return the money she has stolen and mend her life.

Viewers who attribute the shock effect in the film to the actual murder scene in the shower miss the point. In its time (1960), the film startled audiences because its star Janet Leigh was killed off halfway through the film and the viewer was subsequently forced to identify with the only other important character—her psychotic killer! Today, however, people are still moved and disturbed by the film, even though they may have seen it a number of times and are well prepared for the murder, and even though they are indifferent to the forgotten star status of Janet Leigh. Why? I suggest it is because the real shock is the way Hitchcock has so cleverly drawn us into the psyche and emotions of the girl—through the manipulation of point of view—only to pull the rug out from under us, to leave us floundering without the original protagonist to anchor the plot. That he succeeded triumphantly in breaking one of the hardfast rules of genre and then in making us just as concerned and nervous all over again about the killer's fears and emotions—again through the brilliant manipulation of point of view—is a tribute to his cinematic genius.

Let us look at a more recent use—and variation—of point of view that I hope will illustrate that the role played by this important formal device is hardly limited to isolated examples of the A-B-A' type. To indicate how it serves—almost subliminally—to advance the emotional and psychological impact of a popular film, let us use Steven Spielberg's *E. T.* (1981). In this film, as in almost all films, there are plenty of obvious examples of the restrictive A-B-A' model, and perhaps other uses of point of view not immediately apparent. But apart from these, the film reveals an even more pervasive sense of a point of view—a particular perspective and *way of seeing* that governs the mood, the atmosphere, the material content—in short, the world as depicted in the film.

E. T., as everyone must know by now, is a contemporary fairy tale set in suburban California. As a matter of fact, because of the meticulous way in which it establishes the milieu of suburban living and details the manners and speech of hipster kids, it could just as easily have been a straightforward realistic depiction of children in suburbia and nothing about its sets, its acting styles, its dialogue, and its technical aspects (with obvious exceptions, of course) would have needed alteration. Yet within this relatively authentic picture of present-day, middle-class life in sunny California, a perfectly incredible event takes place and the audience is asked to believe that it occurs within an otherwise quite unfairytale-like atmosphere. Although the film borrows from other works of fantasy, it does not attempt to isolate the fantastic event in a separable realm. It is not *The Wizard of Oz* (1939), for example, in which Dorothy's adventures (in the movie as opposed to the novel) are finally encapsulated in a dream. Nor does it, like *Peter Pan*, make an explicit invitation to the world of make-believe. Spielberg's *E. T.* succeeds mostly because it manages to assimilate its fanciful elements without having to reduce them to dream status and without compromising its setting in everyday contemporary reality.

Judging from the universal enthusiastic response to the film, this seemingly paradoxical yoking together of the everyday and the incredible has not posed a problem for general audiences. But this doesn't mean that Spielberg hit upon a lucky formula purely by accident. Close inspection of the film reveals a carefully calculated strategy at work through which Spielberg introduces the fairy tale into the real environment and then sustains its compelling force by a variety of means. Quite cleverly, for more than half the film, he grounds the central experience of the plot exclusively in the imagination and viewpoint of children. Initially through the character of Elliott, and extending to the other children-characters, a sense of wonder and wide-eyed belief becomes the dominant behavior pattern in the film that can legitimately be described as tracing a childlike view of the world. This basic perspective is reinforced on both the narrative and technical levels. On the narrative level, the childlike view dominates simply because of the virtual absence in the first two-thirds of the movie of any full-fledged adult character. The one exception is Elliott's mother, whose authority as an adult is weakened by her vulnerability and insecurity brought on by the apparent dissolution of her marriage. On top of this, she has more than enough to handle with three youngsters—Elliott, his older brother Michael, and their younger sister Gertie. Their father is away, allegedly on a business trip and accompanied by another woman. Thus, the screenplay eliminates the character whose presence and interaction with the mother would certainly have offset the overall atmosphere established in the household, in which the children largely fend for themselves and dominate the scene. But even apart from the household, no male-adult character figures prominently in the narrative at all until very late in the film when the scientist shows up with his entourage of technicians. By virtue of his very absence, therefore, the adult male exerts an important affect that can hardly be considered coincidental.

Spielberg further stresses the significance of this fact by deliberately avoiding any full views of the few men who do appear. They are either seen only from the waist down (like the men searching for E.T. in the opening scene, or Elliott's biology teacher), or are completely enshrouded in shadows (the men in the early scenes, and later the scientists monitoring Elliott's house), or they are seen only from the back (Elliott's teacher and the man who delivers pizza). In all instances, the men are faceless and are evoked through their disembodied voices (heard off screen or through some mechanical contraption), or through the apparatuses connected with their professions (keys, flashlights, monitoring and surveillance devices, steel helmets, trucks, and laboratory equipment). In other words, they do not enter the narrative as full-blooded characters or even as people, but through the symbols of their power and authority in the adult world: carriers of keys, probers of other people's lives, executors of the law, and so on.

In the final section of the film, this pattern is modified, especially in regard to the scientist whose disembodied existence had previously been symbolized only by the keys he carried, but who emerges as a sympathetic friend who actually shares Elliott's enthusiasm when he claims that he has waited all his life for something like this to happen (that is, for evidence of life in outer space). Nevertheless, though modified, the pattern is not entirely abandoned since the children's world must actively assert itself against the male adult world in order to rescue E.T. from life as a specimen and send him back to his home in outer space.

Up until the entry of the scientist, the film is controlled by the children's viewpoint. The very ways in which Elliott, Gertie, and Michael act, react, and interact with E.T. underline this. There are countless images devoted to the reactions of the children to E.T. and E.T. to them. Most of these emphasize awe mixed with confusion and a little fear. E.T. can easily camouflage himself in a closet because his huge eyes resemble those of larger-than-life dolls and stuffed animals; but the amazement that the children experience is equally evoked through the size and luminousness—as well, of course, as a certain innocence—of their eyes. This emphasis on eyes and the multiple exchanges of looks between E.T. and Elliott, E.T. and Michael, and E.T. and Gertie, are appropriate manifestations of the dominant viewpoint in the film—that of the child—as well as of the attitude that logically follows from this—that of wonder and belief. In the child's eyes (and mind, of course), anything is possible, as long as one remains outside of the adult authoritarian world that is understood to be closed and fixed. It is only partly in jest that Elliott tells his sister, in order to keep her from divulging E.T.'s presence: "grownups can't see him . . . only little kids can see him." But it is precisely the child's determination to remain outside the adult world as long as possible that appears to govern the manner in which Spielberg has photographed the film.

In scene after scene, he literally holds the camera at a level to conform to or directly parallel the height of his child characters. There are no looming shots above them to suggest their smallness or vulnerability, nor any low-angle shots from their point of view to frame adults as powerful creatures. The camera chooses instead to remain and move within the horizontal range dictated by the eye level of the children. As if to immediately set the pattern for this camera position, the opening sequence is shot not from the point of view of the men as they pursue the alien ship and search through the wooded area, but from the point of view of the as yet unknown creature, E.T., whose height is that of a small child. As the men with flashlights and keys run about, we barely discern their shadowy shapes and never get a clear shot at the level of their faces. We view them from the perspective of the small pursued and frightened creature. In this way, Spielberg seems to deliberately declare a severance between the adult human world dominated by male authority and institutions, and a world that stands apart from—and physically speaking *below*—the former, a world occupied by strange or imagined beings and children. In so doing, Spielberg cleverly reverses, right from the start, a convention of most sci-fi movies by turning the humans into the aliens and identifying the alien with the child. This identification is later literalized in the narrative when Elliott's behavior and thought patterns are synchronized with E.T.'s and he suffers and almost dies as a result.

So powerfully effective is the rendering of the adult world as an alien one—through the devices already noted and Spielberg's child's-eye-level camera—that when the time comes for that world to fully enter the film via the scientist and technicians, its entrance is presented as the *real* alien invasion. We see a line of helmeted men marching forward like so many wound-up automatons. And when Elliott's hysterical mother opens the door, our first full frontal shot of a man is of one of these terrifying robot-like creatures. Underneath the helmet, of course, is the kind scientist, but the initial impression has done its work: the real threat to the world of the children does not come from outer space, but from the hostile world of adult authority. That the audience does indeed initially experience this arrival as a threat—when it is actually nothing more than the arrival of the very characters who used to be known in earlier science fiction films as the "good guys"—is an indication of how successfully Spielberg has insulated the children's environment and adventure from any outside force. He effectively sustains the point of view of the children and E.T. with a camera that refuses to budge above or beyond the physical range of these characters. And he does this right up to the shot of the men's arrival—seen as a distorted vision through telephoto lenses that render them inhuman and terrifying beings.

Here, then, we have almost an entire film, certainly the larger part of it, controlled by a pervasive sense of a definite perspective: not that of one individual character who tells the story, but that of a shared viewpoint. Point of view here is not limited to the A-B-A' model or to the shot/reaction shot exchange.It is the choice of camera angle (child's eye level), the choice of framing (deliberately excluding full shots of adult males), and the choice of lighting (shadows that conceal the humanizing features of male authoritarian figures) that collectively delimit the range and scope of the world as viewed by children. And since this range is initiated in the film not by one of the children but by an alien creature who befriends them, one is tempted to conclude that E.T. is not the only extraterrestrial in the film. He finds his compatriots in the children—especially Elliott—who embrace him as one of their own, who recognize in his completely alien form the same wide-eyed wonder and amazement with which they confront the world all too briefly.

Naturally the particular interpretations I have given *E.T.* and *Psycho* may not concur with someone else's. But it was not the aim of this essay to demonstrate the inviolability of a particular interpretation. The point that needs emphasis is that to do critical justice to a movie and appraise its achievement—or denounce its failure—one must come to terms with *all* of its facets, particularly those that are unique to the medium's expressibility but that are largely overlooked. A film that advertises itself as having a profound or relevant theme is by no means automatically a good movie or an important one. Many movies once the most talked about of their time are completely forgettable now because their message was their *only* value; they failed to integrate that message into the fabric and texture of the medium's properties. *E.T.* is not an effective movie because its theme is on a par with *Oedipus Rex* or *Hamlet*. It works because it manages to transcribe some fundamental tenets of fairy tales and childhood imagination into the dynamics of film. This, finally, is what must be observed and studied more closely. Spectators react spontaneously to the flashy techniques found in *Star Wars* or *Raiders of the Lost Ark,* but in themselves these dazzling special effects do not constitute good filmmaking either. What we need is a more literate film audience—one that learns to read a film's text and style as one does a novel or a poem—not for its overt content alone but for its special blend of language, images, sound, and sense.

I. VOCABULARY

methodology	genre	rudiments
peripheral	linguistic	entourage
meticulous	milieu	luminousness

II. QUESTIONS ON CONTENT

1. What is the thesis of Pipolo's introduction?
2. How aware were you before reading this essay of the "essential elements" of film?
3. What is "point of view"? Discuss point of view in literature.
4. Why is point of view more difficult to express in film than in literature?
5. What is one extreme solution for expressing point of view in film?
6. What is the most effective way of emphasizing point of view at any one point in a movie?
7. Explain the restricted sense of point of view in film editing.
8. Why does the author use the example from *Psycho* to explain point of view? Had you ever thought of yourself, as Pipolo suggests, as a voyeur, concealed in the dark?
9. According to Pipolo, Hitchcock, because of his "cinematic genius," is able to do what in *Psycho*?
10. What does the author mean by "a way of seeing"?

11. How, according to Pipolo, does Spielberg succeed with setting and fantasy in *E.T.*?
12. Can you recall other films (or books) where "a childlike view of the world" is operative?
13. What does the author say about the depiction of the parents in *E.T.*?
14. What are his comments on the other adults in the film?
15. What is the camera level in the film and how is the audience affected by it?
16. What convention does the use of an unusual camera level reverse?
17. The conclusion reemphasizes what point?

III. QUESTIONS ON FORM

1. In what paragraph does the thesis of Pipolo's introduction appear?
2. Outline the comparison/contrast of film and literature as presented in the first six paragraphs of the essay.
3. Why does this topic, point of view, receive an introduction of this length?
4. Why does the discussion of *Psycho* precede that of *E.T.*?
5. Are content and example mode separable in this essay?

IV. SUGGESTIONS FOR WRITING

1. Analyze point of view in a recent film you have seen.
2. Write a persuasive essay on filmgoing as a cultural experience comparable to reading a novel.
3. Compare and contrast point of view in *E.T.* with other children's movies.

Roger Ebert is film critic for *Chicago Sun-Times* and cohost of "At The Movies," a weekly syndicated television show that reviews current films. He is the recipient of a Pulitzer Prize (1975) and an Emmy Award (1979).

Why the Movie Audiences Aren't Safe Any More

Roger Ebert

In more than a dozen years of professional attendance at the movies, I've never had an experience more disturbing than one I had last summer, in the United Artists Theater in Chicago, during a showing of a movie named *I Spit*

Roger Ebert, "Why Movie Audiences Aren't Safe Any More," *American Film*, March 1981. Reprinted by permission of the author.

on Your Grave. The theater was pretty well filled for a weekday afternoon, but I found a seat in a row toward the back. One empty chair separated me from a white-haired middle-aged man who was, as it turned out, to be my guide through the horrors of this movie.

The film itself was garbage—reprehensible, vile. Its skeleton of a plot existed only as an excuse for a series of violent scenes in which a woman was first ravaged by a pack of four demented men, and then took her vengeance against them. The film's one small concession to artistry was the creation of one male character who was not *merely* a raping and slicing machine, but was given individual attributes: He was portrayed as gravely mentally retarded. To my horror, I realized that he was the comic relief. After scenes in which the movie's heroine was raped or menaced by the other characters, they'd urge on this guy. And he'd slobber and dim-wittedly, impotently try to rape her, too, while the audience laughed.

Watching this film was a terrible experience. As a daily newspaper movie critic who goes to see nearly every movie that opens commercially, I thought I'd seen almost everything in the way of screen violence, but I had not.

What made *I Spit on Your Grave* particularly effective (if that is the word) was its brutal directness of style. Lacking grace, humor, or even simple narrative skill, the filmmakers simply pointed their camera at their actors and then commanded them to perform unspeakable acts upon one another. Although the violence in the film was undoubtedly staged, the directness of this approach took away any distancing effect that might have been supplied by more sophisticated storytelling; the film had the raw impact of those pornographic films which are essentially just documentary records of behavior.

And that, I quickly gathered, was exactly how the white-haired man to my right was taking it. The film marched relentlessly ahead. We saw the woman repeatedly cut up, raped, and beaten. The man next to me kept up a running commentary during these events. His voice was not a distraction, because the level of audience noise was generally high; the audience seemed to be taking all this as a comedy, and there were shouts and loud laughs at the climaxes of violence. And then, beneath these noises, as a subtle counterpoint, I could hear my neighbor saying, "That's a good one . . . ooh-eee! She's got that coming! This'll teach her. That's right! Give it to her! She's learned her lesson. . . ."

And so on. I glanced at this man. He looked totally respectable. He could have been a bank clerk, a hardware salesman; he could have been anyone. He was instinctively, unquestioningly voicing his support for the rape and violence on the screen.

Elsewhere around me in the theater, the vocal responses continued. During the opening scenes of rape, the voices shouting at the screen had been mostly men's. But then, as the movie's heroine began to kill the rapists, a chorus of women's voices joined in. "You show him, sister," a female voice yelled from the back row. "Wooo!"

How does one respond to an experience like the one I had during *I Spit on Your Grave?* As a film critic, I was fortunate, of course: I had a forum in my newspaper to attack the film to deplore its reception. But as a filmgoer sitting there in the dark, that seemed small consolation to me. I wanted to shout back at my fellow audience members—or, more to the point, I wanted to turn to the man next to me and tell him he was disgusting.

I did not. I left. A few days later, talking about *I Spit on Your Grave* with fellow Chicago film critic Gene Siskel, I found that he had been as disturbed by the film as I had. He also sensed that the film was clearly a departure from the ordinary run of summer exploitation and horror movies we critics have come to expect. It was cruder, it was more raw, it was more vile of spirit. And the audience response to it had been truly frightening.

I saw *I Spit on Your Grave* that first time with an audience that was mostly black (although my quiet neighbor was white). I saw it again, a week later, with an almost all white audience in the Adelphi Theater on Chicago's North Side. The response was about the same. But in contrast to the mostly male downtown audience, the Adelphi's crowd on that Friday night included a great many couples on dates; perhaps forty percent of the audience was female. They sat through it—willingly, I suppose.

By now the word was out about *I Spit on Your Grave.* My review in the *Sun-Times* and Siskel's in the *Tribune* had already appeared. And for a piece on the local CBS news, Siskel had stood in front of the United Artists Theatre with a television camera crew and described the movie to customers about to go in. One couple with their small children listened to his description and then said they were going in anyway. "I'd like to know more on the subject," the woman said, an eight-year-old clutching her hand.

Were later audiences influenced by the strongly negative local reviews? Hardly. The Plitt theater chain pulled the movie from the United Artists Theatre on orders from the chain's executive vice-president, Harold J. Klein, who admitted he had not seen it before it opened. But in the theaters where it still played, the movie had a good second weekend—although, curiously, the print I saw at the Adelphi had been extensively cut.

During the month after I saw the film, I became aware that *I Spit on Your Grave* might have been the worst of the summer's exploitation films, but it was hardly alone in its sick attitude toward women. Searching back through my movie memory, and looking at some of the summer's and autumn's new films with a slightly different point of view, I began to realize that a basic change had taken place in many recent releases.

Although the theme of a woman in danger had long been a staple in movies and on television (where television films like John Carpenter's *Someone Is Watching Me!* have racked up big ratings), the audience's sympathies had traditionally been enlisted on the side of the woman. We identified with her, we feared for her, and when she was hurt, we recoiled. But was that basic identification still true? I realized with a shock that it was not, not always, and that with increasing frequency the new horror films encouraged audience identification not with the victim but with the killer.

Siskel had arrived at a similar conclusion, and we decided to devote one of our "Sneak Previews" programs on PBS to the women-in-danger films. On the program we showed scenes from several films (although not the most violent), and we pointed out, in scenes from films like *Friday the 13th*, that the camera took the killer's point of view and stalked the victims. It is a truism in film strategy that, all else being equal, when the camera takes a point of view, the audience is being directed to adopt the same point of view.

We also pointed out that the crime of many of the female victims in the women-in danger films was their independence. The heroine of *I Spit on Your Grave* had gone off for a vacation by herself in the woods. The heroine of *Friday the 13th* was hitchhiking to a summer job as a camp counselor.

"I'm convinced," Siskel said, "that this has something to do with the growth of the women's movement in America in the last decade. These films are some sort of primordial response by very sick people saying, 'Get back in your place, women!' The women in these films are typically portrayed as independent, as sexual, as enjoying life. And the killer, typically—not all the time but most often—is a man who is sexually frustrated with these new aggressive women, and so he strikes back at them. He throws knives at them. He can't deal with them. He cuts them up, he kills them."

All quite true. The more I thought about the women-in-danger films, the more I was disturbed by the way they were short-cutting the usual approach of horror films, even horror films that were frankly exploitative. There was something *different* about these films, something more than could be explained by the degree of violence on the screen, or even by the cynical manipulation of the antifemale theme.

I was bothered by the difference, whatever it was, because I'm not an advocate of censorship, and I have to admit, in perfect honesty, that quite often I *enjoy* horror films—that I am not automatically turned off, let's say, just because a film is about a berserk raving homicidal madman. I admired John Carpenter's *Halloween*, for example, and also Brian De Palma's *Dressed to Kill*, a film that inspired feminist picket lines in many cities. There was artistry in those films, and an inventive directorial point of view. The bottom line is that I believe that *any* subject matter is permissible in the movies, and can be redeemed, if that's the word, by the artistry of the film's treatment of it.

So what bothered me so much about *I Spit on Your Grave*—that it was lacking in artistry? Would the film have been acceptable if it had been better made, no matter how loathsome its subject matter? Well, perhaps; perhaps not. Floundering between my disgust on the one hand and my anticensorship, civil libertarian attitude on the other, I suddenly realized that what was really bothering me about the worst of the women-in-danger films didn't hinge on taste, style, or sexist political content. It was a simple matter of construction. These films were not about their villains. They were about the *acts* of the villains. Dismayed, I realized that the visual strategy of these films displaced the villain from his traditional place within the film—and moved him into the audience.

It is a displacement so basic and yet so subtle that perhaps some of the filmmakers do not yet know their own secret. It explains why so many previous horror films, even those as apparently disgusting as *The Texas Chain Saw Massacre,* somehow redeem themselves, become palatable to large audiences (if not, of course, to the squeamish). Those films are *about* heinous villains and contain them as characters. They are studies of human behavior, no matter how disgusting, and the role of the audience is to witness a depraved character at work within his depravities.

Carpenter's *Halloween* seems to give us a faceless villain—a relentlessly oncoming figure, usually masked, who has superhuman powers to kill, maim, and survive attack. But this killer has been clearly established in the film as a character. We see a traumatic childhood experience that warps him. We learn through his psychiatrist that the unfortunate child has grown up to become the embodiment of evil. As he develops in the film, he takes on a very specific reality, and it's up there on the screen. In the audience, we watch. We are voyeurs. We are not implicated.

The women-in-danger films are, for the most part, not about a specific character at all. They are either about a nameless, dreaded, nonspecific killer on the loose *(He Knows You're Alone, Prom Night)* or about characters so banal that they lack all humanity and are simple stick figures *(I Spit on Your Grave).* These noncharacters are then placed in films where the camera frankly takes the point of view not of the victim but of the killer.

The lust to kill and rape becomes the true subject of the movies. And the lust is not placed on the screen, where it can be attached to the killer-character; it is placed in the audience. The missing character in so many of these films can be found in the audience; we are all invited to be him, and some (such as my white-haired neighbor) gladly accept the role.

While it is true that such movies as *Prom Night* and *Terror Train* supply a rudimentary explanation for the behavior of the killer, that is really just a perfunctory plot twitch. The difference between Carpenter's skill and the ineptness of the makers of *Prom Night* is that the latter movie rips off the device of a childhood trauma but has no idea how to use it to establish identification with the adult who bears it. For most of the movie, innocent people are stalked and killed by a faceless, usually unseen, unknown killer, and the film's point of view places that killer's center of consciousness in the audience.

The same device is used in *Terror Train.* A traumatic experience during a fraternity initiation ceremony causes a character to become so emotionally twisted that he conducts a reign of terror on board a train rented by the fraternity. Although *Prom Night* and *Terror Train* seem to copy the structure of *Halloween* by providing their killers with childhood traumas and then sending them on inexorable killing sprees, there is a crucial difference between Carpenter and his imitators. Carpenter's killer in *Halloween* is clearly seen on the screen, is given an identity, an appearance, and a consistent pattern of behavior.

In *Prom Night* and *Terror Train,* however, the killer is never clearly seen nor understood once the killings begin; a typical shot is from the killer's point of view, showing the victim's face in horror as a knife reaches out. The more these movies make their killers into shadowy non-characters, the more the very acts of killing become the protagonist, and the more the audience is directed to stand in the shoes of the killer.

This is all very creepy. Horror movies, even the really bloody ones, used to be fair game for everyone—diversions for everybody. Pop psychologists could speculate that they were a way for us to exorcise our demons. Terrible things were happening all right—but to the victims who were safely up there on the screen. Now that's not the case in some of these new women-in-danger films. Now the terrible things are happening to women, and the movie point of view is of a nonspecific male killing force. These movies may still be exorcising demons, but the identity of the demons has changed. Now the "victim" is the poor, put-upon, traumatized male in the audience. And the demons are the women on the screen.

I. VOCABULARY

reprehensible   voyeurs   vile

II. QUESTIONS ON CONTENT

1. Do you attend horror films often? Why?
2. Have you ever had an experience like Ebert's? What was your reaction?
3. Did you see the film "Halloween"? Did you enjoy it?
4. Have you been conscious of an antiwomen bias in horror films?
5. What does Ebert say is always true of the camera and point-of-view?
6. What subtle change has Ebert noted in recent horror films?
7. Why is that change so disturbing?
8. Can you recall a film you've seen where this perspective was employed?
9. Do you endorse any form of film censorship? What do you think of the current rating system?
10. Do you watch Ebert and Siskel in "At the Movies"?

III. QUESTIONS ON FORM

1. How much of Ebert's article is concerned with his filmgoing experience? Why?
2. Following the anecdote, how much space does he devote to his reactions to the experience?
3. What is the last part of the article concerned with? Is the essay balanced in organization?
4. Ebert makes what point about film audiences? For what audience is he writing? Are the two similar?

IV. SUGGESTIONS FOR WRITING

1. Write a vivid description of a horror film you have seen.
2. Review (analyze and evaluate) a horror film you have seen.
3. Write a persuasive essay on women as victims in horror films.

Janet Maslin joined the *New York Times* as a film critic in 1977. She was formerly a film critic for *Newsweek* magazine and for the *Boston Phoenix*. Maslin has also served as a music columnist for *New Times* magazine and a freelance reviewer for *Rolling Stone*. She chaired the New York Film Critic's Circle in 1981.

Unreal Heroes for the 80's

Janet Maslin

The superheroes of this summer's movies have accomplished some remarkable feats, not the least of which is temporarily banishing the memory of what movie heroism used to be. Only a few years ago, we watched loner after loner battle the system, proving that one man could make a difference and fight injustice. Now we're watching comic book characters single-handedly save the world from utter destruction. Why have we passed so emphatically from "Serpico" to "Superman"? The answer isn't particularly encouraging.

This is the first summer in recent memory that finds moviegoing a mass habit once again. At multiple movie theater complexes, people line up eagerly and indiscriminately, ready to see "Raiders of the Lost Ark" if the "Superman II" show is sold out, or "For Your Eyes Only" if the others are

Copyright © 1981 by The New York Times Company. Reprinted by permission.

unavailable. The message of movies like these—or "Outland," or "Clash of the Titans," or "Dragonslayer"—is so merrily escapist that audiences adore it. These movies are simple, clear, enjoyable and undemanding. We would rather watch idols than idealists right now.

It's true, of course, that many of these films are tremendously entertaining, and that business is booming because movies are better than they have been in a long while. But it's also true that these films dovetail distressingly with the spirit of the times. When films aren't striving for realism, they're aimed at an audience that would rather not look in the mirror. When they offer superhuman bravado the moviegoer can admire from afar, rather than the grittier kind of courage he or she might actually emulate, their buoyant, upbeat message has a defeatist tinge.

The heroes of the mid- and early 70's, in films like "Serpico," "All the President's Men," "The French Connection," even "Dirty Harry," were crusaders on a smaller scale than the comic book figures we're seeing right now. They were fighting crime and corruption, not mythical monsters or invaders from outer space. And whether they won or not, their sacrifices were those with which audiences could identify. The sight of Popeye Doyle, the policeman played by Gene Hackman in "The French Connection," waiting cold and hungry outside the restaurant where a rich drug smuggler dined in splendor, remains one of that era's most poignant images of dedication.

Nowadays, the film about an individual struggling for something he or she believes in is a rarity. Two years ago, "Norma Rae" had an exhilarating but dated feeling. And who knows how successful "The China Syndrome" might have been without Three Mile Island in the headlines? Besides, most recent films in the solitary do-gooder mode have been failures, like "Brubaker," in which Robert Redford played a prison warden dedicated to reform. "Fort Apache, The Bronx" went so far as to begin investigating police corruption and then virtually abandoned the subject. At the moment, the only viable forum for such crusading is on television, where "Lou Grant" and "60 Minutes" capture an audience the movies miss.

Films are still presenting the occasional earnest and dedicated individual, but generally their battles are being fought at home rather than in public. "Kramer vs. Kramer," a watershed movie in many ways, took a character with all the innate decency of an early 70's hero and devoted him entirely to the task of raising a child—an essential job, to be sure, but one less broadly ambitious than that of exposing a government scandal. Last year's homebody hit was "Ordinary People," an emotionally wrenching but considerably less pointed film than "Kramer vs. Kramer." And this year's version, "The Four Seasons," is a resolutely jolly romp in which all of life's problems are taken lightly.

• • •

So for the time being, up in the sky or in exotic corners of the earth, superheroes reign supreme. And yet they, too, reflect the same discouraging conditions that have sent the little-guy crusader into retreat. In the two biggest superhero films of the summer, "Superman II" and "Raiders of the Lost Ark," America's security is in jeopardy. In "Raiders," the swashbuckling hero Indiana Jones must battle Hitler's henchmen for the Biblical relic of the title; if Indie loses the Ark, Hitler may win the war. And in "Superman II," the President of the United States is brought to his knees by ruthless, all-powerful enemies. In both films, of course, America is ultimately saved—it's unlikely that either would be such a hit if it didn't end more or less happily, with the villains safely vanquished. But saving America requires the spectacular derring-do of Indie, or the intervention of Superman—in other words, it requires the impossible. These are fairy tales in which the menace is real and the rescue is not.

Another worrisome thing about the current superhero stories is that they convey so little sense of community. In "Outland," which tells a version of the "High Noon" story in an outer space setting, Sean Connery plays the same breed of loner Gary Cooper played, the one man willing to defy fearsome villains. In "High Noon," Cooper's sheriff was surrounded by a community of cowards, but at least they cringed in unison; at least they cared about what was going on. In "Outland," Mr. Connery's lawman is so alone that nobody seems interested in what he's up to. When he finally vanquishes the villains and strides into a space-age barroom, no one even shrugs.

In "Superman II," common folk are simply props for the big action scenes, used perhaps as passengers on a bus Superman catches in midair. No one cares what the citizens of Metropolis think or where they stand, even though Clark Kent is, after all, a newspaperman. In "Raiders," Indie is essentially fighting alone, more for his own glory than for humanity's sake. The hero of "Dragonslayer" is supposedly protecting a kingdom that is being terrorized by a dragon, but "Dragonslayer" is the most synical of the current superhero stories. The king is corrupt, the dragonslayer's feat is never publicly acknowledged, and the movie's ending is a shambles.

A modest little summer film opened and closed here several weeks ago. It was called "High Risk," and it was about four likable, believable ordinary Joes who set out to steal $5 million from a Colombian drug smuggler, mostly because they themselves were out of work and had families to support. They didn't perform magical feats or demonstrate superhuman powers, but they did grab their loot and get home alive. They weren't crusading for anything important, but they weren't deluding the audience with wildly improbable bravado, either. They weren't heroes at all, as a matter of fact. Perhaps that's why they were so refreshing.

> **Gerald Clarke** is a New York based free-lance writer who has been published in *Esquire, New Republic,* and *Atlantic Monthly,* and is currently a regular contributor to the entertainment section of *Time* magazine. His biography *Capote* on the writer Truman Capote is to be published in 1985.

In the Footsteps of Ulysses
Gerald Clarke

One of George Lucas' fondest images is this: a group of youngsters sitting around, their mouths open in wonder and suspense, as they hear the story of Ulysses. The adventures of Luke Skywalker bear only a superficial resemblance to the quest of Homer's "kingly man," but both draw from the same deep wells of mythology, the unconscious themes that have always dominated history on the planet.

"Myths are public dreams," according to retired Sarah Lawrence College Professor Joseph Campbell, whose books, notably *Hero with a Thousand Faces,* have established him as one of the world's leading experts on mythology. "Dreams are private myths. Myths are vehicles of communication between the conscious and the unconscious, just as dreams are." The myth of Prometheus, the Titan who stole fire from the great gods on Olympus and gave it to man, can be viewed as a dream of aspiration, reflecting the exuberance and almost celestial confidence of the Greeks. The contrasting and contemporary Hebrew story of Job has the opposite meaning: it symbolizes man's submission to a power above himself, cruel and incomprehensible as it may seem to be.

The myth Lucas is drawing upon in *Star Wars* and *The Empire Strikes Back* is that of the hero who ventures forth into dangerous and unknown territory, who is tempted by his own dark impulses, but who eventually conquers them and emerges victorious. The story thus symbolizes man's ability to control the irrational savage that exists within him and to follow instead the path of justice and love that religions probably were teaching even in the caves from which humanity emerged all those millenniums ago. "Do ye think that ye shall enter the Garden of Bliss without such trials as came to those who passed away before you?" asks the Muslim Holy Book, the Koran.

Luke, with Artoo Detoo as his friend and companion, is the unpretentious cinematic heir to a long line of such heroes: Prometheus, Jason, Aeneas, Sir Galahad, John Bunyan's pilgrim. Luke begins his adventure and soon encounters Ben Kenobi, who, as such figures often do in traditional fairy

Copyright © 1980 by Time Inc. All rights reserved. Reprinted by permission from *Time.*

tales and myths, offers advice and the benign protection of destiny. In classical myth such a role was played by Mercury, or Hermes as the Greek called him, in Egyptian myth the part belonged to Thoth. After Ben is transported to that place where all good Jedi Knights go in *Star Wars*, Yoda takes over his function in *The Empire*.

Following that, however, Luke, like any other such hero, enters what Dante called the dark wood midway in the journey of our life. He must go into it alone and alone face the evils that there reside, the dark forces that are within himself. Yoda knows that, and he tells Luke to leave behind his lightsword when he steps into the tree cave in the Dagobah swamp. Luke refuses and in a dreamlike sequence soon finds himself using it against what seems to be the figure of Darth Vader, whom he decapitates. Vader's mask breaks away and reveals Luke's own face; the symbol of evil was in Luke. Later, when he battles the real Vader, he is again tested, and Vader's evil has a magnetic power that is far more potent than the weapon he carries in his gloved hand. Luke, who is not yet strong or virtuous enough to resist such temptation, escapes only by letting himself fall desperately into the void below.

In the first two sagas of his series, Lucas has thus completed only half of the ancient story of testing and triumph. If he follows the common traditions of mythology and epic history, as he has up to now, Luke will eventually win, and Vader will lose. The larger fight they are engaged in will go on, of course, as long as men exist on earth—or Dagobah—and as long as they continue to invent symbols to cope with adversity and to rein in their own irrational and threatening impulses.

I. VOCABULARY

| dovetail | viable | watershed |
| aspiration | exuberance | poignant |

II. QUESTIONS ON CONTENT

1. Do you agree with Maslin that we have moved from loners to comic book characters and would rather watch idols than idealists?
2. Cite some recent films you have seen that support or argue this trend.
3. What point is Maslin making by using that particular scene from "The French Connection" as an example?
4. How has the focus shifted, according to Maslin, when an embattled individual is portrayed?
5. What is your reaction to her definition of fairy tales: "the menace is real and the rescue is not?"

6. What does the author say about a sense of community in these films? Do you agree?
7. How are Gerald Clarke's views of contemporary superheroes opposed to Maslin's? Which view is more appealing to you?
8. Why doesn't Maslin mention ancient heroism in her article?
9. What does paragraph four, page 374, in Clarkes article do for Luke Skywalker?
10. Explain the essential elements of heroism in the ancient myths.
11. Were you aware of Lucas' use of this heroic tradition in his films?

III. QUESTIONS ON FORM

1. What is the thesis sentence in Maslin's persuasive essay?
2. What modes of development does she employ?
3. What do the last sentences of Maslin's first three paragraphs reinforce?
4. In the second part of her article the author gives two reasons why the heroic superhero films disappoint her. What are they and in what order are they organized?
5. Maslin concludes the essay with an example; what point does it make? Comment on her final sentence.

IV. SUGGESTIONS FOR WRITING

1. Write a persuasive essay supporting either Maslin's or Clarke's views.
2. Write an essay applying the ancient heroic code to another contemporary hero: Captain Kirk, Indiana Jones, James Bond, and so on.

Marilyn Milloy is on the National Staff of *Newsday*.

A Cinematic Schism in Black and White

Marilyn Milloy

Hollywood—Brock Peters established himself as an actor of ample talent in the '50s and '60s in such movies as "To Kill a Mockingbird" and "Porgy and Bess." He portrayed the victimized rural black—proud, defiant, angry.

Now Peters is doing soaps.

Copyright © 1982 by Newsday, Inc. Reprinted by permission.

To call him one of the lucky ones—as some in the film business refer to anybody who gets work—is to miss the issue, say leaders of the National Association for the Advancement of Colored People, who for several months have made blacks' scant visibility in films a matter of public discussion. Peters' race, they say, has more to do with his absence from movies than the fact that work on quality motion pictures is difficult for most anyone to come by.

So minimal is the black presence—both in front of *and* behind the cameras—the group says, that it has been negotiating with movie studios for a "fair share" of the industry's jobs, this amid discussions of a possible movie boycott.

A peek at movie industry statistics, the group says, is telling: Only 12 of the 240 feature films released in 1981 had black men in leading or supporting roles. And only two black women—Cicely Tyson in "Bustin' Loose" and Deborah Allen in "Ragtime"—had major roles.

For black writers, producers and directors, the situation is just as bleak. Only two or three of the 70 black writers in the 5,700-member Writers Guild of America do much work on theatrical films, says Robert Price, who heads the guild's minority committee. And only two black directors—Sidney Poitier and Michael Schultz—seem to capture jobs on both black and nonblack productions.

Black producers, says Leroy Robinson, president of the 22-member Association of Black Motion Picture and Television Producers, "were so long not taken seriously" that their tale is even grimmer. The same seems true for black craftspeople behind the camera, who, according to a 1978 Civil Rights Commission report, made up only 6.6 per cent of the studios' employees.

"We're simply missing from the product" says Sumi Haru, national head of the ethnic equal opportunity committee of the Screen Actors Guild, which has 20,000 members, 11 percent of whom are minorities.

Ms. Haru insists that blacks "should be showing up everywhere" on the screen, and certainly in other than black films, which are rarely produced these days.

The problem, she and NAACP leaders say bluntly, stems from nepotism, greed and racism—albeit an unconscious sort.

"In many of those scripts out there, *any* American could fit the part. But you're dealing with people who are thinking white," Ms. Haru says. "They're thinking white American, white actor . . . And we're just not a part of their social system—the one that allows deals to be started at weekend swimming parties and barbecues."

The NAACP is now presenting movie studios with proposals to get blacks on boards of directors and in other corporate positions—positions NAACP leaders think matter most.

When the roles specifically for blacks do appear, Ms. Haru and the black leaders charge, they are largely stereotypical—weak men, prostitutes and drugged youths. Rarely are they proud. Rarely are they accomplished professionals.

Indeed, Lou Gossett Jr.'s well-received role as Sgt. Foley in "An Officer and a Gentleman" was originally written for a white. Gossett petitioned to have it changed. Says Lil Cumber, a black who has been an agent for 26 years in Los Angeles, "That's the kind of thing you have to do. You're the one who has to constantly make that pitch—and hope to God they go for it."

Delores Robinson, personal manager for LeVar Burton, who played Kunte Kinte in "Roots" six years ago, says that's a good approach, but one you can't bank on. "The industry doesn't want to see blacks as intelligent human beings," she says. "And it's a big problem, because LeVar doesn't *do* street talk, you see. He doesn't *do* 'black humor.'"

The job situation appears so hopeless to Ms. Robinson, who is black, that she has decided for now not to represent any blacks except Burton. "I have to look at business as business," she says. "I can't represent people that the industry won't let work. I represent people I can get jobs for."

Jobs for directors come no easier, says William Crain, who directed "Blacula" and "Roots II." "You can't get work, but then they say since you haven't done anything lately, well, you can't get hired this time around," he says. "They slap you on the back and give you a hearty handshake and, meantime, your house note is due."

So intense has been the pressure on the industry to hire more blacks—and to improve the image of blacks in movies—that the Los Angeles City Human Relations Commission held hearings last week on the issue. But the horror stories had been compiled long before: of some of the most famed black actors vying desperately for a one-day bit part; of white stuntsmen being "painted down" black to double for black actors, despite the fact that 17 blacks belong to the Black Stuntsmen Association; of work rates being cut drastically because, as actor Dick Anthony Williams ("Dog Day Afternoon") explains, "the industry pretty much sees us as interchangeable . . . so, hey, if you don't take it, he will, or she will."

The Los Angeles branch of the U.S. Equal Employment Opportunity Commission has been deluged with discrimination complaints—about 50 of them—against the motion picture industry. But because so few people have permanent jobs, says Margaret Ryan, the attorney handling the cases, "it's hard to determine how pervasive the problem is." Getting statistics, she says, hasn't been easy.

The NAACP has been trying to get those statistics for several months and has been successful with two studios.

Meanwhile, the idea of boycotting one of the industry's promising new releases has been pushed closer to the back burner but not yet abandoned.

While a boycott wouldn't bring a studio to its knees, the NAACP says, it would at least be an unwelcome financial blow: Blacks, the organization claims, pay about $400 million a year for movie tickets and make up about 30 per cent of theater audiences, even though they comprise only 12 per cent of the U.S. population.

The issue of participation by blacks in the movie industry is not new. Except for a period during the early '70s, when Hollywood was having its own economic troubles and began creating cheap, profitable, black-oriented movies, the industry has rarely showcased black actors the way it has whites, according to some people who have studied the business.

"The industry has often had the idea of 'one at a time,'" says Donald Bogle, author of "Toms, Coons, Mulattos, Mammies and Bucks," an interpretive history of blacks in films, published in 1974. "In the '50s and some of the '60s, it was Sidney Poitier. He was the only black actor who was really working consistently. For the '80s," Bogle says, "we have Richard Pryor."

As the awesomely funny comedian whose appeal knows no racial lines, Pryor is what the industry calls "bankable," having been responsible in large part for such hits as "Stir Crazy" and "Live on Sunset Strip." While everything he does may not turn to gold, Pryor, nevertheless, attracts large audiences.

It was not without this thought that Warner Brothers sat down with Pryor one day earlier this year and struck a deal that still troubles many black observers of the industry: Richard Pryor, a comedian, would play Malcolm X in an epic biographical film on the slain civil rights leader—a man who, for many blacks, drums up the same passion and ranks historically in importance with Martin Luther King Jr.

"We're not saying Richard isn't talented," says Robert Price, the writer who also heads the Los Angeles-based Black Anti-Defamation Coalition. "It's just that we're talking about a *national hero.*"

What's worse, other black observers say, is that a white screenwriter and director have been hired to script and make the film.

Robert Shapiro, president of Warner Brothers, thinks the outcry is unjustified. "Pryor's the right age and has the passion that symbolizes Malcolm X," he told The Washington Post. About the selection of a non-black screenwriter: "We wanted someone who could deal with Malcom as a man, a person—not someone who worshiped him," Shapiro said.

Richard Wesley, a black who wrote the screenplays for the successful films "Uptown Saturday Night" and "Let's Do It Again"—and a man who admires Malcolm X—says he was asked to write the script but turned down the offer because "among other things I didn't think any project with Richard Pryor as Malcolm X could be a serious project."

Some industry veterans, such as actor, producer and screenwriter Ossie Davis, view the Malcolm deal as testament to the notion that Hollywood's concern is money and profits—"us as economic entities, you know, like a computer was making all the decisions . . ."

Studio officials who would talk about the scarcity of blacks in the industry reject the suggestion that it has anything to do with race.

"I've never known anybody in the industry to care about what anybody was," said Michael Eisner, president of Paramount Pictures. "We don't think black or white."

"It's the dollar. It's what sells," says Harvey Lehman, director of personnel for Columbia Pictures. "From what I hear from management, they're looking for crossover material," Lehman says. "That's the stuff that appeals to both black and white," because black-oriented films, he says, historically don't do as well at the box office.

Blacks take issue.

"Saying there's no market for black films is based on nothing because there hasn't been any true testing," says Price. "When's the last time you've seen a creative, human, artistic black film that's given the same kind of industry [financial] backing as, say, an 'E.T.'?"

After the box office success of early black-hero movies, such as "Shaft" and "Sweet Sweetback's Baadasssss Song," which were produced by blacks, "Hollywood took the formula and simplified the figures and began tearing those movies out at a rate it seemed of one a month," says Bogle. But few were done in good taste, he says, recalling "blaxploitation" films such as "Hell Up in Harlem" and "Legend of Nigger Charlie." Insulted and dismayed, blacks stopped going to see such films, he says, and Hollywood, in turn, stopped making them.

On those few occasions when there was a different kind of product, blacks contend, Hollywood did not support them with enough publicity to do well.

"Again, we as blacks are being asked to be superhuman," says Curtis Rodgers, assistant legal counsel of the NAACP. "We're being asked to demonstrate our worth far beyond what ordinarly is required by the marketplace and the studios. Can one really argue that because a "Sounder" or a "Buck and the Preacher" didn't do well that there is no market? . . . My God, look at all the bombs that come out of the studios each year. What does that prove, and why does it continue to happen?"

To divorce themselves from the headaches inherent in getting backing from the major studios, a growing number of blacks have been trying to start their own companies and produce their own films.

But most find that getting the minimum $10 million needed to produce what borders on a low-budget picture is not easy. And getting more money to produce Grade A movies is even harder. Investors usually aren't interested until a distribution plan with major theaters is intact. And that is next to impossible, black moviemakers say, given the "unbankability" of black films.

A few independents have been financially successful, however. Fred Williamson, the Clint Eastwood of black films, has been the most prolific black moviemaker, churning out 12 films through his 8-year-old Po' Boy Production Co. Each movie cost less than $1 million to make, and they have been of relatively inferior quality. But they sell.

Because of that, Williamson has managed to get continuous backing from foreign investors. His latest film "One Down, Two to Go," starring the classic hemen of black films—himself, Richard Roundtree, Jim Brown and Jim Kelley—should turn a big profit, Williamson says.

While pleased that Williamson is doing well, many blacks don't want to follow his example. They want to do quality films, they say. And they want to put together companies that use as much black talent as possible, in front of and behind the cameras.

"I'm not really into having blacks come join with me because they're black," says Williamson. "I just want people who can help me put my product out . . . It's simple. I'm about making motion pictures and surviving in this world myself."

I. VOCABULARY

scant   albeit   inherent
schism   nepotism

II. QUESTIONS ON CONTENT

1. Were you aware of this situation in the film industry before reading this essay? How?
2. What is your perception of the present treatment of blacks in film? Has the situation improved?
3. In what areas of the film industry is this discrimination most acute?
4. What is the NAACP's priority in this situation?
5. Are "black stereotypes" still appearing in films? Cite some examples.
6. What is your reaction to Richard Pryor as Malcom X?
7. What is "bankability"?
8. Have you seen any Fred Williamson films? What was your reaction to them?

III. QUESTIONS ON FORM

1. Explain the function of the introductory paragraph on Brock Peters.
2. How does Milloy include statistics in this article? Is the method effective?

382 Popular Writing

3. What is the aim of the piece? Does it succeed?
4. Cite some uses of fact, example, and anecdote as modes of development.

IV. SUGGESTIONS FOR WRITING

1. Compare and contrast Hollywood's treatment of blacks with television's. Which medium offers more exposure and more realistic portrayals?
2. Write a classification and analysis of the roles played by black artists in recent movies you have seen.
3. If films reflect the times, what does the treatment of blacks in movies today reveal about our society? Write a persuasive essay.

For the past many years **Vincent Canby** has been a film critic for the *New York Times*. In addition to reviewing movies, he has written plays, a novel, and a critical work.

Longevity—the Real James Bond Mystery

Vincent Canby

One of the earliest and staunchest supporters of the James Bond films was Bosley Crowther, the late film critic of The New York Times, but by 1967 even he was beginning to suspect that enough was enough. Writing about "You Only Live Twice," the fifth of the phenomenal series started in 1963 with "Dr. No," Mr. Crowther said sadly, "The sex is minimal. But then, Bond is getting old."

Two days later, another critic in The Times described "On Her Majesty's Secret Service" as "the sixth and possibly last installment in the adventures of 007." That writer, mourning his own youth in the 1960's when he had been naive and seduced by the Bond films, decided they were not all harmless and , in fact, "essentially sadistic and cruel."

Today James Bond is not only alive and benign, but the entire Bond phenomenon seems to have obtained an extraordinary new lease on life. At the moment there are two new James Bond films in release, "Octopussy," which opened in June and stars Roger Moore, and "Never Say Never Again," which opened in New York the week before last and returns Sean Connery to the role in which he was succeeded by Mr. Moore in 1973.

Copyright © 1983 by The New York Times Company. Reprinted by permission.

In addition, new, best-selling Bond novels continue to be written by John Gardner under an agreement with the estate of Ian Fleming, who died in 1964.

As attractive as the character of 007 is, and as amusing as most of the films have been, this longevity is as mysterious to me as it is rare. All that one can do with any certainty is describe the phenomenon.

There's never been another series of films that have endured with quite the same élan as the Bond movies. All other films in long-running series have been B-movies, like the various Charlie Chan and Sherlock Holmes mysteries turned out in the 1930's and 40's. Only Bond has always traveled first-class.

Some statistics are in order to understand the series' relation to the decades through which it has passed. Including "Dr. No," there have been 14 Bond films, seven with Mr. Connery in the Bond role, six with Mr. Moore and one, "On Her Majesty's Secret Service" (1969), with George Lazenby, who departed after one try.

In 1967 there was also a huge, all-star Bond comedy, "Casino Royale," produced by Charles Feldman but unrelated to any other Bond movies. The film version of "Casino Royale," based on Mr. Fleming's first Bond novel, was directed by six people, including John Huston, with a cast that included Woody Allen, as "Jimmy Bond," James's nephew, and an actress billed as "Jacky Bisset" playing a character called "Miss Goodthighs."

The first eight Bond films were produced by Albert Broccoli and Harry Saltzman. When Mr. Saltzman sold his interest in the rights after "Live and Let Die" in 1973, Mr. Broccoli carried on alone. Kevin McClory owns the rights to "Thunderball," which he produced with Mr. Connery as the star in a joint arrangement with Mr. Broccoli and Mr. Saltzman in 1965, and which he has now rather freely readapted as "Never Say Never Again."

To recapitulate the titles of the Bond films and their dates of release: "Dr. No," 1963; "From Russia With Love," 1964; "Goldfinger," 1964; "Thunderball," 1965; "You Only Live Twice," 1967; "On Her Majesty's Secret Service," 1969; "Diamonds Are Forever," 1971; "Live and Let Die," 1973; "The Man with the Golden Gun," 1974; "The Spy Who Loved Me," 1977; "Moonraker," 1979; "For Your Eyes Only," 1981; "Octopussy," 1983, and "Never Say Never Again," 1983.

When the film version of "Dr. No" came out, it was shortly after President John F. Kennedy had admitted that the Bond novels were among his favorite reading matter. Whether accurately or not, the first films made from the Bond novels came to characterize a number of aspects of the Kennedy Administration with its reputation for glamour, wit and sophistication, and its real-life drama and melodrama. Indeed, the President himself could be seen as a kind of Bond figure, and the 1962 Cuban missile crisis as a real-life Bond situation.

Even so, the series managed to outlive the era with which it was originally identified, though the films themselves did not radically change in formula:

James Bond, the invincible, sexually omnipotent male, after numerous brushes with death, often in the form of chases, and after sleeping with a minimum of two women before finding Miss Right, with whom he also sleeps but without a clear conscience until the fadeout, saves the world from destruction, often at the hands of S.P.E.C.T.R.E., a terrorist organization with continuing ties to no one nation or ideology.

Just as the Cuban missile crisis did not dim the appeal of Bond movies about nuclear confrontations, the subsequent poltical assassinations, the Vietnam build-up, the antiwar demonstrations, Watergate, the oil crises and the wars in the Middle East have not apparently affected the public's enjoyment of Bond's make-believe world. Somehow Bond movies seem to sail above all realities without actually denying them. Neither do the films argue with critics who charge them with being callous, violent or chauvinist. They neutralize criticism as often as not by being too witty and good-humored to be taken too seriously.

The Bond films have survived all imitators, including the Our Man Flint and Matt Helm adventures. They have survived the sexual revolution that, in a casual way, they once represented in James's perfectly frank enjoyment of casual, promiscuous sex. Now, however, compared to the heroes of other contemporary films, James looks to be a practitioner of courtly love.

For all of Bond's wild, wild ways, no movie containing him has ever gone out with a rating more racy than PG, which is what "King Kong" received. As far as I can remember, Bond has never used drugs of his own accord, not even marijuana. Further, his fondness for the extra-dry martini seems almost to be a throwback to the 1930's. Could it be that he has managed to stay hip by being gloriously square?

One of the major reasons for the series' continuing critical success is not a big secret: Each film costs a fortune to make but virtually every cent of it is on the screen. The magnificent space-war that is the climax of "Moonraker" is as stylish as anything done by Lucasfilm. The outlandish sets, whether Dr. No's underwater laboratory or the volcano landing-pad in "You Only Live Twice," are almost always totally convincing.

The increasing dependence on elaborate physical gags, some of the finest of which often turn up in precredit sequences, does not mark a falling off of the intelligence of the films. On the contrary, these gags are simply glorifying the kind of action in which the Bond films traffic. Bond himself is certainly not an introspective sort. With or without the sometimes heavily facetious quips, he's a man of action, but random action in movies soon becomes tiresome. Eighty years ago, movie audiences may have ducked in their seats at the sight of a streetcar rolling toward them, but they soon collected themselves and demanded more complicated thrills.

It's to the credit of the people who make these films that the physical gags, the looks of the films and their soundtracks have continued to become increasingly spectacular.

Some of the people to be credited include Terence Young, director of "Dr. No," "From Russia With Love" and "Thunderball"; Guy Hamilton, director of "Goldfinger," "Diamonds Are Forever," "Live and Let Die" and "The Man with the Golden Gun"; and Lewis Gilbert, director of "You Only Live Twice," "The Spy Who Loved Me" and "Moonraker."

After seeing "Never Say Never Again," which was directed by Irvin Kershner, I'm not at all sure the public wants to worry about James Bond's getting old, though the film very wittily acknowledges that he—and Mr. Connery—are not quite as young as they once were. Having admitted that fact at the start of the film, where Bond is at a health farm getting back into the shape that too many women and too many martinis have denied him, "Never Say Never Again" goes on to show Bond/Connery performing at the same tireless pace he has displayed in every previous film.

Though Mr. Moore has done perfectly acceptable work as James Bond since he took over the role in "Live and Let Die," the character still seems to belong to Mr. Connery, even though "Never Say Never Again" is not quite as splashy an entertainment as "Octopussy," the Bond/Moore movie.

At times "Never Say Never Again" seems almost somber, which is not unpleasant though it's a contradiction in terms. Bond movies are meant to be escapist, not introspective, which is a quality that Mr. Connery, who's now a better actor than ever, brings to the film.

"Never Say Never Again" also has a terrifically witty villain, Largo, who, as played by Klaus Maria Brandauer, the star of "Mephisto," is a madman to rank with Joseph Wiseman's Dr. No, Gert Froebe's Goldfinger and Geoffrey Holder's Baron Samedi. Appearing in several throw-away scenes is Max von Sydow as Blofeld, the evil genius who runs S.P.E.C.T.R.E., a role that has been played in the past by Donald Pleasance and Telly Savalas.

I still don't understand the appeal of the Bond films, though I respond to them as faithfully as millions of other people. It's not their stories—I can't remember one plot from another without rereading old reviews. They are beautifully cast, but at this minute I'm not sure whether Herve Villechaize appeared in "The Spy Who Loved Me" or "The Man With the Golden Gun." The women in the films are fantastic, but so are the women in Playboy.

It's possible, of course, that the Bond movies, which once seemed so smartly, wickedly sophisticated, now reassure us by their courtly manners and by the orderliness of a world in which S.P.E.C.T.R.E., though never permanently defeated, never triumphs. In an era in which total victory might also mean total defeat, equilibrium is suddenly most alluring.

I. VOCABULARY

benign	élan	chauvinist
courtly love	facetious	introspective

II. QUESTIONS ON CONTENT

1. Do you enjoy James Bond films? Check the article and count how many you have seen.
2. What characteristics does Canby emphasize in his description of Bond?
3. What effect has history had on the Bond films?
4. How, according to Canby, do the films neutralize criticism?
5. What irony does Canby suggest about Bond's sophistication?
6. What are the author's comments about production in the Bond series?
7. Does Canby come to a conclusion about the longevity of the series?

III. QUESTIONS ON FORM

1. Why does Canby refer to earlier film critics in his introduction?
2. What point do the quotations in the introduction reinforce?
3. Outline the article, listing Canby's reasons for Bond's longevity. How are they organized?
4. What is the critic's aim in this article? Does he succeed?
5. Is his tone consistent with the aim?

IV. SUGGESTIONS FOR WRITING

1. Write a satire/spoof of the James Bond character.
2. Is Bond finally passé? Write a persuasive essay disagreeing with Canby.
3. Compare and contrast James Bond and Indiana Jones.

Since 1968 **Pauline Kael** has been film critic for *New Yorker* magazine. She is the author of *Reeling* (1976), *When the Lights Go Down* (1980), *5001 Nights at the Movies* (1982), and *Taking It All In* (1984). In 1974 she received the National Book Award for *Deeper into Movies*.

Movies on TV

Pauline Kael

Movies could easily go the way of the theatre—and faster, since the moneymen have no aesthetic commitment whatever. And probably there'd be less lamentation for movies than for live theatre. Because, of course, there's television. But it's not the same medium. And though if you don't

From *On the Future of Movies* by Pauline Kael. Copyright © 1974 by Pauline Kael. By permission of Little, Brown and Company in association with the Atlantic Monthly Press.

read a book when it comes out you can read it a year later, if you don't see a movie when it comes out, and wait to see it a year later on television, you're not seeing what you could have seen in the theatre. (Nor do you see that movie if you wait to see it in a college, or at a film society in a cheap, grainy 16-mm. reduction.) What's lost on television is the visual beauty, the spatial sense, the fusion of image and sound—everything that makes movies an art form. And movies made directly for television almost never have these qualities; one talks of TV movies in terms of pace and impact and tension, and occasionally—with the prestige ones—subject and performances, but who talks of television movies in terms of beauty? Movies made for TV, or movies made for a big screen and shown on TV, are reduced to just what the businessmen believe in—the bare bones of entertainment. There is something spurious about the very term "a movie made for TV," because what you make for TV is a TV program.

Television as we have it isn't an art form—it's a piece of furniture that is good for a few things. There's a problem of dimensions: no matter what people say, the screen is too small, and that's why the thing TV does best is a closeup of a person being asked a direct question—because both you and that person knew that it operates like a lie detector. For perhaps most Americans, TV is an appliance, not to be used selectively but to be turned on—there's always something to watch. If a hundred million people see a movie in two showings on TV, that doesn't mean what it would if a hundred million people saw it in theatres. Sure, forty-two million people saw "The Autobiography of Miss Jane Pittman," but they saw it sandwiched between two other shows. TV stars with audiences larger than the world has ever before known are eager to appear in a real movie—which, even if a hit, will be seen by only a handful, relatively speaking (until it, too, winds up on TV)—because they know that on TV they're part of the furniture. On TV they're mundane, they're reduced to the routinely, boringly tolerable. There's an aesthetic element in the phrase "larger than life," and the artists working in the movie medium instinctively take that into consideration. What is on the big screen has an aesthetic clarity denied to the box; when you're watching a movie in a theatre, you don't need a voice telling you what you have just seen.

There have been some few subjects filmed for TV which nobody would finance for theatres, because it's generally understood that people won't pay to see a film on a subject like that of "I Heard The Owl Call My Name" or "Jane Pittman" or "The Execution of Private Slovik." But a few TV shows with social themes shouldn't become the occasion for big headlines in the press about how television "has been growing bolder." Bold is just what these shows aren't; even when they're made as well as possible, they're mincingly careful. And they're not a key to new opportunities on TV so much as a key to the constriction of opportunities for moviemakers: moviemakers can't get backing for pictures with social themes—or with any real themes at all. Probably it's true that people wouldn't pay to see the films on social themes which they'll watch on television, but that's because those subjects are treated in the sober, limited TV manner. We have no way of knowing how the public might respond if a hugely talented filmmaker with adequate resources and a campaign to back him took on a large social theme. Nobody has had the chance in decades.

Television represents what happens to a medium when the artists have no power and the businessmen are in full, unquestioned control. People's TV expectations are so low and so routinized that "Brian's Song" can pass for an event, and a pitifully predictable problem play like "Tell Me Where It Hurts," in which Maureen Stapleton plays a middle-aged housewife who joins a women's-lib group and has her consciousness raised, is received by the press as if it marked a significant advance. And what sort of opportunities does *normal* television offer for the development of talent? Here are the words of Brandon Stoddard, A.B.C.'s vice-president in charge of motion pictures for television:

> I am interested in emotional jeopardy, not physical jeopardy. I want the viewer to really care about the people and to feel something when it is over. . . . I have nothing against exploitative material if it is done right, and the way to do it right is to translate it into human drama rather than gimmicks. I don't want to know about the two Vampires in the casino in Las Vegas. I want to know about the man they are attacking and how it will affect his life. . . . We are looking everywhere for story ideas and even calling colleges to get some new blood into this.

Movies as an art form won't die and go to the heaven of television. If they die, they'll be truly dead. Even if the shift in the audience toward the crude and insensitive is only a temporary derangement, it could be sufficient to destroy movies.

I. VOCABULARY

spurious   mincingly

II. QUESTIONS ON CONTENT

1. Why does Kael say television movies are *not* an art form? What aspects are lost?
2. Kael's comments were written several years ago. Are movies made for television still just "television programs" or have they improved? Cite some examples.
3. Does the small screen disturb you as a viewer?

4. Is the "aesthetic clarity" of movies superior to television?
5. Discuss Kael's explanation of television and film financing.
6. Is television still a medium where "artists have no power and the businessmen are in full, unquestioned control?" Cite some examples in support of your view.

III. QUESTIONS ON FORM

1. What are the connotations of labeling television a "piece of furniture" or an "appliance?"
2. Outline this article as a comparison/contrast piece.
3. How would you describe Kael's tone? Select some examples of vocabulary and diction that indicate the tone.
4. Can today's television audience be described as "crude and insensitive"? For what audience is Kael writing?

IV. SUGGESTIONS FOR WRITING

1. Using specific movies for television, write a persuasive essay disagreeing with Kael.
2. Compare and contrast a specific movie for television with a large screen film in terms of production, aesthetic clarity, and impact.

Writer and film and book critic **Charles Champlin** has been a correspondent for *Life* and *Time* magazines, and a commentator on KCET-TV, Los Angeles. He is now entertainment editor and columnist for the *Los Angeles Times*.

The Critic as Image Maker
Charles Champlin

"Is sex necessary?" James Thurber and E. B. White inquired in a book back in the 1930's. "No, but it beats Whist," is a fair summary of their findings, as I recall.

"Are critics necessary?" is a question frequently asked, often through clenched teeth, at cocktail parties in Hollywood, New York and other centers of creativity.

Charles Champlin, "The Critic as Image Maker," *American Premiere*, December 1981-January 1982. Reprinted by permission of the author.

The responses vary, depending on whether a critic has recently driven a crude stake through the responder's heart or has hand-woven a garland of spring flowers and placed it on the responder's brow.

It is interesting to note how highly critics rate in the estimation of the well-reviewed, and how trivial and expendable they are in the eyes of the skewered (not to mention how blind, venal, illiterate, bigoted, and possibly diseased). A correlation between the *slings* of negative reviews and the *arrows* of attack upon the concept of the critic himself could be proved without trouble. After all, it takes a saint to put hand to heart and say, "Thanks for pointing out my grievous shortcomings and o'er-reaching ambition," and saints are as infrequent in this age as in any other.

But, when the wounds have crusted over, if not quite healed, or when yesterday's debacle has been followed by today's soaring and unmitigated triumph (Smythe-Jones, *Ft. Worth Press-Avenger*), the survivors can reassess the matter. Very possibly they will conclude that the critic plays a role that no one else can play, and that he achieves a singular end, unduplicated by anyone or anything else in the image-building process.

Money may not be able to buy happiness (although this is a challengeable bit of folk wisdom), but it can engender fame and procure an image. Strictly speaking, money cannot buy a reputation for high achievement—except possibly in the making of still more money. Reputation, unlike fame, notoriety or public image, arises from achievement, and who is a more authoritative barometer of achievement than the critics—singly or even better, collectively.

The Beatles presumably did not require critics for their earth-rocking popularity, although you could argue that the first disc jockeys who picked Beatles records out of obscurity and cheered them were functioning as critics. But when William Mann, the devoutly serious music critic of *The Times* in London, published a thoughtful piece proving that the Beatles' melodies were derived directly from Elizabethan plain-song and no wonder they were so popular, some sort of symbolic gap had been bridged, and the Liverpool lads were confirmed (Mann was not alone by any means) as far more than a transient teenage phenomenon. From fairly early on, in fact, the Beatles had both popular success and critical acclaim—as well as quantities of analysis about what they revealed about our times.

But reputation and commercial success don't always dance hand in hand. Starting in 1922, *Abie's Irish Rose* ran for 2,327 performances, despite the virtually unanimous cat-calling scorn of the Manhattan drama critics. Robert Benchley, forced week after week to do a capsule listing on the play for a magazine, once simply gave the title and a Biblical citation. Those intrigued enough to turn to Isaiah found that the cited line read, "Jesus Christ, the same yesterday, today and forever."

Anne Nichols wrote the play, which became a film as late as 1946, but no one placed her alongside Eugene O'Neill, whom she may well have outearned.

Where critics may well earn their keep, or at least stifle the wrath of their detractors, is in standing in defiance of the indifference of the paying customers to a work of art. There are treasuries of critical invective which proved that Beethoven was a no-talent bum and Stravinsky's "Rite of Spring" was a joke, no matter how many thousands enjoyed them. Not so colorful, unfortunately, are the brave critical celebrations of work so dark, so avant-garde, so threatening and so true, that the public could not be persuaded to see it with the promise of free beer and sandwiches.

Ingmar Bergman's films altogether will never earn as much as *The Devil in Miss Jones,* yet he is among the most honored filmmakers in the world. His image, as defined by critics and confirmed by a small but discerning public, could not be bought by commercial success nor damaged by the lack of it.

Film critics collectively have saved works as different as *Stevie* and *Sunday Bloody Sunday* from premature burial. The television critics and their near-unanimous raves for *Hill Street Blues* unquestionably helped it override low ratings by identifying it as the prestigious undertaking it was—good for the network image—and, in time, audiences will almost certainly discover the series in high-rating numbers.

Anyone who has read of the derisive hoots and hollers that greeted Cubism, Surrealism and Abstract Expressionism has to agree that it was the critics, along with adventurous curators and collectors, who, in time, persuaded a dubious public that Picasso, for example, was not a prankster but a supreme artistic genius.

Drama critics may be the most potent image-makers, or hit makers, of all, which is less a comment on their perceptiveness than an acknowledgment of the hit-or-stay-home mentality of the occasional theater audience.

In New York, straight plays rarely prosper unless the critics link arms and dance around Times Square singing anthems of praise and glory. Musicals do marginally better, but there is now a tradition of million-dollar turkeys which died of their critical roastings before the public even had a chance to agree that the critics were all too correct.

Images, especially in Hollywood, more often mean individuals rather than whole productions, and film critics have, in the last quarter-century, done a great deal to identify and celebrate a relatively new breed of star-actor. The "star" is known primarily for admirable body and piercingly white teeth; the star-actor is impervious to bad material and spins straw into gold with regularity. The star system has changed, reflecting the rise of television and the decline of the major studios as star-making institutions. Post-television, the star who is principally an actor (or actress, although actor is now a unisex word) has come into his own. Dustin Hoffman, Robert De Niro, Al Pacino, Meryl Streep and a considerable number of others have established their reputations with dazzling performances acclaimed by critics, and have become stars without the need of that kind of carry-over persona (e.g., John Wayne as rugged hero) which was such a convenient shorthand for moviemakers of the Golden Era.

The critics hardly invented the star-actor, and the critics are not really empowered to create a star unless the public is agreeable, too. But in the postwar years, the critics have led the enshrinement ceremonies for the actor as star. The national magazine reviewers in particular, with their influence on cover stories and features, have created an appreciation and a following for a group of actors who, in an earlier Hollywood, would have been shunned by the ruling class; now they are not only the rule, but the rulers.

For critics as image-makers, it has been their finest hour. But, lest the critical body grow feverishly enthused about its powers, it is well to bear in mind something Fred Allen said about Ed Sullivan, when Sullivan had emerged as television's preeminent variety show host. "Ed Sullivan," Allen said, "will be in business as long as other people have talent."

So will critics. Which is not to say they don't have an invaluable function. They *do* make images, based on achievement, and the critical image is accordingly of a much longer-lasting metal than fame or notoriety or even inflated bank balances.

I. VOCABULARY

expendable	unmitigated	venal
engender	stifle	invective

II. QUESTIONS ON CONTENT

1. What does Champlin say about a critic's reception?
2. What does he say about the critic's role?
3. Champlin uses image interchangeably with what word?
4. Why are the Beatles such an apt example?
5. Champlin discusses criticism in what other arts and media?
6. Why does Champlin select Hollywood for his final illustrations of critical power?
7. The conclusion reiterates which idea?

III. QUESTIONS ON FORM

1. Where does the phrase "slings and arrows" come from?
2. To what references do the phrases "crude stake through the respondent's heart" and "garland of spring flowers placed on the respondent's brow" allude?

3. The phrase "brave critical celebrations" reinforces Champlin's thesis about critics. Analyze the organization of the paragraph in which it is found.
4. Explain why Fred Allen's comment is a *non sequitur*.

IV. SUGGESTIONS FOR WRITING

1. Play critic. Attend several films and write up reviews.
2. Recount an occasion when you have been influenced by critics. Were they correct? Write a persuasive essay discussing their current influence on cultural tastes and activities.

TOPICS FOR INVESTIGATION

1. Investigate the evolution of the heroic figure and his "ancient story of testing and triumph" in films from the early epics to today's superheroes.

2. Discuss the roles of the critic as defined by Champlin, DeMott, and the French critic Derrida, as referred to in DeMott's article in Chapter Nine. Research the historical role and power of the critic in different arts at different periods.

3. Critique the critics. Evaluate the print and television film critics of today. How is their new celebrity status affecting their function?

4. Where are all the good musicals? Investigate its development from the heydays of Busby Berkely through Astaire, Kelly, and so on to its current infrequent appearances. Why has it declined?

5. Select one of the following movie genres and investigate its development and current status: comedies, romances, serious dramas, mysteries, or science fiction films.

THE PULITZER HOAX: A CASEBOOK

The Pulitzer Prize hoax of 1980 was a canon misfired at the citadel of journalism. For a variety of reasons the reverberations of that blast are still being felt. Here is a casebook of facts and opinions in different formats and from different perspectives on that cause célèbre.

Readings

Wash. Post Story a Hoax, Paper Returns Pulitzer
Thomas Collins

In what will probably go down as one of journalism's darkest moments, a 26-year-old Washington Post reporter yesterday relinquished the Pulitzer Prize she had won earlier this week, admitting that her harrowing and well-written story about an 8-year-old heroin addict had been a "fabrication."

In submitting her resignation, reporter Janet Cooke said in a signed statement that she had "never encountered or interviewed an 8-year-old heroin addict" and that the story, which ran in the Post in September and caused considerable controversy in the capital, had been "a serious misrepresentation which I deeply regret. I apologize to my newspaper, my profession, the Pulitzer Board and all seekers of the truth."

Post Executive Editor Benjamin C. Bradlee sent telegrams to the 17 members of the Pulitzer Prize Board, advising them of the deception and stating that Cooke would not be accepting the award. He told the board that the story was a "composite" and that "the quotes attributed to a child were in fact fabricated, and that certain events described as eyewitnessed did not in fact happen."

In the story, the child had been identified only as "Jimmy," which the account said was not his real name. His purported mother and her boyfriend, who the story said had administered heroin shots to the child, also had been given fictitious names, the story said.

The incident rocked the journalistic world and reverberated through Columbia University, which administers the prizes. Osborne Elliott, dean of the Columbia Graduate School of Journalism, said it was a "very unfortunate situation, to which the Washington Post has responded appropriately."

Others in journalism expressed serious concern that the incident would hurt the press' credibility with the public. "It cannot help but damage the profession," said Joel Dreyfuss, executive editor of Black Enterprise magazine, who served as a Pulitzer juror this year.

After a majority of Pulitzer board members was polled by phone, the board voted to give Cooke's award to Teresa Carpenter of the Village Voice for a story about Adam Berwid, a Long Island mental patient who is accused

Copyright © 1981 by Newsday, Inc. Reprinted by permission.

of killing his ex-wife. Carpenter had been the original choice of Pulitzer jurors for the award in the features category, but had been over-ruled by the Pulitzer board, which has the last say in such matters.

The Post, which has won journalism's most coveted prize a number of times, most notably in 1973 for the Watergate reporting of Bob Woodward and Carl Bernstein, was deeply shaken by the incident. At a staff meeting yesterday, Bradlee said: "It breaks my heart to tell you what you already know." Post Publisher Donald E. Graham said the paper would apologize to its readers in today's editions.

Woodward, who as metropolitan editor was Cooke's supervisor, and who had questioned her closely when she submitted the story, was obviously upset. "It was my job as an editor; I'm responsible," he said in a telephone interview. "I feel devastated that we put something in the paper that was a fabrication, and which we had stood behind."

Immediately after the story was published, doubts about its authenticity were voiced by the Washington, D.C., mayor's office and by police, who conducted a thorough search of ghetto areas in a fruitless effort to find the child. At one point, authorities considered subpoenaing Cooke, but the Post stood by the story; it said it would fight the subpoena on First Amendment grounds, and the issue was dropped. Yesterday, Mayor Marion Barry, who received an apology from Bradlee, said: "I didn't believe [the story] in the first place."

Doubts about the veracity of the account had also been whispered in journalistic circles for some time, even at the Post, and increased last week when reports began circulating that it was headed for a prize. In a telephone interview on Monday, the day the awards were announced, Woodward said he was "absolutely convinced" the story was true, but declined to say specifically that Cooke had given him the child's name and those of others mentioned in the story.

Yesterday he said that she had given him a name and a vague address of the family but that no one at the Post had tried independently to verify the story. "She was the reporter that we had trusted," he said.

"After a period of time, a relationship of trust is built up between an editor and a reporter," Bradlee said. "And when push comes to shove, you go with your reporter."

It was learned that Cooke had staged a "dramatic playlet," in the words of one source, for the benefit of Post editors to convince them of the truthfulness of the story. She told them in detail how she had been threatened with a switchblade knife by the alleged boyfriend if she told anyone, including her editors, the family's identity. She also recounted how she had thrown up after seeing the boyfriend give the child a shot of heroin.

Cooke was reportedly in seclusion with her family and some friends from the Post. Bradlee, who called her "a promising and talented young reporter," said the paper would help her in any way possible.

Cooke had been with the paper for a little more than a year. Her story for the Post, called "Jimmy's World," began: "Jimmy is 8 years old and a third-generation addict, a precocious little boy with sandy hair, velvety brown eyes and needle marks freckling the baby-smooth skin of his thin brown arms." In describing how the child allegedly was given the dope, she wrote: "The needle slides into the boy's soft skin like a straw pushed into the center of a freshly baked cake."

Cooke's undoing began when an official at Vassar College called Bradlee on Tuesday to say that Cooke had never been graduated from Vassar, as recounted in her resume to the Pulitzer Board. In fact, she had attended Vassar for only a year. Questions raised about her background by reporters in Ohio, where she had worked on the Toledo Blade, also reached the Post, and Cooke was questioned closely by Post editors throughout the day and night about the story. At one point, Bradlee said in a telephone interview, editors accompanied her to the neighborhood where the child supposedly lived, but Cooke said she could not find the house.

Finally, after an exhausting night of questions and denials, she admitted that she had lied, Bradlee said. Another source at the paper said she also had fabricated her notes, a phony name—Tyrone Davis—for the child, and other names for the non-existent mother and boyfriend. She also had made up other aspects of her background, including that she spoke four languages, had a master's degree from the University of Toledo—when, in fact, she held a bachelor's degree—and had studied at the Sorbonne in Paris, which she had not.

The incident had to be embarrassing to the Pulitzer Prize Board, even though some of its members pointed out that it had no reason to disbelieve the story, coming as it did with the imprimatur of a newspaper as prestigious as the Post. There were contradictions as to whether the question of giving the $1,000 prize to a story in which the principals had not been identified had come up at the board meeting.

Dean Elliott said that there had been a discussion of the issue but that the board decided it had to have faith in the Post's recommendations. Another board member, who did not want to be identified, said the question had not been raised, but, "in retrospect," should have.

Another sore point was that if the Pulitzer Board had acted upon the recommendations of the features jury, the incident probably would not have surfaced. Cooke's story originally was submitted in the general local news category, where it came in second, and then had been shifted to the features category, where it won. The board did not consult the features jury, which never saw Cooke's story.

One of those reportedly pleading for the shift was board member Roger Wilkins, associate editor of the Washington Star. Questions were raised as to whether the child addict's case was "representative" of a larger problem, and Wilkins reportedly told the board that he could probably find an 8-year-old addict within a few blocks of Columbia University. Wilkins could not be reached for comment.

The irony is that child addiction no doubt does, in fact, exist, and Cooke's story powerfully focused on that problem and aroused community concern about it. Social workers and others quoted by name in the story attested to the existence of the problem. "There is no question it does," said Bradlee, adding that that did not alter the fact that the story was literally false. "That's no good, my friend."

Aftermath of a Pulitzer Hoax
Newsday, April 18, 1981

Many people in the newspaper business are in a state of shock this week because a Washington Post story that won the Pulitzer Prize has been exposed as a fabrication.

And many people outside of the newspaper business are wondering what kind of journalistic standards exist when editors of one of the country's leading newspapers could be so readily deceived.

We understand the shock and the wondering. But we also think it's important to keep this dismal event in perspective.

What occurred was an aberration, an individual incident that in no way represents what generally occurs at newspapers—no more than Clifford Irving's fraudulent biography of Howard Hughes represents what generally occurs at book publishing houses, or fake experiments with mice represent what generally occurs in research laboratories. And like book publishing and scientific research, newspapers will survive and flourish.

What's really sad in this whole affair is that journalistic standards are in fact higher than ever, and that newspapers have accomplished more in fulfilling their responsibility to inform the public in recent years than ever before. The Washington Post deserves a good share of the credit for these accomplishments.

Now it must examine the damage that has been done, and how it can be repaired. To its credit, the Post quickly reported the fabrication when it was discovered, and the paper plans a full report to its readers of how the event occurred.

Less to its credit is that its editing procedures failed. Reporters don't put stories in newspapers; editors do. And for an editor not to insist on knowing the principal source of such an explosive story when the reporter is new on

Copyright © 1981 by Newsday, Inc. Reprinted by permission.

the job, as this one was, and when the story seems to border on the fantastic, is certainly a lapse of judgment.

Yet the event will have its positive impact. At newspapers all over the country, including this one, procedures are being re-examined to ensure that safeguards against fabrication are made stronger than ever. There is a kind of unwritten contract in our society: Newspapers are protected by the First Amendment; in exchange, they are expected to provide credible information to the citizens of that society. We are hopeful that the end result of this aberration will be a strengthening, rather than a weakening, of that contract.

A widely respected investigative reporter, coauthor of the 1974 Pulitzer Prize-winning series "The Heroin Trail," later published as a book, **Les Payne** has covered numerous controversial issues, both national and international. He is president of the National Association of Black Journalists and has served as a judge for the National Academy of Arts and Sciences and as a member of the Pulitzer Prize selection committee.

The Faked Story: When Ambition Replaces the Truth

Les Payne

When one gets his pockets picked in London, it is attributed to pickpockets. But when one gets his pockets picked in Harlem, ofttimes it is attributed to blacks. Janet Cooke, a black reporter, recently picked the pockets of The Washington Post and some suggest that it reflects on the work of black reporters everywhere.

Cooke's fake story about an 8-year-old heroin addict she named Jimmy had black reporters around the country phoning each other, bracing to defend themselves, expecting to be attacked as co-conspirators of a reporter most of them never met, whose story many never read.

"Blacks in newsrooms all over the country" are the biggest victims of the hoax, said Roger Wilkins, one of the journalists who sat on the board that awarded Cooke the Pulitzer Prize for feature writing. "We blacks are distrusted by many white editors who doubt our perception, our judgment

Copyright © 1981 by Newsday, Inc. Reprinted by permission.

and our ability to be fair and accurate. We struggle against this every day and . . . Cooke . . . made our burden of proof much heavier."

This conclusion clearly is undernourished. It is true that white editors and readers who doubt black reporters' ability and potential will use the Cooke affair to support their prejudices. But the doubt existed long before Cooke's hoax. For bigotry, as Sartre noted, does not feed on evidence or facts. The bigot is someone who has chosen to reason falsely.

The Wall Street Journal incredibly held up Cooke's carcass as a warning to newspapers everywhere about the "broader and troublesome issues" of affirmative action: "To what extent do the pressures facing big city papers to recruit and promote promising minorities cloud the initial hiring procedures—as well as the decisions as to which of their stories should be published?"

Despite delusions to the contrary, the Post is under no real pressure to hire blacks, as the Journal suggested. And clearly it was under no pressure to hire Cooke. If she had earned the Pulitzer fairly, I am sure that the Journal would not have taken her achievement as a confirmation of what passes for newspapers' affirmative-action programs.

What black reporters face here, as do all victims of bigotry, is a society that indicts them collectively for their individual failures but rewards them singularly for individual achievement, because to succeed as a black in America is to stand alone, as an exception, but to fail is to bring into the conspiracy some 32 million other unknowing blacks.

Bigotry aside, the key questions the Cooke affair raises are how widespread are newspaper hoaxes and to what are they attributed? As H. L. Mencken noted, "The journalist can no more see himself realistically than a bishop can see himself realistically. He gilds and engauds the picture, unconsciously and irresistibly."

What emerges too often in the journalist's false view of himself is a figure of heroic dimensions, combining the intellect of Aristotle, the honesty and long-suffering of a Trappist, the courage of Prometheus.

But the truth is that newspaper hoaxes like Cooke's, a Tiffany of the genre, are not all that uncommon. During the September, 1971 rebellion at Attica Prison, a newspaper reporter wrote that he had witnessed prisoners slitting the throats of guards who were held hostage. Later, an investigation showed that no guards' throats had been slit.

In the 1967 uprising in Detroit, overzealous local reporters wrote accounts of black snipers firing at police from rooftops. Most such sniping reports, both in Detroit and in riots elsewhere that year, were either false or exaggerated, according to the 1968 report of the National Advisory Commission on Civil Disorders. Other stories, fabricated at least in part, have no doubt escaped discovery.

But it is the foreign correspondent who has raised story invention to an art. While on assignment abroad, I have seen reporters create stories, sources, quotes, national trends and once even an entire village. Evelyn Waugh wrote the classic treatise on this in his novel, "Scoop," a thinly disguised account of his assignment in Ethiopia for a British daily.

The "Scoop" tradition survives among foreign correspondents assigned to Third World countries, especially Africa. In most hoaxes several elements are present:

- The reporters and readers have a stereotyped view of the subjects.
- The newspaper's readership is largely ignorant about, if not indifferent to, the subjects.
- There exists a vast cultural gap between readers and the subjects.
- The reporter concludes that subjects of the fake story are powerless to expose the false account.

And this practice may not be limited to African countries. In 1978, James Gibbins, a reporter for The Daily Mail in London, was assigned to Washington, D.C., and filed news stories from there that most other Washington reporters believed to be fake. The Mail printed—as a serious story—a Gibbins dispatch describing beggars in front of the White House and wearing bowler hats distributed by the Washington welfare agency. Another said that President Carter's "image-makers," desperate about his low public-approval rating, had, in a "top-secret summit at Camp David," suggested that he emulate Abraham Lincoln by growing a one-inch beard.

Gibbins said his stories were accurate. In defending the Carter beard story, he said in July, 1978: "It took three weeks of digging and sifting before I could establish that story as absolute fact. Two of my sources were impeccable. And I am hopeful that at least one . . . will . . . volunteer to break the confidentiality which was the *sine qua non* of our interview."

However, after the Mail investigated Gibbins' stories and his seven-year career, he, like Cooke, resigned.

All such fabrications are unpardonable in journalism. Cooke and the others like her must not be allowed to put ambition before facts, accuracy and the public trust. In cases where this has happened, the ambition got a leg up on professionalism.

Ellen Goodman is a journalist. A feature writer columnist for the *Boston Globe* since 1967 and a syndicated columnist for the *Washington Post* Writers Group since 1976, Goodman was awarded a Pulitzer Prize for commentary in 1980. In the same year she also received a prize for column writing from the American Society of Newspaper Editors.

Faked News Reports and the Destruction of the Public's Trust
Ellen Goodman

In my city room, and most others, reporters clustered around and shook their heads when the news came in that Janet Cooke had made up the Pulitzer-winning story of an 8-year-old heroin addict, and The Washington Post had returned the prize.

We talked about nothing else all that day and the next. We talked about the psychology of lying, about the apparent scope and nerve of this embezzlement of trust, about what it must feel like to get caught.

We felt sorry for her and sorry for us; we felt that it was a shame and shameful. We tried to figure out how an editor could have, should have, separated her fiction from fact. We talked about unnamed sources, and how this could have happened almost anywhere.

Frauds exist in other professions, and they exist in ours. But it's harder to report our own scams.

The medical reporter remembered the story he'd written about a "brilliant young researcher" who had made up the experiments. A doctor at the Massachusetts General Hospital, the cream of the cream, had been caught fabricating a small detail. Slowly his whole research project unraveled. Janet Cooke had been caught fabricating her academic degrees, and slowly her story had unraveled.

It was so unnecessary. The doctor was brilliant. Janet Cooke was a fine writer. Now, he is running lab tests in a suburban hospital in Michigan, and she has resigned from The Washington Post.

The political reporter remembered a story he had written about a man appointed head of the Massachusetts department of elderly affairs. The first clue of fraud in his resume was that he had misspelled the name of his "alma mater," the university at Heidelberg.

There were other tales exchanged about the people we have covered, the lives we've watchdogged: Rosie Ruiz, who "won" the Boston marathon. Tamara Rand, who "psyched" the Reagan assassination attempt.

Then we talked about our own: about the Oregon reporter caught making up quotes from the governor, about The National Enquirer, about Janet Cooke.

Journalists are dogged soul-searchers. We ask more questions about ourselves than about others. We'll analyze how this story got into print and how it got into the Pulitzer's winning circle. We'll write biographies of one

Copyright © 1982 by The Boston Globe Newspaper Company/Washington Post Writers Group. Reprinted with permission.

young reporter. We'll investigate how a reporter can protect sources, and a newspaper can still protect its reputation. We'll issue new directives on checking and editing.

But it's hard to explain what this means to those of us in the business who have only one credential: our credibility. This is a society running short on trust. Most journalists deal with this fact every day. We're assigned the role of public trustee. We're the ones who uncover Rosie, Tamara, the scientist, the politician.

So, we are all affected by any single reporter who fuels the public doubt: Is this true? Do I believe them? We are all affected by any lie that finds its way to print, let alone to prize. It makes our jobs harder, it makes our lives harder. We feel it.

Journalism will survive this one. The Washington Post will also survive. We may even come out with tougher guidelines and, for better and worse, more internal skepticism.

But Janet Cooke has greased the chute of public disbelief. Frankly, it feels lousy.

Al Cohn came to *Newsday* as an entertainment writer after working on *Newsweek* magazine, the *New Haven Register*, and the *New York Times*. He was the founding editor of the paper's Sunday sports section and interviewed hundreds of celebrities for the Sunday magazine; he now edits *Newsday*'s daily and Sunday People Pages.

Ex-reporter Recalls Costly Fear of Failure

Al Cohn

Former Washington Post reporter Janet Cooke says the fear of failure caused her to make up the story of an 8-year-old her in addict that won her a Pulitzer Prize.

"In my case, the temptation didn't derive from ambition," Cooke told Phil Donahue in an interview to be broadcast Monday and Tuesday on NBC's "Today" show. "I simply wanted to write a story that I had been working on, so that I would not have to go back and say, 'I cannot do it.' I did not want to fail."

When the story appeared in the Post, Cooke recalled, she could not bear to read it. "At the time I wrote the story . . . I felt terrible about it," she said.

Copyright ©1982 by Newsday, Inc. Reprinted by permission.

"When the paper came out . . . I didn't read it. I didn't want to see it. I didn't want to think any more about what I had done."

Cooke's interview, a transcript of which was released yesterday, was her first since the disclosure in April that parts of the story had been made up. The fabrication and Cooke's falsifying of the resume she had submitted to the Post came to light after she had been awarded the 1980 Pulitzer. The Post returned the award and asked Cooke to resign. Benjamin C. Bradlee, the Post's executive, editor, had no comment on the Cooke interview.

Cooke said she was aware that she could not get away with the story. "I knew that I could not cover it up, and that it would come out, and that it would be every bit of a scandal that it was," she said. Asked about her lies on her application to the Post, Cooke said, "I felt that on the strength of my own accurate credentials, I would never have been hired at the Washington Post, regardless of what sort of experience I had had, or what type of writer I was . . . I wanted to be absolutely . . . as close to perfection, on paper, certainly." The Post found that Cooke had lied about her academic background and her knowledge of foreign languages.

She said she was trying to ensure "that I would not be just another one of your typical affirmative action hires." Cooke said she spent two months looking for the child addict, whom she had been told existed, and decided to manufacture the story "over a period of a couple of days when I really began to think, 'I'm never going to find him, if, in fact, he's out there. What am I going to do?' And I felt that the last thing that I could really do was go in and say to an editor, 'I can't do it.'"

She says she felt no pressure from her superiors at the Post to reveal her sources for the story. "As a matter of fact," she said, "at one point I was told that they would rather not know, that the fewer people who knew, the better. And the idea of writing a story and not identifying the person was actually brought to me before I had even been able to come back and substantiate the information that I had first heard."

She added, "I realized at the time that it was the improper thing to do, although obviously if I had thought about it long and clearly, I wouldn't have done it. I like to think that I wouldn't have done it."

A Pulitzer prize winner in 1947 for *Tales of the South Pacific* and recipient of the U.S. Medal of Freedom, **James A. Michener** is a renowned author. His works include *The Bridges at Toko Ri* (1959), *Hawaii* (1959), *Centennial* (1974), *Sports in America* (1976), *The Covenant* (1980). *Poland* (1983), a recent book, was a paperback best seller.

On Integrity in Journalism
James A. Michener

On April 13, Janet Cooke of the Washington Post was awarded a Pulitzer Prize for a poignant account of an 8-year-old boy, Jimmy, who was hooked on heroin administered by his mother's boyfriend. Days later, the story was exposed as a fabrication and the Pulitzer Prize was returned. Miss Cooke resigned. That hoax and how it was allowed to happen in a leading newspaper raise many questions about the state of journalism today. We asked author James Michener, himself a Pulitzer Prize winner, to comment in the following guest appearance on the Editor's Page.

Marvin Stone, Editor

It was one of the saddest weeks in the history of American journalism. It was John Peter Zenger in reverse.

A major newspaper was humiliated. One of the most necessary professions in the world was made to look shoddy. A prize treasured by all who enter that profession was made to look laughable. And a woman reporter of extraordinary talent, who could write as well as Ida Tarbell or Maggie Higgins, was disgraced, bringing ridicule upon two minorities who had long battled for good jobs in journalism. Women and blacks.

When blind Samson pulled down the central pillars of the temple at Gaza, the entire structure fell. When Janet Cooke turned in a fake story, she knocked down the central pillar of her profession—integrity—and the reverberations went far.

Every concept in the above paragraphs merits a chapter of philosophical discussion, and in years to come this will be provided in schools of journalism and in the bars where proud newsmen and newswomen meet after work. I should like to stress a few core ideas.

The Newspaper

A paper such as the Los Angeles Times or the Chicago Tribune is a national treasure, kept alive with difficulty, kept vital only because millions trust it and thousands work to preserve its reputation. This nation would perish if its free press were strangled, which is why I am willing to forgive papers, magazines and television stations the howling errors they sometimes make. We could not live rewarding lives without the media. And anyone who finds glee in the embarrassment of the Washington Post should remember how

---

Reprinted from *U.S. News & World Report* May 4, 1981. Copyright © 1981, U.S. News & World Report, Inc.

avidly one reaches for it when one has been out of the country for a few weeks, missing the news it brings.

Insofar as the Post's carelessness made this debacle possible, it deserves rebuke, and I suppose it is castigating itself adequately without my help. But since no media agency can protect itself fully against downright fabrication, the Post deserves our compassion. It will be a better paper after this wrenching experience.

Sources

Miss Cooke's disaster could be titled "Son of Deep Throat." In the Watergate case, the Post got away with launching a major story without disclosing sources, and a tradition evolved, there and elsewhere, that a reporter did not have to reveal where he got his facts. This was a dangerous precedent, and when Miss Cooke refused to tell even her editors the names of her sources, she was free to write whatever she wished.

For legal and common sense reasons, a newspaper may not wish to reveal its sources to the general public, but the editors certainly should demand that their writers prove the veracity of their stories. In this case, Miss Cooke was responsible to no one.

Newspapers cannot long retain their credibility if they accept unchecked reports. One of the pleasures of my professional life has been working with Life and Reader's Digest, whose editors checked every word I submitted. I mean, until they placed a blue dot over every word as they verified it, the story could not be sent to the printers, and the trouble they saved me, and themselves, was remarkable. That kind of checking would have uncovered the fraud in this case.

The Prize

Custodians of the Pulitzer Prizes must review their procedures, for they administer an award which ennobles the profession. Winning it insures a newsman of a lifetime job, with honor. It encourages small newspapers to keep plugging, and it makes cartoonists bolder. In this instance, the controlling advisory board chose to override the recommendations of its jury of experts composed of editors and specialists and handed the feature writing prize to Miss Cooke, whose article had not even been submitted to the jury on feature writing. So the advisory board got its fingers badly singed, for it is wrong to seek advice and then ignore it.

The Reporter

Two facts are conspicuous. Miss Cooke can write. She would make a fine novelist, because when I read her story I noticed how well she depicted the setting, the characters, the dialogue. With the intensity of her present experience behind her, I suspect that she can apply her talent in some kind of writing other than newspaper work. She need not be mortally wounded by this disastrous beginning.

The second fact is that Miss Cooke progressed so fast in her profession that she did not learn its great traditions. She may have thought she had, but she had not even begun. The traditional news reporter begins slowly under some cantankerous editor with high professional and grammatical ideals. One hobnobs with policemen and bartenders and mayors and congressional aspirants and learns painfully to distinguish between truth and fiction. One is knocked about by one's equally gifted colleagues and watches what happens when either blind ambition or excessive drinking destroys a promising talent.

Always there is the steady accumulation of standards: "I do not betray confidences." "I refuse to touch that kind of story." "I must have two confirmations of a statement like that."

In my own case, one sentence lives with me still and guides my work. "If that stinker says it's Tuesday, even money says it's Friday."

It takes about a decade to make a good newsman. Miss Cooke graduated from the University of Toledo, not Vassar as she claimed, in 1976. In 1979, at the age of 25, she landed a job with the Post. In 1980, at the age of 26, she wrote her famous story about the 8-year-old black boy who shot heroin given him by the man who lived with his mother.

She had used charisma, unquestioned talent and a fierce ambition to attain a position sought after by thousands, but she reached it without two essential attributes: A deep commitment to the historical traditions of her profession and an understanding of what makes a newspaper acceptable to its community.

She had not paid her dues, and in a moment of crisis she was left without self-protection.

The Minorities

When she came to Washington, it was not as mere Janet Cooke. Whether she admitted it or not, she came also as a representative of our two most important minorities: Professional women, and blacks. As a black woman with a pleasing personality, she was doubly valuable to the Post, which publishes in a city with a large black population, for she was what is known as a twofor. The management could cite her twice in claiming that it did not practice discrimination, and the only person better to hire would have been a black female Puerto Rican. That could be called a hat trick, a phrase borrowed from sports indicating that one person covered three constituencies.

It is possible, although the record shows no evidence of this, that the Post grabbed Miss Cooke as the solution to a problem, and that had she been an ordinary white male from the Missouri School of Journalism she might have been investigated much more thoroughly. It is possible that her stories were handled with more tenderness than would otherwise have been the case.

Those whom society nominates as symbols are obligated to perform doubly, because a poor exhibition will do double damage. If Gloria Steinem acts the fool tomorrow, all women will suffer. If Carl Rowan messes up his television program, all blacks are denigrated.

The damage Miss Cooke has done to black and women reporters is incalculable, and she should have anticipated this when she wrote her fake story and allowed it to be nominated for a Pulitzer.

I am a Quaker, a graduate of Swarthmore College, a former naval officer, a former official of the Democratic Party, and a writer, and I am kept in line partly because I would be mortified if my poor behavior brought dishonor to those institutions which served me so generously. I must be watchful that my actions do not diminish them, because in this case we are all members of various minorities.

Credentials

The most curious aspect of this scandal is that the Post did not check Miss Cooke's credentials. Her record, with its shifts and contradictions, had to awaken suspicions, and when my wife read it to me as we drove north on the day the Pulitzers were announced and I heard her history, I cried: "Watch that Sorbonne bit! Watch those four foreign languages!"

Why was I so dubious? For two good reasons. In almost every institution in which I have worked, some misguided person has claimed university degrees he did not have, and I believe you could go to any campus in this country, if checks had been carelessly made, and find some professor using a spurious degree. When someone says she has studied at the Sorbonne, warning whistles should toot.

When I worked with the military police at one point, I found that when young men pose as officers, dressing up in bemedaled uniforms to charm small-town girls, they usually claim to be Marine majors. Colonels or generals would alert suspicions, while mere Army or Navy uniforms would lack glamour.

With military-police impostors it's the Marine major, with academes the Sorbonne.

Apprenticeship

We should insist that young men and women serve proper apprenticeships, because throughout history that is how standards and traditions have been kept high.

The number of attractive-looking young people posing as newsmen on television with never a shred of hard-news experience is shocking. The parade of people reporting to newspaper offices without any knowledge of English or of American history is appalling.

Young people learn their profession, whatever it may be, by studying the best work of their predecessors, and I shall never forget the delight with which I saw a great painting done by Giovanni Bellini which had been copied by his pupil Titian. Rubens had learned by copying Titian to see what his secrets were, and Delacroix had copied Rubens. Van Gogh did a marvelous adaptation of Delacroix, so that we had five of our greatest, most distinctive painters, men of the most intense personal style and integrity, striving to learn what good artists of the past had accomplished.

Recent requirements that a company must have a balanced staff should not be interpreted as meaning that it must have an incompetent one or one ignorant of the great traditions.

The Pulitzers

Suggestions have been made that reporters on a newspaper as important as the Washington Post should not degrade themselves by competing for prizes. Nonsense. People with aspirations have always appreciated recognition from their peers, and I respect John Paul Jones who left the American fleet to serve in Russia's because the former would not promote him to admiral while the latter would. There are legitimate milestones in every profession, and it is not ignoble to mark them off.

I feel especially involved in this case because, as a young man, I won a Pulitzer.

I did not aspire to do it. I did not campaign for it. But when it arrived it remade my life, enabling me to do those things to which I did aspire. Without the Pulitzer, I might never have made it as a writer. With it, excellent things became possible.

I am worried about this debacle because it has befouled institutions that are important to me. I hope things can be worked out.

INDEX

Advertiser's Bag of Tricks, The (Burns), 198–206
Advertising, 195–256
   readings, 198–241
   selected ads for study, 243–255
Aftermath of a Pulitzer Hoax (Newsday), 398–399
Aims, writing, 4
   samples of, 5
Alperowicz, Cynthia, 268–270
American Mass Communication (Sandman, Rubin, and Sachsman), 62–72
American Society of Newspaper Editors, 102–104
American Writing Now (Kazin), 155–161
Assignments, 2
Associated Press, 153–154
Audience, 2–3
Average U.S. Author's Writings Bring in Less than $5,000 a Year (Mitgang), 161–166

Bailey, Jeff, 309–312
Ball Games or Brawl Games? (Friedman), 287–290
Beyette, Beverly, 149–152
Bittner, John R., 142–148
Books, 139–141
   readings, 155–193
Brainstorming, 5–6
Browne, Ray B., 15–21
Burns, Marjorie, 198–206

Canby, Vincent, 382–386
Cartoons, 47, 112, 178, 210, 266, 308
Cause and effect, 9
Champlin, Charles, 389–393
Chaps Cologne ad, 246–247
Charren, Peggy, 268–270
Cheever, John, 220–223
Cinematic Schism in Black and White, A (Milloy), 376–382
Ciolli, Rita, 183–189
Clarke, Gerald, 374–376
Classification, 7
Cohn, Al, 403–404
Collins, Thomas, 110–112, 395–398
Combined News Services, 274–275
Communications, 60–92
   readings, 62–92
Comparison/contrast, 8
Corliss, Richard, 348–350
Country Music Is No Small-Town Affair (Rockwell), 324–328

411

Crichton, John, 233-241
Critic as Image Maker, The (Champlin), 389-393
Culture, popular
  readings, 13-59
  writing about, 2

Decline of Quality, The (Tuchman), 49-59
Definition, 7
DeMott, Benjamin, 329-335
Descriptive writing, 4, 5
Development, patterns of, 6-9
Dexatrim ad, 252-253
Donosky, Lea, 180-182
Don't Leave the Room during the Commercials (Cheever), 220-223
Doscher, Barbara, 167-173
Drawing a Privacy Line Inside Publicity's Glare (Friendly), 129-133

Ebert, Roger, 365-371
Effect, cause and, 9
Examples, 7
Expository writing, 4, 5
Ex-reporter Recalls Costly Fear of Failure (Cohn), 403-404

Faked News Reports and the Destruction of the Public's Trust (Goodman), 402-403
Faked Story, The: When Ambition Replaces the Truth (Payne), 399-401
Film, 352-393
  readings, 354-393
Fiedler, Leslie A., 35-41
Fizz Biz, The: Tiny Bubbles (Kanner), 215-219
Friedman, David, 287-290
Friendly, Jonathan, 129-133

Games That Play People (Skow), 42-48
Goldman, Kevin L., 303-306
Goldsmith, Barbara, 22-32
Goleman, Daniel, 345-348
Goodman, Ellen, 401, 402-403
Goodman, Peter, 275-279
"Grabbers," 2, 3

Hackett, George, 180-182
He Moves in Close to Bring the Big Stories Vividly to Life (Beyette), 149-152
Heavy Metal (Robins), 339-340
Hinckley, David, 283-287
How Politicians Seduce Journalists (Steel), 113-118
How to Detect Propaganda (Institute for Propaganda Analysis), 104-109

In the Footsteps of Ulysses (Clarke), 374-376
Institute for Propaganda Analysis, 104-109
It's Nothing to Smile About: The Decline of TV Sit-Coms (Hinckley), 283-287

Jacoby, Susan, 280-283
Jaguar ad, 248-249
Johnston, Donald H., 95-102
Journalese as a Second Tongue (Leo), 123-126
Journalism, 93-138

Kael, Pauline, 386-389
Kanner, Bernice, 215-219
Kazin, Alfred, 155-161
Keller, Fred A., 290-294
Kohler Greek Bath ad, 244-245

Lapham, Lewis H., 118-123
Leo, John, 123-126
Life According to TV (Waters), 259-267
Longevity The Real James Bond Mystery (Canby), 382-386

Magazine Runs Hydrogen Bomb Diagram (Associated Press), 153-154
Maslin, Janet, 371-373
Magazines, 139-154
  readings, 142-154
Magazines (Bittner), 142-148
Meaning of Celebrity, The (Goldsmith), 22-32
McGowan, Bill, Jr., 189-193
Medium Is the Maximum, The (Corliss), 348-350
Menand, Louis, 341-345
Meyer, Karl E., 298-303
Michener, James A., 404, 405-409
Miller Beer ad, 254-255
Milloy, Marilyn, 376-382
Mind in the Machine, The (Rosenblatt), 84-90
Mitgang, Herbert, 161-166
Modes, 6-9
Morals and Ethics in Advertising (Crichton), 233-241
Morrow, Lance, 317-320
Movies on TV (Kael), 386-389
Music, 315-351
  readings, 317-350
Mystique of the Empire State Building, The (Sargent), 32-35

Narrative writing, 4, 5
New Form of Power: Information, The (Smith), 72-76

News, 93–138
　readings, 95–138
Newsday, 398–399
Nielsen Rating Service, 3
No Verbs Tonight . . . The Reasons . . . The Consequences (Saltman), 126–128

On Integrity in Journalism (Michener), 405–409
Oppenheim, Mike, 270–274
Ordinary Critics: Immanuel Kant and the Talking Heads (DeMott), 329–335
Organization, 3, 6
Orwellian Implications of Two-Way Television (Goodman), 275–279
Outlining, 9–11
　sentence, 10–11
　topic, 10

P. O. V., Psycho, and E. T. (Pipolo), 354–365
Palmer, Robert, 306–309
Payne, Les, 399–401
Peer, Elizabeth, 180–182
Persuasive writing, 4, 5
Pink Floyd Album Marks 10 Years as a Best Seller, A (Rockwell), 336–339
Pipolo, Tony, 354–365
Polskin, Howard, 133–138
Popular culture, *see* Culture, popular
Popular Culture: Notes Toward a Definition (Browne), 15–21
Print (magazines and books), 139–194
　readings, 142–194
Process analysis, 6, 7–8
Psychologists Examine Appeal of Michael Jackson (Goleman), 345–348
Pulitzer Hoax, The, 394–409
　readings 395–409

Radio, 296–313
　readings, 298–313
Radio's Born-Again Serenity (Meyer), 298–303
Radio's Latest Boom: Late-Night Talk Shows (Goldman), 303–306
Robins, Wayne, 339–340
Rockwell, John, 324–328, 336–339
Rosenblatt, Roger, 84–90
Rubin, David M., 62–72

Sachsman, David B., 62–72
Saltman, David, 126–128
Sandman, Peter M., 62–72
Sargent, Robert, 32–35
Save a Life or Get the Story? (Polskin), 133–138

Sculptures in Snow: Notes on the Uses of the Press (Lapham), 118–123
Semantic Environment in the Age of Advertising, The (Skolimowski), 224–232
Skolimowski, Henryk, 224–232
Skow, John, 42–48
Smith, Anthony, 72–76
So Long, Ring around the Collar! Welcome, Paper Blob! (Townley), 206–211
Statement of Principles, A (American Society of Newspaper Editors), 102–104
Steel, Ronald, 113–118
Stereo "Box": Big Bucks in Big Sounds (Bailey), 309–311
Supermarket Erotica "Bodice-busters" Put Romantic Myths to Bed (Thurston and Doscher), 167–173

Television, 257–295
　readings, 259–295
Television and the Slow Death of the Mind (Keller), 290–294
Textbook Wars, The (Ciolli), 183–189
Thesis statement, 4
They're Playing Ur-Song (Morrow), 317–320
Those Packages Aren't Just Selling Deodorant (Wiemer), 212–215
Thurston, Carol, 167–173
Tiger, Lionel, 320–323
Topics, 3, 4
Townley, Rod, 174–179, 206–211
Transforming Elvis into a Suffering Culture Hero (Menand), 341–345
Tuchman, Barbara W., 49–59
Tuning Out Controls on Radio (New York Times), 312–313
TV, Newspaper Journalists Abide by Different Rules (Collins), 110–112
TV Fan, 15, Leaps to His Death (Combined News Services), 274–275
TV Isn't Violent Enough (Oppenheim), 270–274
TV Violence Breeds Violent Children (Charren and Alperowicz), 268–270
25 Million Americans Can't Read This (McGowan), 189–193

Unreal Heroes for the 80's (Maslin), 371–373
Up, Up and Away—The Rise and Fall of Comic Books (Fiedler), 35–41

Wait Till You Read/See the Book/Show (Townley), 174–179
Washing Our Minds Out with Soaps (Jacoby), 280–283

Wash. Post Story a Hoax, Paper Returns Pulitizer (Collins), 395–398
Waters, Harry F., 259–267
Wellborn, Stanley N., 77–84
What Is News? (Johnston), 95–102
Why, It Was Fun! (Tiger), 320–323
Why Movie Audiences Aren't Safe Any More (Ebert), 365–371
Why Writers Plagiarize (Peer, Donosky, and Hackett), 180–182
Wiemer, Bob, 212–215
Will Video Clips Kill Radio as Maker of Rock's Top 10? (Palmer), 306–309

World of Communications Wonders, A (Wellborn), 77–84
Writer's block, overcoming, 1
Writing
  descriptive, 4, 5
  effective, 1
  expository, 4, 5
  free, 1
  good, 1
  narrative, 4, 5
  persuasive, 4, 5

Zena Jeans ad, 250–251